ENTERTAINING
THE THIRD REICH

Post-Contemporary Interventions
Series Editors: Stanley Fish and Fredric Jameson

ENTERTAINING

THE THIRD REICH

ILLUSIONS OF WHOLENESS

IN NAZI CINEMA

Linda Schulte-Sasse

*

DUKE UNIVERSITY PRESS

Durham & London 1996

© 1996 Duke University Press
All rights reserved
Printed in the United States of America on
acid-free paper ∞
Typeset in Sabon by Keystone Typesetting, Inc.
Library of Congress Cataloging-in-Publication Data
appear on the last printed page of this book.

FOR MY PARENTS

EVELYN PEDERSON SCHIELE AND BURTRUM C. SCHIELE

CONTENTS

LIST OF ILLUSTRATIONS

PREFACE

At the risk of imitating Nazi cinema's reduction of history to pathos, I feel compelled to begin with a little confession. Namely, in the course of working through this material, I have been guilty of the very approaches which, much like a reformed alcoholic, I now lambaste. I started out with the usual conviction that Nazi films are of interest only as propaganda, and then advanced to a more sophisticated informed-by-film-theory stage that went something like this: "These movies may *look* innocent, but this is why you, the ordinary viewer, need me, the film critic, to tell you why you shouldn't be enjoying them." In addition to being a bit arrogant, these perspectives are insufficient precisely because they answer our questions too completely, and hence may discourage the asking of further, more complex and disconcerting questions. For this reason, some films on which I published earlier articles (*Jew Süss, Friedrich Schiller,* and *Komö-dianten*) appear here in a vastly more ambivalent light.

I hope in this book to have achieved an epistemological reversal that is simple, but somehow daunting when it's *Nazi* cinema you're talking about: rather than taking ideology as a starting point and looking at how movies show ideology, we can perhaps take movies as a starting point and examine how they harbor, transform, exceed, and undermine political ideology. If we start this way, we may see contradictions where we would most expect ideological homogeneity, and need not be vexed by movies that don't seem to "fit."

I am indebted to a number of people for intellectual stimulation, critical feedback, and moral support at various stages of the project: Ellis Dye, J. Michele Edwards, Sander Gilman, Jürgen Link, Rick McCormick, Roswitha Mueller, Tom Plummer, Dana Polan, Eric Rentschler, Norm

Rosenberg, David Sanford, Clay Steinman, Renate Werner, Caroline Wilbrecht, Jack Zipes, and my two anonymous readers. A special thanks to Nancy Armstrong for her "open knife" theory and to Slavoj Žižek for work that changed my whole approach to movies (and for those jokes and movie examples that give one the pleasurable illusion of having understood Lacan). Thanks to David Bathrick for first telling me to let "competing imperatives" speak in Nazi cinema, and to Gerhard Weiss, my key to the "Frederick" movies. Thanks also to Tom Browne, Brian Longley, Dave Reynolds, and Kristie Wheeler at Macalester College Media Services, to Al Milgrom, Bob Strong, Chris Barsanti, and Chris Nordling at the University of Minnesota Film Society, and to David Bathrick and John Mowitt for help with the still photographs. Thanks to Macmillan, Inc., for permission to reprint the chapter on *Jew Süss*, which appeared in *Perspectives on German Cinema* (1995). I am likewise grateful to Ken Wissoker and colleagues at Duke University Press, whose patience and humor have made collaboration a pleasure, and to the students of Macalester College, whose challenges and low tolerance for gratuitous theory-speak gave me just the kind of pressure I needed.

Finally, thanks to Linn and Daniel for putting up with a mother who blocked the VCR with Nazi movies, and to Jochen, whose ideas and works I have recklessly plundered, taking liberties one only dares with a (preferably current) spouse. His occasional critique, always in the tactful, mild-mannered style of German universities in the late sixties, is most definitely reflected in these pages.

INTRODUCTION

A few months ago, I watched a Hollywood movie called *Swing Kids* about a free-thinking boy in 1930s Germany who pays a price for his resistance to Nazi conformity.[1] Much to my surprise, this predictable film was to inspire a useful little experiment. I began editing together clips from some programmatic Nazi movies produced in 1933 about youth living in the Weimar Republic. My first clip, which I'll call *hero is beaten for liking the wrong kind of music,* was from *Hitler Youth Quex.* The second, *hero makes a scene in a nightclub when someone defiles his kind of music,* was from *Hans Westmar,* based on the story of Horst Wessel, Nazism's favorite martyr. Another Nazi movie called *S.A. Man Brand* accommodated me with two clips: *man from the wrong political movement beats helpless woman* and *hero's convictions are reconfirmed after a woman reads him a letter from his dead father.* When I showed this montage to some students, they realized right away that the film I had concocted was none other than *Swing Kids*—in structure at least. Re-creating *Swing Kids* didn't take much imagination, since it follows to a "t" the formula of Nazi youth films, especially *Hitler Youth Quex,* with the small narratological difference that their allegiances are reversed. Had I expanded my Nazi repertoire a bit, my pastiche could have become a full-length feature: *Swing Kids'* last-minute conversion of a figure seemingly lost to the "other" side echoes the German movie *Holiday on Word of Honor* (1937); *Swing Kids'* equation of loving Beethoven with resistance to Nazism mirrors *Request Concert's* (1940) equation of loving Beethoven with *fidelity* to Nazism;

1. Directed by Thomas Carter, 1993.

while *S.A. Man Brand* tells us that people who read books are Nazis, *Swing Kids* tells us that people who read books fight the Nazis.[2]

Few would contest that the Nazi movies mentioned above are propaganda. But while we might decry *Swing Kids* as another exercise in the Culture Industry's reduction of history to kitsch,[3] propaganda would likely not be our charge. What makes the Nazi films propaganda, we'd say, is that they're trying to "make you" sympathize with a terrible cause, while *Swing Kids* champions freedom. I won't be the first to point out that such distinctions depend upon context, upon which "cause" has been valorized by history or by a group fighting for hegemony. Lewis Milestone's film version of *All Quiet on the Western Front* was propaganda of the most virulent sort in the eyes of the Nazis, which was why they staged massive protests at its Berlin premiere in December 1930.

The lesson to be gleaned from *Swing Kids* is, of course, the infinite corruptibility of narrative formations, whose structures can be filled with whatever content serves a given purpose. But it also illustrates another problematic that underlies this study: how to draw the line between propaganda and entertainment; more specifically, how to deal adequately with propaganda when it *is* entertainment. When *Swing Kids* shows us kids being brainwashed by Fritz Hippler's "documentary" *The Eternal Jew* (quite amazingly, a year before the film was produced), it is not showing Nazism at its most cunning, since Hippler's film is as tedious as it is heinous. Such Hollywood representations, which have become a form of memory as we collectively imagine "Nazi Germany," do more than just deprive the era of its contradictions and heterogeneity; they rob it of the one thing even the most murderous state cannot live without: its normalcy. What I want to do here is fight movies with movies, to examine National Socialism's fusion, via its feature films, of the "political" with "normal" entertainment, which means with desire. My strategy will be to look at Nazi propaganda movies, only not as propaganda movies.

Not so very long ago an interest in propaganda was the only reason anybody had for giving Nazi movies a second thought. The pleasure

2. In the Nazi movie a landlord gives a destitute war widow money he hides from his greedy wife in Hitler's *Mein Kampf;* in *Swing Kids* underground resistance messages are hidden in books by Goethe.

3. *Swing Kids* does have one redeeming feature: its focus on unharnessed music (the "racially suspect" jazz that Nazism objected to) and sensual, frenetic dance as a form of bodily liberation from the lockstep synchronized by the Nazi drill machine. In one scene the protagonist almost literally shucks off National Socialism through dance, as if having a seizure that says "get this *thing* off of me."

of propaganda studies lay in their blissful orderliness and simplicity. A scholar needed only to describe Nazism's film industry and the rest of his/her book organized itself as a series of film stories told either chronologically or according to genres; chapter titles like "Goebbels Shows His Teeth" or "Götterdämmerung" offered their own narrative flavor.[4] The subject position of both writer and audience was defined beforehand as one of moral and aesthetic superiority, and thus never needed to be problematized or even articulated. The propaganda experience was not marred by complexity of any sort.

I want to resist the fashion of trashing early studies of Nazi film, like Erwin Leiser's *Nazi Cinema* (originally 1968) or David Stewart Hull's *Film in the Third Reich* (1969), as untheoretical or superficial. Their work was an important first step that could not yet benefit from developments in film studies (or even from VCRs, for that matter), and few works on Nazi film fail to cite them. Yet early studies left much space for further exploration, having told us a lot about what surrounded Nazi films, such as the circumstances of production and distribution, and very little about the films themselves. As film studies has evolved since the mid-seventies, so has a theoretical apparatus that acknowledges the importance of "low" as well as "high" textual forms and that has furnished tools for reading them. Recent writing has thus begun exploring the Nazi entertainment genres usually ignored by early scholars who lacked either the tools or the reasons to investigate what was not "overtly" political. The result of new methodologies has been a blurring of boundaries: Even if we study propaganda, no longer can we restrict ourselves to unmasking the "intentions" behind films or to explicating their manipulation of presumably malleable subjects. By the same token, no longer can any feature film escape the political, since we've come to understand the inscription of ideologies in classical realist narrative form, regardless of what a director might have intended.

Essential though the move away from "political" Nazi films has been, I want to backtrack a bit and demonstrate that the last word has not been spoken on those state-commissioned propaganda vehicles that so consumed Hull and Leiser. To be sure, they were a minority among all Nazi-era films, yet they offer exemplary documentation of Nazism at work, of the ways it gives form to its fantasies and works through its anxieties.

4. Chapter titles from David Stewart Hull's *Film in the Third Reich* (Berkeley: University of California Press, 1969) and Erwin Leiser's *Nazi Cinema* (New York: Macmillan, 1974).

Furthermore, they function in much the same ways as "regular" entertainment films, which is why my study will also cross boundaries and include films that are not easily categorized as propaganda, yet exhibit many of its structures. Indeed, Nazi cinema drives to an extreme the problem of how to distinguish propaganda from entertainment, because the German film industry was at once heavily regulated and heavily profit-oriented. Moneymaking and ideological dissemination were perceived as one and the same; hence a disproportionately large number of popular Nazi films were simultaneously political films. Productions commissioned by the state for purposes of "public enlightenment" were privileged with huge budgets to ensure they became monumental, star-studded spectaculars. Once on the market, "politically correct" Nazi films were promoted by various means: while a 1936 law prohibited journalists from seriously critiquing them, a system of "predicates" like "culturally especially valuable" or "valuable for youth" gave them a public exposure and status commensurate with today's multi-Oscar-winning films. Indeed, many of Nazi cinema's top-grossing and most entertaining films, from *The Great Love* and *The Golden City*[5] to *Request Concert,* are readable as propaganda, and at least one, *Jew Süss,* is an outright hate film.

To say that *Jew Süss* is a hate film is not to prove, however, that it was always received as a hate film or was popular for this reason. It and many similar films "worked" because they met certain social and psychological needs and reflected deeply rooted narrative traditions. If one dispenses with preconceived ideas and *looks* at these films, one finds that not only are they riddled with the same ruptures and internal subversions that beleaguer virtually all narrative texts, but that the popular success many enjoyed may be tied precisely to these ruptures, which compromise — if not necessarily contradict — their "Nazi message." The struggle to make the "Jew" Other ends up making him ambivalent if not appealing; films about Genius/Leader figures may overshoot the mark, rendering their hero so insufferably perfect as to make his adversary more sympathetic; many films thrive on a melodrama not necessarily accommodated to Nazi totalism, which, as we will see, involves an exorcism of the private sphere. In other words, it could be that what works as film competes with the working of indoctrination — even if all films have ideology as their by-product.

5. Stephen Lowry offers an excellent, differentiated close reading of these two films in *Pathos und Politik: Ideologie in Spielfilmen des Nationalsozialismus* (Tübingen: Niemeyer, 1991). His is the first study to concentrate on the public success of films, rather than on an exclusively "political" agenda.

For better or for worse, then, the evolution of film studies, combined with the peculiarities of Nazi cinema, has left us with a framework that is a far cry from the simplicity of Hull's and Leiser's day. Nazi movies, regardless of genre, need to be studied in themselves *and* anchored in the context of their culture's moral and aesthetic values. To begin understanding these we have to consider the anxieties and fantasies that find their way into aesthetic products like movies. Such fantasies and anxieties are, of course, informed by social, political, and personal realities, and at the same time are reinforced when they are recycled in movies and other cultural texts. We have to ask where the stories in which these fantasies are couched come from and to consider how a specific aesthetic medium, in this case film, forms or transforms the ideas, values, and narrative forms underlying it. How, moreover, did the public attitude toward movies and the ways it experienced them affect the reception of the "political" ideas these movies might have harbored? Finally, we have to be willing to modify the image we have of Nazi culture, to let its internal contradictions as well as its continuities to earlier and later cultures speak. One might summarize the study of Nazi films as a series of relationships, only some of which have been addressed: of the Nazi state to both filmmakers and the public, of filmmakers to their cultural sources and resources, of contemporary filmgoers to films, and last but definitely not least, of today's public with our twenty-twenty hindsight to the same films.

To address the above considerations is not to dispense with the propaganda question, but to look at it through a different lens that stresses texts and how they answer public needs. Nor does this framework negate the understanding of National Socialism the reader likely has already. One can certainly find in the films a series of recurrent thematic oppositions (like the unsophisticated peasant with common sense versus the manipulative capitalist) and "master" narratives that permit them to be ordered in the (seemingly) coherent and predictable ideological edifice we call "Nazi ideology." A good deal of my own analysis consists of an ideology critique[6] sorting out such configurations, establishing unities among film texts as well as references between texts and various subtexts. I have tried, though, to make ideology critique only a first step, since every critique of ideological configurations in a given narrative, through its very methodology, is forced to act as if meaning is fixed for once and for all within a given text. Far from being able to achieve or "reach" an ultimate meaning, narrative merely moves toward a meaning propelled by desire (whether

---

6. I am using this term here with reference to the Frankfurt School.

the desired "intention" of the author or what is "read in" by someone else). Like realist narrative itself, ideology critique falls prey to the illusion that narration can be an accurate representation of "reality," of something external to representation and desire. Ideology critique is thus propelled by a desire to erase contradictions within a text and between text and reader; it indulges the critic's own desire for mastery of the text (which is also a means of gaining a comfortable distance *from* the text).

What is "going on" in Nazi cinema is to be found not only in its ideological patterns but in a broader social-psychological function that encompasses and transcends ideology. In trying to connect all of the above I will draw on the work of Slovenian theorist Slavoj Žižek, who understands "politics" itself in terms of fantasies we expect to find in movies. His notion of social fantasy, which is central to my study, proceeds from Ernesto Laclau's and Chantal Mouffe's proposition that "society" doesn't exist, that any vision of society as a harmonious whole is always a delusion.[7] Societies are marked by ruptures that prevent the utopian visions that hold them together from ever being realized, whether this vision is Marxism's classless society or National Socialism's corporatist community. In response to this fundamental rupture or blockage, societies "invent" social fantasies to mask the impossibility of the ideals by which they identify themselves. National Socialism epitomizes this structure with its social fantasy of the "Jew," who is essential to Nazism's understanding of itself because he masks the impossibility of its corporatist ideal of an "organic," racially "pure" society.[8] He does so, paradoxically, by providing a palpable, material embodiment of the very qualities supposedly hindering social perfection. In other words, through a process of displacement and condensation, all social negativity is projected onto the "Jew." Building on Žižek, I have theorized a dialectical relationship between the "Jew" as social fantasy and its counterpart, the "positive" fantasy of the Leader or the Leader-People unity, which assumes an endless variety of historical equivalences. These two essential fantasies, both of which respond to a modernity perceived as hostile, will be the point of departure for my film readings.

7. Slavoj Žižek, *The Sublime Object of Ideology* (London: Verso, 1989), esp. 87–130. See also Laclau and Mouffe's *Hegemony and Socialist Strategy: Towards a Radical Democratic Politics* (London: Verso, 1985), 93–148.
8. I am consistently referring to Nazism's constructed "Jew" as "he" because Nazism is male-centered both in its Leader fantasies and its imagined antagonists. This is not to distract from the fact that femininity is one of its greatest anxieties and that specifically the Jewish woman was imagined as threatening.

What distinguishes Žižek's approach from traditional ideology critique and what makes it so useful in contemplating Nazi films as movies is that it does not content itself with laying bare discursive features of an ideology, like anti-Semitism's myths about Jews being avaricious, cunning, etc. It aims, rather, "at extracting the kernel of enjoyment, at articulating the way in which — beyond the field of meaning but at the same time internal to it — an ideology implies, manipulates, produces a pre-ideological enjoyment structured in fantasy."[9] What does Žižek mean by *pre-ideological?* In approaching a phenomenon like anti-Semitism we persistently use rational categories to define something that is not "rational" and thus escapes such categories as "meaning." Anti-Semitism tries to organize itself according to recurring ideas about Jews, but something is missing if these ideas become its definition. A discursive analysis overlooks how Nazism's "Jew" is a source of pleasure, how he "captures desire" because he both embodies and denies the impossibility of "society," of a perfect community. It is only through the Jew that Nazism can believe in itself, that its multiple contradictions can be masked.

It is important to note, moreover, that Žižek (whose work draws heavily on Jacques Lacan's psychoanalytic theory) conceives fantasy not as an imaginary fulfillment of desire, but as the frame in which desire becomes possible. It becomes "possible" in fantasy because the latter provides a framework (often a narrative framework) that organizes and channels choatic feelings; it thus helps "manage" emotions. Fantasy is indispensable because it conceals the fact that desire is unfulfillable. In Lacanian terms, this begins with the fact that we can never fathom the desire of the Other (which might mean an individual person who places demands on us, a social context, or the "world" in which we must "measure up"). We are constantly subjected to demands by our reality but can never fully understand what this reality "wants" of us; nor, of course, can we meet this demand.[10] Fantasy masks the fact that desire is by definition never satisfied (it will, at best, give way to new desires); it helps us live with the insurmountable gap between the self and the symbolic order or what Lacan calls the "big Other." Just as individuals need fantasy as the only pos-

---

9. Žižek, *The Sublime Object of Ideology,* 125.

10. Žižek thus defines fantasy as a "defense against '*Che vuoi,*'" Lacan's term (meaning "What do you want?") describing the gap between the subject's desire and fantasy as an imaginary site where one indeed can comprehend the demand of the symbolic order, where the question receives an answer. Though this gap is unbridgeable, fantasy helps the subject mask it. See Žižek, *The Sublime Object of Ideology,* 118.

sible means of experiencing harmony — however fantasmatic — so groups fantasize an "impossible" social harmony.

These negative and positive fantasies of "Jew" and Leader typify Nazism's habit of articulating social harmony and social disruption through images of the human body. We would land ourselves back in the propaganda camp, however, if we considered Nazism's imaginary "body politic" to be exhausted with such images (we would be stuck looking for Leaders and caricatures of Jews). Nazism's fantasies "take shape" simultaneously in more abstract terms, through an imaginary social body, a construction called "Germany" that is vaguely defined (or, more accurately, presumed) in the spatial and temporal terms of narrative.[11] National Socialism conceives "Germany" as a geographic space that needs to be molded as one, maintained as one, or retrieved as one, depending on the historical juncture. Inseparable from this geographic wholeness is a temporal dimension writing "German history" as a familiar narrative of struggle whose pain is overdetermined by an ultimate telos, or imaginary presence, of harmony. In other words, the painful history Nazism dredges up can be enjoyed because it is organized in the form of stories guaranteeing harmonious closure; hence, the greater the pain, the greater the pleasure.

All of these notions of body pervade many Nazi discourses, from *Mein Kampf* to speeches, media cartoons, or literature, which likewise have elements of narrative. This study explores them through the movies, where they are couched in specific narratives and in a medium that maximizes the pleasurable dimension of fantasy stressed by Žižek. In order to elucidate the necessary connection between time and space in Nazism's construction of its social body, I will concentrate on films that recycle German history as part of a larger master narrative. Ironically, my earlier, overarching question — Where do the film stories that give expression to Nazi fantasies and anxieties come from? — will be answered by a restricted

11. Neither the construction of a social body nor the formation of social fantasies is, of course, unique to National Socialism. In the imagery of political cartoons and the metaphors of speeches or media headlines, societies tend to envision themselves as some kind of a vessel (a house, ship, airplane, car, or living body) whose borders must be protected against potential threat from internal or external forces, often symbolized as rats, rough waters, turbulence, a virus, or cancer. See Jürgen Link's work on collective symbolism in "Collective Symbolism in Political Discourse and Its Share in Underlying Totalitarian Trends," trans. R. Westerholt and L. Schulte-Sasse, in *The Public Realm: Essays on Discursive Types in Political Philosophy,* ed. R. Schürman (Albany: State University of New York Press, 1989), 225–38.

focus: on film representations of eighteenth-century German history. Although this was only one setting among many in historical films, which themselves were one genre among many, they offer a unique insight into how Nazism's particular social body came to be constructed. Namely, it is grounded and legitimated in the bourgeois culture that emerged in the eighteenth century, although it also violates that culture, most obviously through the theories of "race" we know only too well. As always with historical films, we will learn much more about the era that makes them than about the era portrayed. An eighteenth century viewed most literally through the lens of National Socialism is a particularly instructive means of grasping Nazism's relationship to a cultural framework it both exalted and contradicted.

I will focus, however, not only on what National Socialism does to the eighteenth century, but on what features of early modern aesthetic culture lend themselves to such appropriation. Long before Nazism seized power, the eighteenth century produced the body of cultural texts that became a retroactive focal point for a German "identity." These texts include canonized works by Goethe, Schiller, or Lessing, and eventually the writers themselves as figures of symbolic identification. While the Enlightenment project espoused by such thinkers, with its notions of educability, humanity, and tolerance, seems to represent the opposite of Nazism, this same culture generated the antecedents of Nazism's notion of a social body whose harmony is impeded by modernity's alienation. If eighteenth-century culture "gave birth" to the modernity National Socialism so reviles, it also generated the first sentiments of antimodernism that found their logical extreme in National Socialism and that we will see emphasized even in films espousing authoritarianism. To anticipate one example: even though film biographies of Frederick the Great advocate unconditional subordination to authority and the molding of the body into a military machine, the ideological grounding of this centralism is to be found in anticentralism, in a naturalization of Frederick's state as the embodiment of the People, resisting, with Schillerian fervor, the machine state of Frederick's enemies. Thus we'll find in Nazi movies features we expect, authoritarianism and militarism, mixed with elements that seem at least superficially "democratic."

As implied by the discussion of social fantasy, the social body, and Nazism's alignment with early modern aesthetic culture, my stress in examining Nazism's historical films will be less on history and its distortion than on the fact that the films tell history in the form of stories, that they actively construct an imaginary history as a source of pleasure. The stories or story fragments with which they construct this history are often drawn from the eighteenth-century canon, especially the bourgeois tragedy — hence a sometimes "democratic" feeling. The bourgeois tragedy provided the family-based narratives and binary value system underlying the films, as well as the supposedly timeless, universal notion of virtue with which they align themselves. We'll see how Nazi cinema "waters down" the bourgeois tragedy to a form of kitsch, but also how it repoliticizes the genre by reversing its "message." Finally, since the bourgeois tragedy was a major precursor of melodrama, we will see its patterns echo in Nazi films set in other eras.

At the heart of my project are questions of translation or transformation. What happens when an early moment of bourgeois culture is reappropriated by a later moment? What formal consequences ensue when a narrative style that was often experienced in private is translated into a mass visual form — when what Diderot calls "cinema of the mind"[12] becomes classical realist cinema? In using active verbs like *translate* or *appropriate* I mean to encompass both the deliberate manipulation implied by the word *propaganda* and a much broader process of cultural inscription that has nothing to do with propaganda, yet is a precondition for it. Nazism's uses and abuses of the eighteenth century reveal not only historical dependency but a curious affinity with the world of autonomous Western art in which we like to think that "cultural barbarism" does not belong. If eighteenth-century narrative strategies aimed at sublating difference in favor of a "family of man" can be maneuvered to reinforce a biologically defined difference, perhaps it is the tools of eighteenth-century narrative, especially its mechanisms of identification, that allow this "perversion." If, moreover, Hollywood-style cinema serves National Socialism so well, perhaps there is an implicit affinity between the subject effect of this cinematic style and of fascism (at least with respect to the pursuit of harmony). It is my hope that literally watching the worlds of "light" and "darkness" interact will make these affinities clearer.

Although this book is ambitious in situating Nazi cinema within such a broad framework, it is also modest in contrast with traditional propaganda study. I frankly do not know the extent to which the Nazi film industry generated the ideologically solidified, "brainwashed" collective

12. See Dorothea von Mücke's discussion of the eighteenth century's aesthetic project of *Anschaulichkeit* in *Virtue and the Veil of Illusion: Generic Innovation and the Pedagogical Project in Eighteenth-Century Literature* (Stanford: Stanford University Press, 1991), 18–61.

that much scholarship assumes and that National Socialism tried to make believe existed by constantly reproducing images of such a collective. What I *can* demonstrate through textual analysis is how cinema reinforced Nazism's "impossible" harmony by organizing desire, by creating what Benedict Anderson calls an imagined community[13] of watchers feeling "at home" (with various narrative paradigms, with historical events and figures who "come to life," with movie stars). In what may seem a contradictory move, I want to argue that film under National Socialism was important as a collective mirror less because of its ideological homogeneity than because of the familiarity of its underlying literary paradigms, because of the inconsistencies and contradictions that give films a "human" face, and because all of the above was packaged in a medium that guarantees a pleasurable illusion of wholeness. In other words, even where it is most propagandistic, film may have been more useful to the state in its management of desire than in its management of ideas; even *Jew Süss* may have gotten more mileage out of pleasurable suffering than out of hate. As recent scholarship on melodrama has maintained, its effect lies not in message or moral but in another, emotionally oriented register. It is in seeking out this "other" register that I hope we can find out what propaganda study won't or can't tell us.

Early on I described Nazi cinema as a series of relationships. I want to conclude my introduction by returning to the relationship that for historical reasons was taken for granted in early studies of the subject: between "us," a post–World War II public, and these historically compromised film texts. A — perhaps *the* — major challenge when reflecting back on National Socialism is to prevent it from becoming a narrative. By narrative I mean a tendency to project homogeneity upon Nazism, to assume not only that "it" all fit together, but that it worked on everybody. As already suggested, if we approach Nazi cultural products with firmly fixed expectations, we will surely find what we are looking for and nothing more.

More disturbing, though, is the general function a narrativized Nazism takes on for contemporary cultures: it can easily become another kind of social fantasy, a convenient Other against which we can find our own, untroubled identity. Over and over contemporary societies exhibit how identity depends on something perceived as opposite. The post–cold war era has occasioned a reformulation of prevailing social fantasies; having

---

13. *Imagined Communities: Reflections on the Origin and Spread of Nationalism* (London: Verso, 1983); Anderson stresses that this notion does not imply " 'fabrication' and 'falsity,' " but rather " 'imagining' and 'creation' " (15).

lost the Soviet Union *qua* "evil empire," the U.S. political Imaginary inflates the mass-mediated image of minityrants or it stages "contained" wars that permit a brief, make-believe cohesion. If National Socialism becomes a historical narrative likewise affirming the identity of contemporary societies (who doesn't look good next to the Nazis?), the only "good" thing emerging from this era is lost: the lessons it offers as to how fantasies based on illusionary identification can erupt into very real terror.

Finally, the most compelling feature of narrative is what makes it so problematic as a mode of history: narrative always involves enjoyment, suggested by Nazism's unflagging popularity as a subject of films and TV dramas.[14] In the name of "enlightenment," contemporary discourses too often evoke Nazism as a source of what Saul Friedländer calls a frisson or titillation that neutralizes its horror.[15] Ironically, to the extent that we homogenize and "smooth out" Nazism as a horrifying Other, we are repeating the operation of the films in this study: constructing a seamless narrative which we project into the past with the ultimate purpose (whether we know it or not) of bolstering the present and ourselves. It is for all of these reasons that my film readings attempt to stress not only the familiar Nazi ideology (from which we can distance ourselves), but the unfamiliar and perhaps disconcerting side of the films: their heterogeneity, their internal contradictions, and their appeal.

In part my assertions about Nazi cinema's appeal as movies are based on personal, though hardly scientific, observations during an extended stay in Vienna. In researching this book, I frequently attended the film theater Bellaria, specializing in German films from the thirties and forties.

---

14. Precisely this dimension receives scant attention in public discussions of "enlightenment" regarding the Holocaust. In Stephen Spielberg's *Schindler's List,* female concentration camp workers are diverted by mistake to Auschwitz, where they are herded into what turns out to be a regular shower, but not until after they and the audience suffer drawn-out agony in anticipation of cyclon B. A justification of the scene as a "factual" account based on an inmate's chronicle of her experience does not account for the changed status of the story when re-presented in the trappings of a Hollywood film (indeed, by a director who has specialized in mythologizing Nazism as adventure). The "real" event is transformed into a "cheap trick," building up an artificial tension, worse, a titillation — all the while "knowing" the showers are really just that. The audience is led into a trap of tension *qua* enjoyment. To my mind, the scene is, notwithstanding the accolades the film enjoys, an insult to the real people who died in a real Auschwitz. The Washington, D.C., Holocaust Museum, with its issuing of a "personal identity" card to each visitor, suffers from the same problem.

15. *Reflections of Nazism* (New York: Harper, 1982), 18.

I found myself among scores of senior citizens who not only had memorized key passages of the films but engaged in active dialogue with them and with each other. The spectacle they offered to one separated by age and culture rivaled that of the films themselves: before my eyes a generation cathected its film culture and, in so doing, "retrieved" its youth. One has to wonder what propels the Bellaria "regulars," many on crutches and in wheelchairs, continuously back to the theater if Nazi film really can be grasped solely for its long discredited Moral. Although it wouldn't surprise me to find a few old Nazis among these people, I suspect that what drives them back has very little, if anything, to do with "politics." When I tried to "interview" one of the old men, it became clear that a "political," "ideological," or "documentary" interest in these films was not within the horizon of his thinking; hence he read my queries as a sign of total ignorance. "My dear," he began explaining, "first there was World War I, then there was World War II." I got my deserved comeuppance upon noticing that a group of curious seniors had gathered; I had turned myself into the bizarre spectacle the old man and his peers had been for me. Though it proves nothing, Bellaria served for me as potent evidence that despite the fascist discourse discernible in many feature films from this period, when they succeeded, they spoke to people (and not just to "fascists").

My opening chapter examines representational practices informing the study: Nazism's general fusion of the political with the aesthetic, its historical discourse, and its classical cinematic style. Although I treat them separately by way of introduction, all three are inextricably connected: "history" is nearly always invoked in Nazism's choreographed spectacles; indeed, it becomes a spectacle when made into a movie. Whether considered together or separately, all three components are linked by a common subject effect: the illusion of reconciliation, coherence, "wholeness." In other words: just as I am arguing that the effect of political films occurs on an unpolitical level, here I draw on many theories showing how "unpolitical" Nazism was as a movement. The chapter thus shifts the accent away from Nazism's *exploitation* of illusion as a means of indoctrinating the masses, and toward an understanding of National Socialism as virtually *synonymous with* illusion, theater, or spectacle. As suggested by Walter Benjamin's notion of "aestheticized politics," Nazism broke down a series of modern boundaries; above all, by allowing "politics" to thrive in aesthetic form, it offered a reconciliation of antagonisms only possible in the imaginary.

The study's three main sections deal, via film paradigms, with the central social/political fantasies of National Socialism (the "Jew" and the King or Leader), with its recycling of cultural history in artists' biographies, and finally with the transferability of the eighteenth-century model. The first examines Veit Harlan's infamous anti-Semitic film *Jew Süss* and several film biographies of Frederick the Great as cinematic articulations of social fantasy. *Jew Süss* illustrates how Nazism fantasizes the "Jew" as a literal embodiment of an "abstract" modernity threatening a healthy organism. I attempt to elucidate the contradictions that a representation of the "Jew" in classical cinema encounters: the film "wants" to make him irreducibly Other, but in trying to do so must draw on its own literary and film culture, thereby implicitly revealing its projections to be just that. It ends up, furthermore, making him curiously admirable by ascribing to him immeasurable sexual, political, and economic power. My reading elaborates the film's appropriation (and simultaneous inversion) of the bourgeois tragedy in a way that serves as a model for other films in the study. *Jew Süss*'s repoliticization of eighteenth-century drama brings it closer to the very different genre of horror, an affinity I explore with respect to the film's linkage of Jews and women as representing a threatening sexuality that needs to be contained by a male collective.

The "Frederick" films popular from the twenties through the forties exemplify the problem of trying to locate a filmic strategy exclusive to National Socialism; indeed the mythology constructing Frederick as a *völkisch* monarch dates back to the nineteenth century. Frederick is one embodiment of the necessary other side of the coin, the counterpart of the "Jew." I approach the Frederick myth in Nazi film using Ernst Kantorowicz's (and others') analysis of premodern political theory, according to which the King possesses two bodies, a mortal one and a second, immortal one that is a sublime object, that is, "more" than just its material self. In their specularization of Frederick, the films engage in a kind of revival of the King's Body as a visual manifestation of social well-being. This revival, however, is indelibly marked by modern tensions. Unlike in the medieval cathecting of the King's Body, its renewal attests to a desire to reconcile, via narrative, the perceived division between alienation and community, between the rationalization of everyday life and a sphere of fulfillment, between the public and the private as a site of decentering. The second Frederick chapter, a reading of *The Old and the Young King*, traces Frederick's evolution into a King as a disciplinary process, in Foucault's sense. Ironically, it is a series of spectacles that effect the disciplining; thus the film foregrounds the contradiction between Nazism's endorsement of discipline, which is an operational principle of "modernity," and its ideological antimodernism.

The second, larger section of the study deals again with the social fantasy of a historical Personality who compensates for real-life deficiencies. However, these films shift the nature of the fantasy from the manifestly political/military to the artistic, all of which have in common the struggle against alienation and the banality of the everyday. In other words, the tempestuous "world of the artist" assumes a similar function as aestheticized war or aestheticized politics. Three film readings, drawn from the plethora of Genius film biographies produced in the early forties, elaborate how Nazi cinema mobilizes a familiar canon of eighteenth-century culture to concoct a myth of history in which the spectator can feel part of a collective of "cultured" Germans. Herbert Maisch's *Friedrich Schiller — Triumph of a Genius* is the "model" Genius film, with its celebration of a perfect male Genius who is, moreover, a textual enunciator of his own fictionalized story. Gender is a central factor in G. W. Pabst's biography of actress Caroline Neuber, *Komödianten*. The film at once acknowledges Neuber as historical agent and refuses her as an embodiment of Genius. Finally, Traugott Müller's *Friedemann Bach* turns the Genius genre upside down, telling the story of what Althusser might call a failed interpellation,[16] of a figure who, though fetishized as body and biological Genius, self-destructs while running from one space to another. Although this genre is a form of "ideological rearmament" (Julian Petley) to counteract the trials of World War II, my readings explore a certain ambivalence in all three films, which at times threaten to ironize the seriousness of their "dominant ideology." Each has a counterpoint which is the source of its fun (e.g., the lovable tyranny of Duke Karl Eugen as a necessary prerequisite for Schiller's achievement) or which accommodates "female" desire at the expense of Nazism's hyperbolic maleness.

Having identified Nazi cinema's concomitant imitation and inversion of eighteenth-century culture and history, I am ready to proceed beyond this explicit model. The final section of the book extends the logic of Nazism's "translation" of the eighteenth century, demonstrating how little it has to do with a particular historical setting, figure, or event. The basic narrative patterns, the alignment of spectators with or against certain figures and value systems, above all the dominant social fantasies enjoyed via narra-

16. *Interpellation* is Louis Althusser's term for the way in which ideology "recruits" subjects among individuals. Althusser envisions the working of ideology as analogous to a policeman's hailing an individual on the street. The individual becomes a subject when she/he turns around 180 degrees, recognizing the hail was "really" addressed to her/him and nobody else, although of course the process of ideology does not occur in succession. See "Ideology and Ideological State Apparatuses," in *Lenin and Philosophy and Other Essays* (London: New Left Books, 1971), 127–86.

tive in the "eighteenth-century films" remain intact in virtually all of Nazi cinema. The reason is, to put it simply, that the eighteenth century did not "go away," that its narrative organization continued to live on in Germany of the thirties and forties, as it does in modern societies today. The first two chapters that comprise this section are structured parallel to the book's first section on "negative" and "positive" social fantasies. The first examines more film embodiments of social forces that, much like the "Jew" in *Jew Süss,* undermine community with principles of abstraction, circulation, and exchange value. In addition to an anti-Semitic comedy, *Robert and Bertram,* the chapter focuses on early films in which "Weimar," as a discursive phenomenon equated with dissolution, plays a major role (*Gold, Hitler Youth Quex,* and other early programmatic films). The second chapter addresses National Socialism's paradoxical reconciliation of its "antimodern" orientation with the tools of modernity; with industry and machines in *The Ruler* and *Diesel* and with radio in wartime "homefront" films like *Request Concert.*

My final chapter engages what has often been called Nazi cinema's most fascinating film, *Münchhausen.* Josef von Baky's spectacle celebrating the film studio Ufa represents both a revival and an upheaval of the human and social bodies running through the book. The film is an allegory of cinema itself that indulges a very different, perhaps incompatible, fantasy of total liberty and moral abandonment, yet also tries to harness what it unleashes. As a film almost in battle with itself, *Münchhausen* provides a fitting finish to a book about contradictions. At the very least it belies another fallacy ingrained by Hollywood, that the real problem with the Nazis was that they had no sense of fun.

ONE

Mass Spectacle, History, Cinema:
Embodiments of Social Fantasy

The Spring of festivals was to be followed by a Summer of festivals, and when with the approach of Fall the miserable condition of the country had still not improved, the decision was made to celebrate the triumph of the regime in a festival that would surpass all others, a powerful party rally. Since enough fireworks were available, there was nothing to prevent such an event. — Bertolt Brecht[1]

When, at the end of his famous essay, "The Work of Art in the Age of Mechanical Reproduction," Walter Benjamin wrote that communism responds to National Socialism's aestheticization of politics by politicizing art,[2] he surely did not mean to imply that Nazism did *not* politicize art. In this chapter, I want to lay some groundwork by examining both sides of this chiasmus, Nazism's infusion of the political with aesthetics and of aesthetics with the political — the latter of which has been the basis of propaganda study and the reason why Nazi art has often not received the attention it warrants ("political" art is not "real" art, etc.). The chapter offers a theoretical grounding for what I will subsequently demonstrate on a case-by-case basis: that the most important "political" lesson in Nazi cinema is not to be found in its political content but in its generation of a subject effect that would seem to have little to do with politics. This subject effect of wholeness and mastery depended on "imaginary" experience, which we can take in an everyday sense or in Lacan's psychoanalytic sense.[3] It is the

---

1. "Briefe um Deutschland," *Gesammelte Werke,* 20 vols. (Frankfurt: Suhrkamp, 1967), 20:234.
2. *Illuminations,* trans. H. Zohn (New York: Harcourt, Brace and World, 1968), 242.
3. Lacan's notion of the imaginary designates that order of the subject's experience which is dominated by identification and duality. It is the system of images absorbed

common factor in the representational practices — mass spectacle, historical discourse, and cinema — that this chapter addresses and that come together in my film readings. An excursus at the end of the chapter examines the importance of anchoring Nazism's beautiful illusion within the Western cultural heritage it appropriates. I will draw throughout on theories attesting to the inadequacy of viewing Nazi culture only in terms of cynicism, thus underscoring that Nazism's project encompasses both cynicism and "authentic" need. As Philippe Lacoue-Labarthe and Jean-Luc Nancy remark in discussing the myth that was Nazism, "exploitation . . . remains within the logic of the belief: for it is necessary to awaken . . . the Aryan dream in the Germans."[4] By no means should we assume that masters of manipulation are masters of themselves.

NAZISM'S BEAUTIFUL ILLUSION I: SPECTACLE
FOR AND BY THE MASSES

However historians of fascism may otherwise differ, they seem to concur on the affective character of Nazi "politics," on Nazism's emotional rather than intellectual appeal (whether or not they theorize that the "emotional" constitution of subjectivity is the very precondition for "intellectual" judgment). Equally familiar is its deemphasis of written texts or manifestos in favor of the spoken word, to which Hitler, following Gustave Le Bon's *Psychologie des foules* (1895), ascribed "all great, world-shaking events."[5] In his psychoanalytic study of fascism, *Male Fan-*

---

before entry into language and which continue to play a role throughout life. Christian Metz has defined the cinematic signifier as an imaginary one — as one which induces by means of visual images the same sorts of identifications that occur early in the subject's life, and within which absence plays the same structuring role. The symbolic order refers to the subject's entrance into language (discourse, narrative). The imaginary establishes similarity, e.g., of one image to another, or one thing to its image. The symbolic establishes difference — words "mean" not because they "imitate" a thing or thought but because they belong to a system in which they're distinguished from other words. The above condenses Kaja Silverman's lucid introduction to Lacan in *The Subject of Semiotics* (New York: Oxford University Press, 1983), esp. 149–93.

4. Philippe Lacoue-Labarthe and Jean-Luc Nancy, "The Nazi Myth," *Critical Inquiry* 16.2 (Winter 1990): 312.

5. Hitler's *Mein Kampf,* trans. Ralph Manheim (1925; Boston: Houghton Mifflin, 1943), 469. For a discussion of Hitler's tactics, see Klaus Vondung, *Magie und Manipulation: Ideologischer Kult und politische Religion des Nationalsozialismus* (Göttingen: Vandenhoeck & Ruprecht, 1971), 35, and Klaus Theweleit, *Male Fantasies,* vol.

tasies, Klaus Theweleit describes fascist oratory as therapy, as a "monstrous form that . . . emerges from the mouth of the *Führer* and closes around . . . open wounds."[6] Theweleit takes pains to argue that a disparagement of fascist language for lack of "substance" overlooks the very source of its effectiveness. Similarly, Saul Friedländer describes fascist language as circular rather than linear: it replaces interconnected argument with accumulation, repetition, and redundancy, launching "a play of images sent back, in turn, from one to the other in echoes without end, creating a kind of hypnosis by repetition."[7] By no means is fascist language "just" a tool, "just" the form that gives body to contents. Rather, this form is the content; it is, as Brecht puts it, "most cunning when it is most confusing."[8]

Not surprisingly, then, National Socialism's party conventions, where speech joined forces with music and visual plenitude, stand out as its "greatest aesthetic accomplishments."[9] Nor is it an accident that Leni Riefenstahl's film of the 1934 NSDAP congress, *Triumph of the Will,* has provided *the* images with which we conceive of the Nazi public sphere today. Few if any documentaries about this period have failed to include clips from the film, which attests to the true *Gesamtkunstwerk* character of these rallies and to Riefenstahl's ability to capture, even transcend, "real" experience through cinema. As many have commented, it is unclear in the film where the text begins and reality ends, since the "reality" she filmed was pure "text," an event staged for the very purpose of being filmed.[10]

How does this kind of spectacle, for which Nazism spared neither cost nor effort, figure in the grounding concept of the movement, its rejection of modernity? In *Mein Kampf,* Hitler describes in astonishingly clinical terms the subject effect he expects of mass rallies:

2, trans. Erica Carter and Chris Turner (Minneapolis: University of Minnesota Press, 1989), 118–29, "The Speech."

6. Theweleit, 2:126–27. I have modified this translation somewhat.

7. *Reflections of Nazism* (New York: Harper, 1982), 50.

8. *Arbeitsjournal,* 380, entry of February 28, 1942, quoted in Rainer Stollmann, "Fascist Politics as a Total Work of Art: Tendencies of the Aesthetization of Political Life in National Socialism," *New German Critique* 14 (Spring 1978): 57.

9. Ibid., 44.

10. See, for example, Susan Sontag's "Fascinating Fascism," in *Under the Sign of Saturn* (New York: Farrar, Straus and Giroux, 1972), 83, or Siegfried Kracauer's *From Caligari to Hitler: A Psychological History of the German Film* (1947; Princeton: Princeton University Press, 1971), 300–301.

20

The mass meeting is . . . necessary for the reason that in it the individual, who at first, while becoming a supporter of a young movement, feels lonely and easily succumbs to the fear of being alone, for the first time gets the picture of a larger community, which in most people has a strengthening, encouraging effect. . . . The community of the great demonstration not only strengthens the individual, it also unites and helps to create an *esprit de corps.* The man who is exposed to grave tribulations, as the first advocate of a new doctrine in his factory or workshop, absolutely needs that strengthening which lies in the conviction of being a member and fighter in a great comprehensive body. And he obtains an impression of this body for the first time in the mass demonstration. When from his little workshop or big factory, in which he feels very small, he steps for the first time into a mass meeting and has thousands and thousands of people of the same opinions around him, when, as a seeker, he is swept away by three or four thousand others into the mighty effect of suggestive intoxication and enthusiasm, when the visible success and agreement of thousands confirm to him the rightness of the new doctrine . . . — then he himself has succumbed to the magic influence of what we designate as "mass suggestion" (italics in original).[11]

The central opposition structuring the passage is that of isolation ("lonely" man's "fear of being alone") versus a "larger," "strengthening, encouraging" community imagined as a literal and metaphoric body ("comprehensive body," *"esprit de corps"*). With this opposition Hitler makes recourse to a critique of modernity that dates back to Rousseau, Sentimentality, Storm and Stress, and Romanticism, and that has been theorized many times since. As modernity becomes increasingly rationalized and instrumentalized, the individual feels driven into a position of isolation.[12] In response to this isolation, social institutions like art, the nuclear family (with its relatively new ideal of love "as passion," to cite Niklas Luhmann[13]), and other forms of communal experience began to take on a compensatory function; they provided a sanctuary in which other, noncompetitive standards exist. The institutions of art and the fam-

11. Hitler, 479.

12. For a non-mainstream yet interesting psychohistorical reading of this development with extensive documentation, see Fred Weinstein and Gerald Platt, *The Wish to Be Free* (Berkeley: University of California, 1969).

13. *Love as Passion: The Codification of Intimacy,* trans. Jeremy Gaines and Doris Jones (Cambridge: Harvard University Press, 1986).

ily may be very different, but within both the individual forced into a perpetual agonistic struggle can be "decentered" or dissolve individual boundaries, merge with an Other.[14] As *institutional* practices, however, these decentering experiences are simultaneously centered or contained in a manageable framework. They compensate, rather than disrupt, the everyday pressures of modern life.

The precondition for this process of isolation and its compensation is what Luhmann describes as a shift from "stratified" to "functionally differentiated" societies that occurred in the seventeenth and eighteenth centuries.[15] The first term refers to hierarchically organized premodern societies, the second to modern societies in which social stratification has increasingly given way to functional differentiation; the economic becomes a sphere separate from the political or the aesthetic, and a given individual comes to be defined more as a doctor or merchant than as a baron or peasant (though obviously class remains an important factor to this day). This process of differentiation also separated the fine arts from the crafts, which had earlier been subsumed under one category; a watchmaker was in social terms the equivalent of a painter or composer. Thus the compensatory effect of the aesthetic and of "community" is a function of modernity's compartmentalization or functional differentiation; the aesthetic reacts to an overemphasis on rationalization in the structurally predominant realms of modern societies — to our perception (today more than ever) that we're "just a number."

We can find reference to the compartmentalization Luhmann theorizes in another of Hitler's juxtapositions: that of the economic sphere (the "little workshop or big factory," where the man feels "very small" and is "exposed to grave tribulations") versus the "strengthening" mass meeting. Here, however, we run into a problem: if Hitler codes the economic sphere as isolating, what label should we give the mass meeting that remedies this isolation? The meeting's association with a political movement would seem to make it "political," yet another glance at Hitler's language clearly belies this presupposition. His emphasis of seeing (the "picture of a larger community," "an impression of this body," "the visible success") and implicitly of hearing moves the experience he describes into the sphere of the

---

14. For an illustration of the importance of this term, see "The Transitional Space of Literature," chapter 2 of Gabriele Schwab's *Subjects without Selves: Transitional Texts in Modern Fiction* (Cambridge: Harvard University Press, 1994), 22–48.

15. See, for instance, *The Differentiation of Society,* trans. Stephen Holmes and Charles Larmore (New York: Columbia University Press, 1982).

sensual and the aesthetic; the speech is a kind of show. More ominously, words like "swept away," "suggestive intoxication," "succumb," and "magic" leave no doubt that we've entered the realm of the religious and erotic; more precisely the religious *as* erotic — an effect driven to an extreme in Goebbels's novel *Michael,* when the narrator's description of his experience of a mass meeting is nothing short of orgasmic: "Shivers of hot and cold ran through me. I had no knowledge of what was happening inside me. But all at once I seemed to hear cannons thunder. . . . Revelation! Revelation! I no longer knew what I was doing. I was almost out of my mind. . . . In this instant I was reborn. . . . I was intoxicated."[16]

Either Hitler's or Goebbels's quotations alone would back up Theweleit's point that National Socialism does not lack "substance"; on the contrary, it rests on a profound, if purely intuitive, insight into the social and psychic structure of modernity. It turns modernity's constitutive experience of lack into political capital, and, as suggested by Žižek's term "social fantasy," it turns "society" into a kind of narrative or fiction. In order to pretend that social harmony is possible, it makes up the idea of a Leader as well as his antagonists, using the kind of displacements and condensations discussed earlier. Even its source of legitimation, the People symbiotically fused with the Leader, is a construction that fits into this fiction, and into the power structure that this fiction sustains. Whether we choose to call it Nazism's fiction or its "big lie," it worked by reconciling incompatible discourses, by pretending to retrieve a community perceived as "lost."

This is the essence of Benjamin's notion of "aestheticized politics," which is crucial to understanding not only fascism but all modern political forms. In "aestheticizing" politics, National Socialism went a step further than the early modernity that allowed the aesthetic to *compensate* for a rationalized world; it attempted rather to let the aesthetic become "reality" by breaking down traditional boundaries and turning the political experience into an aesthetic experience of community (which is by nature aesthetic).[17] Certainly no political practice in modernity has been devoid of aesthetics, but National Socialism infused aesthetics into the political

---

16. *Michael: Ein deutsches Schicksal in Tagebuchblättern* (Munich, 1929), 102; translation from Theweleit, 2:121f.

17. It is not, of course, my intention here to reduce the success of National Socialism to structural characteristics of modernity alone. In order for the NSDAP to achieve a mass basis, many other factors, such as the swift proletarianization of the petty bourgeoisie, had to intersect.

and public sphere to an unprecedented degree, trying to turn "life" into a work of art. While real life is subject to destabilizing contingencies and numbing banalities, "life as a work of art" represents the realm of the beautiful, a delimited realm of harmony.

In the process of aestheticizing politics, Nazism elided many other boundaries as well. Following Benjamin, Alice Kaplan aptly labels fascism a "polarity machine" that is in its very essence contradictory, particularly with respect to its "antimodern" ideology and its "modern" political practice: "Since fascism can be characterized formally as an entry of aesthetic criteria into the political and economic realms . . . it makes way for the possibility that a social defense against modernization can itself be (aesthetically) modern."[18] Besides effecting what Jean Pierre Faye calls a "cross-pollination" of revolutionary and conservative ideologies, fascism fuses elitism with populism, the individual with the collective. In this respect the passages from Hitler's *Mein Kampf* and Goebbels's *Michael* speak for themselves, elaborating how the individual experiencing the fascist public sphere gains a sense of identity paradoxically through the very sublation of individual identity, through "succumbing" and fusing with the "great comprehensive body."

This sublation of part and whole is manifested visually in a compositional principle that was dominant in the ritualized Nazi public sphere and that turns up at times in films: the "mass ornament" or merging of individuals into ornamental groupings in which they lose the appearance of individuals. Siegfried Kracauer invented the term with reference to new aesthetic forms that seemed to reflect rationalized modern economic forms. He wrote his famous essay "The Mass Ornament" in 1930, describing the synchronization of bodies in modern entertainment, in which chorus lines like the American Tiller Girls echoed the Taylorization of the modern production process, with synchronously working and dancing body parts corresponding to each other.[19] Only later did Kracauer apply the term to Nazi aesthetics, epitomized again by *Triumph of the Will* with its "officially fabricated mass ornaments" or "tableaux vivants."[20]

Like Nazism itself, the mass ornament tries to achieve an illusory reconciliation of oppositional experiences in modernity: of the rational and the beautiful, difference and sameness, the mechanized and the organic.

18. Alice Yaeger Kaplan, *Reproductions of Banality: Fascism, Literature, and French Intellectual Life* (Minneapolis: University of Minnesota Press, 1986), 26.
19. "The Mass Ornament," *New German Critique* 5 (Spring 1975): 70.
20. *From Caligari to Hitler*, 302.

Indeed, its integration of individuals into an aesthetic totality recalls eighteenth-century discussions on the relations of the manifold (*das Mannigfaltige*) to the unity of the whole. In his *On the Aesthetic Education of Man,* for example, Schiller sees the aesthetic state as unique in its ability to harmonize individual and society: "The aesthetic State alone . . . carries out the will of the whole through the nature of the individual. . . . Taste alone brings harmony into society, because it establishes harmony in the individual. All other forms of perception divide a man, because they are exclusively based on the sensuous or on the intellectual part of his being; only the perception of the Beautiful makes something whole of him, because both his natures must accord with it."[21]

Nazism, of course, *functionalizes* the perception of aesthetic harmony, the illusion of reconciliation experienced via the mass ornament, which comes to manifest in visual and spatial form its ideal subject position, described by Alice Kaplan as a dialectic of "selfishness" and "selflessness," and by Susan Sontag as one of "egomania and servitude"[22] (whereby we must remember that images of ornamentalized masses not only reflected life in the Nazi state but were disseminated to create that very disposition). Nowhere is this double effect of spectacle or the dialectic of egomania and servitude better captured than in the ambiguous title of Robert Brasillach's French fascist newspaper: *Je Suis Partout,* meaning both I am everywhere and I follow everywhere. Kaplan reads the slogan as an abdication of nineteenth-century liberalism with its illusion of individual autonomy, which is "succeeded in fascism by a sense of being able to *follow* and *belong* to a limitlessly large world. To be everywhere is to see or hear images of one's own progenitor everywhere."[23]

To this point I have focused on what people see and hear at mass rallies, yet another imaginary and narcissistic dimension is at work in mass experience that we can glean from comments made by less charitable viewers of Nazi events like Benjamin and Kracauer: the pleasure of being seen. Benjamin ascribes the paralyzing effect of mass rallies ironically to the grandiose delusion they offer: participants come "under a spell in which they must appear to themselves as monumental, which means incapable of reflected and independent action."[24] Similarly, Kracauer describes how

21. Trans. Reginald Snell (New York: Frederick Ungar, 1965), 138.
22. "Fascinating Fascism," 91.
23. Kaplan, 34.
24. "Pariser Brief" (1936), in *Gesammelte Schriften,* 3:489.

the masses are "forced to see themselves everywhere; thus, they are always aware of themselves, often in the aesthetically seductive form of an ornament or an effective image."[25] In addition to stressing the often remarked pacifying effect of fascist events, both statements point to their double function: the spectators at Nazi rallies and festivals were essentially the spectacle as well. Put in more theoretical terms, Nazism's mass gatherings accommodated themselves not only to scopophilia, the pleasure in looking, but to what is usually perceived as a threat: the subject's own specularization within the symbolic order. Thomas Elsaesser makes explicit this connection when he asks: "Might not the pleasure of fascism, its fascination have been less the sadism and brutality of SS officers than the pleasure of being seen, of placing oneself in view of the all-seeing eye of the State? Fascism in its Imaginary encouraged amoral exhibitionism, as it encouraged denunciation and mutual surveillance. Hitler appealed to the Volk but always by picturing the German nation, standing there, observed by 'the eye of the world.'"[26] Elsaesser suggests an erotic dimension to the fascist experience that differs from what we find in Hitler's or Goebbels's discourse; while the latter describe an experience whose erotic effect is grounded in active looking, culturally coded as "masculine," the exhibitionism Elsaesser describes implies a passive pleasure in being looked at, coded "feminine."[27] These need not, of course, exclude each other; they have in common the experience of erotic decentering.

Yet Elsaesser's implication that one of fascism's pleasures lies in being seen by the "eye of the world" may come as a surprise when we consider

25. "Masse und Propaganda: Eine Untersuchung über die faschistische Propaganda" (Paris, 1939), quoted in Karsten Witte, "Introduction to Kracauer's 'The Mass Ornament,'" *New German Critique* 5 (Spring 1975): 62.

26. "Primary Identification and the Historical Subject: Fassbinder and Germany," in *Narrative, Apparatus, Ideology,* ed. Philip Rosen (New York: Columbia University Press, 1986), 545.

27. This gender coding of the look finds an interesting narrative manifestation in Helmut Käutner's *Big City Melody* (1943). The film tells the story of a provincial female press photographer who captures the essence of Berlin in her work. When hired to photograph horse races, she breaks with convention by photographing the exhilarated spectators rather than the spectacle itself. We might read her reversal of standard procedure either as the expression of a female gaze that forgoes pomp in favor of the "human," or of a (Riefenstahlesque) fascist gaze aware that the importance of spectacle lies as much in letting people watch themselves as something else. Her photographs metamorphose Berlin from "just a city" to a "country" with its own People, and from a lifeless object to a human being: "Berlin sleeps just like we do."

that fascism is usually understood as a reaction against modernity, and that thinkers have consistently conceptualized modernity precisely in terms of the subject's visibility. Visibility is the principle underlying Foucault's notion of "discipline,"[28] which I will discuss in more detail in connection with film biographies of Frederick the Great. Foucault describes discipline using, as a metaphor, Jeremy Bentham's panopticon, a prison designed with a central tower surrounded by cells visible from the tower. A prisoner isolated in the panopticon can be watched at any and all times, but since the watcher is invisible and anonymous, one cannot know when one is being watched. The state of permanent visibility exemplified by this architectural model embodies for Foucault the operation at work in modern social institutions from prisons to schools, factories, hospitals, and even the family. The subject's visibility disciplines behavior in a positive as well as negative sense: since she or he must always count on being observed, the subject internalizes expected behavior; deviation from a given norm is prevented before it occurs.

Lacan, whose thought informs Foucault, reads visibility in psychoanalytic terms as the terror of the modern subject.[29] His theory of the gaze *qua* object reverses our perception of ourselves as the point from which the gaze emanates. In locating the gaze on the side of the object, Lacan suggests that, for all subjects, to see is simultaneously to be seen, to be part of the "spectacle of the world, [which] appears to us as all-seeing."[30] This all-seeing world is the symbolic order, the big Other that looks back at us, placing demands on us we can neither fulfill nor even grasp. Lacan's reversal of Renaissance conceptions of perspective thus destabilizes the subject's perception of the self as outside of the spectacle at which she or he looks, as in a position of (at least mental) mastery over what is seen.

If we add Luhmann with his notion of functional differentiation, we have three thinkers who, despite vastly different approaches and terminologies, implicitly or explicitly equate modernity with the very thing National Socialism reacted against: helpless exposure, agonistic pressures,

---

28. *Discipline and Punish: The Birth of the Prison,* trans. Alan Sheridan (New York: Vintage, 1979).

29. Lacan's theory is, of course, often considered ahistorical. For an argument that his theory indeed refers to the modern subject, see Teresa Brennan, *History after Lacan* (London: Routledge, 1993). Joan Copjec's *Read My Desire: Lacan against the Historicists* (Cambridge: MIT Press, 1994) argues that Lacan's psychoanalytic theory offers an explanation of historical progress superior to that of historicism.

30. "The Eye and the Gaze," in *Four Fundamental Concepts of Psychoanalysis,* ed. Jacques-Alain Miller, trans. Alan Sheridan (New York: W. W. Norton, 1973), 75.

instrumentality, commodification — in short, some antagonistic and abstract big Other. So how, in light of these famous theories, are we to understand Elsaesser's remark that fascism offers *pleasure* in being seen? His proposition seems all the more strange if we consider that in many ways National Socialism *intensified* the operations of modernity especially as described by Foucault: everything from the Gestapo to *Gleichschaltung* to the ritualized public sphere depended on a meticulous system of surveillance. Not coincidentally, for example, in articulating the importance of spatial organization to discipline, Foucault describes compositional forms that recall Kracauer's mass ornament; he even uses Kracauer's term "tableau vivant": "the constitution of '*tableaux vivants*' . . . transform[s] the confused, useless or dangerous multitudes into ordered multiplicities."[31]

The reason Nazism's gaze can be pleasurable, even erotic, lies again in *aestheticized* politics. When Elsaesser speaks of the state's "all-seeing eye," he refers not to real-life surveillance but to Nazism's imaginary, in which the state is an organic being under whose gaze modernity's experience of void becomes one of pleasure. The subject perceives a harmony between his/her own look and a benevolent gaze of the Other, which creates an aesthetic experience of wholeness. Using feature film as one kind of vehicle for imaginary experience, I intend, especially in my first two film readings on the "Jew" and King or Leader, to build on Elsaesser's insight. National Socialism answers the annihilating visibility that is modernity not only by changing, in its imaginary, the nature of the gaze, but by resurrecting the importance of the spectacle that characterized premodernity (albeit with a different agenda). Since both its "negative" and "positive" social fantasies involve an all-seeing, omnipotent watcher who is anything but anonymous, Nazism subjectivizes a gaze that is by its very nature in modernity anonymous; the gaze belongs to *somebody*. The "Jew" and the Leader become the subjects of a malevolent and benevolent gaze, respectively, but simultaneously *objects* of the gaze who need to be represented in order for this imaginary to work. The result is that "life" becomes a fantasy in which the subject knows the answer to what Lacan calls "che vuoi?" ("What do you want?"); knows with what symbolic mandate she or he must identify.

I have traced some complex thought to underscore a rather simple point: Once we understand Nazism's imaginary, its existence as aestheticized politics, we can no longer reduce its spectacles and symbolism to a

31. Foucault, *Discipline and Punish*, 148.

purely negative function of "disguising" repression and terror; nor can we reduce the most propagandistic film to "pure" propaganda or intention. Nazi spectacle must be seen as at once creative and camouflaging. It fulfills the all-important positive function of *renewing* the sensations described by Hitler, of incessantly reinforcing an imaginary collective identity via rituals sustaining the illusion of social harmony. Whatever form it takes, spectacle becomes more an end in itself than a means to an end. It negates social negativity *and* a reasonable social and political discourse. For all of these reasons it becomes clear why National Socialism is a "lived" and not a "political" movement, why it is religion and "not substitute religion,"[32] It also becomes clear why it is not enough to conclude that the subject of fascism is "stripped of his will, . . . an instrument of the ruling powers."[33] What if subjugation to an Other is indeed the "will," or, more precisely, the desire of this subject? What if such subjugation offers a narcissistic pleasure outweighing the desire for deliverance from what Kant called "self-incurred tutelage?"[34]

All of the representational practices with which National Socialism sustained itself operate on the same principles of aesthetics; all aimed at generating an experience of harmony and wholeness. In what follows, I want to briefly highlight in these terms two representational practices of importance to my study: historical discourse and feature film.

NAZI HISTORICAL DISCOURSE

"History" assumed a crucial role in National Socialism's endlessly re-cycled dramaturgy; whether invoked in a speech, marked by a holiday, or reproduced in a biography or a movie, it fulfilled the same psychic function as mass rallies and other spectacles. I referred in my introduction to history as a temporal "body" to which a coherence and wholeness is ascribed that carries over into the present. Nazi "history" serves to delimit boundaries, anchoring the subject in an imagined time and space, separating "German" from other histories and telling some versions of that history while silencing others. At the same time, experiencing this history cinematically allows for the same pleasurable sublation of boundaries discussed earlier; Nazi cinematic history "rewrites" individual desire as collective desire; its ready-made closure anticipates closure yet to come,

32. Theweleit, 2:413.
33. Stollmann, "Fascist Politics," 56.
34. Immanuel Kant, "What Is Enlightenment?" in *Philosophical Writings,* ed. Ernst Behler (New York: Continuum, 1986), 263.

which is already written as victory (whether in a military or cultural war). Nazism, in short, constantly invoked history while suppressing trauma and hegemonic struggle in favor of an imaginary, narrative struggle culminating in the wholeness Nazism projects into the present.

The reader's likely expectation that Nazi films about history "falsify" the past will not be disappointed. As early studies never tire of pointing out, Nazi films distort the motivations for wars, change the outcome of battles, the age and characters of historical figures, and so on. But it would be as misleading to reduce the films to historical "falsification," thereby implying the possibility of a pure or "correct" version of history, as it is to see only lies in Nazi rallies. The "deliberate" twisting of history in itself tells us little about the function of that history in organizing desire and identity, although factual distortions may indeed play into that organization. If the protagonists of *Lady von Barnhelm* (1940) ride by the Brandenburg Gate thirty years before it was built, we can assume that the arsenal of connotations the gate evokes outweighed concerns about historical sloppiness.

By no means, of course, are historical "distortions" unique to the cultural products of National Socialism or other "totalitarian" systems. An inevitable disparity exists between history, which remains unknowable, and historical discourse, which affords our only access to history. Historical discourse thus cannot help but "falsify," if by this we mean selecting, reconstructing, interpreting, hierarchically ranking, and filling in the gaps around historical data which at some point becomes congealed (if not ossified) into "knowledge" about history. As Hayden White reminds us, the reality of real events lies not in their occurrence but in their being remembered, and in their ultimate location in a chronologically ordered sequence.[35] In other words, "history" means events and phenomena that have gained meaning retroactively and are always already subject to processes of ideology, to a construction of an illusory national "identity," "essence," or "roots." As has so often been discussed in connection with "cultural pluralism" in the last decades of the twentieth century, a critical view of any history has to account for what's left out as much as what's left in. Even Nazi film directors Wolfgang Liebeneiner and Veit Harlan openly acknowledged that their films consist "to a great extent of omission," which, however, "should nevertheless remind us of the great events."[36]

35. "The Value of Narrativity in the Representation of Reality," in *On Narrative*, ed. W. J. T. Mitchell (Chicago: University of Chicago Press, 1980), 19.

36. *Filmkurier*, December 1943, reprinted in Joseph Wulf, *Theater und Film im dritten Reich* (Reinbek bei Hamburg: Rowohlt, 1966), 396.

Its intimate relationship to narrative gives historical discourse both its unreliability and, paradoxically, its authority. Again, it was the eighteenth century that rendered barriers between the "camps of the historians and creative writers osmotically porous."[37] A new experience of time demanded that historians construct their history "on an artful, moral, and rational basis,"[38] which forced them into a fictional mode. Yet historical narratives are at the same time unreliable because different narrative reconstructions compete, and "our desire for the imaginary . . . must contest with imperatives of the real."[39] Narrative cannot be "true" to history, since it imposes an organization on disorganized happenings, pulls together fragmentary sentiments and ideas, and structures disperse events in a narrato*logical* context. It allows social fantasy access to the realm of popular memory, disguising both past and present social contradictions (while also dialectically reinforcing social fantasy).

Ironically, it is precisely the violence narrative does to history that makes history seem to "come to life." Though fragmentary representations of history are arguably most "accurate," they seem incomplete and lacking in "meaning." Western historiography since the eighteenth century has responded to this perception by personalizing historical conflicts as interaction among individuals, thus precluding counterhegemonic histories and allowing "great" men to stand in for broad structural factors. National Socialism's cult of the personality both depends on and perpetuates this personalization of history, driving Heinrich von Treitschke's famous phrase "men make history" to its logical extreme. Hitler, aping von Treitschke, opposes "the mass man with the notion of personality. Only men make history, not the masses. . . . Without the masses being firmly led, major historical decisions are inconceivable."[40]

Nonetheless, Nazi historical films are not all that different from Weimar or Hollywood historical spectacles in making literal and figurative capital

37. Reinhart Koselleck, "Terror and Dream: Methodological Remarks on the Experience of Time during the Third Reich," in *Futures Past: On the Semantics of Historical Time*, trans. Kenneth Tribe (Cambridge: MIT Press, 1985), 214.
38. Ibid.
39. White, 4.
40. E. Calis, *Ohne Maske: H-B Geheimgespräche* (1931; Frankfurt, 1938), 47. Cf. Fritz Hippler, Reich film director from 1939 to 1943, on film: the "only possible subjects for successful historical [Nazi] films are personalities . . . with which people of the present are familiar or with which they can identify," who possess "timeless authenticity" and give "meaning to life." *Betrachtungen zum Filmschaffen* (Berlin: Max Hesses Verlag, 1942), 79.

out of history. As feature films, they occupy a space somewhere in between historical scholarship, with its imperative of authenticity, and "pure" fiction, with its license to invent, rearrange, and dramatize.[41] Like other forms of historical fiction, they assume a foreknowledge on the part of the reader or viewer, and their pleasure generally derives less from teaching new material than in affirming the audience's foreknowledge, allowing it to savor what it already "knows." As already suggested, this "foreknowledge" is the product of other ideological discourses and is anything but neutral. Ironically, the better "prepared" we are for a given historical fiction, the more it is likely to affirm a delusory subjective stability, to let us "misrecognize" ourselves in a glorious past.

I hope that in the course of individual film analyses the most important feature of the process by which Nazism (but, again, not only Nazism) "treats" history will become clear: that with the help of its narrative form "history" becomes a compilation of displacements, condensations, and projections — in short, in place of "historical" processes steps a psychoanalytic process. Through period costumes, setting, well-known figures, and the organization of dispersed events via underlying literary paradigms, the films rely on temporality, yet their effect is to detemporalize. Moreover, the Otherness of historical events not tamed in a particular narrative continuum is suppressed. Narrative figures and thematic oppositions will be "coded" in ways that are inextricably linked with one another: sociological coding borrowed largely from eighteenth-century literature is tied to moral coding, which in turn is tied to gender coding, whereby the "feminine" is nearly always negated or punished, to "racial" coding, and "specular" coding (how a given figure wields, or does not wield, the gaze).

These various levels coalesce to assign "value" rather consistently to an "antimodern" ideological model — indeed, it is here that psychoanalytic critique meets, and cannot do without, "old-fashioned" sociohistorical groundwork. "Nazi Germany" dreams of a lost world projected into the past, but that somehow has been rendered "timeless." At the same time, Nazi historical film narratives constantly reveal the ruptures in this ideal; constantly the "premodern" and most distinctly "modern" are in competition. The desire for the "timeless past" is conditioned by modernity's split; it can only be achieved through the brutal methods Foucault calls discipline, and can only be disseminated as an ideal by modern technology.

41. See Renate Werner's "Der Zeitgeschichtsroman in der Weimarer Republik," *Heinrich Mann Jahrbuch* 1 (1983): 121–44.

I want to look briefly at the medium that gave historical films their special power: the cinema that allows what Stanley Aronowitz calls "the never-was" to become history.[42] A public sphere so wholly structured around aesthetic experience as National Socialism naturally depended on technologies that allowed its orchestrated harmony to transcend a particular time and place. The importance of technologies like film and radio can also be understood in terms of the double function of Nazi spectacles I discussed earlier: the pleasure of seeing and being seen by a ubiquitous enveloping Other. Like mass rallies, movies not only offered a feast for the eyes but contributed to the oceanic feeling of a public space pervaded by uniforms, flags, posters, microphones, parades, festivals, monumental art and architecture. Mass-mediated sounds and images functioned literally as what Hitler refers to as "comprehensive" (umfassend, better translated as enveloping or all encompassing) embodiments of an Other in whose gaze or sound the subject could wrap him/herself and which "clos[ed] around open wounds." The experience of media like film did not have to be "political" to contribute to this healing effect; it only needed to be satisfying. As Alice Kaplan puts it, new, "authorless" forms recuperate "modern man's lost rituals with the help of the very factor that has threatened them in the first place: technology."[43]

In this context, then, it becomes evident why the Reich Film Chamber was established (July 14, 1933) before the Culture Chamber (September 22), of which the former became a subsidiary, why films were aimed at youth and disseminated in remote areas, why Goebbels ordered that film theaters be reopened immediately following air raid attacks, why films became most extravagant when they could least be afforded, etc. Goebbels spent, for example, 8.5 million Reichsmarks, twice the normal even for a major film production, and withdrew 187,000 soldiers and 4,000 sailors from duty when Soviet forces were crossing the East Prussian border in order to make the film Kolberg (1945). According to Kolberg's director, Veit Harlan, both Hitler and Goebbels were convinced that the impact of this film on the population would potentially outweigh that of a military victory.[44]

42. "Film — The Art Form of Late Capitalism," in The Crisis in Historical Materialism (New York: Praeger, 1981), 203.

43. Kaplan, 30.

44. Veit Harlan, Im Schatten meiner Filme: Selbstbiographie (Gütersloh: Sigbert Mohn Verlag, 1966), 262 f, quoted in Welch, 234.

Goebbels's well-known avoidance of "overt" propaganda again under-scores the inadequacy of locating the significance of Nazi cultural prod-ucts wholly in "message" or false consciousness. Stating his opposition to films "beginning and ending with National Socialist parades," he banned the early programmatic film *Hans Westmar,* seeing "no particular value in having our stormtroopers march about on stage or screen," and dis-paraged "sledgehammer" tactics.[45]

> At the moment that propaganda is recognized as such it becomes ineffective. However, the moment that propaganda, message, bent or attitude as such stay in the background and appear to people only as storyline, action, or side-effect, then they will become effective in every respect. . . . All art has a message. Art has an aim, a goal, a direction. . . . Thus I don't want art for the sake of a message but to insert that message into the greater overall design.[46]

What I want to highlight here is that Nazi cinema's adherence to genre and stylistic conventions of classical cinema is not the result of artistic deficiency, but is wholly consistent with the subject effect to which Nazism aspired. As theorized by film critics like Christian Metz, classical cinema offers its spectators an illusory wholeness and compensatory satisfaction that compliments a public sphere dependent on the imaginary. Cinema, like the human subject, is structured by the loss of some "original" object but compensates this loss through its "impression of reality" as plenitude, which disavows the absence of the profilmic object (the "actual" object being filmed). Likewise, cinema compensates the spectator's exclusion from the site of production with mechanisms of identification that restore to the subject a sense of imaginary wholeness. The most obvious form of identification (referred to by Metz as "secondary" identification[47]) is that

45. Quoted in Erwin Leiser, *Nazi Cinema,* trans. G. Mander and D. Wilson (London: Secker & Warburg, 1974), 35.

46. Speech at the Berlin Krolloper on March 5, 1937, quoted in Gerd Albrecht, *Na-tionalsozialistische Filmpolitik: Eine soziologische Untersuchung über die Spielfilme des dritten Reiches* (Stuttgart: Ferdinand Enke, 1969), 456. Cf. a similar Goebbels speech: "This is the really great art — to educate without revealing the purpose of the education, so that one fulfills an educational function without the object of that educa-tion being in any way aware that it is being educated, which is also indeed the real purpose of propaganda. The best propaganda is not that which is always openly reveal-ing itself; the best propaganda is that which, as it were works invisibly, penetrates the whole of life without the public having any knowledge at all of the propagandist initia-tive." Quoted in Albrecht, 468 f.

47. See *The Imaginary Signifier,* trans. C. Britton et al. (Bloomington: University of

with film characters through whom the spectator gains a sense of authority and wholeness lacking in real life. Metz terms "primary" the identification with the film itself; we see through the camera's eye, which transcends the diegetic characters' view and knowledge. This illusion of "omniscience" leads us to ignore the constructed nature of cinema: "Insofar as it abolishes all traces of the subject of the enunciation, the traditional film succeeds in giving the spectator the impression that he is himself that subject, but in a state of emptiness and absence, of pure visual capacity."[48]

It is this illusory compensation for perceived loss, this identification with someone else's authority, and this oscillation between narcissistic experience of self and communal experience that lend the subject effect of classical cinema its affinities with that of fascism. This is not, of course, to equate the two. Constant exposure to movies and other media clearly helps "construct" individuals as subjects, helps shape perceptions of the world and consequent behavior. Presumably, however, the filmgoer knows that movies are "only movies"; there is a vast difference between being ideologically shaped by the media and being "swept away," as Hitler would say, by National Socialism or a modern-day cult. Since, moreover, classical cinema relies on a codified system, it is questionable how fit that cinema is to represent some of Nazism's more pathological fantasies, as we will see in the case of *Jew Süss*. But these differences should not minimize the importance of the affinities between the world offered by classical cinema and by fascism; at the very least they suggest why fascism invested so heavily in that cinema. Conversely, we can read in these same terms Nazism's rejection of modernist art and the avant-garde, with its estranging of the "normal," as a fear of any art form that might undermine the subject's imaginary coherence. Such art had to be rejected by a movement whose very existence depended on an illusion of a harmony allegedly transcending social class and history; it had to privilege forms that allow this harmony to be experienced euphorically.

I want to close with a final admonition that, although cinema was doubtless an effective tool for National Socialism, its significance does not stop there. An often quoted statement by Goebbels to film executives in

Indiana Press, 1977). Although one can challenge Metz's implicit positing of a chronology to different forms of identification, as has Teresa de Lauretis (*Alice Doesn't: Feminism, Semiotics, Cinema* [Bloomington: Indiana University Press, 1984], 149), his distinction is useful in articulating a sense of empowerment generated by Nazi cinema that can include but goes beyond identification with a Hitler surrogate.

48. Metz, 97.

1945 may serve to illustrate that Nazism had such a predilection for film because its vision of reality was fundamentally cinematic:

> Gentlemen, in a hundred years' time they will be showing another fine color film describing the terrible days we are living through. Don't you want to play a part in this film, to be brought back to life in a hundred years' time? Everybody now has a chance to choose the part which he will play in the film a hundred years hence. I can assure you that it will be a fine and elevating picture. And for the sake of this prospect it is worth standing fast. Hold out now, so that a hundred years hence the audience does not hoot and whistle when you appear on the screen.[49]

Goebbels's remark demonstrates the ultimate trajectory of aestheticized politics; the *imagination* shapes political reality according to the *imaginary*. Goebbels seems to be already "living" his reality in terms of a future representation. As in movies, history assumes for him the form of a teleological narrative to be captured in a spectacle of visual and acoustic plenitude. Goebbels invites his peers to identify narcissistically with a film in which they will not only function as historical icons but as figures of identification for future audiences. He is, moreover, imagining the double pleasure of Nazi spectacles discussed earlier: Just as National Socialism affords its converts the pleasure of being subjects as well as objects of spectacle, Goebbels's compensation for his literal vulnerability lies in a fantasy of being watched by a future "Germany." At the same time, by prophesying the production of such a film, he seems to locate himself as agent of history and as the subject of an all-perceiving, omniscient look capable of transforming "Europe into a cinema screen," to use Paul Virilio's words.[50] This cinema screen is but another manifestation of the subjectivized gaze I talked about earlier, the benevolent gaze Nazism invents to counter modernity. It encompasses not only a harmonization between the subject's look and that of the Leader who returns the gaze, but also a broader gaze "looking back" upon the subject: that of an imaginary, whole "German history" that was at once produced by and that in turn produced the German "race."

Again in this case, the Nazis have documented themselves best. In one remark Goebbels says what this book is about: an imaginary grounded in

49. Quoted in Welch, 234.
50. *War and Cinema: The Logistics of Perception,* trans. Patrick Camiller (London: Verso, 1989), 53.

aestheticized politics, history as promised future, and an art form sustaining the subject. Above all, he articulates National Socialism's project of reconciling the contradictions of modern society. His is a vision that collapses all kinds of oppositions: art and reality, life and death, helplessness and transcendence, present and future, war and peace, spectator and spectacle, a whole, "organic" community and a fragmented machine product. The crucial point is that this reconciliation can only happen one way: as a big, expensive movie.

NAZISM'S BEAUTIFUL ILLUSION II: EXCURSUS ON NAZISM AND THE CLASSICAL AESTHETIC OF AUTONOMOUS ART

In my introduction I developed the fundamental argument that even at its most propagandistic, Nazi film works largely on a level of pleasure, that this pleasure is derived from a fantasy of social harmony, and that the latter in turn is derived ultimately from eighteenth-century thought and is couched in narratives recalling eighteenth-century literature. This excursus, though it will be necessarily oversimplified, is intended to reinforce my basic proposition by looking at how the beautiful illusion toward which all of Nazism's artistic praxis aspires is to be anchored vis-à-vis Art as we understand and valorize it (hence the capital A). I will approach this question initially from a different angle, examining some ways postwar Western cultures resist seeing the connections between the cultural tradition in which we and National Socialism are grounded.

As suggested by the term *cultural barbarism,* our repudiation of Nazism is based not only on values of humanity and democracy but on our sense of art, which has been an articulator and upholder of humanistic values. We reject Nazism because it was murderous *and* because it was kitschy — producing a kitsch all the more repugnant in its disguise of brutality. This criterion has its validity but also its pitfalls: while much is to be learned from discussing the nature and function of National Socialist kitsch, its dismissal is what has left us with so few serious readings of all but a few key Nazi art works, especially films. Because they aren't Art, they were long disqualified as objects of *textual* analysis — being objects at best of contextual analysis found in early studies of Nazi cinema.

The basis for this dismissal is not spoken, because it is taken for granted, even unconscious. Underlying it is a notion of "autonomous" art that emerged in the late eighteenth century and is still deeply inscribed in Western culture (ask anyone who has ever challenged this notion with upper-middle-class students). The early Enlightenment saw literature as capable of intervening in social practices, as a behavioral model for an emerging bourgeoisie. Hence J. C. Gottsched's *Critical Theory* of 1730 reads something like a recipe book: take a worthy pedagogical principle and stir in a narrative structure spiced with two ounces of humor and a dash of eroticism. The pedagogical benefit ascribed to such literature was the sole legitimation for its indulgence of narrative pleasure, which, to the consternation of many theologians, was tolerated as the spoonful of sugar that made the medicine go down. The early Enlightenment assumption was that dissemination of reading and of morality went hand in hand. As reading proliferated in the later eighteenth century (in part due to developments in printing), for the first time the modern notion of "high" versus "low" culture developed. Many thinkers began decrying what they perceived as the narcissistic, self-indulgent consumption of romantic novels and other genres that became the eighteenth-century version of schlock. By late in the century, "high" art was no longer perceived as capable of "moralizing" society but was valorized as an "autonomous" sphere all its own, a sanctuary from society in which ideals were preserved that countered but could not correct the real world. The notion of "autonomous" art is thus connected with the functional differentiation of the aesthetic I discussed earlier, and refers specifically to the retreat into the aesthetic that accompanied this growing pessimism. Concomitant with this development was the growing mythologization of the artist as person, the emergence of the genius aesthetic. In short, art became the Art that still intimidates us or that we use to bolster our egos; it became what Nazi films weren't.

I am more than aware of having turned this complex process into a narrative, but have done so to foreground an important irony: namely, the very notion of art with which we repudiate Nazi art is the notion of art that Nazism itself exalted, as especially the "Genius" films in this study demonstrate. There can be no question that National Socialism "used" the German cultural heritage or that Goethe and Schiller must have rolled in their graves at the way Nazism "used" them. But we'll never understand this usage by artificially severing National Socialism from its cultural framework. In what follows I will address three (albeit overlapping) strategies with which we dissociate at least high culture from Nazism's: aesthetic distance, art as social criticism, and fascist art as irrational. While none of these strategies is exactly "wrong," all are problematic, as I hope individual film readings will clarify.

One of the lasting effects of the process by which art became autonomous is the notion of aesthetic distance. It has stood since the eighteenth century as a major criterion distinguishing "high" art from kitsch. Both artist and "receiver" are expected to maintain distance toward the artwork, to contemplate the work rather than be excessively "involved." The aesthetic of distance entails thus an intellectual effort that to a degree disturbs the pleasure of reception,[51] yet presumably rewards the beholder of art with a degree of "freedom," a "deeper" understanding. Fascist aesthetic practice, which, as has already been discussed, encompasses the ritualized public and political sphere as well as art in the usual sense, is conceived as a surrender of aesthetic distance; note how Benjamin and Kracauer referred to fascist subjects as "under a spell" and "seduced," respectively. Fascist art betrays aesthetic distance by being "too close," by arousing "cheap" emotion. It shifts the emphasis from the symbolic to the imaginary, as the fascist subject mirrors him or herself "uncritically" in it.

Certainly this critique is valid; fascism and its art work on a "gut," emotional level, which is why one can't "argue" with them. It nonetheless is useful to problematize Western cultures' entrenched reception of high art before we use aesthetic distance as a "line in the sand" between the art we revere and the fascist art we disdain. The "proper" contemplative stance toward high art may in fact differ from the involvement fascist art (or kitsch in general) invites, but this does not mean that contemplative reception lacks the latter's imaginary dimension. From the 1930s on, culture critics began deconstructing the narcissistic potential of contemplative art, suggesting that the very distance posited by the aesthetic of the beautiful is itself an illusion covering up, among other things, its implication in sustaining class hierarchy. One might conceive "contemplative" reception as a dialectical shifting: as a subject contemplates the work of art, she or he simultaneously allows that work to reflect back upon the self as a mirror in which she or he pleasurably "recognizes" the self as a member of an exclusive club — all the while disavowing any narcissism (recalling Brecht's famous line, there's more reality "in the bad taste of the masses than in the taste of the intellectuals"[52]). This irreverent perspective on aesthetic distance holds a key to understanding Nazism's narcissistic identification with high culture and its canonical figures like Friedrich Schiller. It is the eighteenth century's own Genius aesthetic, its dichotomization of high and low, and its elevation of creator and receiver of

51. See, for example, E. M. Wilkinson, *Über den Begriff der kritischen Distanz: Von Schiller und Wordsworth bis zur Gegenwart*, Deutsche Beiträge zur geistigen Überlieferung, no. 3 (1957).

52. "Der Dreigroschenprozess," in *Gesammelte Werke*, 18:165.

greatness that opens the way for Nazism's "genius" films, for example, to invoke Culture as a collective mirror.

Connected to the idea of aesthetic distance permitting a "higher" form of reflection is another widespread assumption regarding the *function* of fascist art versus that of the humanistic tradition. Bourgeois, humanist Art, we assume, "opens our eyes," is a thorn in the side of the social status quo, while fascist art "blinds," is pure affirmation of what is. This relationship is often presented in chiasmic terms, suggesting that fascism is a kind of reversal of a classical aesthetic: "Where [in National Socialism] free art should be, politics reigns, namely terror, proscription, repression. Where emancipatory politics should be, pseudo-art reigns, namely the illusions of beauty, sensual joy and sublimity."[53] Apart from the quandary of how to separate "free" from "pseudo" art or to define what an "emancipatory" politics free of aesthetics would be, the binary oppositions in such a statement provide too easy a topography for grasping the relationship between Nazism and its heritage. This topography fails to account for Nazism's constant "borrowing" of narratives and semiotic configurations from a literature that aspired at once to "free art" and "emancipatory politics." Nor does it account for the fact that some films, *Friedrich Schiller* being again a good example, have generated contradictory readings as "pro-" and "anti-Nazi" films. Finally, if we can agree that Nazi art does indeed have an affirmative social function, this does not guarantee that the "beautiful illusion" of classical aesthetics successfully challenged "reality."

Even if the *contents* of autonomous art are subversive and expose social ruptures, the *institutionalization* of art may render its critique compensatory and affirmative, encouraging its receiver to engage in the narcissistic self-heightening in the mirror of Art described above. This has particularly been true since art has been institutionalized as an autonomous subsystem compensating other realms of modern life. To state this more accessibly: as long as high art belongs to the (financially and educationally) privileged, it can be ever so subversive and still be defused, even coopted as "rad chic." (This disparity between content and institutionalization again dates back to the eighteenth century, although the idea of an institutional framework was not yet within the horizon of contemporary thinkers, who took for granted that the aesthetic could exercise a critique of reality independent of art's institutionalization.) "High," autonomous art, then, is yet another framework for social fantasy, for something that makes it

53. Stollman, "Fascist Politics," 59 and 51.

possible to live with social antagonism — a tendency Brecht assailed with his attack on "the old, untechnical, anti-technical, 'radiating' art tied to religion,"[54] Benjamin with his analysis of "aura," and later Marcuse with his critique of "affirmative art." This defusing of subversion via institutionalization gives us another key to how "freedom" and rebellion against tyranny could be a "master narrative" in the SS state.

The very assumption that art can serve as a potential agent of social intervention derives from an Enlightenment notion of reason, which leads us to another conceptualization of fascism as espousing an "irrationalism" that can be in effect "blamed" on German Romanticism, as in the following statement from a book on Nazi cinema: National Socialism grew out of the "*Völkisch* tradition, which is essentially a product of late eighteenth century romanticism."[55] Probably the best-known proponent of such a linear model was Georg Lukács, whose *Destruction of Reason* (1954) traced the development of Romanticism through National Socialism. The moment of truth in this model lies in the historical link between reactions to modernization beginning in eighteenth-century Germany, to which I have already referred, and subsequent "conservative" movements. What has often passed as an affinity between early Romantics and fascists was in the case of the former a refusal to acquiesce to what they perceived as the pitfalls of rationality when it becomes a pervasive, ossified force. Romantic "irrationality" was, in other words, based on insight into the potential of a totalized rationality to shift into its opposite, to become the basis of oppression and terror as it did in the French Revolution and later in Stalinism. Nazi irrationalism, on the other hand, derives from the slippage of (political, aesthetic, erotic, religious) discourses we have seen, and is complemented by a chilling rationality in practice. Furthermore, Nazi narrative and practice depended on closure, while Romantics objected to, undermined, and deconstructed all closures.

Again, the fallacies in this model, which also allow a kind of distancing from fascism even if it concedes a linkage to the Western cultural tradition, lie in the transformation of history into a totalizing narrative in which one movement becomes the offspring of another, which also lends each a homogeneity it did not have. An understanding of Nazism either as a functional inversion of humanist art or a logical extension of Romanticism operates on the binaristic assumption that something "good"

54. "Dreigroschenprozess," 158.
55. David Welch, *Propaganda and the German Cinema, 1933–45* (Oxford: Clarendon Press, 1983), 1.

(Enlightenment "reason") has been invaded by something "bad" ("irrationality")—a structure that is the foundation of a narrative and that invariably aligns the subject telling the narrative on the "good" side. Most ironic in this respect was the Lukács position, which, in suppressing the closeness between rationality and irrationality, is itself closer to the "irrational" and exclusionary tactics of fascism than are the so often maligned Romantics. This is perhaps why we find Nazi feature films relying more on the narratological patterns of Enlightenment literature than (especially early) Romantics with their constant destabilization of cultural assumptions, centered subjects, and accepted oppositions like illusion and reality.

This still leaves unanswered the question of exactly what the relationship is between the "good" Germany of poets and thinkers and the "bad," fascist Germany. One attempt at an answer was made in the seventies by Rainer Stollmann, who, also building on Benjamin, complicates the above alternatives and resists an uncritical affirmation of Great Art.[56] Stollmann juxtaposes a quotation from Schiller's *Letters on the Aesthetic Education of Man* distinguishing between the creative artist, who shapes "a formless mass," and the political artist, whose materials are human, with a strikingly similar quotation from Joseph Goebbels (in a letter to conductor Wilhelm Furtwängler) also referring to politics as an art. The difference lies in Schiller's distinction between things and people as material—a distinction to which Goebbels is indifferent. While Schiller insists that the political artist must respect his materials and create "true political freedom" as the "most perfect of all works of art," Goebbels regards the political artist's human subjects merely as "raw material" out of which "a solid, well-wrought structure of a Volk" must be formed.[57]

Stollmann builds on the juxtaposition to argue that the "intentions and perspectives of idealistic aesthetics have established themselves 'perversely'" in fascist art, which is the "heir" to classical art in form rather than content.[58] Fascism's exploitation of aesthetic illusion was made possible by the petty bourgeoisie's "flight" from reality and by the fact that attempts to reconcile the beautiful illusion of classical art with the "ugly reality of bourgeois society always transcended that society."[59] Fascist art is a reversal not of bourgeois art but of socialism's intent to restructure

---

56. See footnote 8 and Stollmann's larger study *Ästhetisierung der Politik: Literaturstudien zum subjektiven Faschismus* (Stuttgart: Metzler, 1978).
57. Letter of April 1933, quoted ibid., 202.
58. Ibid., 48 and 51.
59. Ibid., 49.

social relations. It is a "pseudo-socialist changeling" aimed at constructing a beautiful "illusion" that disguised, rather than subverted reality. Though Stollman's reading suffers, I think, from an overemphasis on the negative function of fascist aesthetics (of disguise and fakery), as well as from an implicit assumption of "genuine" art and a "genuine" socialist identity that recognizes "reality,"[60] it was significant in problematizing the institutionalization of an autonomous art that indeed opened itself up to "perversion."

It is, I think, no coincidence that Paul de Man—though doubtless miles away from Stollmann's leftist position—reiterates Stollmann's rhetorical strategy. In an unpublished lecture on "Kant and Schiller," de Man begins with the very same maneuver of juxtaposing Schiller's "aesthetic education" with a quotation from Goebbels's *Michael* whose content (politics is an art akin to plastic arts) mirrors the quotation Stollmann cites. Though de Man readily concedes that Goebbels grievously misreads Schiller, his point is to suggest, cautiously, affinities between the implications of their aesthetics.[61] De Man gleans from Schiller's aesthetic, which is largely indebted to what he sees as his misreading of Kant, a "violent streak."[62] His suspicions are raised by Schiller's (and other German philosophers') a priori valorization of art as "primarily a social and political model."[63] While art may define the human, it is characterized by a "principle of formalization" that generates its own codes and systems, ultimately allowing only for a reproduction of that system. Recalling Marcuse's critique of "affirmative" culture, he cites aesthetic form's tendency "to substitute the spectacle of pain for the pain itself, and thus sublimate it by drawing away from the pains of experience, focusing instead on the plea-

---

60. A case in point is Stollmann's discussion of National Socialism's well-known appropriation of leftist symbolism. Because these symbols had a "long tradition" on the left, Stollmann accords them the ability to "strengthen [the workers'] collective identity," while in the case of "frantic[ally] clustered" subjects of fascism, such symbols could only enhance "an artificial identity" (58). Such a reading again tries to understand National Socialism as an "irrational" phenomenon, and assumes that any identity can escape the status of fiction, any symbolism that of an imaginary mirror.

61. For a critical discussion of de Man's thesis, see Martin Jay, "The 'Aesthetic Ideology' as Ideology; or, What Does It Mean to Aestheticize Politics?" *New German Critique* 21 (Spring 1992): 41–62.

62. Paul de Man, "Aesthetic Formalization: Kleist's *Über das Marionettentheater*," in *The Rhetoric of Romanticism* (New York: Columbia University Press, 1984), 280.

63. Ibid., 265; see also de Man's "Kant and Schiller."

sures of imitation."[64] Beneath Schiller's perfect aesthetic project, de Man detects an intrinsic flaw and risks "a more perverse reading," that aesthetic distance may be a ruse to "enjoy . . . pleasures that have to do with the inflicting of wounds rather than with gracefulness."[65]

Whether or not de Man goes "too far" in deconstructing Schiller's aesthetic republic, the aesthetic ideology he identifies as ideology is what inhibits a traditional "propaganda" approach to all parts of the Nazi cultural apparatus, including film, from really engaging its object, which is dismissed as not worth the effort.[66] Most important is de Man's refusal to let us weasel out of the uncomfortable fact that even if Nazism is a bad relation, a relation it is. Its subject position of wholeness, of fusion with a cohesive social body, with its implicit exclusion of an Other, has its roots in eighteenth-century literature, however "perverted," biologized, or pathological a shape these may take. Without the classical aesthetic we rightfully revere as a historical expression of culture, the movies in this study, and indeed Nazism itself, most literally could not have been.

---

64. Ibid. Cf. Marcuse on the humanistic tradition: "To the need of the isolated individual it responds with general humanity, to bodily misery with the beauty of the soul, to external bondage with internal freedom, to brutal egoism with the duty of the realm of virtue." "The Affirmative Character of Culture," in *Negations* (Boston: Beacon Press, 1968), 98.

65. "Aesthetic Formalization," 280.

66. Note David Stewart Hull's dismissal of Nazi films as "tedious," "bombastic," "corny," "heavy and vulgar." In indicting Nazi nationalism, Francis Courtade and Pierre Cadars exude their own chauvinism in *Geschichte des Films im dritten Reich,* trans. Florian Hopf (Munich/Vienna: Carl Hanser, 1975). Although they celebrate a few actresses whose "feminine ease and magical presence" permitted one to forget "Teutonic moroseness," they conclude their Nazi film history with the remark that film in the Third Reich was "deeply German in spirit and style" (285 and 284, respectively). "German" or "Teutonic" become in their discourse as unproblematic as "Aryan" and "Jewish" were in the Third Reich they attack.

I

TWO SIDES OF A COIN:

THE "JEW" AND THE KING

AS SOCIAL FANTASIES

*

TWO

Courtier, Vampire, or Vermin? *Jew Süss*'s Contradictory

Effort to Render the "Jew" Other

Hate implies a kind of love, or at least an inability to rid the mind of obsessions with the hated other. . . . There is no fruit like forbidden fruit; there is nothing more delicious to enjoy and punish freely than the crimes of sex and aggression which authoritarian repression has forbidden. — Joel Kovel, *White Racism*

Veit Harlan's *Jew Süss* (1940), which is based on the life of the eighteenth-century financier Joseph Süss Oppenheimer, has been branded one of the "most vicious . . . motion pictures of all times,"[1] appealing to "the lowest instincts of man."[2] *Jew Süss* owes its notoriety to its singular production history as a film commissioned to help prepare Germany for the "final solution," the extermination of European Jews. Consequently, most studies of the film restrict themselves to a discussion of the film's subtext, of Goebbels's intervention in the production process, and his coercion of actors.[3] Unlike other major anti-Semitic films made in the Third Reich,

1. Cited from commentary preceding the film on its video release in the United States by Video City Productions, prepared by David Calvert Smith and released by the Jewish Media Services JWB. The film is given the subtitle *The Indoctrination of Racial Hatred.*
2. Helmut Blobner and Herbert Holba, "Jackboot Cinema," *Film and Filming* 8.3 (1962): 16.
3. A wealth of literature exists on *Jew Süss*, and the following studies provide detailed examination of its complex relationship to Nazi culture and politics: D. S. Hull, *Film in the Third Reich* (Berkeley: University of California Press, 1969); E. Leiser, *Nazi Cinema* (New York: Macmillan, 1974); P. Cadars and F. Courtade, *Geschichte des Films im dritten Reich* (Munich: Hanser, 1975); J. Wulf, *Theater und Film im dritten Reich* (Reinbek bei Hamburg: Rowohlt, 1966); D. Welch, *Propaganda and the German Cin-*

however, *Jew Süss* was also a box office success featuring a host of stars.[4] I want to concentrate on the film text itself, exploring both sides of the equation: how the film constructs the "Jew" as Nazism's constitutive social fantasy and how it spoke to ordinary moviegoers.

Like other films in this study, *Jew Süss* fictionalizes history not only by distorting facts but by appropriating a literary paradigm deeply rooted in German culture. The eighteenth-century bourgeois tragedy by writers like G. E. Lessing and Friedrich Schiller serves as a vehicle helping the film align its viewers with some narrative positions over others. The first section of my reading focuses on the film's narrative paradigms, beginning with the recycled bourgeois tragedy. It sets up a model for the analysis of other films, which similarly borrow eighteenth-century literary codes and blend historical events with fiction to rewrite "German history" as a bourgeois narrative in which spectators can pleasurably "recognize" themselves.

From here I explore a narrative slippage specific to *Jew Süss* and necessary to its anti-Semitism: into the structure of horror. *Jew Süss* modifies the historical-philosophical presuppositions of the bourgeois tragedy by locating the source of social antagonism in the "Jew" rather than in feudal powers. It thus aims its critique at a "racially" rather than a socially defined group — one presumed to be "outside" of German culture, though spatially located within its boundaries. This structure resembles horror, which imagines an assault upon the social body by something alien that must be destroyed for the social equilibrium to be restored. The Jew's supposed vampiric Otherness is articulated with the help of a specular regime in which he is both possessor of a "castrating" gaze and the object of the gaze.

The second section of the chapter charts *Jew Süss*'s incorporation of anti-Semitic mythology. I introduced earlier the role of the "Jew" as Na-

---

ema, 1933–1945 (Oxford: Clarendon, 1983); D. Hollstein, *"Jud Süss" und die Deutschen* (Frankfurt/Main: Ullstein, 1983); F. Knilli et al., *"Jud Süss" Filmprotokoll, Programmheft und Einzelanalysen* (Berlin: Spiess, 1983).

4. *Jew Süss* was one of the most popular films of 1940, drawing 20.3 million viewers. Its profits were exceeded in 1940 only by *Request Concert;* for the years 1941–1942, it was the sixth most popular film, reaping 6.2 million Reichsmark. See Stephen Lowry, *Pathos und Politik* (Tübingen: Niemeyer, 1991), 269–71. Especially in the late thirties and early forties, many Nazi feature films had strong anti-Semitic elements, such as *Linen from Ireland* and *Robert and Bertram* (both 1939). Yet few concentrate on the "Jewish question." These include *The Rothschilds* and the "documentary" *The Eternal Jew* (both 1940).

tional Socialism's essential social fantasy: He embodies all obstacles to Nazism's harmonious corporatist society, yet, paradoxically, empowers the illusion that this harmony is possible. Since the social antagonism generated by modernity is displaced onto the "Jew" and condensed in him, he is necessary for society to believe in itself, to disavow its internal contradictions. While *Jew Süss* depends on preexisting anti-Semitic ideas, it also provides the type of fantasy space necessary in order for the fantasmatic "Jew" to exist. Régine Mihal Friedman captures this relationship in the title of her book on anti-Semitic films, *L'Image et son Juif* ("The Image and Its Jew"): the fantasy image itself constructs the "Jew," rather than a preexisting truth being ideologically distorted by anti-Semitism.[5] Like any other ethnic, religious, or national identity, the "Jew" does not exist apart from his hypostatization by someone, although, as Sander Gilman reminds us, the self-construction of any group is affected by the discourses and images by which others define it.[6]

Jew Süss is a complicated case of identity construction for the following reason: to say that it is the kind of fantasy vehicle anti-Semitism needs is not to say that the film's construction of "the Jew" is identical to anti-Semitism's fantasy. The reason is that Nazism's fantasized "Jew" is riddled with contradictions (he is both rich and dirty, intellectual and vermin, impotent and licentious, communist and capitalist, etc.), and his essential sexual, mental, moral, and ultimately racial difference is imagined and not representable in concrete terms. (Unlike other forms of racism, anti-Semitism cannot even call upon reliable bodily markers.) *Jew Süss,* on the other hand, is *nothing but* a form of representation that follows the imperatives of classical cinema. Its exhaustive catalog of anti-Semitic stereotypes has to be forced into this formal framework that, despite a formidable repertoire of villains, is hard put to demonstrate the "essence" of Jewishness. Often when we say the film shows that the Jews are vermin, we are reading our historical knowledge of anti-Semitism and the Holocaust into the film. What the film *shows* are certain codified narrative types that are found in cinema and that, though identified as "Jewish" by the film story, have a much more universal application.

My aim is to explore from a variety of perspectives how anti-Semitic ideas, canonized literary paradigms, and classical cinema come together in this one infamous text attempting to represent Nazism's "Jew." Scholars writing on *Jew Süss* generally take for granted that the film is an effective

5. Paris: Payot, 1983.
6. *The Jew's Body* (New York: Routledge, 1991), 1–9.

anti-Semitic document, which is doubtless true, especially if an audience is predisposed to anti-Semitism.[7] Yet I would stop short of assuming either that the film's popularity among Germans was necessarily a *result* of its anti-Semitism or that the construction of the "Jew" as Other is without ruptures. I will argue that whatever power *Jew Süss* wields is to be found in its cinematic address, which is based on old narrative paradigms onto which anti-Semitic ideas are "grafted." In other words, the film's (from today's perspective) obvious organization of anti-Semitic ideas, its logic of ideas, is only part of the picture. Moreover, because the film juggles ideology and a codified cinematic mode of organizing desire, it sometimes entangles itself in contradictions that shed light on the compensatory function of anti-Semitism itself.

The historical Joseph Süss Oppenheimer (1692–1738) was a controversial figure during his lifetime, and the subject of documentations and literary works throughout the nineteenth and twentieth centuries.[8] He held the position of financial advisor to Duke Karl Alexander of Württemberg (then an independent duchy) from 1733 to 1737. Württemberg had a

---

7. There is ample evidence to support a claim that *Jew Süss* was capable of inciting anti-Semitic activities. The SS Security Service's monthly "Reports from the Reich," which attempted to gauge public reaction, especially to prestigious films, corroborate the film's inflammatory effect. See Leiser, 152–54. The film was shown to SS units before they were set into action against Jews, to non-Jews in areas from which Jews were to be deported, and to concentration camp guards, some of whom testified at the Nuremberg trials that inmates were subsequently mistreated. I would be more cautious in contemplating how universal such a reaction was among the general movie-going public. To my surprise, the older Germans I've talked to who saw the film in its day tend not to be apologetic about having liked *Jew Süss,* although they all, at least retroactively, condemn the Nazis. Their admission that the film was, of course, terrible Nazi propaganda may well be accompanied by a major *but:* "but today's actors aren't nearly as good as Werner Krauss," "but today's movies are violent and trashy." The only explanation I can find is that to many of its original audience *Jew Süss* will always be regarded in a way impossible for anyone born later: as a movie that somehow will always remain in a separate category from something as traumatic as the Holocaust. I mention this admittedly anecdotal evidence not to exculpate anyone or trivialize the historical importance of the film, but because I think this schizoid "yes, but" attitude might offer a more complicated lesson about the way such texts "work" or, in some cases, don't.

8. Besides Harlan's film, the best-known versions are Wilhelm Hauff's novella of 1827, Lion Feuchtwanger's novel of 1925, and a British film, also called *Jew Süss,* by Lothar Mendes of 1934. See also Manfred Zimmermann, *Joseph Süss Oppenheimer: Ein Finanzmann des 18. Jahrhunderts* (Stuttgart: Rieger'sche Verlagsbuchhandlung, 1874), Selma Stern, *Jud Süss: Ein Beitrag zur Deutschen und zur Jüdischen Geschichte* (1929; Munich: Gotthold Müller, 1973).

dualistic constitution, and the powerful Estates felt undermined by Süss Oppenheimer's efficient and sometimes ruthless service to the sovereign.[9] As Protestants, they were also distrustful of Karl Alexander's Catholicism. The Duke planned a coup d'état, of which Süss was not informed, that would increase his power and hence make Württemberg Catholic. When the Duke died suddenly just before the coup, Süss was arrested for treason and hanged on February 2, 1738, after a trial that "mocked all justice."[10] The film's script by Harlan, Wolfgang Eberhard Möller, and Ludwig Metzger, allegedly based on "an exact study of the trial protocol in the Württemberg State Archive,"[11] makes Süss solely responsible for the coup attempt and the rift between the Duke and the people of Württemberg:

> The film begins in 1733 with Karl Alexander's accession to power as Duke of Württemberg. Lacking enough money to buy a celebratory gift for his wife, the Duke sends his envoy von Remchingen to Joseph Süss Oppenheimer in Frankfurt's Jewish ghetto. Süss ingratiates himself with the Duke by extending him credit on a necklace in exchange for permission to enter the capital city of Stuttgart, which heretofore has been prohibited to Jews. Süss becomes the Duke's financial advisor, and continues to finance the latter's representational excesses (an opera, a ballet, and a retinue) denied by the Estates. To compensate Süss, the Duke grants him control of the roads of Württemberg. Süss enrages the people by taxing every bridge, gate, and street heavily. He persuades the Duke to lift the ban on Jews entering Stuttgart, as well as to seek absolute power by staging a *coup d'état* with the help of foreign soldiers hired with Jewish money. When Estate-Counselor Sturm rejects Süss's offer to marry his daughter Dorothea, Süss has Sturm arrested as a traitor. Dorothea is hastily married to her lover

9. The Estates were an elective assembly representing the social "Estates," or orders in a number of European countries from the fourteenth through the eighteenth centuries. Until weakened or abolished by absolutist rulers in the eighteenth century, the Estates considerably restricted the powers of provincial rulers. The Württemberg Estates were among the most powerful and resilient in Germany; they included almost no nobility and were dominated by Lutheran ministers and burghers. The Württemberg Estate constitution, which the Duke vows to respect in the beginning of *Jew Süss*, was in place until 1805.

10. Hollstein, 78. For a more detailed summary of Süss's life, see Hollstein, 77–78.

11. *Hamburger Tageblatt* 18.11 (1939), as quoted in Hollstein, 76. Hollstein, who has researched the sources for the film, concludes that the script virtually ignored both historical and literary versions of the Süss story and produced an "independent version of the . . . topic" (78).

Karl Faber, who is also arrested for planning a revolt. She visits Süss in his chamber, begging him to free her husband and father. Süss rapes her, after which she drowns herself. The Duke dies suddenly, whereupon the power of Württemberg falls into the hands of the Estates, who arrest Süss and hang him for having carnal relations with a gentile woman.[12]

LITERARY PARADIGMS: THE REPOLITICIZATION OF THE BOURGEOIS TRAGEDY

How does a narrative provide a fantasy space in which a figure like the "Jew" is constructed, or in which an existing cultural fantasy can be enjoyed? It generally does so by writing a story its audience already knows; in the case of *Jew Süss*, this story derives from the eighteenth-century bourgeois tragedy, a genre not only entrenched in the German school curriculum since the nineteenth century, but familiar as part of a literary canon often performed on the stage. Although, as I will elaborate, *Jew Süss* rewrites the bourgeois tragedy in ways inimical to itself, the film's indebtedness to the genre not only has a crucial connotative value but preconditions the audience to identify with certain characters and narrative events. By using the bourgeois tragedy as a narrative framework, the film aligns itself with a tradition connoting freedom, virtue, "heart," and a flight from an inhumane modernity. Whatever "conclusions" the narrative invites appear to emerge from the same framework. It is, in other words, its allusions to the bourgeois tragedy that allow *Jew Süss* to be a racist film and yet feel — at least to contemporary audiences not disposed to see movies politically — like an antifeudal invective. In discussing this literary anchorage, I will restrict myself largely to narrative analysis, turning later to its filmic realization.

As one expression of an increasingly self-aware bourgeoisie in the mid–eighteenth century, the bourgeois tragedy attempted to dissolve the absolutist separation of politics from morality. Its stated aim was to "moralize" all citizens, especially the aristocracy, by demonstrating via narrative the tragic consequences ensuing from an absolutist power structure.[13] The

12. The historic Süss Oppenheimer also had a reputation as a womanizer, but he was not condemned for that reason because this would have implicated numerous courtly women involved with him.

13. See, for example, Lessing's debate with his contemporaries about how tragedy affects its reader or viewer: *Briefwechsel über das Trauerspiel: Lessing, Nicolai, Mendelssohn,* ed. Jochen Schulte-Sasse (Munich: Winkler, 1972).

genre is organized around two competing value systems: one whose central signifier is (bourgeois) virtue and another centered around an aristocratic notion of power.[14] This essential binarism reverberates in the paradigmatic title of Schiller's 1784 drama *Kabale und Liebe* (Cabal and Love) and might be schematized as follows:

Aristocracy/Court	*Bourgeoisie*
intrigue/*Kabale*	love, fidelity, honesty/*Liebe*
politics	dedication to community
ambition (power, personal glory)	humanity, sympathy, conscience
materialism	"virtue" above the material
sexual pleasure (*amusement*)	tenderness, love
women as sexual objects	women domestic, virtuous
use of French terms	straightforward language
gallantry, *politesse*	kindness
revenge	forgiveness, trust

Although historically a clear expression of growing bourgeois self-consciousness, the bourgeois tragedy disavows references to social class; it casts the virtue represented by the "bourgeois" world as "human," and not class-specific virtue. Just as reference to class remains covert within the bourgeois tragedy, its political implications are couched in family stories. The Sentimental family serves as a metaphor for the potential harmony of society at large; social conflict takes the narrative form of disrupted family harmony. Typically, tragedy results from an aristocrat's attempt to seduce a virtuous bourgeois woman.

This family tragedy is exemplified by G. E. Lessing's drama *Emilia Galotti* (1772), which illustrates particularly well the narrative affinities between the bourgeois tragedy and *Jew Süss*. In Lessing's play, a prince has become infatuated with a bourgeois woman, Emilia Galotti, who is about to be married to the virtuous Count Appiani, an aristocrat of lower rank. The courtier Marinelli persuades the Prince to have Emilia kidnapped on her way to her wedding, so that he may indulge his desire before it is too late. During the kidnapping, Marinelli (unbeknownst to the Prince) murders Appiani. When Emilia becomes a prisoner at court and recognizes the machinations behind the episode, she persuades her father to kill her. While Marinelli is the play's real villain, he is merely a tool of absolutist cabal; the play is more interested in the Prince, whose egotism and libido are the precondition for tragedy. Lessing assails the tyranny of a system in

14. The genre does allow for ambiguities that complicate the narratives and allow for convincing characterizations.

1-2 Karl Faber (*top*) bears a great resemblance to the young Friedrich Schiller.

which a master's arbitrary whim can lead to multiple deaths, and juxtaposes it with the autonomous, bourgeois (read: "human") will embodied in a father-daughter alliance.

The characterizations of *Jew Süss*'s males are clearly drawn from the repertoire of dramas like *Emilia*. Germans who did not literally see in the volatile Estate Counselor Sturm bourgeois patriarchs like Emilia's father, Odoardo Galotti, will have recognized the type. Even Sturm's name suggests the eighteenth-century literary movement *Sturm und Drang* (Storm and Stress). Karl Faber, Sturm's future son-in-law and functional double, recalls the "hot-headed" protagonists of early Schiller Storm and Stress dramas. Moreover, the actor playing Faber, Malte Jäger, bears a striking resemblance to idealized portraits of the young Friedrich Schiller (photos 1–2). Duke Karl Alexander (Heinrich George) echoes *Emilia Galotti*'s ambivalent Prince. Both *Jew Süss* and *Emilia* critique the infantile narcissism coded as aristocratic, the fact "that princes are human beings" (*dass Fürsten Menschen sind*), to quote the famous closing line of Lessing's play.[15] Although the film portrays the Duke as a vehicle rather than as a

15. *Emilia Galotti*, 5.8. The prince, unable to see his own culpability, lays the blame on Marinelli: "Is it not enough—to the misfortune of so many—that princes are human

source of evil (again parallel to *Emilia*), it hints at his puerility as he revels in watching a young woman being molested in the street procession through town. The syntactic linkage of the molested woman with Dorothea Sturm, who first appears with the next cut, intensifies the Duke's responsibility for social disharmony by anticipating the violation of woman even before the "Jew" enters the narrative. The role of evil is, of course, reserved for the "Jew," whose precarious positioning in this narrative paradigm I will discuss shortly.

Women and the Family Narrative. The film's taxonomy of women corresponds as well to eighteenth-century class coding: male projections of bourgeois female virtue like Dorothea Sturm are juxtaposed with idle aristocratic women (the Duchess, Süss's mistress) who were sexualized by bourgeois discourses in the course of the eighteenth century. The virtuous woman is crucial to the bourgeois tragedy's family narrative, which *Jew Süss* mirrors but also extends. The film tells two stories, a family one and a political one, but the two are clearly parallel, and the nuclear family again stands for social harmony.[16] Patriarch Sturm is at once spokesman for the Estates, whose rights are abused, and father of a daughter who is abused; the rape of Dorothea *is* the rape of Württemberg.[17] In fact, *Jew Süss*

---

beings; must there also be devils disguised as their friends?" "Ist es, zum Unglücke so mancher nicht genug, dass Fürsten Menschen sind; müssen sich auch noch Teufel in ihren Freund verstellen?"

16. This interweaving of private and public reconciles the bourgeois tragedy to Nazism's "totalization" of the private, to its recasting of divergent individual desires as one collective desire. At the same time, the eighteenth century began to discursively equate the public sphere with family, as suggested by the term *Landesvater,* or father of the country, for the ruler.

17. The film ingeniously preserves the emancipatory "feeling" of the bourgeois tragedy by emulating its anticentralistic, antiabsolutist ideology, encoded in Süss's plan to instate Karl Alexander as an absolute, centralistic ruler "like the Sun-King in Versailles" (a step that National Socialism codes within a destructive process of modernization). Geraint Parry analyzes the failure of Enlightenment rationality to anchor itself firmly in German cultural life ("Enlightened Government and Its Critics in Eighteenth-Century Germany," *Historical Journal* 6.2 [1963]: 185). Under the influence of Rousseau's reception in Germany, Sentimentality and Storm and Stress (e.g., Lessing, Herder, the early Goethe) reacted against the potential tyranny inherent in an excessively centralized, rational view of society and politics. Increasingly eighteenth-century artists and theoreticians came to focus on the "heart" as a category of humanity, to valorize intuitive knowledge over purely discursive learning. Süss's plan to modify the governance of Württemberg alludes to the historical competition between rulers seeking

mirrors the family metaphor doubly by including a story fragment anticipating the trajectory of the entire film. The bourgeois Fiebelkorn family
appears only once, disputing whether daughter Minna should attend a
masked ball arranged by Süss in support of the Duke's lascivious desire for
"springtime wildflowers." Mother Fiebelkorn is susceptible to the lure of
the court, while the volatile father correctly anticipates the daughter's
sexual violation: "The Jew is arranging a meat market and our daughters
are good enough to provide the meat." This constellation, like the Sturms'
father daughter relationship, is typical of the bourgeois tragedy, in which
the mother is often either absent or morally compromised. In Lessing's
Emilia Galotti and Schiller's *Kabale und Liebe,* the social-climbing mother
is oblivious to the danger threatening her daughter; in Lessing's *Miss
Sara Sampson* and *Nathan the Wise,* the mother is dead (like Dorothea's
mother).

The "corruptibility" of *Jew Süss*'s women and their objectification by
the camera leads Regine Friedman to assail the film as no less misogynous
than anti-Semitic. Citing Horkheimer and Adorno's equation in *Dialectic
of Enlightenment* of Jews and women as objects of similar hatred, Friedman labels *Jew Süss* a "shockingly anti-feminine denunciation" whose
"repudiation of women . . . proves to be no less than that of the Jew."[18] I
concur with Friedman's charge of misogyny and its linkage with anti-
Semitism, but prefer to distinguish the film's class-specific "repudiation"
of courtly woman from its *functionalization* of bourgeois woman as a
metaphor for the social body, which is another extension of an eighteenth-
century construction of gender and class. The recurrence of the desirable
female in eighteenth-century narrative and her merger with the private
sphere was a constitutive element in the assertion of bourgeois power
throughout European culture. As Nancy Armstrong has shown with reference to England, the construction of female virtue was part of an attempt

---

absolute power and the Estates during the eighteenth century, and typifies centralistic,
rationalistic thinking in three ways: (1) it aims at dissolving the Estates, which compromise the sovereign's power; (2) it involves borrowing foreign soldiers to suppress popular revolt — a strategy historically typical of absolutist governments; (3) the idea of
replacing the Estates with a ministry emulates the absolutist cameralistic practice of
hiring an elite of trained specialists to administer the people's "welfare" — a practice
that subordinates community experience to theoretical "expertise." This construction
of a political "machine" is also typical of rationalist philosophy, in which the metaphor
of the machine is commonly employed to describe the function of politics.
18. "Male Gaze and Female Reaction: Veit Harlan's *Jew Süss* (1940)," *German Cinema
and Gender,* ed. Sandra Frieden et al. (Province, R.I.: Berg Publishers, 1993), 2:125–26.

to transform a blatantly political struggle into a psychological one, and to evaluate psychological motives according to a set of values in which the bourgeois woman became exalted over the aristocratic woman. It was, above all, the female "on whom depended the outcome of the struggle among competing ideologies."[19] This narrative association of the bourgeois woman with virtue is part of the construction of sexuality Foucault traces in *History of Sexuality*. Contrary to popular belief, Foucault argues, Western culture did not repress sexuality, but actually produced it as a means of disciplining individual and social bodies. Normative sexuality became crucial to bourgeois identity; the bourgeoisie's sexuality was the "fragile treasure"[20] by which it distinguished itself from the aristocracy, as well as lower classes. Dorothea von Mücke corroborates Foucault's point by demonstrating how a disciplined, bourgeois subjectivity depended on abjection of the female body, at least on a level of representation. Thus, for example, Lessing's Miss Sara Sampson (the title character of his first tragedy, 1755) becomes an object of pity, the crucial category of Sentimentality, only after she "has overcome the carnal passions by rejecting the corporeality of the body, female sexuality, and a tyrannical maternal love."[21]

We see in all of the above a historical basis for *Jew Süss*'s narrative strategy of making Dorothea Sturm's body a contested territory that, like the "Jew's" body, is killed off by the narrative. The film adds, however, a "racial" dimension to this threat that is inconsistent with the bourgeois tragedy, which assumes that everyone is amenable to moral improvement. This is a crucial departure from the eighteenth-century genre to which I will return; moreover, I will elaborate how *Jew Süss* strips bourgeois woman of the autonomy her eighteenth-century precursors have, even if this autonomy is viewed through the lens of male projection. We will see how *Jew Süss* most consistently defaces the very woman it pretends to privilege; the rape of Dorothea is "really" a rape of Stuttgart men.

It is significant to note, however, that *Jew Süss*'s xenophobic equation of the virtuous female body with a biologized notion of "race" is not without its foundation in the eighteenth century. Repeated shots in the film showing Dorothea at a harpsichord quote an eighteenth-century iconographic

---

19. *Desire and Domestic Fiction* (New York: Oxford University Press, 1987), 5.

20. Michel Foucault, *History of Sexuality*, vol. 1, trans. R. Hurley (New York: Random House, 1978), 121.

21. *Virtue and the Veil of Illusion: Generic Innovation and the Pedagogical Project in Eighteenth-Century Literature* (Stanford: Stanford University Press, 1991), 113.

tradition that attests to a similar, if more subtly racist equation of domestic harmony with a "racially" superior community. By analyzing the semiotics of eighteenth- and nineteenth-century British colonialist painting, Richard Leppert has demonstrated the significance of the harpsichord throughout Europe as a standard-bearer of Western culture, one that was linked with women.[22] As an instrument that produced harmony, the harpsichord functioned as a subtle legitimator of British colonialist supremacy and complemented the philosophical notions of reason, order, and racial hierarchy. Contemporary conduct literature prescribed the harpsichord as an appropriate instrument for women, and its foregrounding in paintings of domestic life had a special representational status, suggesting the cultural and racial perpetuation of the British. Women grouped around a harpsichord are essential as "the producers of the race," rendering the scene familial as well as musical.[23]

We can see repercussions of the harpsichord's connotative value for early modernity in Nazi films like *Friedrich Schiller, Lady von Barnhelm, Friedemann Bach,* or *Romance in a Minor Key,* which display their female protagonist sitting at a harpsichord or piano. In *Jew Süss,* not only do we first see Dorothea beside a harpsichord, but the film's musical theme, the folk song *All mein Gedanken, die ich hab,* traverses the spheres of public and private intermingled by the film (with its double story of a raped Dorothea and Württemberg). Sung by Dorothea and Faber, the song signals the literal and figurative harmony of the private sphere. Yet it also pervades the film as nondiegetic "background" music, and in moments of pathos shifts into a minor key as if penetrated (like Dorothea) by Eastern sound.

22. "Music, Domestic Life, and Cultural Chauvinism: Images of British Subjects at Home in India," in *Music and Society: The Politics of Composition, Performance, and Reception,* ed. Richard Leppert and Susan McClary (Cambridge: Cambridge University Press, 1987), 63–104.

23. Ibid., 87. Elsewhere Leppert has analyzed the complementarity of music and violence. Proceeding from the painting of war and hunt scenes on pianos, he argues that musical aesthetics, "marked female, serve as the peaceful product of violence"; the two are linked "answering the cause of mutual justification." "Sexual Identity, Death, and the Family Piano in the Nineteenth Century," in *The Sight of Sound: Music, Representation, and the History of the Body* (Berkeley: University of California Press, 1993), 127 and 128. Nazi cinema makes this connection most explicitly in *Lady von Barnhelm,* when the music Minna plays on the harpsichord becomes a kind of nondiegetic accompaniment to the war-montage sequence that follows.

The "Jew" in the Bourgeois Tragedy Narrative. Jew Süss's most fascinating maneuver is its location of the "Jew" within a scenario in which neither race nor religion generally plays a role.[24] The film both divests the "Jew" of "racial" difference and insists vehemently on that difference — depending on whether we examine the semiotics of Süss Oppenheimer for the majority of the film or the structure of the *Jew Süss* narrative. In exploring this paradox, I will begin with semiotics, with the characterization of Süss. If his persona is as familiar as the characters already discussed, it is because this persona is not really "Jewish" (even as constructed by anti-Semitism), but belongs to courtly *intrigeurs* exemplified by Lessing's villainous Marinelli in *Emilia Galotti*. Like Marinelli, Süss pushes the reticent Duke to indulge his licentious fantasies and to forsake community for self-aggrandizement. Süss's own machinations and sexual appetite, though again passed off as "Jewish" traits, are thoroughly inscribable in the bourgeois tragedy's sociological coding of "court" as synonymous with an amoral world of debauchery. Süss neither dresses nor talks "Jewish" through most of the film. Whereas anti-Semitism's "Jew" is, as Gilman writes, deemed unable to "truly command the national language of the world in which he/she lives,"[25] Süss masters courtly discourse and is vastly more elegant and courageous than the Duke himself. The French vocabulary Süss brandishes (*demoiselle, amusement, par exemple, souper,* etc.) likewise aligns him verbally with the bourgeois tragedy's courtly figures rather than with German Jews, whose dialect Nazi cinema satirizes in films like *Robert and Bertram*.[26] From the eighteenth century on, the use of French, especially on the part of aristocratic literary figures, was a signifier for an "international" orientation, i.e., for those lacking "heart."[27] France was not only culturally important for the aristocracy but exemplified the most successful embodiment of enlightened absolutism.

24. The play that comes to mind when one thinks of the eighteenth century in these terms is Lessing's *Nathan the Wise* (1779), with its famous plea for religious tolerance. While an important step in the development of bourgeois literature, *Nathan* is a "Dramatic Poem" and not a tragedy.

25. Gilman, 12.

26. *Robert and Bertram* and *The Rothschilds* also ascribe aristocratic hedonism and egotism to Jews; moreover, both films mock Jews' imitation of an aristocratic lifestyle (see chapter 8).

27. Karl Alexander's preference for a "no-nonsense" (*klipp und klar*) discourse contrasts with the embellished and insincere rhetoric of courtly language, and works along with his frequent reference to the people of Württemberg as "my Swabians" to establish

Of course, the point of the film is to make us believe that Süss's "courtly" self is a mask, a ruse to slip himself into a space where he does not belong. The film couches in narrative form the warning that is directly spoken in Fritz Hippler's infamous 1940 documentary *The Eternal Jew:* Be careful! Only the discerning eye can identify an assimilated Jew. Nonetheless, it is telling that there is so little that is "different" about this supposedly racially different character; it suggests the contradiction to which I have alluded. In wanting desperately to make the Jew an Other, to make him fit the fantasy, it has few options outside its own narrative culture in which to do so. Consequently, it keeps making him act like a "bad" Aryan, while finding ways to equate this behavior with something called "Jewishness." It thus unwittingly acknowledges one of Slavoj Žižek's important insights into anti-Semitism: "In 'going through the fantasy' we must in the same move identify with the symptom: we must recognize in the properties attributed to 'Jew' the necessary product of our very social system; we must recognize in the 'excesses' attributed to 'Jew' the truth about ourselves."[28] It is as if the film were revealing its projections onto the "Jew" to be nothing but projections. I will return to this narrative impasse and the film's attempts to resolve it in the second section of the chapter.

Jew Süss's narrative structure, combined with a number of cinematic techniques I will discuss later, tries to remedy the above problem: it indeed locates the "Jew" as originating from a different space and culture, and it is here that we run into the limitations of the bourgeois tragedy as a model for the film. Even though Süss Oppenheimer is coded as a courtly type, it is not without consequences that the film makes him a Jew and an Outsider (which are synonymous in anti-Semitic terms). *Jew Süss*, namely, forgoes the bourgeois tragedy's binarism in favor of another binarism in which "Jewish" culture is pitted against "Aryan" culture. To be sure, the old class opposition of the bourgeois tragedy is present as the precondition for the Jew's success, and the aristocratic realm remains important as his sphere of operations. Nonetheless, the threat to narrative equilibrium is not the invasion of family by aristocracy (notwithstanding the Duke's dalliances; he is, as I will show, an essentially emasculated figure), but of "Aryan" by "Jewish" culture. What counts, then, in the final analysis, is the "same-

---

him as a fundamentally redeemable character. Military language as well as shared military experiences link him with Colonel von Roeder, whose "soldierly" virtue the film incessantly emphasizes.

28. Žižek, *The Sublime Object of Ideology,* 128.

Table 1. Social Coding in *Jew Süss*

"Jewish" Culture	Württemberg ("Aryan" Culture)	
	Court	Burger
Süss	Duke Karl Alexander	Sturm
Secretary Levy	Duchess	Dorothea
Rabbi Loew	Süss's mistress	Faber
Butcher Isaak	Ballerina	von Roeder (soldier)
Old man	von Remchingen	Miller
Rebecca		Blacksmith Hans Bogner
Masses		Members of Assembly
		Fiebelkorn family

ness" of aristocrat and bourgeois against an Otherness that we're supposed to believe is "racial." In distinction from the bourgeois tragedy, a diagram of the film's social coding might resemble table 1.

Ultimately, then, *Jew Süss* aligns its audience with the bourgeois tragedy's codified morality only to turn that genre inside out, subtly reversing its "message."[29] We saw how the bourgeois tragedy targets structural flaws within the absolutist system, how *Emilia Galotti* exposes the failure of an autocratic system to account for human fallibility. In replacing the traditional aristocratic villain with a Jew (a transfer historically grounded in the tradition of the "Court Jew" as financial advisor at absolutist courts), *Jew Süss* submerges a challenge to an autocratic social system in a *disavowal* of internal contradictions, which are instead projected onto an outside. In so doing, *Jew Süss* works not toward the depoliticization we associate with kitsch[30] but toward a *repoliticization* of the bourgeois trag-

29. This does not mean we need to assume the bourgeois tragedy was successful in its political agenda, or that it was without its own internal contradictions and misogyny. For a feminist critique of the genre see von Mücke or Silvia Bovenschen in *Die imaginerte Weiblichkeit: Exemplarische Untersuchungen zu kulturgeschichtlichen und literarischen Präsentationsformen des Weiblichen* (Frankfurt: Suhrkamp, 1979).

30. Certain characteristics of *Jew Süss* borrowed from nineteenth-century melodrama-like the quotation of *Tosca* in the rape scene or the allusion to the "Dead Girl from the Seine" in the drowned Dorothea, give the film a feeling of kitsch. It is important, however, that the melodrama we think of as "depoliticized" grew historically out of genres like the bourgeois tragedy. Jürgen Link has traced historical connections between popular cultural texts and "high" literary genres like the bourgeois tragedy. Since the nineteenth century, popular narratives have emulated the structure of the bourgeois tragedy, but tended to diminish its articulation of social antagonism by foregrounding

edy: it becomes a racist narrative permitting the "Jew" to function as a social fantasy who makes possible the belief in community. The film's strategy is to frame this racism within the model of the bourgeois tragedy, thereby disguising it as racism. Killing the Jew off as an imaginary source of social disruption becomes thus legitimated as self-defense.

At the same time, this fundamental alternation, the desire to locate the source of antagonism "elsewhere," requires *Jew Süss* to take on structural features of a narrative form that, unlike the bourgeois tragedy, is able to accommodate irreducible Otherness: the horror story. Without invoking the supernatural at all, *Jew Süss* repeats the horror narrative's fantasy of a social body penetrated by a monster defined as sexually, biologically different (recall that in many compelling horror genres the monster is assumed *to be* different, but does not *look* different[31]). In its classic forms, the horror narrative drives toward the resolution we find in *Jew Süss;* that the Thing must be "eradicated!" — to use a word ironically spoken by Süss *(ausrotten!).* This is why the scenes showing torch-bearing crowds frenetically hunting down Süss Oppenheimer so vividly recall horror film classics like *Frankenstein.*

Horror. It is no coincidence that in *Mein Kampf* Hitler assails the alleged tyranny of Jews as "blood-sucking."[32] The structural similarities between *Jew Süss* and vampire stories, especially Bram Stoker's *Dracula* of 1898, are compelling. Like Dracula, at least in most portrayals since the 1920s,[33]

the "natural-human" traits (chastity vs. promiscuity, trust vs. calculation, eroticism vs. lack of eroticism, etc.) defining literary characters while reducing the "social" factors (class, wealth) defining them. Link regards the "black and white" structure of modern popular narratives essential to their affirmative social function; the general devolution of what he calls the social-psychological drama to "kitsch" is not to be sought either in the incompetence of author or public, but in the genre itself and in the society which functionalizes it. J. Link, "Von 'Kabale und Liebe' zur 'Love Story' — Zur Evolutionsgesetzlichkeit eines bürgerlichen Geschichtentyps," in *Literarischer Kitsch,* ed. Jochen Schulte-Sasse (Tübingen: Niemeyer, 1979), 121–55.

31. Žižek's analogy of anti-Semitism's "Jew" and body snatchers rests on the impossibility of distinguishing the latter from "normal" humans and on the unfathomability of the alien's desire; *The Sublime Object of Ideology,* 89.

32. Trans. Ralph Manheim (Boston: Houghton Mifflin, 1943), 309.

33. Dracula first appears in his familiar elegant evening clothes in a drama from the late 1920s by Hamilton Deane and John L. Balderston. The play was set in London, and theatrical conventions of the time prescribed that the villain had to be a person one could believably invite into one's living room. See David Skal, *Hollywood Gothic: The Tangled Web of Dracula from Novel to Stage to Screen* (New York: W. W. Norton, 1990), 69–70.

Süss demonstrates a great mobility with respect to his physical appearance. As already discussed, he becomes indistinguishable from nobility, indeed, surpasses in physical appeal the legitimate ruler of Württemberg. Süss also recalls Dracula's spatial mobility, his sexual threat to the male order, his predominant choice of female victims, his contamination of these victims (not explicit in the film but suggested by references to "the blood of our children and children's children"), and, as I elaborate later, his role as an ambiguous figure located somewhere between the self and the Other. Finally, the narratives of *Jew Süss* and Stoker's novel are strikingly similar in trajectory. Both revolve around the transgression of oppositional spaces associated with an alien East ("Jewish" culture and Transylvania, respectively) and a domesticated West (Württemberg/London) with their concomitant cultural associations. Both begin with a figure (the Duke's envoy von Remchingen; Jonathan Harker) traveling from the familiar Western space to the space of Otherness. The initial transgression, compromised by the economic grounds by which it was motivated, provides the conditions for the second major journey from East to West, which unleashes evil upon Western culture. Finally, both Süss and Dracula are eliminated by a male collective, but not until at least one woman has been sacrificed.

It is obvious that there are also significant differences between *Jew Süss* and *Dracula*. While the Dracula legend harkens back to folklore and superstition, *Jew Süss* is not only a realist narrative but one which invokes the additional authenticity of history. Second, the alien "Eastern" space in *Jew Süss* exists as a microcosm *within* Western culture. Süss lives in the Frankfurt Jewish ghetto, a space that, unlike the distant Transylvania, persistently threatens to erupt as a menace to its "host nation." The citizens of Stuttgart do not need to be educated by a "Book of the Jews."

These differences underscore rather than mitigate the importance of structural affinities between *Jew Süss* and the horror story. Namely, the presence of so many vampire motifs in a film calling itself "historical" raises some key questions. What are vampire motifs doing in a historical film? What function do these motifs have in horror, and what might the incorporation of such motifs into a realist narrative tell us about National Socialism? Critical readings of Dracula as a narrative figure in literature and film have concentrated on two general spheres: the narrative negotiation of a real or imagined political threat and of a sexual threat.[34] A

34. See, for example, James Donald, ed., *Fantasy and the Cinema* (London: British Film Institute, 1989), or James Twitchell, *The Living Dead: A Study of the Vampire in Romantic Literature* (Durham, N.C.: Duke University Press, 1981).

political reading of Süss *qua* Dracula sustains what I have already discussed as the film's reconfiguration of the bourgeois tragedy, and lends itself to familiar associations of the "Jew" with money and power.[35] A reading focusing on sexual threat, while by no means excluding the political, opens up perspectives neglected by a study of political implications, which tend to be "rational." Racist obsessions are hardly rational, but, in Joel Kovel's words, "invariably tinged with sexuality: a preoccupation with, a deadly curiosity about, the sexual excesses of the hated group, etched in the imagination by the acid of a harsh moralism."[36] As I hope to illuminate below, a psychoanalytic analysis of Süss as a horror figure offers possibilities of understanding central pathologies underlying National Socialism and how a film like *Jew Süss* attempts to respond to these pathologies.

The connection established by Régine Friedman between women and the "Jew" can be carried further in light of the horror genre, whose gender configurations and organization of looks reverberate in *Jew Süss*. Linda Williams's article "When the Woman Looks" explores why horror film so consistently features female victims, why the genre seems to punish women for looking at the monster.[37] Williams theorizes a number of affinities between woman and the monster. On the one hand, the woman recognizes in the frightful body of the monster her own difference, her mutilation in the eyes of patriarchy; on the other, both woman and monster pose a potential threat to male power. The connection Williams posits transfers in a number of respects to *Jew Süss*. Although Süss does not have a monstrous appearance, his courtly look is, if we read it with anti-Semitic logic, only a mask covering up his "real" debased body. Moreover, circumcision renders the Jew visibly mutilated in the eyes of anti-Semitism — not unlike the woman in Freud's paradigm. Above all, as Theweleit's *Male Fantasies* attests, the "Jew" represents a threat to male hegemony commensurate only with that posed to the fascist man by devouring women.

Friedman stresses how for the majority of the film Süss controls vision. His possession of the look is inscribed in the film as one of political and

35. Dracula has also been read as a metaphor for fascism itself. Just after World War II, Richard Wasson claimed Dracula was an unconscious parable of old Central Europe attempting to destroy new Western Europe. For Wasson, Dracula is a fascist besieging Western civilization; his first victim is Lucy Westenra (light of the West). See Twitchell, 139.

36. *White Racism* (New York: Columbia University Press, 1984), 57.

37. *Re-vision: Essays in Feminist Film Criticism,* ed. Mary Ann Doane et al. (Los Angeles: American Film Institute, 1984), 83–99.

economic power, but is also associated with a reduction of others, especially women, to helpless objects of an erotic and humiliating gaze. Indeed, power relations are closely linked with verticality throughout the
film, in which power belongs to the figure looking down upon others (cf.
the Duke peering over a balcony at ballerinas; the Duke and Süss looking
over a balcony at Stuttgart ingenues; the two peering at Minna Fiebelkorn's exposed leg; Süss spying on Württemberger; Süss on a balcony at
the execution of Bogner, etc.). Ironically, this principle of verticality will
be reversed at Süss's execution, as I will elaborate later.

It is important to stress that, despite the prominence of Süss's abuse of
women, not only women are victimized by his look. When Estate members invoke Martin Luther in urging the Duke to cast out the Jew, Süss
spies on them through a molding in the ceiling. He peers through a mask
(literalizing anti-Semitism's "mask" motif), gaining a god's eye view of
subjects who, though perceiving themselves as autonomous, appear to the
film viewer, via the Jew's eye, as miniature puppets, as incredible shrinking
men. The scene gives narrative form to anti-Semitism's fundamental paranoia, the conviction that nothing escapes the Jew's eye and ear; he is a
malevolent, all-knowing Other whose eye signals his murderous intent.[38]
In particular it testifies to the anti-Semite's perception of himself as the
object of a penetrating gaze, his feeling of being "photographed" by an
abstract force whose desire cannot be fathomed. Mary Ann Doane argues
that paranoia, with its obsessive sense of being watched, is linked with a
feminine subject position in that the perception of being on display is
equally symptomatic of femininity: "There is a sense . . . in which paranoia is only a hyperbolization of the 'normal' female function of exhibitionism and its attachment to the affect of fear."[39] Doane's analogy transfers smoothly to Süss's destabilizing effect on Württemberg culture. By
subjecting males to a powerful and humiliating look, he casts them in a
culturally feminized position. The Duke, to be sure, often shared this look,
but only when it is orchestrated by Süss.

The Duke's dependency on and simultaneous distrust of Süss likewise
recalls a feminine constellation Doane analyzes with respect to the gothic
women's film of the forties. In the latter, the (female) protagonist is never

38. Cf. Mary Ann Doane's discussion of the eye as a metonymy for murderous intentions in gothic women's films of the forties, such as *Suspicion* (1941), *Gaslight* (1944),
or *The Spiral Staircase* (1946), in her *The Desire to Desire* (Bloomington: Indiana
University Press, 1987), 127.
39. Ibid., 126.

sure whether her husband is a murderer. The films "adopt" the woman's subjective vision, but often prove it unreliable, just as the Duke's delusion of power is unreliable (cf. the scene alluding to Schiller's *Wallenstein,* in which the rabbi tricks the Duke into thinking he can control his fate by consulting the stars. Süss not only controls what the Duke looks at, but gives it meaning). The Duke is a feminized figure who must rely on other men to enlighten him (significantly, most important in this respect is the "soldierly" von Roeder); he can never be sure what the "Jew" really wants, and Süss's seduction of his wife signals his effective emasculation.

Even the film's "manly" men are feminized by the Jew's control and panoptic eye, by his appropriation of their women, and his invasion of their "home," the quintessential woman's space. Süss remains what Lacan would call a "stain" in the field of "Aryan" vision that looks back and destabilizes the self. At best the "Aryan" can recognize the stain, as does Faber when he instantly "sees" that Süss is "a Jew." Soon thereafter the camera dollies into a close-up of Süss's face, a technique used repeatedly in the film to intensify his threat. In his detailed analysis of shots used in the film, Friedrich Knilli has pointed out that the film devotes a full seven minutes of close-ups to Süss.[40] Indeed, the very first scene in which we see Süss begins and ends with close-ups of him, which in effect frame the scene and elicit the sense of discomfort Westerners feel when someone stands "too" close. This difference is underscored by a hapless attempt to exhibit "racial" physiognomy in two scenes when Süss confronts Sturm and Faber, respectively. In each case "Jew" and gentile appear close-up in profile, highlighting the contrast between supposedly delicate "Aryan" features and more pronounced "Jewish" ones[41] (notwithstanding the fact that the Austrian actor playing Süss, Ferdinand Marian, was not Jewish but merely a swarthy type not uncommon among Austrians and, especially southern, Germans).

As suggested by the above, then, Süss is not only the subject but the object of the look throughout the film. This status does not contradict but complements his own visual power; he becomes virtually Lacan's gaze *qua* object, the thing that looks threateningly at us (see chapter 1). This status relates to another point Linda Williams makes with respect to horror, that the monster displaces woman as the site of spectacle. Despite the film's profusion of objectified women, Süss's specularization is no less impor-

40. "Die Gemeinsamkeit von Faschisten und Antifaschisten gegenüber dem N.S. Film 'Jud Süss,'" in Knilli, 66.

41. See Sander Gilman's discussion of the Jewish nose as phallus, 126–27.

tant. In addition to being an obsessive focus of the camera, Süss ornamentalizes himself with opulent clothing, the effect of which is heightened by the contrast between his courtly self and his "original" appearance in caftan and beard.[42] Yet, far from being an object the viewer can master visually, he acts as a threatening voyeur.

The strategy of *Jew Süss* will be to wrestle the look away from the Jew and back into the eyes of the "Aryan" male collective. This restoration of visual power to the film's privileged males is, in effect, its restoration of their potency overall. The film's conclusion, which I will discuss at the end of this chapter, turns Süss's own self-specularization against him in an execution in which he becomes a spectacle of a degrading sort and is himself forced to assume a feminized position. Again, in its restoration of male hegemony, *Jew Süss* follows the paradigm of the vampire narrative. From Bram Stoker's *Dracula* on, the trajectory of vampire stories has been to exorcise the threat to the male order usually by means of male authority (especially by Professor van Helsing, standing for the rationality of science). This authority manifests itself in the spectacle of the vampire's execution, which similarly casts him in a feminine position: the pounding of the phallic stake into the vampire's heart.

THE PROJECT OF "JEWISH" OTHERNESS

In what follows I specifically examine *Jew Süss* as an anti-Semitic text, proceeding step by step through the myths with which anti-Semitism constructs its "Jew." These myths linking Jews with money, abstractness, a distorting rationality, rootlessness, deception, and sexual degeneracy can all be connected to social, economic, and psychological fears of modernity. I will refer back to the preceding analysis, attempting to show how the film's narrative paradigms and cinematic techniques assist or impede its projection of these myths upon Jews.

Money and the Abstract. Essential to *Jew Süss,* as to anti-Semitism in general, is its sociohistorical understanding of the history of moderniza-

---

42. Kaja Silverman, following C. J. Flugel, has discussed the importance of the eighteenth-century shift in male clothing as a kind of "revisualization of sexual difference," resulting in a despecularization of the male subject and a concomitant hyperspecularization of the female subject. *The Acoustic Mirror* (Bloomington: University of Indiana Press, 1988), 24–27. I will return to this in my chapter on *The Old and the Young King.*

tion. The film depicts the development of capitalism, for which absolutism appears as the first step, as a process caused by and to the primary benefit of Jews. A key passage from Hitler's *Mein Kampf* describing the position of the Jew in eighteenth-century Germany anticipates the plot of *Jew Süss*:

> [The Jew] begins slowly to become active in economic life, not as a producer, but exclusively as a middleman. . . . His usurious rates of interest finally arouse resistance; his increasing effrontery, indignation, his wealth, envy. . . . Since he himself never cultivates the soil, but regards it only as a property to be exploited . . . the aversion against him gradually increases to open hatred. His blood-sucking tyranny becomes so great that excesses against him occur. . . . At times of bitterest distress, fury against him finally breaks out, and the plundered and ruined masses begin to defend themselves against the scourge of God. In the course of a few centuries they have come to know him, and now they feel that the mere fact of his existence is as bad as the plague. . . . Proportionately as the power of the princes begins to mount, he pushes closer and closer to them. He begs for "patents" and "privileges," which the lords, always in financial straits, are glad to give him for suitable payment. . . . And so, his ensnarement of the princes leads to their ruin. . . . The Jew well knows what their end will be and tries to hasten it as much as possible. He himself adds to their eternal financial straits by alienating them more and more from their true tasks, by crawling around them with the vilest flattery, by encouraging them in vices, and thus making himself more and more indispensable to them. With his deftness, or, rather, unscrupulousness, in all money matters he is able to squeeze, yes, to grind, more and more money out of the plundered subjects. . . . Thus every court has its "Court Jew" — as these monsters are called, who in intervals go the way of all flesh.[43]

Hitler is referring to the phenomenon of the "Court Jew," with which *Jew Süss* legitimates historically its association of Jews with money and nascent capitalism. It was common practice in eighteenth-century courts to hire Jews as financial and commercial agents in the ruler's service. This service included procuring personal luxury items, as we see in the beginning of *Jew Süss,* or attending to state policies dealing with currency, provisions, or investments. By gaining control of the Duke, Süss incrementally gains control of the social fabric, taking steps to transform the Würt-

43. Hitler, 309–11.

temberg community into a market. In scenes like the following, Jews epitomize the hated "middleman" described by Hitler: a disgruntled miller entering Stuttgart complains to Süss's secretary, Levy, about the increase in road tolls since the Duke has given Süss control of the city streets. Levy attempts to persuade the befuddled miller to be grateful since he is allegedly reaping greater profits from the inflation caused by the higher tolls. As illustrated by the subsequent scene in which Dorothea complains about a sharp rise in food prices, the inflation resulting from Jewish policies will burden the entire community.

In its "anticapitalist" critique, the episode attacks a development that was historically necessary for the transition from a feudal to a capitalist economy: the increasing complexity of systems of product distribution, which required that an ever greater role be played by "middlemen" not directly involved in production. Large-scale distribution, financing, transportation, and eventually public relations increasingly interfered with what had originally been a one-to-one exchange of commodities. "Late-blooming" nations in this process such as Germany frequently needed centralized controls to accelerate the capitalist process, in order to compete with more advanced countries like England and the Netherlands. The film narrative distorts this process, making it appear as simple exploitation by (Jewish) middlemen, who use verbal acrobatics to disguise this exploitation. The display of such acrobatics is a central diegetic function of secretary Levy, whom one figure calls a "talmudic Jew brain." The leitmotif of "Jewish reasoning" as a negation of common sense sustains romantic anticapitalism's attack on the abstractness of money and finance capital. It simultaneously contradicts the idea of Jews as subhuman "vermin" — a problem the film tries to explain away by labeling the Jew as "clever, but not smart"(*schlau* versus *klug,* which connotes a deeper intelligence or wisdom).

I will be dealing in coming chapters with Nazism's contradictory attitude toward the modernizing process resulting in what Foucault calls "discipline." I want to suggest here, however, that although *Jew Süss* portrays Jews as lacking "discipline" in a bodily sense (their sloppy dress, unleashed drives, lack of internalized "values," etc.), it indeed links them with "discipline" to the degree that this is a process of structural, temporal, and spatial organization necessary to modernity and capitalism. We saw earlier how discipline's anonymous gaze becomes projected onto the "Jew." Second, as part of Süss's "rape" of Aryan space to be discussed below, he engineers, as in the scene with the miller, a spatial organization of Württemberg that ensures his personal profit. He uses "Jewish" reasoning in another spatial maneuver that destroys tradition in the name of "nature": he demands that blacksmith Hans Bogner pay Süss eighty talers because his house, located where the blacksmith's house "always" was, overlaps with the "natural" line of the street; Süss orders half of the house demolished when Bogner refuses. Bogner is executed after attempting to avenge himself in a physical attack on Süss. The episode sustains the film's anticentralist, antidisciplinary position, since Bogner's self-defense constitutes an exercise of the "club law" (*Faustrecht*) associated with individualistic late medieval heroes (epitomized by Goethe's *Götz von Berlichingen*, 1773) who rejected formal legal codes as tyrannical. The "club law" symbolized eighteenth-century critiques of centralists who favored a unified legal code applicable to everyone, which was partially achieved by the Prussian Law Code (*Allgemeines preussisches Landrecht*) of 1794. Codified law was part of the proliferation of writing that, as Foucault stresses, supported the emergence of a "disciplined" world sustained by organized and classified documents. The same association underlies Sturm's remark later that the Jews "twist and *verklausulieren*" everything, or put it in an enigmatic "legalese." His verb *verklausulieren* stems from the word *Klausel* or paragraph, as in a legal code or another contractual document. Sturm can link *verklausulieren* with distortion, because in antidisciplinary ideology they both amount to the same "Jewish" thing.

It is no coincidence that the film juxtaposes a miller and a blacksmith, that is, small businessmen who produce essential commodities, with Jews who produce nothing. Moische Postone's analysis of German anti-Semitism is helpful in understanding why the finance capital of the middleman rather than industrial capital was the target of romantic anticapitalist attacks. Postone explains anticapitalism in terms of the Marxist notion of the fetish, the distinction between what modern capitalism is and the way it appears, illustrating the similarity between the characteristics Marx ascribes to the value dimensions of social forms and the characteristics modern anti-Semitism ascribes to Jews: abstractness, intangibility, mobility, universality. He recalls Marx's notion of commodity form, which shows how the dialectical tension between value and use value requires that their "double character" be materially externalized in value form, appearing "doubled" as money (the manifest form of value) and as the commodity (the manifest form of use-value). Although the commodity is really a social form expressing both value and use value, it appears to contain only the latter, to be only material and "thingly." Money, by contrast, appears to be the sole repository of value, the manifestation of the purely abstract: "The form of materialized social relations specific to capitalism appears . . . as the opposition between money, as abstract, as the 'root of all evil,' and 'thingly' nature. Capitalist social relations appear to find their expression only in the abstract dimension. . . . One aspect of the fetish, then, is that capitalist social relations do not appear as such, and, moreover, present themselves antinomically, as the opposition of the abstract and concrete."[44]

"Volkish" ideologies understood capital itself only in terms of the manifest form of its abstract dimension: finance and interest capital, which, then, is held responsible for the concrete social and cultural upheaval provoked by the swift development of modern industrial capitalism. Since concrete labor appears to be the opposite of the abstract realm of money, it is not perceived as part of the capitalist process but rather as the descendant of artisinal labor, which, by contrast to "parasitic finance capital," seems to be "organic" and rooted in nature.[45] This understanding of capitalism as an abstract force is increasingly biologized during the nineteenth century, manifesting itself in theories of race, especially anti-Semitism, in which the "racial" opposition between Aryans and Jews supplants that of the concrete material and the abstract. Hence Jews do not merely *represent* capital; they come to personify its intangible, pernicious power.[46]

Jew Süss repeatedly affirms this antinomy between the abstract and the "thingly." Although money is crucial to Süss, what the film foregrounds is its value to him as something abstract, power. In contrast, the citizens of Stuttgart attach value to things money buys, albeit a differing value depending on their social status. The film's bourgeois figures even invest

---

44. "Anti-Semitism and National Socialism: Notes on the German Reaction to 'Holocaust,'" *New German Critique* 11 (1980): 109.

45. Others have of course pointed out that "petty-bourgeois anticapitalism" attacks finance capital. See, for example, Daniel Guérin's 1936 study, *Fascism and Big Business:* "Throughout the nineteenth century, the petty-bourgeois theoreticians attacked not *producing* capitalism, but *idle* capitalism — the lender, the banker. . . . Fascism, in its turn, concentrates its attacks on 'loan capital,' and thereby expresses the aspirations of the middle classes while diverting the working masses from the struggle against capitalism as a whole" (New York: Monad Press, 1973), 82f.

46. A certain irony is at work in the film narrative and in Nazi discourse; the abstractness of capitalism is represented by the Jew, although he is a particularly *specularized* object. This recalls the paradox Kaja Silverman calls attention to with respect to cultural gender coding: "Man, with his 'strikingly visible' organ, is defined primarily in terms of abstract and immaterial qualities such as potency, knowledge, and power, whereas woman, whose genitals do not appeal to the gaze, becomes almost synonymous with corporeality and specularity." *The Acoustic Mirror,* 164.

money itself with a certain deictic value, as suggested by the implication throughout the film that "Jewish" money is somehow materially different from other money. The same idea underlies Faber's accusation that Süss's money is "blood" money, acquired at the price of our "wives and daughters'" racial purity. In the same scene, Süss playfully affirms the abstractness of money for him: "Money does not stink."

Another example of this contrast is the motif of jewels, the objects through which Süss gains access to the Duke, but which are for him objects of barter. The "magical" (*märchenhaft*) jewels that Süss keeps hidden in a massive chest (a metonymy for hidden Jewish wealth) at once entrance the Duke's envoy Remchingen and become textual metaphors for Jewish power. A tiny jeweled crown topped by a cross that we see enveloped by Süss's hand anticipates Jewish hegemony over Christians. Towering over the seated Remchingen, Süss dangles a string of pearls that Remchingen eagerly grabs; the "reins" by which Süss gains access to and ultimately control over "Aryan" space. Jewelry, especially rings, assumes a different, thingly value for bourgeois figures; Dorothea offers Süss her wedding ring to save Sturm and Faber, while the latter refuses to part with his during torture. Süss, by contrast, gives the Duke a ring to "buy" the ballerina, and later taunts Dorothea with an opulent ring.

Of course, Süss's attitude toward money and power fits the paradigm of the corrupt aristocrat and is only "Jewish" if we believe it is Jewish. A scene in the Jewish ghetto preceding the introduction of Süss plays on anti-Semitism's contradiction between Jews as slobs and as rich, thus imagining a specifically Jewish relation to money. When Remchingen has entered Süss's house, two Jews in the ghetto street discuss in a distinct Jewish dialect the appearance of "such a fine goyish dandy" at "our Oppenheimer's." A kosher butcher or *Schächter*[47] wearing a bloody apron and carrying a large butcher knife, which he wipes off on his apron, explains the nature of the visit to an old man: "[Oppenheimer] will give him a lot, he will, because he's got brains. He *should* give, so we can *take, take, take!*" While the verbal exchange signals the "Jewish" equation of money with power, the slovenly appearance of the men suggests that Jews are too uncouth to even be interested in personal luxury. The Schächter's bloody apron evokes the kosher slaughter of animals, conjuring up a similar revulsion to Jewish "cruelty" as do gruesome slaughter scenes in *The Eternal Jew*.

---

47. *Schächten* (from Yiddish *schechtn*, Hebrew *schachat*) refers to the slaughter of animals and poultry according to a prescribed Jewish ritual, prohibited by the Nazis in 1933. Cf. *Brockhaus Enzyklopädie*, 16:528 (Wiesbaden: Brockhaus, 1973).

The same scene typifies the film's persistent linkage of money with a free sexuality that, like money, circulates and has the status of an abstract transaction in which the "partner" is merely an interchangeable sign. Next to the old man in the ghetto street is a wanton-looking young woman with long, black hair leaning out of the window, chewing on something resembling a weed. Since she is not involved in the conversation and never appears again, her presence has no function other than to underscore the talk about money with an image of dissolute "Jewish" sexuality, also associated, as both Theweleit and Gilman illustrate, with sickness.[48] The only spoken reference to her, the old man's comment "Get dressed, Rebecca!" is unrelated to the rest of the dialogue, but merely stresses her exhibitionism.

The film suggests effectively in filmic terms that money is an *abstracting* force, one which strips individuals, particularly women, of their value and renders them commodities. Nowhere is this better illustrated than when Süss throws a purse full of coins onto a table in front of Karl Alexander, which then dissolve into the skirts of spinning ballerinas shot from a bird's eye view (signaling that Süss has financed the ballet which the Estates refused the Duke). The dissolve renders visual not only the courtly reduction of art and women to *divertissement*, to a mass ornament, but the link between the Jew and the intangible power of money. Süss uses money to buy the concrete woman for the Duke, but her visual fusion with coins simultaneously renders the woman abstract. Money voids her of content; she is as interchangeable as the coins. Her twirling skirt and circling figure recall the shape and circulation of money itself; her feet in constant movement further link her with the myth of the "wandering" Jew (photos 3–5). Consistent with the historical fact that ballet remained a courtly, not a bourgeois art form, the ballerina represents the ultimate commodified woman in the film's discourse, as I will illustrate with respect to *Friedemann Bach* as well.

The film's linkage of all its courtly women with the Jew likewise voids them, in keeping with the bourgeois tragedy's negative coding of courtly women as heartless. In their opulent attire and shrill hysteria, the Duchess, who seemingly becomes Süss's mistress, and his "official" mistress are barely distinguishable. The nameless mistress laughs with erotic titillation upon seeing a house Süss had ordered half demolished in a metaphoric gesture anticipating his destruction of family and reduction of "men" to

48. See Theweleit, *Male Fantasies*, vol. 2, trans. Erica Carter and Chris Turner (Minneapolis: University of Minnesota Press, 1989), 13, and Gilman, "The Jewish Murderer," 104–27, and "The Jewish Disease," 210–33.

3·5 A dissolve equates spinning ballerinas with coins. The ballerinas are rendered, like coins, abstract, circulating, interchangeable.

puppets: "Such a cute doll's house. . . . You're *so* cruel!" Her enjoyment of the spectacle is one of the film's only "honest" responses, mirroring the pleasure the film audience takes in all its sadistic spectacles.

The "Wandering Jew." As suggested by its analogies to vampire narratives and by the importance of money as a circulating sign, *Jew Süss* is the story of crossed boundaries, of mastered space. The "Jew" seeks to subjugate everything to money or circulation, poisoning "home" (in the double sense of the private and public) as the space that guarantees quality or "self-sameness." The film's opening shot following the credits shows an engraving of Württemberg with Stuttgart encased by a city wall; hereafter we see a variety of Jewish figures entering the city gates. In his first appearance, Süss vows to "open the door" to Württemberg for Jewish domination: "It may be tomorrow, it may be the day after, but it will be!" The two times he literally falls down in the film (when his coach overturns on his way to Stuttgart, and when he is about to rape Dorothea) suggest a revolt of "nature" against the Jew's penetration of "Aryan" space.

The spillover of Jewish culture into Aryan culture even occurs on a formal level, most conspicuously in Harlan's use of the lap dissolve at key moments. For example, after the film has established the initial harmony between the two dominant "Aryan" milieus of court and bourgeois home, it shifts to a "Jewish" milieu by means of a dissolve. Karl Alexander appears before the people of Stuttgart, standing directly above Württemberg's coat of arms. The camera travels to the coat of arms, which slowly dissolves into a sign with Hebrew writing. On a denotative level the dissolve signals a change from one setting to the next, the Jewish ghetto in Frankfurt. On a connotative level, however, the sign stands for "Jewishness"; it is presumably illegible to the viewer and underscored by ominous music. The scene change could have been achieved with a cut, but the lap dissolve allows the Hebrew letters to "swallow" Württemberg and, by implication, Karl Alexander.[49] The same spillover occurs at times on the level of soundtrack, when sound from one scene at times overlaps briefly with the next. The synagogue scene, for example, concludes with Dorothea's singing voice briefly preceding the cut to her at the harpsichord.

Once this spillover has occurred, "Aryan" spaces are stifled, deprived of *Lebensraum*, suggested by Sturm's act of opening a window and proclaiming "Fresh air!" after an explosive argument with Süss. The film's two brief mass "Jewish" scenes, repeating on a macro-level what Süss achieved as an individual, have in common a compositional principle of clutter that lends them a claustrophobic quality. They likewise mobilize sound (loud Hebrew chanting) and (often frenetic) movement to alienate the gentile spectator the film anticipates. The brief scene in which droves of Jews enter Stuttgart shows a long caravan of chanting Jews appearing

---

49. Cf. Christian Metz's commentary on the lap dissolve in *The Imaginary Signifier*, trans. C. Britton et al. (Bloomington: Indiana University Press, 1982): "The moment of travel is emphasized and expanded, and this already has the value of a meta-linguistic commentary. Moreover, by *hesitating* a little on the threshold of a textual bifurcation, the text makes us attend more closely to the fact that it performs a weaving operation" (276); "it has a remarkable *capacity to metonymise*" (279).

dusty and dirty, with their possessions piled high upon wagons. Most shots are composed so that we cannot perceive the beginning or the end of the long line extending diagonally across the frame. The appearance that there is no end to the entering swarm is underscored verbally as a Württemberger cries that the Jews are entering Stuttgart "like locusts."[50] The Sabbath celebration begins with Jews opening a chest and removing a Torah topped by a crown. It thus mirrors on a mass level the early scene in which Süss fondles the jeweled crown (= Christianity); only here the pace of the scene intensifies to an orgiastic mass frenzy.

The claustrophobic effect of mass "Jewish" scenes is intensified by the fact that prior to Süss Oppenheimer's entrance into the narrative the film is marked by compositional and narrative equilibrium. As we hear, in the opening scene, Karl Alexander's off-screen voice vowing to rule "with fatherly (landesväterlicher) care," we see a massive portrait of the late Duke Eberhard Ludwig, out of which the voice seems to flow. This counterpoint of voice and image suggests continuity in the spirit nurturing Württemberg, or in the terms of Ernst Kantorowicz,[51] though each king's physical body dies, his second, transcendent body lives on in his successors. The camera pans swiftly from the icon of the deceased patriarch to Karl Alexander, again linking them metonymically. Each shot is correspondingly orderly and symmetrical, centered around the patriarch flanked by deferential Estate members; the light emanating from windows high above lends the figures' heads a radiant appearance, as if divinely sanctioned. The first family scene in the Sturm home is composed with similar tableau shots of Dorothea and Faber poised at the harpsichord, likewise illuminated by natural light. As we have seen, the Jew's arrival disrupts such compositional harmony, which will seldom recur until the court scene in which Süss is condemned.

Anti-Semitism transformed the literary motif of the wandering Jew victimized by modern existence into one burdening the Jew with the blame for modernity. Already by the late nineteenth and twentieth centuries, the motif of the traveler had in part forfeited the positive associations of self-realization accompanying it in the eighteenth and early nineteenth cen-

50. *Jew Süss*'s analogy of Jews to parasites is also central to *The Eternal Jew*, which compares the Jews to rats spreading the plague and juxtaposes scenes of rats to scenes of Jews, who "always remain alien bodies in the organism of their host nation."

51. I am referring to Kantorowicz's well-known analysis of medieval political theory in *The King's Two Bodies: A Study in Mediaeval Political Theology* (Princeton, N.J.: Princeton University Press, 1957). See chapter 3 herein on film biographies of Frederick the Great.

turies; a new motif of the traveler developed alongside the older one of the bildungsroman. A precondition for the valorized traveler of the latter is the protagonist's possession of a homeland or *Heimat* to which he or she can return, as in Tieck's *Franz Sternbalds Wanderungen*. This *Heimat* is a space of rest guaranteeing that all movement can be arrested and that the traveler will not lose the self in eternal movement. The competing motif of the restless traveler signifies the aimless roaming of an alienated, uprooted subject unable to find its own space in a world dominated by exchange value. Like money, as the embodiment of alienation through movement par excellence, the traveler without a home is a mere element within an all-present process of circulation characteristic of modern societies. Frequently this motif was merged, as in the case of Kundry in Wagner's *Parzifal*, with the ancient motif of the wandering Jew, which dates back to the Middle Ages but which changed its character substantially during the nineteenth century.[52] In a secular context, this motif often symbolizes the consequences of materialistic attitudes and actions (see, for example, Lienhard's novel *Ahasver am Rhein* of 1903) and the impossibility of redemption as long as materialism determines human actions.

Süss fits smoothly into anti-Semitism's figure of the wandering Jew turned master of a movement aimed at commodifying space and conquering the abstract realm of circulation and exchange (again like Stoker's Dracula). Hence his juxtaposition with Dorothea, a nurturing potential mother standing for presence, for *Heimat* as a geographical projection of the need for security. Dorothea and Süss become allegories for stasis and movement, respectively, as they enter Stuttgart together. Dorothea fails to comprehend how Süss can be at home "everywhere": "Don't you have a homeland? . . . But there must be some place you feel the happiest!" Her "natural" movement is strictly confined to the private home, by which she is utterly absorbed (note, for example, her failure to guess in whose honor her father is proposing a toast on the day of the Duke's coronation). At times she appears literally framed by window, a stance Mary Ann Doane links with the social and symbolic positioning of woman: "The window is the interface between inside and outside, the feminine space of the family and reproduction and the masculine space of production."[53] It is her de-

---

52. Indeed, all of Wagner's protagonists since his first "Wagnerian" opera fit the prototype of a figure who does penance for some original sin by wandering aimlessly, longing fervently for redemption by a woman. Moreover, a number of Dracula renditions code him in a similarly sympathetic way (cf. Werner Herzog's *Nosferatu* and Francis Ford Coppola's *Bram Stoker's Dracula*).

53. *The Desire to Desire*, 138.

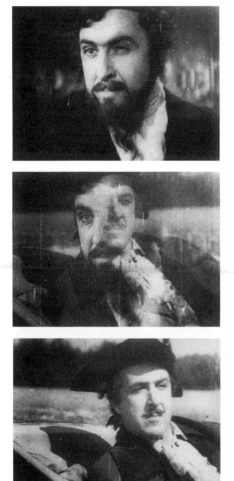

6-8 *Jew Süss* literally "dissolves" the bodily markings that reveal Süss Oppenheimer's "Jewish essence." Above he is transformed from a Jew to a courtier ready to penetrate Stuttgart.

partures from the walls of her home that imperil her, especially her two autonomous acts, bringing Süss into Stuttgart and visiting him to seek mercy.

"Jewish" Masquerade. The all-pervasive power that anti-Semitism projects into the Jews is not readily apparent; it lurks behind events, but is not identical with them. Again the film signals "Jewish masquerade" formally through the lap dissolve in which the bearded Süss of the *Judengasse* emerges as a clean-shaven, wigged courtier en route to Stuttgart (photos 6–8). The reverse occurs in a final dissolve at the conclusion of the film, when Süss is arrested and forced to own up to his "true" appearance. Steve

Neale has articulated effectively how bodily marks signify racial order within the film; racial difference needs to be "inscribed and readable, immediately intelligible," which is only possible if racial characteristics are visible.[54] The same semiotic and ideological technique is used to identify the "Jew" as a bodily metaphor for the abstract domination of capital. Complex interdependencies are thus reduced to easily comprehensible bodily constellations. National Socialism masks this reduction by "turning the tables" and implying that the "real" issue is the concealment of bodily indicators by the enemies of society.[55]

Underlying the need for "Jewish" masquerade is the presupposition that the undisguised Jew is fundamentally and visibly different from gentiles, and simultaneously homogenized with other Jews by his parasitic nature — a presupposition the film tries unsuccessfully, as I'll elaborate shortly, to "prove." Such "proof" would seem to be offered by the scenes depicting a parasitic "mass" stifling "Aryan" racial health, and by the film's employment of one actor to play all Jewish figures except Süss: Werner Krauss portrays the secretary Levy, Rabbi Loew, the butcher Isaak, and even the old man in the same scene.[56] The collapsing of nearly all Jews into one unclean, coughing, or cackling body tries to efface Jewish humanness, in keeping with Joel Kovel's elucidation of racism as a process of dehumanization via abstraction (e.g., from "body" to "penis" to inanimate "thing") until the group in question reaches the "final point of nothingness."[57] Nazism fantasizes Jews as a kind of void; Jewish "identity" is posited merely as negativity, existing in transgression and social destabilization.

However the film endeavors to suggest the subhuman nature of Jews,

---

54. "Propaganda," *Screen* 18 (Autumn 1977): 26. Significantly, as Neale points out, the Aryan character who falls short of the bourgeois moral standard, the Duke, is fat and ugly: "The disorder that is centered on his sexual appetite and which inaugurates Süss' rise to power is marked on his body and reinforced by the contrast between his appearance and that of the other 'Aryan' characters in the film" (27).

55. Süss's masquerade extends beyond the visual. His adoption of the francophile courtly discourse I discussed earlier serves as another kind of mask, concealing his "real" intentions.

56. According to an interview with Harlan in *Der Film* on January 20, 1940, the choice of one actor for these roles was intended to show the similar roots of Jewry: "It was meant to show how all these different temperaments and characters — the pious patriarch, the wily swindler, the penny-pinching merchant and so on — are ultimately derived from the same roots." Quoted in Welch, 287.

57. Kovel, 92.

the bulk of its narrative time and its images is devoted to Süss Oppenheimer — a figure who belies precisely the presupposition the film wants to
reinforce. Jürgen Link's theorization of different varieties of "enemy images" in Western culture is useful in exploring Süss's precarious status as a
figure whom the film refuses to code as identical to its "Aryan" figures, but
who also fails to conform to the above description of a Jewish mass. Link
posits a distinction between enemies with and without what he calls "subject status."[58] An enemy with subject status, exemplified by Soviet communist as viewed by the postwar West, is perceived as possessing the
autonomy and rationality one accords one's own system. Although this
enemy may be "evil," he plays by the rule of the metaphoric game, be it
poker, chess, or war. The enemy lacking subject status is symbolically
coded as "chaos"; he is located outside the boundaries of a system centered on reason. These enemies, for whom "Muslim fundamentalists"
might serve as an example, cannot be conceived as partners or even really
as opponents. Their lack of subject status disqualifies them as rationally
thinking beings "like us"; they are excluded from the start as co-players in
an antagonistic game.

Nazism's metaphoric coding of Jews as rats or vermin is a gesture di-
vesting them of subject status, and this, in turn, is a precondition for
engineering consent to their extermination (they don't suffer like we do,
etc.). However, the desire, exemplified by *Jew Süss,* to perpetuate anti-
Semitic thinking via narrative results in the inescapable dilemma to which
I have alluded. Namely, in order for Süss to function as the central narrative antagonist, he must be accorded subject status, albeit coded as the
devil (cf. the Duke's playful reference to him as *Teufelskerl*). Indeed, central components of anti-Semitic mythology presume not only subject status but even a kind of superiority on the part of the Jew (the agility of
Jewish reasoning; the persistent ability to dupe the Aryan, etc.). This superiority over others is indeed magnified in the case of Süss, making him a
profoundly ambivalent figure — a problem the film tries to resolve by the
"other" Jews and the frame device permitting Süss's "true" Jewish essence
to emerge.

The selection of the "Aryan" Ferdinand Marian to play Süss only exac-
erbates the quandary, as the Nazi journal *Der Film* unwittingly admitted
in 1940: "Naturally a film like this will encounter casting difficulties in

58. "Fanatics, Fundamentalists, Lunatics, and Drug Traffickers — The New Southern
Enemy Image," trans. Linda Schulte-Sasse, *Cultural Critique* 19 (Fall 1991): 33–53.

Germany."[59] Although ghetto Jews were used in *The Eternal Jew,* Nazi policies would not have permitted a Jew to star in a feature film; yet without a Jew in the role, it forfeits at least some of its alleged genuineness (invoked elsewhere by, for example, predictable claims of authenticity at the film's beginning). Finally, no "Aryan" male in the film appears as Süss's narrative counterpart; no individual is his equal and only as a group do the citizens of Stuttgart defeat him. Although this narrative configuration encodes Nazi collectivism, it simultaneously enhances Süss's status as a figure essentially unchallenged and unchallengable.

Another complicating factor is Süss's portrayal as sexy or at least ambivalent. He contradicts the normal coding of the Jewish man in Nazi films as ludicrous and repulsive (cf. Nathan Ipelmeyer in *Robert and Bertram*) — perhaps as a concession to historical legend, which calls for a sexual appeal on the part of Süss Oppenheimer, but more likely to the erotic imperatives of classical cinema. The screen persona of Ferdinand Marian predisposed him to be regarded as an erotic object. Described as a "rather oily matinee idol,"[60] Marian embodied the "characteristics of the attractive, gallant lover intensified by his southern looks, which in the Third Reich were considered foreign and forbidden."[61] According to Veit Harlan's memoirs, Marian received baskets of love letters from fans after appearing in *Jew Süss.* If there is a moment of subversion to be found in the film, it is in the titillation he offers, which Friedman reads as "an instance of rebellion against the denial and sacrifice of the female self demanded of the regime."[62] Although I find Friedman's reading overly optimistic, clearly the prowess and sexuality of the "Jew" that threaten to dislodge the film's "intention" are crucial to its entertainment value. One might say that precisely what makes *Jew Süss* work as film, with its codified organization of desire, undermines it as anti-Semitism.

A further dimension in this casting of an attractive "Aryan" in the role of Süss ties into the film's reliance on horror: its suggestion that the "Jew"

59. January 20, 1940; quoted in Leiser, 152.
60. Hull, 165. Marian's screen personae were often morally compromised, as is Cagliostro in *Münchhausen,* which I discuss in chapter 9, Cecil Rhodes in *Ohm Krüger* (see chapter 8), and the lover and husband in *Romance in a Minor Key* and *La Habanera,* respectively.
61. Siegfried Zielinski and Thomas Maurer, "Bausteine des Films 'Jud Süss'," in *"Jud Süss": Filmprotokoll, Programmheft und Einzelanalysen* (Berlin: Spiess, 1983), 32.
62. Friedman, "Male Gaze and Female Reaction," 132.

be read as an ambiguous figure located in the space between self and other. Süss occupies what Hélène Cixous describes as the space of ghosts: "It is the between that is tainted with strangeness. . . . What is intolerable is that the Ghost erases the limit which exists between two states. . . . It is his coming back which makes the ghost what he is, just as it is the return of the Repressed that inscribes the repression."[63] Just as the ghost, like the vampire, is somewhere between being alive and dead, Süss resists easy localization: he is somewhere between Jewish culture and Aryan courtly culture; no longer truly part of the first, and supposedly not integratable in the second. He is also between as an "Aryan" playing a Jew; he is a figure somehow *with* subject status and *without;* he is, above all, in between the me and the not-me. As the figure who is meant to embody the society's own antagonism, he cannot be seen as totally outside, but rather as the repressed that persistently returns.

Freud's reading of paranoia as characterized by an elision of subject-object relations holds for Nazism's paranoid construction of the "Jew" as well. The projection of the society's own antagonisms onto the "Jew" is one attempt to restore that distinction between subject and object, to allow the "Jew" to exist only as Other. This can only be a strategy that works to a limited degree within narrative; the "Jew" will never be relegated fully to an outside beyond the social totality. As such a creature who is me and not me, and who both embodies for others and pursues for himself forbidden desire, the narrativized "Jew" is a creature of simultaneous repulsion and fascination, and hence a symptom of "the instability of culture, the impossibility of its closure or perfection," the same ambiguity James Donald articulates with respect to monsters: "The dialectic of repulsion and fascination in the monstrous reveals how the apparent certainties of representation are always undermined by the insistent operations of desire and terror. The lurid obsession with archaism and liminality in horror films, and their play on the uncanny ambivalence of *heim* and *unheimlich,* highlight the fragility of any identity that is wrought from abjection."[64]

Contagious Lust. Klaus Theweleit uses the term "contagious lust" (*Lust-seuche,* literally an "epidemic of lust") to describe anti-Semitism's projection of "Jewish" sexuality as insatiable and perverse. No specter was more

63. "Fiction and Its Phantoms: A Reading of Freud's '*Das Unheimliche*' ('The Uncanny')," *New Literary History* 7 (Spring 1976): 543.
64. Donald, "The Fantastic, the Sublime, and the Popular," 247.

disturbing to Nazism than that of "parasitic Jews" (*Aussaugejuden*), whom Julius Streicher saw "sitting with blonde German girls in bars and cafes, sapping the sexual and racial strength of their host people and destroying them."[65] The myth of "Jewish" lust again involves an implicit demarcation of boundaries that are transgressed by Jews. *Jew Süss* encodes "contagious lust" most prominently in the rape of Dorothea Sturm that literalizes the rape of Württemberg. The representation of Dorothea's rape is, however, like so many aspects of *Jew Süss*, ambivalent. The film's historical role in anti-Semitic policies encourages us to read the rape in anti-Semitic terms, as racial poisoning. Occasional dialogue references to "Jew children" and threatened "blood," as well as the citing of carnal relations with a gentile as grounds for Süss's execution, sustain this interpretation. Viewers familiar with film history, moreover, will be reminded of D. W. Griffith's racist film *The Birth of a Nation* (1915), in which a girl commits suicide to escape being raped by a freed slave. Yet again, from a cinematic or narrative perspective, Süss's sexually exploitative ways are not particularly "Jewish," but fit into a long tradition. To recall my earlier discussion, his sexuality is typically "courtly," as is his lust for revenge, the motivation he articulates for raping Dorothea.[66] My point is not to suggest that Dorothea's violation is not "intended" as a demonstration of "Jewish" racial defilement, but that little in the film text explicitly points to "race." What is definitely clear, whether or not we foreground an anti-Semitic reading of Süss's sexuality as deviant, is that it threatens male hegemony. Crucial to the portrayal of this threat is the series of spectacles involving not only Süss and women, but other men.

The titillating rape scene, whose mise-en-scène borrows from Sardou's nineteenth-century drama *Tosca* (1887, better known today through Puccini's opera), constitutes Süss's final and definitive opportunity to position another man as feminized spectacle. Dorothea seeks mercy from Süss for the imprisoned Faber, while in a close-by cell the latter is tortured every time Süss displays a white handkerchief outside of his window. Unlike in

---

65. As quoted in Theweleit, 2:9–10. Streicher was one of Nazism's most virulent anti-Semitic propagandists.

66. The film attempts to explain revenge as "Jewish" when Süss refers to the Jewish "God of revenge—an eye for an eye, a tooth for a tooth." It also disavows that revenge is Christian, when Sturm contends he does not seek "retribution, but what is right. An eye for an eye, a tooth for a tooth; that's not our way." Ironically, revenge is precisely what is sadistically and pleasurably carried out in the execution scene that follows Sturm's remark.

traditional stagings of *Tosca,* where the constraints of the stage permit the viewer only to see Tosca's anguish and eventual murder of her assailant, *Jew Süss* cross-cuts between Süss's bedroom (dominated by his giant bed) and the sight of Faber being tortured. It thus highlights the simultaneity of woman's abuse and man's impotence, and shows on the man's body a violation that conventions of the time do not permit to be shown on the woman's body. Faber's hands, mutilated by thumbscrews, are another bodily mark signaling "Aryan" male inadequacy, his inability to prevent the violation of nature and his "territory."

Significantly, the narrative has persistently disrupted the consummation of Faber's desire; every scene in which he kisses Dorothea is interrupted. Though stylized as a Schillerian hero, he appears throughout as unequal to the Jew or Sturm, even as slightly feminized. During his first appearance at the harpsichord, Dorothea strokes his hair, then walks away and is replaced by Sturm, who repeats her gesture. The replacement of Dorothea by the father anticipates the disruption of the heterosexual couple not only by the Jew but by the all-pervasive father, whose arrest will even inhibit the couple's union after their marriage. Indeed, Süss's prime opponent in his battle over Dorothea is Sturm, who wields complete control over his daughter's body (another motif left over from the bourgeois tragedy). After proclaiming that Dorothea "will not bring Jew-children into the world," he arranges her marriage to Faber, if not to ensure his own sexual domination over her, then to shield her from the Jew's more potent sexuality.

If we read the film with anti-Semitic ideology in mind, "Jewish" sexuality is fully consistent with the horror analogy I introduced earlier. Desire, narrative contingency, and editing destine Dorothea and the Jew for each other, as numerous readings of the first Dracula film, Murnau's *Nosferatu* (1922; as well as of Werner Herzog's 1979 remake), have claimed for the relationship between Nina (Mina in Stoker's novel) and the vampire. Several times when Dorothea encounters Süss the camera tracks into a close-up of his face, allowing the spectator to share with her the titillating sensation of being the object of his look. As Friedman points out in illustrating women's "corruptibility,"[67] not only does Dorothea first transport Süss to Stuttgart, she veritably runs into Süss's arms. While the naiveté that delivers her to Süss is readable against the background of eighteenth-century codings of innocence, it is also readable as a sublimated desire to be raped, especially in light of her abortive relationship

67. See also Neale, 26.

with Faber. The *Illustrierte Film-Kurier,* with which the film was promoted, consistently shows stills of Dorothea and Süss together, or of Dorothea alone dressed as in the rape scene. One montage of production stills
in the pamphlet forms a triangle in which Süss and Dorothea face each
other, with Faber in the background, as if he, not Süss, were the intruder in
the dyadic relationship. The only shot of Faber and Dorothea together
shows the latter as a corpse.[68]

Just as *Jew Süss* exerts pressure to eliminate the Jew, Dorothea's rape is,
in anti-Semitic terms, synonymous with her death. Rape by the Jew effects
an irreversible contamination of the victim, much like vampirism, as described by Linda Williams: "The vampire's power to make its victim resemble itself is a very real mutation of the once human victim."[69] Bram
Stoker's Mina becomes aware of herself as "unclean" once Dracula has
forced her to drink blood from an incision in his chest. The self-disgust she
expresses is simultaneously a striking articulation of the threat vampiric
sexuality poses to male hegemony: "I must touch him or kiss him [hus-
band Jonathan Harker] no more. Oh, that it should be that it is I who is
now his worst enemy, and whom he may have most cause to fear."[70]
Stoker's novel explicitly associates vampirism with female sexual arousal.
Dracula's first victim, Lucy Westenra, turns from a prim Victorian into a
sexualized woman after her attack by Dracula. She receives transfusions
by a variety of men, which have been read by numerous critics as a covert
metaphor for semen.[71] Anti-Semitism reverses this symbolization, though
to the same effect; here the Jew's semen stands for contamination of
woman by Jewish blood, as remarked by Julius Streicher: "During coitus
the male semen is fully or partially absorbed into the lining of the female uterus, where it enters the bloodstream. A single act of intercourse
between a Jew and an Aryan woman is enough to poison her blood
forever."[72]

Again here, however, the film is not explicit—there is no verbal explanation for Dorothea's suicide (except "the Jew has her on his conscience")
and cinematically it is only implied by editing. Unlike in both horror and

68. The *Film-Kurier* also highlights Süss's threatening gaze, having on its cover a close-
up of him (in his "original" caftan and beard) looking up so as to expose much of the
whites of his eyes. Inside is a still photograph (that does not appear in the film), in which
he looks through magnifying spectacles used to examine jewelry.
69. Williams, 89.
70. *Dracula* (New York: Barnes & Noble, 1992), 305.
71. See Twitchell, 136–37.
72. Gilbert: *Nürnberger Tagebuch* (Frankfurt, 1962), 119, quoted in Theweleit, 2:12.

the bourgeois tragedy, *Jew Süss* also denies any explicit suggestion of sexual pleasure on the part of Dorothea, who seems to have Aryan "blood" but not the "blood" of sensuality Lessing's Emilia Galotti speaks of. The rape is as much a rape of Faber as it is of her, and although the narrative credits her with the will to die, the film's actual narration does not permit us to see a display of the female will common in the bourgeois tragedy.[73] While we do not see her drown herself (even elliptically), we do see Faber struggling with his wounds. Dorothea is merely stranded between two scenes in which she is *acted upon* by males; the rape and Faber's emergence from a lake bearing her corpse. (Only a brief clip showing her wandering in a state of derangement and, typically, looking for Faber separates the two.) Dorothea is essentially stripped of her subject status, becoming the thing suggested by actress Kristina Söderbaum's nickname "Reich Water Corpse" (*Reichswasserleiche*).[74]

The cinematic celebration of Dorothea's limp body is at once the height of pathos and the first step in the exorcism of a sexuality imperiling male stability. As her corpse is retrieved from a lake, black night is offset by torches creating a dramatic chiaroscuro effect which recalls the often remarked Nazi love of pyrotechnics, especially in connection with funerals. The camera lingers on the final close-up of Dorothea laid on the ground, her childlike face illuminated, divested of the sexuality that made her the object of "Jewish" lust, and returned to a harmless, de-eroticized state. The dead Dorothea calls to mind Saul Friedländer's analysis of the fusion of "kitsch and death" as typical for National Socialism,[75] but this in

73. The filmic articulation of Dorothea's death reveals a shift away from relatively autonomous eighteenth-century women like Emilia. The latter similarly exists to be the object of desire and likewise bears a "guilt" (of desiring) which has been the focus of much scholarly discussion. See, for example, Harry Steinhauer, "The Guilt of Emilia Galotti," *Journal of English and Germanic Philology* 48 (1949): 173ff. Emilia articulates, however, her own "guilt," which thus becomes linked with her integrity, complexity, and character development; she essentially evolves from narrative object to subject. She atones for her guilt by forcing her father to kill her (a fully autonomous act reversing the *Virginia* tradition on which the drama is based, in which usually the decision to kill the daughter rests with the father).

74. Söderbaum was Harlan's wife and one of Nazi cinema's most popular actresses (see Lowry, 60–61). Her screen persona was strongly marked by continuity in type and fate, suggesting sadomasochistic elements in her appeal.

75. Friedländer refers to the "frisson" created by this opposition between the harmony of kitsch and the evocation of death and destruction as a "bedrock of Nazi aesthetics." *Reflections of Nazism* (New York: Harper & Row, 1982), 27.

turn is indebted to an older tradition of nineteenth-century aestheticism and kitsch motifs like reproductions of the famous "Dead Girl from the Seine."

Dorothea's death seemingly empowers the film's male collective to begin its process of reasserting itself. The scene in which Estate members confer on a punishment for Süss restores the compositional symmetry of the film's beginning, as well as ensuring the final narrative resolution exorcising the Jew. Anecdotal accounts of the film cite Veit Harlan's memoirs, which contend that his original ending showed Süss facing death boldly, hurling a curse on the people of Stuttgart. Goebbels allegedly demanded that the scene be reshot with Süss appearing cowardly — a change in full accord with the film's attempt to restore the look to its destabilized men, and by extension, to the spectators (quasi-literally taking "an eye for an eye," a revenge Sturm insists the Aryans are not after).

Süss's execution is a mirror reverse of the earlier execution of blacksmith Bogner, in which the humiliation inflicted by Süss is inflicted *upon* him. The pleasure of seeing Süss made the object of his own staged spectacle is enhanced by the similar cinematography of the two execution scenes. Both are punctuated by the sound and image of drums counting the moments to death; both alternate extreme high- and low-angle shots reversing the film's vertical coding of power (i.e., diegetic and film spectators *look up at* the humiliated and disempowered figure). Süss ultimately becomes the object of a spectacle more humiliating than any he "executed" himself. Several bird's eye shots encompassing the scene invite a feeling of spectator omniscience.

The original version of the scene with Süss cursing would have portrayed Süss as an ethical hero, a Don Giovanni adhering to a Kantian radical evil, an evil so ethical as to remain inexorably resolute even in the face of death. Such an ending would have allowed Süss to retain his narrative ambivalence, ensuring his spectator appeal and permitting him one final assertion of phallic supremacy. Spectators of the execution would have remained his objects. The "Jew," as the stain too close and yet too different from the self, needs not only to be exorcised (in narrative and in life) but to be rendered a thing. Goebbels's alleged revision of the scene complies with this need; it allows male lack felt throughout the narrative to be transferred to Süss. The ultimate feminization of the Jew compensates for his feminizing effect on the Aryan male; consequently it is Faber, rather than Sturm, whom the scene privileges. The actual hanging of Süss is framed by close-ups of Faber, the last object of the Jew's humiliating spectacle and now a bold watcher of another spectacle. As Süss is raised in

9·11 Shots foregrounding Karl Faber, whose injured hands signal his "castration," suggest that the Süss's execution is staged for his gaze (*top*). As Süss is hoisted into the air, a subjective shot shows Faber, from Süss's point of view, as he fades into the distance. The Jew must watch Faber watching his execution, but the film does not accord Süss a reaction shot (*middle*). Alternately, the execution is staged for the eye of God (*bottom*).

his cage the camera tracks out and up from a shot of Faber, as if from the point of view of Süss himself. This subjective shot adds to Faber's compensation by suggesting that Süss sees Faber watching his death, although in accordance with its aim of dehumanizing Süss, the scene does not permit a reaction shot. Immediately following Süss's death, the camera again tracks into a close up of Faber, completing the effect that the spectacle was staged primarily for his look (photos 9–11). The reassuring effect of this transformation of phallic power at once complements and exceeds the importance of restoring Süss's "true" Jewish appearance.

The final close-up of Süss's body shows his bare feet hanging limp from out of his cage, resembling a slaughtered chicken, a thing lacking subject

12 The last shot of Süss, slaughtered like a chicken, attempts to rob him of the subject status that was necessary for him to function as the center of the narrative.

status (photo 12). This fragmentation, degradation, and effacing of his body contrasts starkly with the individualizing "death mask" (to borrow Eric Rentschler's phrase) iconography with which Dorothea is celebrated. It represents the film's attempt to cancel out the disquieting appeal of the Jew throughout, and to relegate him to the subhuman being he is supposed to be.[76] Purifying light snow as well as the recurrence of the "Dorothea" song signal the return of narrative harmony. The "Jew" is comfortably restored as Other, as the "You" Lacan maintains is essential to taming the Other. Only Faber's prominently displayed hands hint that the restoration is incomplete; his wounds (i.e., emasculation) loom as a stain reminding the viewer of male lack.[77]

OTHERNESS, NARRATIVE, AND CINEMA

Jew Süss's meticulous encoding of anti-Semitic mythology offers a historical documentation of attempted indoctrination that will remain impor-

76. Apropos of the vampire parallel, in John Badham's film version of *Dracula* (1979) with Frank Langella, Dracula is "executed" in a strikingly similar, ignominious manner. Professor van Helsing throws a hook into Dracula's back, by means of which he is hoisted high onto the mast of a ship, where he dangles helplessly until the sun destroys him. The finality of this purgation is called into question, however, like that of *Jew Süss*, as a bat flies into the horizon.

77. Steve Neale has analyzed how the film threatens to rupture its own boundaries at the end, when Sturm exhorts that future generations should uphold the ban on the Jews. The exhortation is spoken to a diegetic audience, but "really" to the film audience, and hence borders on undermining the narrative closure. Sturm's semi-direct audience address allows the film to approach a mode of address Neale argues is constitutive of "propaganda": it aligns "the subject as in a position of struggle vis-à-vis certain of the discourses and practices that have been signified within [the text], and signified in such a way as to mark them as existing outside and beyond it." Neale, 31.

tant for the analysis of ideology. Yet I hope to have demonstrated in this chapter that a discursive recounting of ideology in the film does not even begin to grasp it as a totality. This requires a sorting out of the components that make up *Jew Süss*: narrative paradigms with their inherent modes of identification and ideology, the anti-Semitism woven into these narratives, and their filmic articulation. All of the preceding elements need to be not only de- but reconstructed in a consideration of how they mutually reinforce or work against each other.

The manifold textual components that collaborate to make *Jew Süss* (and I am including here anti-Semitism and history, which come to us in textual, usually narrative form) are able to work together because of a common narrative delimitation of an "inside," which provides an imaginary fulfillment of the desire for harmony, and an "outside" that threatens harmony. No matter what the narrative form, this dichotomization of "inside" and "outside" is a mere rhetorical strategy, since the inside and outside projected through narration into different, opposite spaces are inextricably related and dependent upon one another. They are each other's Other and cannot exist independently; the "Jew" with his excesses is but the alter ego of those who construct him. The appeal of narrative lies in an imaginary mastery over the "outside" that lives off the certainty that it can never be eradicated, as it is merely the dialectical opposite of the "inside." This illusion of mastery has (and wants) to be renewed—which further suggests that the Other supposedly impeding community cannot be overcome, that the void will never be entirely filled in. The fact that the Nazi state did not content itself with trying to eliminate the Other via narrative raises the "what if?" question, whose answer is clear: If Nazism had survived the war and succeeded in exterminating European Jews, it would have deprived itself of its necessary Other. Either that state would have totally reconstituted itself, or would have had the daunting task of generating an Other to replace the Jews.

The inconsistencies that plague *Jew Süss* derive from the different terms in which this outside is defined by its competing narrative paradigms. The moral terms of eighteenth-century literature (making the Other amenable to improvement) clash with the biological and nonrecuperable Otherness of horror and anti-Semitism. Moreover, cinema, with its reliance on representation and codified paradigms, gives *Jew Süss*'s anti-Semitic ideology its power yet falls short in trying to represent the essentially "different" Jew who exists only in the imagination. Although there are doubtless perspectives on *Jew Süss* that I have left out, what is clear is that a reading going beyond ideology critique yields a far more complex mode of textual operation than a listing of anti-Semitic myths in the film would suggest.

The danger in approaching such a notorious film is, I believe, that our knowledge of the terrible events in which it was implicated compel us to use its anti-Semitism as our starting point and to view everything else about the film as secondary. As long as our focus is the film's production history, this approach is indeed appropriate. It becomes more problematic the moment we turn our interest toward how the film worked on an audience. In imagining the response of a paying, movie-going public, I suspect the starting point of analysis should be reversed, proceeding from the experience of cinema and working toward the specific narratives and ideologies that figure into cinematic pleasure. Knowledge that *Jew Süss* was part of an apparatus, ultimately of extermination — while crucially important — should not lead to "automatic" conclusions about what made the film successful and the degree to which its anti-Semitism translated into real-life anti-Semitism. Even the most zealous anti-Semitic ideologue will have responded to *Jew Süss as a movie*. Assumptions of cause-and-effect impede rather than further understanding of the complex ways in which ideology and practice function.

The following chapters on Frederick the Great will constitute both the opposite of *Jew Süss* and an extension of it. Thematically, they imagine the "Jew's" mirror reversal, the positive social fantasy of a Leader figure who embodies the social harmony threatened by the "Jew." Yet, we will encounter very similar textual operations: These films will again offer a "viewer-friendly" encapsulation of history that allows the modernization process to be grasped in terms of familiar personae and accessible narrative events, while affording the narcissistic experience of transcending lack, time, and space. We will continue to be challenged by the need to understand that when these films exhibit Nazi ideology, they do so within the framework of classical cinema.

THREE

Frederick, the Movie; or, The Return of the King's Body:

Fridericus and *The Great King*

Österreichischer Offizier: Aber Majestät! Sie befinden sich im österreichischen Lager!

Friedrich: Gewesen, meine Herrschaften, *gewesen!*

Austrian Officer: "But your Highness! You're in the Austrian camp!"

King Frederick: "You mean this *was* the Austrian camp, sirs, it *was.*"

—Most exciting dialogue from *The Chorale of Leuthen,* as remembered by my professor, Gerhard Weiss, about nine when he saw the film

No film genre can take us further in answering the question I raised at the beginning of this study, where Nazi fantasies come from, than the next: film biographies of Frederick II of Prussia, the "Great" (1712–1786). Most importantly, this genre thwarts any illusions that "Nazi" fantasies were unique to National Socialism, even if their political realization was unique. On the one hand, the "Fridericus" movies, as they were called, display a Führer worship, xenophobia, and militarism that seems to qualify them as *the* fascist projection. On the other hand, the cinematic Frederick cult dates back to the beginnings of German cinema, which had a predilection for glamorized Prussian history,[1] and to an even older literary

---

1. Especially privileged were periods of struggle, for example, against Napoleon and for the German unification of 1871, although Frederick emerged early on as the "Prussian film's" most fetishized persona. See the collection *Preussen im Film,* ed. Axel Marquardt and Heinz Rathsack (Reinbek bei Hamburg: Rowohlt, 1981), or Bruce Murray, "The Past as Metaphor for the Present and *Der alte Fritz* (Old Fritz) as an Example," in *Film and the German Left in the Weimar Republic: From Caligari to Kuhle Wampe* (Austin: University of Texas Press, 1990), 75–79.

and historiographical tradition. Although a film named *Old Fritz* appeared as early as 1896, the genre began in earnest with the release of Arzen von Cserépy's phenomenal hit of 1922–23, *Fridericus Rex*. The film, whose "success and consequences resembled a mass psychosis,"[2] spawned profitable "spin-off" merchandise and multiple sequels: *Fridericus Rex* itself had four parts and was followed in the Weimar years by another two-part film, Gerhard Lamprecht's *Old Fritz* (*Der alte Fritz*, 1927–28), *The Flute Concert of Sanssouci* (*Das Flötenkonzert von Sanssouci*, 1930), and *The Dancer of Sanssouci* (*Die Tänzerin von Sanssouci*, 1932) — to name only the major "Fridericus" films. As already mentioned, all of these films carry on a voluminous popular literature about Frederick led by bestsellers like Franz Kugler's *History of Frederick the Great* (*Geschichte Friedrich des Grossen*, 1841) and Adolf Neff's collection of anecdotes *About Old Fritz* (*Vom alten Fritz*, 1916). A 1918 biography by Walter von Molo, one-time president of the Prussian Poets' Academy, had sold 500,000 copies by 1936 and served as a basis for three films.

The four features produced under National Socialism, Carl Froelich's *The Chorale of Leuthen* (*Der Choral von Leuthen*, 1933), Hans Steinhoff's *The Old and the Young King* (*Der alte und der junge König*, 1935), Johannes Meyer's *Fridericus* (1936), and Veit Harlan's *The Great King* (*Der grosse König*, 1942), cannot be separated from this tradition. *The Great King*, which I will examine together with *Fridericus* in this chapter (before moving on to the special case of *The Old and the Young King* in the next) is stylistically the most striking and approximates more than any other film a cinematography we might call "fascist." Not only was Veit Harlan, who made *Jew Süss, Kolberg,* and other fascist milestones, Nazi cinema's premiere director of feature films, but *The Great King* was commissioned by the state at a critical juncture of World War II. Goebbels's diary calls it "an excellent expedient in the struggle for the soul of our people and in the process of creating the necessary German resistance needed to see us successfully through the war."[3] Nonetheless, this film, too, continues Weimar cinema's recycling of the Frederick legend, whose basic formula, as we will see, fuses the incompatible discourses of eighteenth-century Sentimentality with twentieth-century "soldierly nationalism."

My intention is to explore Nazi cinema's renditions of Frederick as

2. Hans Feld, "Potsdam gegen Weimar oder Wie Otto Gebühr den Siebenjährigen Krieg gewann," in *Preussen im Film*, 69.
3. Goebbels's diary entry for 19 February 1942, as quoted in David Welch, *Propaganda and the German Cinema, 1933–1945* (Oxford: Clarendon Press, 1983), 176.

another example of a "body politic" manifesting itself in a modern-day obsession with the Body of a King, as the reverse of anti-Semitism's obsession with the Jew. Ernst Kantorowicz's study, *The King's Two Bodies,* has made familiar the medieval notion of the King as a person possessing a mortal, human body subject to laws of nature and a second body that transcends nature, "that cannot be seen or handled, [that] is utterly void of Infancy, and old Age, and other natural Defects and Imbecilities, which the Body natural is subject to."[4] Because of this duality, the premodern King's Body was a sublime object; it was at the center of social being, constantly displayed as an insignia of state power. Access to this Body was a form of privilege so great that, as Norbert Elias has shown, only individuals of the highest standing were allowed to watch the King defecate.[5]

This expression of power through the body and the visible is eroded around the mid-eighteenth century by a process Foucault describes as a transition from spectacle to "discipline," and Luhmann as a transition from "stratified" to "functionally differentiated" societies (see chapter 1). As this process takes hold, power relations cease to manifest themselves in an "outside," in the spectacle of the King's Body or in the public torture of criminals, which was merely another manifestation of the King's power. The new operations of power shift to an "inside"; they rely on the socialization of constantly visible subjects, who, because they know they may be watched at any and all times, internalize the behavior expected of them, increasingly obviating the need for external force. The body disintegrates as the category defining power; even clothing loses ground as a signifier of class, and particularly the male subject becomes "despecularized."[6] In place of the body steps the "soul"; social relations depend on the production of discourses, that is, on ideological reproduction.

Why then, in the twentieth century, do we begin seeing a particular King's Body, albeit fictional *representations* of that Body, as a ubiquitous specular presence staring down from film posters, postcards, briefcases, and piano music, and coming to life in films like *Fridericus Rex,* the

4. Edmund Plowden, Commentary on Reports (London, 1816), 212a, quoted in Ernst Kantorowicz, *The King's Two Bodies: A Study in Mediaeval Political Theology* (Princeton, N.J.: Princeton University Press, 1957), 7.

5. *Die höfische Gesellschaft: Untersuchungen zur Soziologie des Königstums und der höfischen Aristokratie mit einer Einleitung — Soziologie und Geschichtswissenschaft* (Berlin: Luchterhand, 1969), 178–221.

6. See Kaja Silverman's discussion of C. J. Flugel's *The Psychology of Clothes* in *The Acoustic Mirror* (Bloomington: Indiana University Press, 1988), 24–27. I will return to Silverman's discussion in the following chapter.

photos of which accompanied a new edition of von Molo's biography?[7] If the "original" sublime status of the King's Body is inextricably linked with a premodern stratified order that relied on visible bodily inscriptions, how are we to understand the resurrection of the King's Body, the return to spectacle in modernity?

As the allergic reaction of contemporary culture critics, especially on the left, to the Frederick cult suggests, we can understand this resurrection in part as a brilliant move of reactionary propagandists. Already in 1906, Franz Mehring lambasted nationalistic Prussian historiographers like Leopold von Ranke, Heinrich von Sybel, and Heinrich von Treitschke for painting the king with a "whitewash" of "national rebirth" that is "as tasteless as it is primitive."[8] Siegfried Kracauer condemns the films as "pure propaganda for the restoration of the monarchy";[9] *Fridericus Rex* justified "the aversion of an authoritarian public to enlightenment-reason."[10] Social Democratic and Communist newspapers like *Vorwärts* and *Freiheit* admonished their readers to boycott the Frederick films, and, more recently, numerous film historians have argued that they encouraged the reactionary trends that led to National Socialism.[11]

Although Frederick undoubtedly was exploited for political purposes, I think we must again conceive the enduring fascination with his legend as an expression primarily of desire — which Kracauer corroborates with his

7. Gerhard Schoenberner, "Das Preussenbild im deutschen Film: Geschichte und Ideologie," in *Preussen im Film,* 18.

8. "Vorrede zur zweiten Auflage" of *Die Lessing Legende: Zur Geschichte und Kritik des preussischen Despotismus und der klassischen Literatur* (1893; Stuttgart: Verlag das neue Wort, 1953), 47.

9. *From Caligari to Hitler: A Psychological History of the German Film* (Princeton, N.J.: Princeton University Press, 1947), 115.

10. Quoted in Wilhelm van Kampen, "Das 'preussische Beispiel' als Propaganda und politisches Lebensbedürfnis: Anmerkungen zur Authentizität und Instrumentalisierung von Geschichte im Preussenfilm," in *Preussen im Film,* 169.

11. See, for example, Stephen Lowry's *Pathos und Politik* (Tübingen: Niemeyer, 1991), Julian Petley, *Capital and Culture: German Cinema, 1933–45* (London: British Film Institute, 1979), W. Becker, *Film und Herrschaft* (Berlin: Spiess, 1973), and J. Spiker, *Film und Kapital* (Berlin: Spiess, 1975). According to Gerhard Schoenberner, already in the period from 1910 to 1916, German film displays the "complete catalogue" of themes that dominate film until 1945. Topics such as the community of the people, that is, the eradication of class differences and conflicts in favor of a general harmony, pervaded films during World War I, as is suggested by titles like *It Should Be All of Germany (Das ganze Deutschland soll es sein,* 1914). "Das Preussenbild im deutschen Film: Geschichte und Ideologie," in *Preussen im Film,* 12–13.

diagnosis of "powerful collective desires" as the reason why the "true" Frederick excavated by critical historians "never succeeded in upsetting the legendary one."[12] This desire relates to the individual and social stability that Nazism and earlier antimodern movements perceive as "lost." What seems to be a "premodern" fetishization of the King's Body in cinema is conditioned precisely *by* modernity with its gap between reality and some Other sphere (see chapter 1). The sensation in modernity that the subject's anchorage is "lost" is predicated on the assumption that some earlier era must have had it; "antimodern" ideologies project this anchorage retroactively onto some time or someone who promises reconciliation between the everyday and desire. The fact that this projection is — has to be — retroactive betrays its dependency on time, on an organization of the past as a narrative from which the present can draw strength. Narrative is, as so many theorists have discussed, a function of desire — a desire which propels modern individuals to organize their lives temporally (including the past and anticipated future) as a narrative, and to organize social formations in the same fashion. Without narrative, the individual could not perceive his/her identity as whole; nor could there be projections of social utopia.

Kracauer again cogently summarizes Frederick's psychoanalytic function when, in his December 1930 review of *The Flute Concert of Sanssouci,* he writes, "The masses are searching for an object to which they can cling."[13] Kracauer's reference to Frederick as an object puts in plain terms what psychoanalytic theory might describe as his substitution for the Thing. Both Freud and Lacan used the term *Thing* (*das Ding*—a term Lacan considered untranslatable) to describe the element "lost" by the subject at the moment of its integration into language or what Lacan calls the symbolic. The first point to make clear is that the Thing is, in a sense, a hallucination for the subject, since it is outside of the symbolic and cannot be represented. As Lacan puts it, "at the level of the *Vorstellungen* [representations], the Thing is not nothing but literally is not. It is characterized by its absence, its strangeness" (yet also by pleasure).[14] Nevertheless, the Thing is a *necessary* hallucination that helps the subject maintain a sense of coherent reality. Despite the fact that the Thing cannot be represented, the subject tries compulsively to retrieve it, since it seems to represent lost

---

12. *From Caligari to Hitler,* 117.

13. *Frankfurter Zeitung,* December 22, 1930, quoted in Schoenberner, 22 f.

14. Jacques Lacan, *The Seminar,* Book 7, ed. Jacques-Alain Miller, trans. Dennis Porter (New York: W. W. Norton, 1986), 63.

harmony or fulfillment of desire. The subject's life becomes a kind of never-ending chase after various signifiers that stand in for what cannot be named. Such signifiers ("things" like a man or woman, a political ideal, an idealized figure) are never "it," but allow the subject to pursue what can never be retrieved. Chasing, as anyone can tell you who has ever seen a chase movie (the *Terminator* series being a good example), is temporal, is a fundamental driving principle of narrative. Frederick can be seen in these terms as one important cultural signifier standing in for the lost Thing, the pursuit of which must ever be renewed. To this degree, his popularity covertly acknowledges the impossibility of the reconciliation he promises; since it exists only via narrative representation, his resurrection is "artificially produced" (Kracauer).

Herein lies the crucial difference between the modern and premodern cathexis of the King's Body. Although both disguise the fact that the monarchy is a network of social relations, that there is no such thing as the "essence" of a King (any more than of a Jew), the king's modern representations are part of a narrative, and thus never stand by or for themselves. They project onto him a character, an "inside" which reflects the imaginary identity of those doing the projecting and, as we will see, is tied to an all-seeing, nurturant gaze. The Frederick myth is, in other words, part of another social fantasy masking a fundamental social antagonism; he is a necessary, positive counterpart to, or inversion of, anti-Semitism's "Jew." If the "Jew" embodies the paranoiac, terrifying side of the big Other tormenting the subject, Frederick is a historical embodiment of the big Other as a higher instance of benevolent knowing and guidance that found its political reality in Hitler.[15]

Such a parallel between Hitler and the cinematic Frederick depends on an understanding of both as representational, essentially fictional figures. This "Frederick" has almost nothing to do with the historical monarch, but is the product of a mythification process that began in the nineteenth century with the nationalistic historiography that Franz Mehring and others attacked. Mythification means constructing one fortifying story around someone like Frederick with the help of many smaller stories; hence the collections of literary and filmic Frederick anecdotes that

---

15. Obviously, this does not mean that everyone to whom Frederick appealed was an anti-Semite, especially given the long tradition of Frederick myth. I am referring to the structural interdependencies of positive and negative projections. It is no coincidence that the same *kind* of sociopolitical thinking that produced "Frederick" produced the "Jew."

became bestsellers along with extended stories like the Seven Years' War or his youthful disputes with his father, which will be the basis of the next chapter. What may not be apparent is that the "Hitler" I am referring to is less the real-life political figure than the one constructed by National Socialism's aestheticized political sphere, which likewise weaves a macro-narrative of Hitler as redeemer along with individual stories (the beer hall putsch, the trials of prison, etc.).

In probing the relationship between a fictionalized historical figure at the brink of modernity like Frederick and a modern totalitarian Leader persona like Hitler, Slavoj Žižek's distinction between two kinds of social/political "masters" is useful.[16] He defines the traditional master or monarch according to Lacan's matheme S_1, which stands for the master signifier and is distinguished from S_2 or knowledge. The traditional King embodies S_1; he is autoreferential, an empty signifier, a signifier without a signified. To make this clear one must only consider the tautology with which his rule is legitimated: "I submit to the King because he is King." The suggestion that one submit to the King because of certain qualities is tantamount to blasphemy, to doubting his Kingliness. The same logic holds for family relations, in which we've all heard "just because" as a response to our questioning of paternal prohibitions — because I'm your father and I say so. The rule of the "totalitarian" master is legitimated in a very different way, which Žižek describes as S_2 or knowledge. While the King simply *is the King,* there are supposedly *reasons* why the Leader is a Leader; his understanding of historical laws and principles of community predestines him to serve as a driving force in narratives.

As already suggested, the Frederick films and the legend that preceded them project a modern structure retroactively onto a premodern, more accurately, a transitional, early modern one. Theoretically, Frederick is the traditional King, his legitimacy is purely monarchical, his word automatically Law. (The films are sprinkled with narratives revolving around the imperative of unconditional obedience). Yet the entire Frederick myth is erected around qualities belonging to S_2; qualities that make Frederick "the Great" and comprise what I referred to earlier as his "inside," the ideological discourse that gives his image meaning, embeds it in stories, and promises he can reconcile modernity's split. As a representation constructed *by* the present as a pleasurable mirror *for* the present, Frederick embodies S_2, which allows him to take on a social-psychic function recall-

16. See *For They Know Not What They Do: Enjoyment as a Political Factor* (London: Verso, 1991), 235 f.

ing Hitler's. Though he bears remnants of an old feudal order, he cannot be Lacan's S_1, the traditional King, because the latter is a nontemporal, non-narrative presence whose body signifies power, not desire. The traditional King's "thereness" demonstrates but it does not interpellate: this presupposes a modern structure dependent on narrative. Even when the Frederick movies suggest that he possesses a nontemporal presence, as in his own remark in *The Great King* that "one doesn't become a king, one *is* a king," they refer to biologically infused qualities of "leadership" that are grounded in stories (not to mention the fact that such comments are dialogue in stories, that is, part of Frederick's narrative construction).

Finally, "leadership" itself encompasses "knowledge," an understanding of historical, that is, *temporal* processes. The centrality of temporality to "leadership" can be illustrated by the quotation I cited at the beginning of this chapter, the one that thrilled my German professor as a little boy. Frederick's "You mean this *was* the Austrian camp" (more dramatically captured in the original German by one word, the spine-tingling past participle *gewesen*) is a narrative tour de force that not only puts Austrian hegemony in the past tense but implies a past perfect. Before the prissy Austrians could say "Maria Theresa," Frederick had already seen through their war strategy and taken over their space, despite their vastly greater numbers. Over and over the movies celebrate this gesture of looking ahead, doing, and having done as an event that is at once transgressive, male, and aesthetic: Frederick's art is, to use another of his phrases, breaking "all the rules of the art of war."

To the degree that he depends on a modern narrativization of society and on representation, critics' frequent reference to the Frederick of Nazi films as a surrogate Hitler is accurate. But this still does not legitimate reducing Frederick to pure "manipulation." Not only did Frederick long precede Hitler as a social fantasy, but he appears to have functioned as such a fantasy object for the Führer himself. Hitler repeatedly invoked Frederick as a historical model, likened the early struggle of National Socialism with Frederick's assertion of Prussia against great powers, and kept a picture of Frederick above his desk, which gave him "new strength, when bad news threatens to oppress me."[17]

We still need to examine the kinds of stories in which the myth has "planted" Frederick. Like *Jew Süss*, the Frederick films draw on two narrative paradigms whose compatibility is at least questionable: a war story

17. Quoted in Francis Courtade and Pierre Cadars, *Geschichte des Films im dritten Reich*, trans. Florian Hopf (Munich: Carl Hanser, 1975), 68.

and an eighteenth-century bourgeois "family" story, which I will discuss first. The films do not "tell," even covertly like *Jew Süss*, a bourgeois tragedy. Their indebtedness to eighteenth-century literature lies in the moral binarism they borrow, "bourgeois" virtue versus aristocratic cabal, and above all in their projection of a bourgeois value system (coded as "universal") onto the absolutist monarch Frederick. The cinematic Frederick becomes Prussia's *Landesvater,* the eighteenth-century notion expressing the desire to reconcile politics and morality (which were clearly separate in absolutist political theory). What gives the films their repetitive story is the war he fights, to which I will return. Suffice it to say here that Frederick's bourgeois moral coding permits his war to be legitimated ideologically as a great big bourgeois tragedy in which the harmony of a macro-family, Prussia, is disrupted by the "courtly" states, Austria, France, and Russia, ganged up against it. The ultimate question will be whether this model aims at protecting or obliterating family.

In connection with *Jew Süss,* I discussed the subversive implications of antifeudal eighteenth-century tragedies like Lessing's *Emilia Galotti*. The sentimentalization of rulers like Frederick in the nineteenth century testifies, by contrast, to the epistemological and political limitations of Sentimentality's project of moralizing humanity. In his popular legend, Frederick embodies the ultimate aspiration of eighteenth-century moralization; a king so moral as to obviate the need for limiting his power, for imposing structural political change. Rather than undermining a feudal structure, the projection of "bourgeois" qualities onto enlightened despots like Frederick affirms it. It naturalizes class difference and authority, both of which are sublated in common "human" ideals.[18] In the case of Frederick, this moralization literally perpetuates his monarchy, as suggested by the recurrent motif in the films of the "close call," Frederick's miraculous evasion of death (a motif played upon by Hitler as well) that results from his rejection of luxury. In *The Great King*, Frederick's refusal to drink a (poisoned) cup of hot chocolate out of disdain for luxury saves him from an assassination

18. Although the paradigm of the bourgeois king remains essentially the same from *Fridericus Rex* on, it is interesting to note that in the 1922 film Frederick uses a large number of French expressions in the intertitles, whereas by the Nazi period virtually all French has been expunged from Frederick's discourse. This no doubt relates to the same privileging of the "no-nonsense," soldierly discourse I discussed with respect to *Jew Süss,* as well as to a disparagement of "international" thinking. According to Courtade and Cadars, however, the films distance Frederick from the ordinary or regional. Allegedly, scenes in which the king spoke in Berlin dialect (as well as in French) were dubbed over. See Courtade and Cadars, 77.

attempt; the servant who he insists should enjoy the chocolate dies instead. Unlike in bourgeois literature, where moral characters constantly die off, "bourgeois" virtue protects Frederick's mortal body, or, in medieval terms, intertwines it with his mystical body.

Not surprisingly, the retroactive construction of imaginary "bourgeois" monarchs became a specialty of nationalists in the nineteenth and twentieth centuries. Another important example is Frederick's female counterpart in the Volkish imagination, Queen Luise of Prussia (1776–1810, wife of Frederick William III), who gained fame as spokeswoman for the Prussian people during their occupation by Napoleon and is alleged to have died of a broken heart over her people's suffering. The spatial metaphor with which Wulf Wülfing analyzes the Luise myth can serve as well for Frederick: it replaces "the vertically structured image of 'authority' and 'subject,' which denotes *contrast,* with the mythic image of the 'circle' aimed at a *harmonization* of these contrasts."[19] Like Frederick, Luise was the subject of a Walter von Molo biography, and of four feature films from 1913, 1927, 1931, and 1956. She also shows up, significantly unnamed (as a figure who needs no name), in Nazi cinema's last major historical epic, Veit Harlan's *Kolberg* (1945). Nondiegetic choral music, light radiating from above, and soft focus stylize the queen's chamber as "celestial." In a gesture literalizing the reconciliation of monarchy and Volk, Luise presses an awe-struck peasant girl to her bosom, whose needs she intuitively "reads." Luise's mythification was gender specific; her appeal lay in her maternal passivity, as is amply clear from Heinrich von Treitschke's remark: "It is a touchstone of [Luise's] greatness that one can say so little of her deeds."[20] We will see, however, how Frederick's film persona has an enveloping, maternal appeal of its own.

The simultaneous maintenance and elision of class difference in these mythifications is essential to the structure Žižek describes as "totalitarian." The necessary counterpart to "totalitarianism's" Leader is the "People," which is no less an invention.[21] Frederick's cinematic People are his mirror reflection. They might consist of aristocrats with "heart," middle-class or, most often, peasant figures and soldiers, but the "bourgeois" virtue they share with the King transforms a relationship of author-

19. "Die heilige Luise von Preussen: Zur Mythisierung einer Figur der Geschichte in der deutschen Literatur des 19. Jahrhunderts," in *Bewegung und Stillstand in Metaphern und Mythen,* ed. Wulf Wülfing and Jürgen Link (Stuttgart: Klett-Cotta, 1984), 236–37.
20. Quoted in Wülfing, 272.
21. See Žižek's *The Sublime Object of Ideology* (London: Verso, 1989), 146.

ity into one of symbiosis; as with Luise, class and privilege become meaningless. This totalitarian structure differs from the monarchical structure in that the deception is not so much the fact that the King is "really" no more than himself, but that the *point of reference* with which he legitimizes his rule is imaginary. One might apply Lacan's famous statement about "woman" to Frederick's cinematic People; they "don't exist" except as a fantasy apparition invented by an agency for whom this apparition is necessary. Their pristine innocence is, as Žižek put it in another context, a "staged" identification on behalf of an Other.[22]

The most obvious narrative component of the Frederick genre is the *Glanzkriegsstück* or "lustrous war drama," to use Kracauer's term describing *The Flute Concert of Sanssouci*. Although even in legend Frederick is remembered as a musician, a francophile philosopher and friend of Voltaire, and a proponent of religious tolerance and codified law, all of the movies force him "into the straight jacket of the uniform,"[23] and most are set in the Seven Years' War of 1756–1763 (including all of the Nazi features except *The Old and the Young King*, which *prepares* Frederick for his warrior status). Like the nineteenth-century historiography to which they are indebted, the films rewrite the Seven Years' War as, in Franz Mehring's words, a "fairy tale" about a nationalist underdog with only the People's interest at heart, ignoring the fact that the historical Frederick was an eighteenth-century despot "without a trace of nationalist sentiment"[24]—indeed, he predated the very notion of nationalism.

Although the Frederick legend evolved in connection with nineteenth-century nationalist ideologies, by the 1920s when the Frederick films emerged, his militarization was inscribed in a broad cultural move to erase the cultural discourse of war that evolved in World War I and to replace it, not with a discourse of peace, but a bigger and better one of War. The "Great War" had not only humiliated Germany but had transformed war into a mechanical and technological event rendering obsolete autonomy and heroism.[25] The new discourse of War, to which Karl Prümm gives the name "soldierly nationalism,"[26] offers another means of imaginary escape

22. See *The Sublime Object of Ideology*, 107.

23. Feld, 69.

24. Mehring, 37.

25. See, for example, Stephen Brockman, "The Cultural Meaning of the Gulf War," *Michigan Quarterly Review* 31.2 (Spring 1992): 169.

26. See Karl Prümm, *Die Literatur des soldatischen Nationalismus der zwanziger Jahre (1918–1933): Gruppenideologie und Epochenproblematik*, 2 vols. (Kronberg/Ts.: Scriptor, 1974). Even given the pervasiveness of social militarization in the Wilhel-

from the *agonia* and social atomization of modernity. This War promises to suspend social dispersal by anonymous economic ("Jewish") forces, and again makes recourse to a premodern warrior caste (and yet perfects the most modern of all operations, discipline and what F. T. Marinetti calls the "dreamt-of metalization of the human body,"[27] a contradiction I address in the next chapter).

Rather than securing the private sphere and civil society, the War imagined in this discourse substitutes for it, becoming itself a consummate object of desire, the apotheosis of an aesthetic experience in which the subject can decenter himself. The imaginary space of War not only transcends civil society but is defined against the femininity the latter represents, especially against the dissolution that became projected onto Germany's first democracy, the Weimar Republic. As I will elaborate in chapter 8, Nazism constructs "Weimar" as a historical phenomenon whose representational function comes to exceed "real" memories of it, much like Pearl Harbor for the America of the forties: "Weimar" comes to Germany "already shaped as a representation."[28] Nazism reacted vehemently to, among other things, Weimar culture's blurring of gender boundaries, trying to "cancel out" Weimar by fetishizing maleness in virtually all social spheres and by aggressively projecting the perceived lack onto others, as we saw in the preceding chapter. Precisely this pathological dread of feminization is Klaus Theweleit's focus in *Male Fantasies*, which

---

mine years, there was a new quality to the militarism that emerged during and after World War I out of which National Socialism's concept of the military grew. In "soldierly nationalism" the old Prussian militarism merges with late-nineteenth-century "irrationalism" and Nietzschean elitism. The military and war itself were transformed increasingly into an escape from alienation and from the social domination of exchange value. Intellectuals welcomed World War I as a chance to escape from the drudgery of everyday bourgeois existence, characterized by alienated work. The "front" offered a chance for heroism, for heightened experience, for *die Tat* ("the deed"), and an experience of *Rausch* ("intoxication"). War involved the "whole man," not just a part of him, as did factory work, producing some small part of a product. Cf. the mystification of soldierhood in Harlan's 1945 film *Kolberg*. When an aristocrat decries the idea of a citizen's army because war is a "craft that has to be learned," a soldier responds: "Learned yes, but a *craft*, Colonel, it is *not*. It's something that comes from the heart and the citizens of Kolberg have got that."

27. Quoted in Walter Benjamin, "The Work of Art in the Age of Mechanical Reproduction," in *Illuminations*, trans. H. Zohn (New York: Harcourt, Brace, and World, 1968), 241.

28. Dana Polan, *Power and Paranoia: History, Narrative, and the American Cinema, 1940–1950* (New York: Columbia University Press, 1986), 60.

traces the path from this discourse of war and maleness to National Socialism and beyond. The fascist male that Theweleit studies constitutes his
very identity by dissociation from the feminine, which, however, never
ceases to be a threat to the male self, and is symbolized by recurrent
images in fascist language of enveloping liquid, such as floods, swamps,
tidal waves, seas, or rivers of blood. Ritualized forms of socialization like
the army and military drills, the nation, and the battle help the male form
a substitute for his fragmented ego, making him into an "armored man"
whose body becomes part of a war-machine.[29]

In this sociohistorical context, it is not surprising to find especially
distant wars like Frederick's fought over and over on the cinema screen.
The events of 1756 to 1763 were an antidote to World War I, restoring
war's "glory" and offering a reassuring closure attested to by film critic
Oskar Kalbus's endorsement of *Fridericus Rex:* "A vanquished country,
thrust from sublime heights to the depths of misery, enjoys remembering
glorious times past. . . . We see that the lives of the Potsdam kings were
often more difficult than those of their subjects, and we experience that it
is the fulfillment of duty and obedience that made Prussia, that made
Germany great and strong."[30] Consequently the films' repetitive trajectory, usually beginning with a low point in the war and ending with Frederick's "impossible" victory at Schweidnitz (1762), doubtless enhanced
rather than impeded their popularity. Moments like the disastrous battle
of Kunersdorf (1759) beginning *The Great King* only reinscribe defeat as
a negative moment in a larger positivity — again as an "answer" to an
uncertain, "humiliated" present. Like most war stories, moreover, the
films display the misogyny so essential to Theweleit's model (and that is
one of the few traits the cinematic Frederick shares with his historical
counterpart).[31] As I will elaborate, Frederick recuperates wholeness and
phallic strength perceived as lacking in modernity by abjecting the female
Other, which might thus be linked indirectly to the "Jewish" Other. If, as
he remarks in *Fridericus,* Frederick writes history "with Prussia's blood,"
this blood will take a metaphorically "feminine" form.

It is here, however, that the war story's uneasy marriage with the

29. Theweleit, 2:154.
30. Kalbus, quoted in van Kampen, 170.
31. See Thomas Mann, "Friedrich und die grosse Koalition," in *Gesammelte Werke*
(Berlin: Aufbau Verlag, 1956), 11:66–126. Mann labels Frederick's relations with
women an "unrelationship" (80). The King is rumored to have become impotent after
some early affairs. He urged his officers not to marry, and his palace Sanssouci was
known as a "monastery."

eighteenth-century family drama threatens to unravel in the films. The Enlightenment project on which Frederick's bourgeois *Landesvater* coding draws aims at protecting family as a metaphor for a civilian social order, at ensuring a private sphere marked by community. The warrior Frederick assures community, ironically, through the *destruction* of family and the private sphere, though ostensibly, of course, to "save" it (Frederick fights "for peace," "for Mother"). The films' constant disavowal of such a contradiction does not, I think, counter the feeling they generate that women are tiresome ornaments inhibiting the fun of a world where men do what they've "got to," but really want to "do" (at least from the security of the movie theater).

In what follows I will examine Nazism's Frederick films within the parameters of social fantasies, of the King's resurrected body. However, I want to first insert a cautionary remark that may seem blasphemous to film specialists: the Frederick films are *only movies*. By this I mean to emphasize that, as was the case with *Jew Süss,* the films' exhibition of ideologies and pathologies is framed within, and at times harnessed by, classical cinema's codified system. Moreover, their anchorage in the tradition of "Prussiana" to which I have referred should serve as a useful reminder that their interpellation is not *necessarily* fascist — or, conversely, that fascist texts are not produced only by fascist states. In their infantile indulgence of a virtually womanless world, they recall figures like G.I. Joe; indeed they had a great, though not exclusive, appeal to boys.[32] School teachers capitalized on their popularity among boys by making field trips to the Frederick movies. Not only is there "something" in the fascist psyche, especially as evoked by scholars like Theweleit, that eludes the films, but divinely sanctioned "Leadership" is no more easily representable than the essence of "Jewishness," leaving these films, too, to draw on the iconographies and stylistics within the arsenal of classical cinema. Apropos of representing "divine" Leadership, the Nazis knew what they were doing when they prohibited any actor from playing Hitler.[33] A fictionalized portrayal of, say, Hitler's rise to power might unwittingly have proven a deconstruction calling attention to the fictional nature of both "real" and represented Leader. In order to *be* Hitler, he had to remain beyond narrative representation.

32. Hans Feld describes his reaction to Frederick as a seventeen-year-old; Feld, 68 ff. In particular, I am indebted to Gerhard Weiss for information on the films' popularity among children.

33. When *The Great King* was released, journalists were admonished not to draw direct parallels to Hitler or the times. Courtade and Cadars, 76.

The other point I want to reiterate is that *only* movies could give a historical myth like Frederick such a compelling form of "life." No one had to play Hitler because he was there to constantly play himself, whereas Frederick and the imaginary history he embodies depended on the series of representational forms that culminated in the movies. In this sense, whether inherently "fascist" or not, the Frederick genre served National Socialism, since the community Frederick stands for, like that of National Socialism, is a performative act existing only in the moment it is acted out. Even if "everybody" knew that the movies embellished history, they could enjoy the reenactment of community. In the words of Hans Feld, "it was too beautiful to be true. And that is precisely what made it so effective."[34]

I begin in this chapter with a discussion structured around Frederick as a mirror reverse of anti-Semitism's "Jew," moving from his iconic representation to the narrative spaces in which he operates. In addition to discussing *Fridericus* and *The Great King*, I will draw upon scenes from some films that only allude to Frederick. Because of their redundancy, I am omitting a plot synopsis for each film and will describe the general paradigm instead.

FREDERICK AS THE INVERSION OF THE "JEW"

As embodiments of oppositional social fantasies, Frederick and Nazism's "Jew" in *Jew Süss* bear a curious resemblance to each other. Both are described by other figures as a "devil," both function as the central subject (as well as fetishized object) of the narrative and historical juncture; both are essentially unchallenged by an opponent of equal stature and are characterized by an imagined, indescribable essence ("Jewishness," "Kingliness") that in turn gives them a transformative power over others. Like *Jew Süss*, the Frederick films face the challenge of representing this "specialness," which they generally do with realist cinematic codes, enhanced by some stylistic effects discussed below. Frederick is, like the "Jew," as much the subject as he is the object of spectacle,[35] only the effect of this specular relation is the exact reverse of *Jew Süss*.

---

34. Feld, 69.

35. Cf. Claude Lefort's description of the premodern king: "[He] possesses the gift of clairvoyance as well as that of ubiquity; but, at the same time and even as he escapes the gaze of his subjects, he has the gift of attracting the gaze of all, of concentrating upon himself the absolute visibility of man-as-being." *Democracy and Political Theory*, trans. David Macey (Minneapolis: University of Minnesota Press, 1988), 245.

As object of the look Frederick stands largely for paternal or what Alice Kaplan calls "father-bound" desires.[36] He offers the kind of phallic identification Wilhelm Reich defined long ago as the basis of a "national narcissism" in which the subject can perceive "*himself* in the führer, in the authoritarian state."[37] The films develop an iconography borrowed from earlier media and from each other, a system of images serving as a pleasurable mirror for the spectator, and simultaneously underscoring the gap *between* the spectator and the historical/cinematic icon. Again here, the secret seems to lie in *lack* of variation, in the pleasure of familiarity and recognition. As modern icons, cinematic representations of Frederick tie the King's Body to a structured ideological discourse; that is, his body is never reducible to mere spectacle but is dependent on its syntactical order in the text and on verbal motifs functioning as a *subscriptio* to the *pictura* (he is a "born king," a "robber captain,"[38] etc.).

Jean-Louis Comolli describes historical film as handicapped by "one body too much," when the physical appearance of the actor playing a well-known historical figure interferes with the audience's preconceived image of that figure.[39] The Frederick films obviated this problem by finding a "reel" Frederick, an actor who came to seem more "real" than the king himself. Otto Gebühr, a former Max Reinhardt actor who played Frederick in sixteen films over a period of twenty years, starting with *Fridericus Rex,* became synonymous in the public eye with the king. Kracauer and Hans Feld write that he "resurrected" Frederick,[40] and a joke made its way through Berlin that Gebühr planned to call his memoirs "How I won the Seven Years' War."[41] His frequent appearance in full military regalia at public events further suggests his equation with Frederick and the latter's embodiment of the imaginary national body. When

36. *Reproductions of Banality* (Minneapolis: University of Minnesota Press, 1986), 20–25.

37. *Mass Psychology of Fascism* (1933; New York: Farrar, Straus and Giroux, 1970), 63.

38. The reference to Frederick as a "robber captain" by his Austrian enemies alludes again to Storm and Stress, especially Schiller's Karl Moor (*The Robbers*), who epitomizes rebellion against the machinations of the absolutist state. Cf. my discussion of *Friedrich Schiller.*

39. "Historical Fiction: A Body Too Much," *Screen* 19 (Summer 1978): 41–53.

40. *From Caligari to Hitler,* 116, and Feld, 71. When Veit Harlan wanted to cast Werner Krauss as Frederick in *The Great King,* Goebbels intervened and insisted Gebühr play the role (Veit Harlan, *Im Schatten meiner Filme* [Gütersloh, 1966], 181 f.).

41. Feld, 72.

13 "White horse" iconography mythologizes Frederick in *The Chorale of Leuthen*. **14** Frederick appears unidentified in *Lady von Barnhelm*, based on Lessing's play *Minna von Barnhelm*.

Gebühr was unavailable, lesser-known actors substituted for him, becoming "surrogates of the surrogate."[42]

Though Frederick exists as, and only as, a cinematic spectacle, the last thing the films do is to "hyperspecularize" his body, as they might women or feminized men. They reverse, in fact, the iconography of many mythologizing genres that give their superheroes superbodies. The strategy of the Frederick iconography is to emphasize the *contrast* between the frailty of his aging, gout-plagued body and the magnitude of his "spirit." His codified clothing (a dark, simple military jacket with the royal insignia, the oversized hat that dwarfs his face) lends him a low-key consistency, a kind of visual reliability — enhanced by the familiarity of Otto Gebühr — that complements his narrative reliability. His clothing is that of duty, of a man in a perpetual state of war — recalling Theweleit's warrior who "carries the front" with him. In his most ubiquitous image, found on book jackets as well as in films, an all too human fragility collides with a titanic iconography: dominantly framed from a low angle, Frederick appears alone in the dusk or dark on a pure white horse, seemingly a renegade from mythology (often he will assume this posture in his first appearance,

42. Ibid.

as in *Fridericus* and *The Chorale of Leuthen;* photo 13). The subject effect of this body recalls that of the medieval King as described by Claude Lefort. Precisely weakness and suffering establish a "carnal unity" between the King and his People that cannot be separated from the King's mystical self: "Far from being shocked at seeing the human element in him, they were grateful for it. They believed that it would bring him closer to them."[43]

Just as the "Jew," as a narrative representation of abstractness, needs to be given a cinematic body, so Frederick, as a narrative representation of the concreteness antimodern ideologies value (blood and soil, nation, *Heimat*) needs to be represented in abstract terms that underscore his historical inscription. In foregrounding this historical inscription, making the king "more than himself," the films depart at key moments from their realist narrational mode. Stylized configurations abstracting Frederick from his mortal self seem designed to "materialize" his second body for cinematic purposes, to split him into a public and a private side. I have listed a few such recurring constellations, most of which arrest narrative movement in favor of a "painterly" tableau. Invariably, these moments have little or no diegetic function, but invite contemplative reflection on an imagined history:

1. Frederick is alone in a massive Gothic cathedral at the end of the Seven Years' War, an emaciated, stiff figure visually dominated by super-dimensional architecture. The icon lives off of the same tension between the super- and mini-dimensional as the horse icon and foregrounds at once Frederick's isolation from humans and his affirmation by a transcendent authority. Both *The Great King* and *Fridericus Rex* end with such a shot, but most interesting is its occurrence in the 1940 Nazi film adaptation of Lessing's *Minna von Barnhelm* titled *Lady von Barnhelm.* The brief scene is of great significance to Nazi cinema's "translation" of Lessing's play, which occurs mainly through a manipulation of story and plot. Lessing's comedy of errors about the destitute war hero Tellheim takes place after the Seven Years' War. It satirizes Tellheim's rigid code of honor, which, but for the subversive intervention of fiancée Minna, would have ruined their personal happiness. The film version *Lady von Barnhelm* begins its narration in the *middle* of the Seven Years' War, thus savoring every moment of a war story that remains "background information" in Lessing's play. Lessing's deconstructive indictment of militarism for its own sake becomes here a euphoric affirmation unfolded in dramatic pictures. Crucial

43. Lefort, 244.

15-17 Iconography abstracting Frederick from himself: his shadow visits his lost private sphere (*top*); his shadow confronts his portrait (*middle*); a soldier's caricature ridiculing the King effects its opposite (*bottom*). All from *The Great King*.

to this affirmation is the appearance of Frederick (only an off-stage figure in Lessing's play) in his cathedral icon at the end of the war, walking along a dramatic shaft of light toward a statue of an angel whose arm is stretched out as if in welcome (photo 14). The film's omission of any verbal reference to him in the symbolically loaded scene attests to his significance as ideological capital whose identity is taken for granted. No diegetic character, furthermore, witnesses the scene; it is there exclusively for the film spectator, for whom Lessing's irony is submerged in Frederick mythology.

2. In a constellation borrowing a stylistic earmark of Weimar cinema, Frederick appears occasionally as a shadowy silhouette. A dream se-

quence from *The Great King* permits a glimpse of the peacetime "life" denied him, as his shadow walks into his palace Sanssouci, past bookshelves revealing volumes of Plato and Voltaire. The private sphere, the space of reconciliation in which the body "armor" can dissolve, is pushed back not only into the realm of the imaginary, but of nostalgia. Just as Frederick's frailty makes him more of a Thing, his solitude paradoxically augments our sense of community with him. We identify with elements that function as signifiers of their own opposite — an effect enhanced by the fact that, since the shadow has no body, we inhabit that body.

3. Frederick encounters himself as historical icon, as in *The Great King,* when he enters a house largely demolished by war, where the peasant girl Luise is salvaging her few remaining belongings. Unaware of the King's identity, she directs her anger at the portrait of him hanging on the wall, which is the only item she leaves behind: "You should burn with everything else — the one who burned our mill! . . . Look what he's made out of his country! (*sarcastically*) A wonderful *Landesvater*!" On the one hand, the portrait stands for Frederick's "tragic" human self, abandoned like a child by an angry mother. On the other hand, the portrait stands in for his sublime body, which his mortal, physical body painfully confronts at a time when his stature as object of symbolic identification is uncertain. The split is redoubled as Frederick walks silently toward the picture, his shadow cast on the wall, slowly approaching until the shadow finally reaches the picture, effectively uniting the mortal with the transcendent body (photos 15–16). The shadow mediates between the two representations of Frederick, suggesting the uncapturable essence of a private man "doomed to sacrifice himself" for history.

4. Most extreme is the "portrayal" of Frederick's constitutive absence, exemplified by the empty chair beside his wife during the triumphal parade at the end of *The Great King,* or more dramatically by the empty gilded coach that rolls by (crosscutting shows Frederick attending to peasants' needs). Veit Harlan's *Kolberg* (1945), which takes place during Napoleon's occupation of Germany, ascribes the resistance of the town Kolberg to the strength conveyed by Frederick's second body, long after the death of his mortal body. The film savors Napoleon's error in assuming this second body to be dead; standing by Frederick's grave, he asks (in subtitled French): "Would I be standing here if you were still alive?"[44] The archway to Frederick's crypt conspicuously frames Napoleon, as if de-

---

44. The same scene occurs in Gerhard Lamprecht's *Old Fritz* (1927). Again Napoleon stands before Frederick's grave with his generals and remarks, "Hats off Messieurs! If he still lived, then we would not be standing here today!" Quoted in Murray, 78.

termined to contain him in a limited historical framework. After Napoleon's departure the camera's gaze lingers on the coffin of the ruler whose "ghost," as a French officer puts it, "lives on" in his People (already the next cut will show a woman calling the name "Frederick," in reference to a young soldier literally carrying forth his "spirit").

Ironically, although as a film icon Frederick has to be "played," within the world of the films he is privileged as unrepresentable, much like Hitler in the eyes of the Nazis. A caricature of Frederick drawn in *The Great King* by disgruntled soldiers whom he has punished for their cowardice serves only to enhance the contrast between the picture and reality. Another soldier quickly erases the picture as if it were an obscenity (photo 17). It is, however, not a Frederick film but Herbert Maisch's *Friedrich Schiller* that most explicitly confers Hitler's "too-special-to-be-played" status upon Frederick. When Schiller amuses the Duke of Württemberg by imitating his buffonish tyranny at a dinner party, he refuses the Duke's invitation to mimic the (absent) "Great King" — clearly with the suggestion that this would be tantamount to blasphemy.

As I suggested earlier, not only women like the mythologized Queen Luise have what Alice Kaplan calls a "mother-bound" appeal; this maternal function is, rather, a key to fascist and "authoritarian" fantasies. To articulate Frederick's "mother-bound" appeal, we have to turn to his function as *subject* of the look. This may seem contradictory, since, for example, Theweleit theorizes the fascist look as quintessentially masculine, based on his survey of fascist literature, which often describes the Leader in terms of his powerful "look." Expressive eyes appear to hold the key to the fascist concept of Personality: "If its beam is hard and active, it is phallic."[45] Photographs of Nazi leaders were often touched up to accentuate the eyes, as in Schirach's *Pioneers of the Third Reich*. Indeed, the focus of *The Old and the Young King*, to which I turn in the next chapter, is almost entirely on the acquisition of this steely "fascist" gaze. By calling Frederick "mother-bound," however, I refer to the "feminizing" subject effect of his gaze (upon diegetic characters and the film audience) and not to the possessor of that gaze. Frederick's all-seeing look permits (like Nazi spectacles) his subjects a pleasurable dissolution of boundaries, an "oceanic" pleasure in merging with King and collective.

Most of the time, however, the notion of such a gaze is conveyed in the films in narrative rather than iconic terms, as we are *told* he "sees" farther

45. *Male Fantasies*, vol. 2, trans. Erica Carter and Chris Turner (Minneapolis: University of Minnesota Press, 1989), 134.

than anyone else. It is indeed hard to disentangle the cinematic Frederick's status as subject of the look from his status as object, another feature he has in common with Süss. Virtually all scenes in which Frederick interacts with peasants allow him to look and be seen, fusing his mother-bound nurturance with father-bound authority. The scene described above, in which Luise denounces his portrait, lends an interesting dimension to this dual role. Because Frederick's identity is hidden from Luise (ironically because she thinks he's "just anybody"), he sees her from a point at which he never would be able to see her as king; he penetrates her thoughts like a transcendent being. Although the effect is of course one of irony (it flatters the audience with its superior comprehension of historical "necessity" and of Frederick's "tragic" existence), the scene unwittingly exposes the social relations underlying the monarchy: the king is only a king because people think he's a king. As long as Luise doesn't "think he's a king," she not only acts like "herself," freely venting her disgruntled feelings, but the camera allows her an "equal" status with him. From the inevitable moment on (sadistically enjoyed by the "knowing" spectator) when she understands he's a king, he becomes a cinematic "icon" vis-à-vis her and, essentially, *for her benefit*. She becomes a *subject* permitted to view Frederick only from a distance and a hyperbolic low angle, as she looks up at him on his white horse, or in the window of a large building — she is all but muted by his gaze.

In all of the films, I have located only two sequences that actually attempt to render visual this gaze by abandoning cinematic realism and approximating an articulation of the "fascist" fantasy of a Leader *qua* Christ. One of these is from *The Old and the Young King* and will be dealt with in the next chapter; I will return to the other, the montage ending *The Great King*, at the conclusion of this chapter.

NARRATIVE SPACE AND MISOGYNY

I want to turn to the space in which Frederick operates, the space he makes whole, implicitly countering the Jew's dispersal of space. It is perhaps no coincidence that the historical Frederick compared himself to the "wandering Jew." No less than Süss Oppenheimer, the cinematic Frederick is a master of space (and, indeed, of time). Only if we look at each figure's relation to the imaginary social body does *Jew Süss* again prove to be an exact inversion of Frederick's master narrative. In *Jew Süss*, Woman and a whole, delimited German body are simultaneously penetrated and contaminated by the "Jew," forcing the narrative to work for a restoration of its initial state. The Frederick genre depicts a social body already in a state of siege by another space marked as female (i.e., the obstacles he faces are only ostensibly "political"). Its narrative works, then, to liberate the contaminated social body by a reverse penetration, an explosion into the aggressive "female" space. If both narratives strive for a restitution of self, they do so with oppositional gestures: the "Jew's" act of poisoning has its parallel in Frederick's purgation of the social body through an imaginary war that exorcises metaphorically "female" bodies.

As already suggested, it is hardly a revelation to note that the Frederick genre is not "female" oriented. "Romantic interest" in the films is marginal at best; women appear only archetypes or obstacles to be contained, as in *The Flute Concert of Sanssouci* when Frederick abducts the capricious wife of an officer in order to prevent her from committing adultery.[46] In particular the films sentimentalize "Mother" while reducing her to a machine for producing cannon fodder, as has often been remarked of Nazism with its medals for German motherhood. For example, unable to resist the entreaties of a deserter's mother in *Fridericus*, Frederick pardons the boy whom she carried "with pain in her womb"; "mothers are always right." The abstract and archetypal Mother exists, however, as a mere foil for Frederick, and indeed disappears from the diegesis once her structural function has been fulfilled, displaced by Frederick's mother-bound functions.

The films' misogynous implications go vastly further if we consider that, from whatever perspective one looks, it is femaleness against which Frederick is fighting. The films work to exorcise three levels of "femininity," the first being the body, which is synonymous with enemy territory. He is most literally surrounded by a circle of female bodies, the "Three Whores of Europe" (to quote the historical Frederick)[47] aligned against him in the Seven Years' War. Like Theweleit's soldierly man, he is enveloped by a feminine "flood." *Fridericus* in particular masochistically savors this suffocation by crosscutting among the three type-cast women: Austria's Empress Maria Theresa becomes a dependent child (pouting over "that naughty man!");[48] the Russian Czarina Elizabeth embodies

46. The films were likewise perceived by Austrians as "too Prussian." Boguslaw Drewniak, *Der deutsche Film, 1938–45: Ein Gesamtüberblick* (Düsseldorf: Droste, 1987), 193.

47. Frederick evidently used this expression for the benefit of spies he knew to be present. Mann, 82.

48. This was a well-known phrase used by the historical Maria Theresa. Frederick enraged her when, after his success at the battle of Mollwitz, he quoted the twelfth verse

the Eastern barbarism that will recur in *Komödianten;* the portrayal of France's Mme. Pompadour as conniving hypocrite draws again on eighteenth-century literature's indictment of courtly cabal (photos 18– 20). Each of the scenes retains the "original" language, not only couching xenophobia in a pretend "documentary" mode but removing women from a world of "rational" male discursive communication. The female body is most distasteful when it transgresses its own boundaries, as does the masculine Czarina Elizabeth, whom we see slumped over on her throne in a drunken stupor and relishing a vicarious penetration of Frederick's space (using recognizable cognates: *command, Soldat, marschier, Berlin!*).

These female bodies literalize a threat to *Lebensraum* already suggested by the written text beginning *Fridericus:* "Encircled by the hereditary Great Powers of Europe, rising Prussia has aspired for decades to her right to live. The whole world is amazed at the king of Prussia who, first ridiculed, then feared, has maintained himself against forces many times superior to his own. Now they seem to crush him. Prussia's fateful hour has come." Word pairs like "encircled"/"crushed" versus "rising"; "ridiculed" versus "amazed" typify oppositions constitutive of the Frederick narrative: strictures versus freedom, stasis versus dynamism, an underdog versus centralistic, devouring machine-states perpetuating the status quo. Yet the same oppositions, especially "encircled" versus "rising," are equally readable in terms of gender, of a suffocating female biology. Lloyd De-Mause refers to fantasies of encirclement as "birth canal" imagery, a common "group fantasy," that is, a condition perceived by a group that is a "psychic," as opposed to material, reality.[49] Leaders in nations about to embark on a war often enlist the imagery of being "strangled" or "choked," although the imagery is less common among nations actually threatened with foreign occupation.

The second level of femininity the films exorcise is men who are really women. Already Siegfried Kracauer called Frederick's French and Austrian enemies "effeminate operetta figures."[50] Maria Theresa's prissy hus-

---

of 1 Timothy 2: "I do not permit woman to teach, nor to rise above man, but rather to behave in a peaceful manner." See Mann, 85.

49. Lloyd DeMause, *Foundations of Psychohistory* (New York: Creative Roots, 1982), 93. DeMause contends that the imagery of war's progression occurs in the same sequence as that of birth: that of a "dormant volcano," "rupture," and relief when war is finally decided upon, when the leaders realize "war was a group-fantasy of birth against which one struggled in vain" (96).

50. Kracauer, *From Caligari to Hitler,* 268.

18·20 The "three whores of Europe" surrounding Frederick in *Fridericus:* A pouty Maria Theresa (*top*); Czarina Elizabeth tossing down vodka (*middle*); Madame Pompadour sketches plans to conquer Prussia, explicitly linking the female body with threatened *Lebensraum* (*bottom*).

band in *Fridericus* avoids diplomatic activities on the grounds that he "doesn't understand a thing about politics" (a line the Duchess speaks in *Jew Süss*). Austria's female-gendered position is further conveyed by the films' recurrent (verbal or visual) juxtaposition of music with guns. *Fridericus* introduces the Viennese court by cutting from firing Prussian guns to trumpets blowing a fanfare. In *The Great King,* which introduces the same Viennese court with a cut to a large bouquet of flowers, an Austrian general expresses his disdain at Austrian men heading off for a minuet while Frederick is planning military strategy: "they are marching while we dance!"

Since enemies are only there to be beaten by Frederick, the more grievous threat to his spatial-temporal project lies in the encroachment of femininity within his own space. *Fridericus* equates having the "wrong values" with impotence, exemplified by a greedy local magistrate who has no children, while a peasant has fourteen. Frederick's "You ought to be able to learn it [from the peasant]" diagnoses such impotence as imperiling Prussia's forward trajectory (in addition to compensating ideologically for class difference). Each film includes a story of one or more deserter whose "cowardice" constitutes a personal assault on the king, a symbolic castration of him that is punishable by the same (a reciprocity in keeping with the symbiotic relation of King and People). Frederick's remark in *Fridericus* that if the young deserter does not want to kill, he should "put on a skirt" and find a man who will kill for him echoes with striking precision (as does the behavior of Maria Theresa's husband) Theweleit's analysis of men "hiding behind women's skirts" as a signifier in fascist discourse for bolshevism and its equivalences of dissolution, lechery, savagery.[51] *The Great King* repeats the desertion narrative on a macro-level involving an entire regiment; Frederick "castrates" the men by stripping their uniforms and confiscating their flag, reducing them to tears of shame and driving one to suicide.

In this very punishment, however, lies the transformative power that again reverses the Jew's. While the "Jew" feminizes men, Frederick reinstates men as men, but ironically through a process of total subjugation, self-humiliation, and eradication of personal identity. This transformation suggests the dialectical nature of "fascist" experience; subjugation to the Leader constitutes a "feminine" experience of decentering, which, however, reverses dialectically into a "hardening" of the male subject, a masculinization and abjection of the female Other, either within or outside of the self. Like Heini Völker in *Hitler Youth Quex* (1933), the young deserter in *Fridericus* abandons the skirts of his mother and submits himself to the collective — again suggesting Nazism's real denigration of family despite its rhetoric to the contrary. By suffering what Theweleit calls the "drill," he mechanizes his body and becomes "a true child of the drill-machine, created without the help of a woman, parentless"[52] — a self-violation we will see repeated by the young Frederick in *The Old and the Young King*.[53]

The restitution of phallus for the boy (and hence Frederick and Prussia),

51. See Theweleit, 2:27–35, "Women to the Fore."
52. Ibid., 2:160.
53. Such socialization is common in Nazi cinema; see my discussion in chapter 8 of the allegorical "German Michel" in *Robert and Bertram* (1939).

when Frederick hands him the Prussian flag to carry against the enemy, simultaneously means his sure death; he soon falls in battle, to be mentioned—like his mother—no more in the film. The films thus disavow death *as death* by recoding it as the highest form of life. War is rebirth, a symbiosis in which one can "explode" the boundaries of the self, as implied in *Fridericus* by Frederick's reference to battle as the "day of Last Judgment," the day when the earth will die and be "reborn" in the Second Coming. By the same token, the films transcode sanity (self-preservation) into a discourse of "insanity" implicitly equated with femininity, as when Luise in *The Great King*, having nothing else with which to wrap a soldier's wounds, wants to rip up the Prussian flag (an "insane" act "excused" only by her youth and gender), or when her husband contemplates desertion after Frederick punishes him for disobeying an order while unilaterally saving the battle.

I hinted earlier at the final sphere of the "feminine" exorcised by the films, the private sphere inhabited by women, emotions, heterosexual eroticism, weakness. While home and family exist in *Jew Süss* to be violated by the "Jew," they exist in the Frederick films to be erased by war and, in the same gesture, sublated by a macro-family under the paternity/maternity of Frederick. As is already clear from the iconic configurations I discussed, Frederick's cinematic "life" is a radical denial of the private sphere; he lives according to the "Must." "Sacrifice" here, both within the diegesis and for the film audience, functions not only in its everyday meaning of giving something up, but in the manner analyzed by René Girard with reference to sacrificial practice in cults and religions, as something in the mirror of which "community" can consolidate itself.[54] As such, "sacrifice," whether experienced personally or vicariously in the form of narrative, not only reverses its negative implication but becomes a source of profound enjoyment.[55]

What characterizes Frederick's enemies (including a few of his "own" men lacking "bourgeois" values) is their quest for a different sort of enjoyment in War. These non-People define war with metaphors of a game or sport (cf. references to playing "cat and mouse," to putting Prussia in one's "pocket," or a comparison of Frederick to a deer mounted on the wall). When in *The Great King* Frederick's brother, who is coded as a "courtly"

54. *Violence and the Sacred*, trans. Patrick Gregory (Baltimore: Johns Hopkins University Press, 1977).
55. See Stephen Lowry's discussion of pleasurable suffering as a constitutive element of "mother" films; Lowry, 205–10.

aristocrat, attempts to persuade him to make peace with France, the brother's head is framed so as to appear next to several sets of mounted antlers, clearly with the suggestion that he is "cuckolded," the enemy's booty.

One can further illustrate the genre's exorcism of the feminized private sphere by comparing the treatment in two films of one actress, Kristina Söderbaum, who (as Veit Harlan's wife) played Luise in *The Great King* and Dorothea Sturm in *Jew Süss*. In both films Söderbaum's character is a metaphor for the social body, for *Volk* — the name Luise echoes Frederick's mythic counterpart Queen Luise. Both play on the bourgeois tragedy's father-daughter bond (albeit symbolically in *The Great King*); in both her character is sadistically tortured. In *Jew Süss* her character's private sphere, including her body, is penetrated and destroyed. Arguably, though, *The Great King*'s sadism exceeds the swift punishment by death she undergoes in *Jew Süss;* it allows her to live, but slowly and tortuously kills off the private sphere that is the only space of women, leaving her symbolically transformed into a man (though her "natural" role as mother compensates ideologically for this). She evolves from a daughter and sister to a lover, wife, and mother (a condensation of the various sides of woman and always in relation to men); yet for each "loved one" she gains, she loses one or more. Only her child is spared as another signifier of rebirth through War. (Söderbaum's character Maria in *Kolberg* undergoes a similar series of tortures and has no one at all in the end.) By the end of the film Luise has donned the jacket of her husband's uniform, has been called a "soldier-woman" (*Soldatenfrau*) likely to "put on the pants, too," and has assumed a public role (as miller).[56] As Frederick's counterpoint throughout the film in the private sphere, her "suffering" is intended to parallel his; yet in her final encounter with the king, we are reminded of Kalbus's remark that "the lives of the Potsdam kings were often more difficult than those of their subjects." Her losses are trivialized beside Frederick's as he tells her, "You see, *I* am alone."

Not only does family and personal desire need to be contained as a threat to a sacrificial collective; it threatens to arrest Prussia's forward trajectory (even if this forward trajectory aspires to retrieve a timeless past of community). Desire stops time, temporarily derailing even Frederick in a "moment of happiness" with the "only" person he loves, when (in *Fridericus*) he receives a visit from his moribund sister or (in *The Great King*)

56. This symbolic transformation reflects the changing role of women due to the war, which I will discuss in connection with *Komödianten*.

from his moribund nephew. Temporal retardation becomes more threatening when, in each film, Frederick's "loved one" dies and he becomes momentarily immobilized. After the death of his nephew and heir in *The Great King,* we hear Frederick's steady footsteps pacing inside his bedroom. Two guards outside are alarmed when the steps momentarily stop; it is "as if time stood still." Though the films "enjoy" their momentary lapses into melodrama, their ideal subject position is subjection of personal desire to time and collective, exemplified by the death scene of the soldier Paul Treskow. Treskow's death scene "shows" him as subject and object of the gaze: we see his close-up face superimposed over a subjective shot of boots marching forward over space and in time. The shot again sublates death as pleasurable "sacrifice," yet might be read deconstructively as an admission of the film's "real" intention: the boots literally walk *over* Treskow's face, trampling his life and desire.

It is not as if the films did not arrest narrative time themselves; quite the contrary, they depend on temporal suspension to articulate ideology, exemplified by tedious "talky" scenes expounding paranoid "stab-in-the-back" narratives, or to generate euphoria, exemplified by the various compositions I discussed earlier enjoying the sight of the King's suffering body and the "show" of aestheticized War. All of the films offer battle scenes which substitute forward movement with specular plenitude, heterosexual eroticism with the eroticism of battle and male bonding. As a consummating strategy for warding off the feminine Other within, each film invokes battle as a form of intoxication, as an experience decentering the individual and fusing him with the group. Without ever explicitly marking the male body as an object of erotic spectacle, such scenes permit the audience to revel voyeuristically in a display of maleness, which doubtless enhanced their appeal to men and boys.[57] Significantly, in both films battle provides the personal, implicitly sexual decentering experience that Frederick so radically forfeits in the private sphere; his personal tragedies always seem to coincide with a crucial point in the war, allowing him to surmount a temporary lapse into emotion: "The battle is the only thing that can help me now!"

The films' aestheticized war is not a means of achieving peace, but an end in itself, a source of enjoyment. Of course, the key to this enjoyment is

---

57. The erotic implications in Frederick's imminent purgation through battle are readable in *Fridericus* by a row of flagpoles raised from a horizontal (prostrate) position to a vertical (aggressive, male dominant) position, as he declares the beginning of battle. This recalls the Labor Service scene in *Triumph of the Will.*

the imaginary; the film audience is never in danger and all of the "threats" in the film — external and internal enemies — are always already overcome by Frederick. The fun lies in watching what one knows will happen. Still, the film's ideological framework needs a Sentimental discourse that disavows this enjoyment by giving the war at least an inferred causality, and that distracts from the "impossible" narrative combination of destruction *and* redemption of society, family, woman, heterosexual love. Somewhere in the course of the films, this Sentimental discourse turns against itself, cedes to an endless series of reversals that forces the question: is all of this about a "normal" male adolescent dread of female ickiness, or are we dealing with the essence of "fascist" interpellation in which sacrifice does not serve an objective, but is enjoyed for its own sake? (Or are these two complementary?) We have seen how the films transcode death as birth, sacrifice as fulfillment, pain as pleasure, and insanity as sanity. Once this inverted discourse is in place, it follows a consistent logic: isolation is *really* community, the public private, the Führer family, the human a machine, and so forth. One has to read against this Sentimental discourse of bourgeois virtue to realize that Frederick is fighting not *for* Mother, but Mother herself.

I want to conclude by looking at a scene that shows the "fascist" potential of the Frederick legend if any does, one which epitomizes this disavowal of War as Beauty and simultaneously synthesizes the genre's attempted sublation of modernity and premodernity: the montage sequence ending *The Great King*. It is a coda that is "tacked on" to the rest of the film after the story is definitively over, after a spectacular (and specular) battle has at once destroyed and saved the social body. It stands out from the rest of the movie and from the rest of the Frederick genre by dispensing altogether with cinematic realism in favor of a style that recalls the work of Leni Riefenstahl as well as Hollywood's religious epics. It is, moreover, an attempt to *show* Frederick's omnipotent gaze in cinematic terms. Multiple exposures superimpose Frederick's giant eyes over the windmill that throughout the film stands metaphorically for *Heimat*, over a plow cutting the earth, and over peasants plowing and sowing fields. Finally, the Prussian flag flaps in the wind and a poem appears on the screen whose text is sung by a (nondiegetic) chorus: "You black eagle / of Frederick the Great / Like the Sun / Cover / The abandoned and / Homeless / With / Your golden / Wing." (Du schwarzer Adler / Friedrich des Grossen / Gleich der Sonne / Decke du / die Verlassenen und / Heimatlosen / Mit / Deiner goldenen / Schwinge zu.)

By superimposing Frederick's eyes over privileged icons of romantic anticapitalism, nation, and *Volk*, the sequence amalgamates Mother and Father, nurturance and discipline, the bodily and the abstract, icon and verbal text. Although Frederick appears as "pure gaze," seeing merges, as in other forms of Nazi spectacle, with being seen: the object of our look (presented exclusively to the film audience and denied the diegetic characters) is precisely the subject of the look, the pair of eyes that not only see, but nurture everything (Frederick is linked to the spreading of seed). The scene virtually fuses the two bodies of the King by eliminating all of his physical body but the part most conventionally associated with the "soul."

The poem condenses what each of the films aspires to in a fictionalized narrative. It at once describes the King's compensation of lack in the modern spectator and constitutes an appeal directed at the King. Its use of imperative (which is unambiguous in the German *Decke*) suspends time while its imagery conquers space. The "father-bound" metaphor of the black eagle, which also appears on the Prussian flag, links Frederick explicitly with an imaginary social body possessing strength, farsightedness (as suggested in the German expression *Adlerblick* or "eagle's gaze"), and the ability to span great distances.[58] The simile "like the sun" evokes a plethora of associations from strength, life-giving warmth, vitality, to the Sun King or Germany's historical aspiration for a "place next to the sun" (the phrase with which Kaiser Wilhelm legitimated his imperialist politics). With the eagle's "wing" covering the "lost" and "homeless," Father again merges with Mother as an anchor surmounting rootlessness, abstraction, exchange value, "Jewishness." It verbalizes the shadow of the plane flying over Nuremberg in *Triumph of the Will*, another "wing" suggesting an all-encompassing, protective presence.

The coda not only ruptures *The Great King*'s textual boundary[59] but creates the very state of ubiquity and timelessness to which National Socialism itself aspires (an effect enhanced by ethereal cumulus clouds rolling behind the words of the poem, speeded up by time-lapse photogra-

58. Reifenstahl equates Hitler filmically with the eagle as well; when delivering his nocturnal speech to the NSDAP in *Triumph of the Will* he stands directly in front of an illuminated eagle. As the camera revolves around him from an authoritative low angle, the eagle appears as a literal extension of Hitler, with wings sprouting from his shoulders.

59. This transgression recalls, but far surpasses the exhortation ending *Jew Süss* or Frederick's concluding remark in *Fridericus*, "Gentlemen — do your duty!" which he directs as much to the spectator as to his generals inside the text.

phy). It not only shifts from narrative to prayer, but effectively transforms the film narrative retroactively into a prayer. Again recalling the famous opening sequence of *Triumph of the Will*, the Leader is invoked here *as* God (as opposed to other scenes which merely posit a privileged relation to God).

It is striking that the poem's main symbols, the eagle and sun, are the same symbols with which Foucault describes an old specular world rendered obsolete by a modern panoptical order: "The pomp of sovereignty, the necessarily spectacular manifestations of power, were extinguished one by one in the daily exercise of surveillance, in a panopticism in which the vigilance of intersecting gazes was soon to render useless both the eagle and the sun."[60] The striking comeback these symbols make in the National Socialist Imaginary attests to the paradoxical nature of its recourse to a spectacle determined by the very modernity it wants to escape. It is because the "Frederick" resurrected by Nazism and its Weimar precursors is pure projection that he is able to straddle S_1 and S_2, traditional monarch and Leader. Unlike in the fully modern exercise of panopticism, which derives its power from the anonymity and internalization of surveillance, in this projection authority rests in an individual, the gaze is subjectivized, Frederick's eyes look and no one else's.

I would like to conclude the chapter by juxtaposing the preceding sequence with a scene in *Jew Süss* that can serve as a paradigm for the complementary function of Frederick and the "Jew": it is the scene in which Süss Oppenheimer spies on the citizens of Württemberg through a molding in the palace ceiling. Alternately we see close-up shots of Süss's and his secretary Levy's eyes through the gaping mouth of a plaster face that is part of the molding, and subjective shots showing the god's-eye view the Jews have of the men below, who are imperiled by, but oblivious to, their look (photos 21–22). Set against Frederick's omnipotent gaze in *The Great King*'s coda (photos 23–24), the scene exemplifies National Socialism's personification of modernity's threatening gaze, for which Frederick's benevolent gaze compensates. Both projections, "Jew" and King/Leader, which culminated in, but did not begin with, National Socialism, try to flee the anonymous and annihilating gaze that Foucault describes as panopticism. They do so by bifurcating the impersonal, panoptic gaze into a "good" and "bad" one, and by "inventing" two subjects of that gaze: the "Jew" and the King/Leader around whom a modern

60. Foucault, *Discipline and Punish*, 217.

21-24 Nazism subjectivizes panopticism's anonymous gaze. 21-22: The malevolent gaze of the "Jew" threatens the "Aryan" male in *Jew Süss;* 23-24: Frederick's eyes superimposed over icons of "romantic anticapitalism" in *The Great King.*

religion is born. This is why the visual reproduction of Frederick's eyes and body is as essential to National Socialism as is the representation and abjection of the "Jew's" body. Both are necessary in supplanting a reasonable political discourse with aestheticism; hence both must be represented over and over, hiding the fact that aesthetic experience is an end in itself. For this reproduction Nazism depends not only on a modern structure but on modern technology and, as the next Frederick chapter stresses, on the very inhumane operation of "discipline" that contradicts Nazism's so cherished antimodernism.

FOUR

Building the Body Armor: Hans Steinhoff's

The Old and the Young King

I will regress in this chapter and discuss a film that precedes *Fridericus* and *The Great King* both in production date and in the chronological point it represents in Frederick's life: Hans Steinhoff's *The Old and the Young King* (1935). Even the most tenacious holdout against psychoanalysis could scarcely avoid "psychologizing" this film which, though again articulated almost entirely in conventional cinematic terms, is in my view the most bizarre Frederick movie of all. It deviates from the pattern of the others in portraying the bitter struggle between the young Frederick and his father, the "soldier-king" Frederick William I, which culminated in the execution of Frederick's best friend. The film's story is based on real historical events, which made their way into Frederick's legend and were well known to every German schoolchild. With respect to its semiotic coding, *The Old and the Young King* plays a game of musical chairs: the opposition between a "bourgeois" ruler and his "courtly" enemies in the other films remains the same but the character configuration changes; namely, foreign political enemies are replaced by an ultimately more perilous enemy of narcissistic self-indulgence "inside" the Crown Prince. In other words, while the Frederick of the other films is always already a King, here we witness the making of a King, a kind of perverse body-building achieved through a violent process in which Frederick learns to see and not just to be seen.

*

Young Frederick or Fritz (Werner Hinz) and his father (Emil Jannings) are constantly battling over Fritz's dissolute, francophile lifestyle. He shuns the uniform, incurs gambling debts, and lies. Because of his father's harsh reprimands, Fritz begs his best friend, Hans Hermann von Katte, to help him flee to France. Katte at first refuses, but agrees after witnessing a brutal fight between father and son. When the plot is discovered, the King decides to have Katte executed before Fritz's eyes. The extreme measure transforms Fritz, who pledges obedience to his father and adopts an ascetic lifestyle. Though he becomes a model son, Fritz does not reconcile emotionally with his father until the latter is on his deathbed. Fritz tearfully admits that the King's disciplinary measures were an expression of love. The King dies saying the words "Make Prussia great."

*

The Old and the Young King tells the story of a necessary and successful interpellation, of a subject's acquiescence to the demand of a Father standing in for the symbolic order (to be sure, the film presents a kind of perfect interpellation possible only in narrative representation). Rather than be consumed by the call of the Other, however, Frederick appropriates the symbolic order for himself and in turn becomes its agent. This theoretically "impossible" transition (impossible since, as the name suggests, the big Other is necessarily, irreducibly Other for the human subject and can never be "mastered" except in fantasy) finds its logic in National Socialism's biologism: we are to assume that from the start a King is buried within Frederick and needs to be unveiled, liberated from overdetermination through courtly culture and a kind of *ancien régime* peer pressure. The presupposition of biology modifies the bildungsroman scenario underlying the film: Frederick's process of education, his finding of self is not achieved by traveling, but by returning "home."

Again this film's source of pleasure is in watching the transformation we already know has got to unfold. The radicality of this transformation is, however, fundamentally a delusion in the first place. No matter how profoundly Frederick's life changes, his pleasure does not give way so much to self-denial as to the much more profound enjoyment alluded to in the preceding chapter: that afforded by "sacrifice" for the sake of "sacrifice." Frederick internalizes his father in the form of a superego or Law that does violence to the self. However, this violence conceals an "obscene superego injunction — 'Enjoy!'"[1] The enjoyment lies not in the content of the sacrifice (its supposed value to the People), but in its form.

Again *The Old and the Young King* passes off as "historical" a process that is really, in its discourse, psychoanalytic and gendered. Much like the deserter episodes in the other films, Frederick's "path to Leadership" is

1. Slavoj Žižek, *Sublime Object of Ideology* (New York: Verso, 1989), 81.

128

defined as a progression from femininity to masculinity, from excess to containment — all of which are (con)fused with sociological discourses like eighteenth-century class coding and anticentralism. As already suggested, Steinhoff's film exhibits a political anatomy different from the other Frederick films. First, the function of stand-in for the "impossible" corporatist community which the mature Frederick embodies in the other films is assumed by Frederick William, who mirrors in every respect except bodily shape Otto Gebühr's Frederick: bourgeois virtue, soldierly asceticism, and "heart" beneath indestructible body armor

More importantly, young Frederick's body is the site not of timeless reconciliation, but of a temporal evolution condensing the transition from a society of spectacle to a modernity in which power is internalized. The film projects, moreover, a gender perspective onto this process by displaying the young Frederick as the ornamental, hyperspecularized object Otto Gebühr's Frederick never is (no matter how "specular" the latter's appeal may be). Young Frederick's transformation into a "contained vessel" manifests itself in his *retreat* from spectacle, his adoption of a nonornamental, "soldierly" appearance, which is synonymous with his adoption of his father's masterly look. Ironically, though, this transition is achieved by means of a spectacle, that of Katte's execution, which disembodies Frederick's other (feminized) self. In finding his own anchorage, Frederick, at once individual and a social body, becomes a social anchor for the People and for the film spectator.

In its reliance on notions of the sort that Michel Foucault analyzes, *The Old and the Young King* exemplifies another facet of National Socialism's contradictory negotiation of time that was only implicit in the last chapter. I have tried to make clear how Nazism's desire to "return" to a harmony that, though projected into premodern time, assumes a timeless stature, is the product of the split that modernity generates (or at least becomes cognizant of). Paradoxically, a society can only be organized around this harmonious, premodern vision because of modernity's technological possibilities like radio and film, which, among other things, specularize cathected bodies like the cinematic Frederick. What has yet to be untangled is the contradiction between the modern discipline so important to the militarism embodied in the Frederick legend (and that we know is so extreme in Nazism's real-life *Gleichschaltung*) and the longing for a world predating the enslavement of discipline, which is all but synonymous with the "modernity" Nazism constantly assails. Nazism is, in other words, both "for" and "against" discipline and modernity. This contradiction is already implicit in Frederick's "straddling" of a modern and a premodern world, of traditional monarch and Leader. It is more pronounced here, however, with this film's stress of discipline *as process* (while in the other films it is a "given," at least for Frederick; we do see soldiers being socialized by him in other films).

An important clue to the epistemological contradiction within *The Old and the Young King* is the way in which it endears Frederick William to the spectator; not only by displaying his "good heart," for instance, when he examines his youngest child's sore throat, but by allowing him to display an antimodern, anticentralist ideology at odds with his mastery of "modern" discipline. This display is the major — indeed the only — function of an early scene in which Frederick William grants an audience to court functionaries to review domestic affairs. The King complains to an advisor about the behavior of egotistical local magistrates (*Räte*, whom he calls *Diätenräte* or "per diem counsels"[2]) in rural areas, who exploit farmers and demand privileges (something like the impotent magistrate in *Fridericus*). When the advisor laments that the court has too few scribes to keep track of affairs, the King launches into an antibureaucratic tirade: "Too few? Too many! These quill-drivers, these — these ossified scribblers, these ink-shitters (*verknöcherte Federfuchser, Schreiberseelen, Tintenscheisser*) who squash healthy common sense between the covers of their files! They're a plague on our country!" Like Frederick's juxtaposition of blood and ink in *Fridericus*, the invective mimics Karl Moor's polemics against the "ink-spattering century" in Schiller's *Robbers*, referring to the domination of scribes and centralistic bureaucrats, to rationalistic attempts to organize society hierarchically and develop codified laws.[3] In other words, it assails one of the most central operations of discipline that already provoked resistance in the eighteenth century: the writing with which a rationalized modern society feeds its obsession with "the accumulation of documents, their seriation, the organization of comparative fields making it possible to classify, to form categories, to determine averages, to fix norms."[4]

One hears such attacks on modern methods of recording and classification constantly in Nazi cinema (like the attack in *Jew Süss* on the Jew's

2. The German term *Diätenräte* implies pejoratively a class of functionaries who receive an allowance for doing nothing.
3. Cf. the allusion to the medieval club law or *Faustrecht* in the blacksmith episode in *Jew Süss.*
4. Michel Foucault, *Discipline and Punish: The Birth of the Prison,* trans. Alan Sheridan (New York: Vintage, 1979), 190.

verklausulieren or "putting everything into legalese"). Rarely is the purely ideological, rhetorical function of this "antimodernism" so clear, however, as in *The Old and the Young King,* when the obstacle to be surmounted, Frederick's "inner enemy," is contaminated by an outdated world of spectacle, leaving discipline (i.e., modernity) as the only possible narrative solution. For once Nazism seems to be admitting the disciplinary tyranny and bodily violence that "really" underlies it. At the same time, the role of spectacle in disciplining Frederick is itself a contradictory mixture of the modern and premodern. On the one hand, he is, like every modern individual, subjected to surveillance. More important, however, is his own humiliating specularization and the staging of a sublime spectacle of death, both of which teach him to see, to become the subject of the imagined benevolent gaze with which National Socialism "answers" modernity's anonymous panoptical gaze.

THE DICHOTOMIZATION OF SPACE AND TIME

The film's opening sequence captures in both form and content the narrative's logic. Through the most conventional technique of crosscutting (actually cross-dissolving) from the austerity of the Prussian palace to the milieu in which the unbridled Frederick gambles, it articulates the opposition between the King and the Crown Prince. This opposition is at once spatial and temporal, since the Crown Prince represents an "earlier" form of socialization (or, conversely, a "later" socialization by a dissolute, "Weimar" modernity, which amounts to about the same thing); both distances will be sublated in the narrative's temporal process. The first image after the credits is a low-angle shot traveling slowly up the massive bell tower of the Potsdam Garrison Church, whose bells ring loudly; already here image and sound suggest the interpellation of the phallus (in a literal as well as in Lacan's sense of symbolic order).

The bell tower, a ubiquitous presence in "Prussian" films, veritably fuses state apparatus (Prussia and its military) with ideological state apparatus (church). As if to affirm the suggestion of military *as* religion, the bells give way to the sound of loud drumming, and a line of soldiers marches into the palace in the following scene, functioning as a military alarm clock for the royal family (at the same time the regimentation is so hyperbolic as to risk reversing into a parody deconstructing not only the military but Nazi totalization; presumably the scene was "supposed" to be understood as a good-natured look at how tough "they were back then"). The tall slim soldiers, whose tall, pointed hats and uniforms contain bodily excess, repeat and multiply the phallic shape of the bell tower. The military's forceful penetration of the private, domestic sphere literalizes the militarization of Prussian society described by historians like Eckart Kehr.[5] The humor-punctuated tension created by the rhythm of the drums and by the camera's tracking movement from door to door culminates as Crown Prince Frederick is discovered absent from his chamber (a conspicuous absence whose function is the exact reverse of the other Frederick films, where his absence always means symbolic presence). His absence renders the drums "speechless" and signals the first dissolve to the "foreign world" of his gambling orgy.

Already the composition of the frame in Frederick's first appearance echoes the suffocation of *Lebensraum* by feminized bodies I discussed in the last chapter. Frederick, dressed in an embroidered jacket (i.e., in a courtly "feminine" manner, as opposed to either military dress or plain dark jackets worn in the palace), is at the center of the frame, draped — indeed overpowered — on each side by two Frenchmen with long wigs (who are later to collect a huge gambling debt from the King) obsequiously attending his game and egging him on. Although the soundtrack here is much louder than at the palace, little coherent dialogue is perceptible, only fragmented phrases, all — significantly — in French and signaling Frederick's losses: *"Quel dommage!" "Vous n'avez pas de chance ce soir!"* etc.[6] The set appears cluttered and cramped by the opulent decor with its circular shapes, as well as by the closeness of the people decorated

5. See, for example, "The Genesis of the Royal Prussian Reserve Officer," *Economic Interest, Militarism, and Foreign Policy*, ed. Gordon Craig (Berkeley: University of California, 1965). Kehr defines a militarized society by two factors. First, the officer class does not see itself as a class of public servants. They do not regard their work as a service, after which they will return to citizenry; rather, they regard their profession as a lifelong calling, making them part of a "warrior caste" with its own code of honor, laws, and beliefs. This caste is a privileged one, superior to that of the bourgeoisie. The second factor is the voluntary affirmation of this standard by a substantial sector of the bourgeoisie. According to Kehr, one of the means by which this militarization was achieved was the recruitment, first of members of lower nobility, then of the bourgeoisie, into the Prussian Reserve as officers in the 1880s and 1890s. This solved the army's need for expansion and gave members of the bourgeoisie a sense of pride and identification with the state, thus preventing them from developing a bourgeois class consciousness. He regards the system as a "final capitulation of the bourgeoisie, which had renounced political revolution and was striving to attach itself as firmly as possible to the existing state power structure, for fear of an overthrow of the propertied classes" (Kehr, 105).
6. Cf. my discussion of French as the courtly language in *Jew Süss*.

by curly wigs and lace (chaos, indulgence, eroticism, debauchery). The camera travels along the table, as if drawn toward bodily apertures, to a wigged woman with voluptuous breasts sensuously putting a piece of food in her mouth, underscoring the unleashing of "drives" and decadence the scene as a whole connotes. The camera's slow tracking movement links Frederick to the eroticized woman, although he does not look at her (he has yet to *learn* to look, whether at women or anything else).

Much as editing allows "Jewish" culture to "spill over" onto "Aryan" culture in *Jew Süss*, here raucous noise, barely distinguishable "foreign" sounds, clutter, artificial lighting, and nervous, frenetic action encroach upon the tranquility, steady rhythm, comprehensible dialogue, simple shapes, and natural lighting of the palace. Before we ever lay eyes on the old King, his world of masculine, "Prussian" discipline battles for cinematic domination over a historically and psychoanalytically "dated" world of feminized, indulgent, lustful pleasure.

The clock foregrounded with the next dissolve back to Frederick William's court signals a return to discipline, as the royal family prepares for breakfast. As the royal children enter the room they stand in perfect symmetry, from the tallest to the shortest, waiting to be inspected by the King much as he inspects his regiments in parallel scenes (suggesting parallels in disciplinary society's organization of space in seemingly different social spheres like family, military, school, etc.). In this scene, as in the entire film, Frederick William exists to be Father in every conceivable sphere, both private and public (he is a father to his nuclear family, to the extended family of the royal palace, to the army, and, as *Landesvater*, to Prussia; cf. the "spanking" he gives his dishonest cook or his lecture to the preacher on the virtue of brevity, his paternal treatment of his troops, whom he calls "my blue children"). As the family sits at breakfast, again the frame is uncluttered, the composition orderly, dominated by the large rectangle of the table. The natural light streaming through windows upon the family members suggests health.

In eliciting an affective response to "breakfast" as a time for family community, the film ahistorically "naturalizes" a bourgeois conception of nuclear family and private sphere that in fact, as we saw in other "Fridericus" films, cedes to the call of the collective within National Socialism. Family serves its purpose here, however, not only as an ideological value dating back to the eighteenth century, but as another locus of discipline: familial relations have absorbed "since the classical age external schemata, first educational and military, then medical, psychiatric, psychological, which have made the family the privileged locus of emergence for the disciplinary questions of the normal and the abnormal."[7] Hence it comes as no surprise that the film's diagnosis of Prussia's "sickness" begins with the malfunctioning of family. Once again the camera relentlessly surveils the space and searches for what is not there; for the second time a scene culminates in a shot of Frederick's empty (set) place, multiplying its symbolism of the "place" he must take.

The paternal voice links the polar spheres of action visually juxtaposed in the opening sequence: we hear the King reading a biblical parable to his family about the sower who goes out to spread his seed, only to have it fall into a patch of thorns which grow big and suffocate it. As the King reads these words, the next dissolve shows the Crown Prince seated beside French courtiers looming over him in the frame, obviously the pictorial response to the King's verbal cue, a process that will continue several times. On one level, the parable merely manifests the King's insight that Frederick is being "devoured" by alien, foreign elements associated with dissolute pleasure. More importantly, in its "omniscience" the camera confirms his fears, becoming an extension of the father's eyes — a crucial theme in the film, to which I will return. On a more general level, the parable suggests the threat posed by a dissolute culture to the phallic order, to the male as spreader of seed and thus as reproducer of a healthy species necessary to a corporatist, "organic" vision of society. Finally, the juxtaposition of word and image illustrates Frederick William's possession of the power of language, of the symbolic. He narrativizes, evaluates, and gives meaning to actions merely carried out thoughtlessly (i.e., through the body) by Frederick, who as yet lacks a language, a subjectivity of his own.

One more dissolve shifting from the palace to the gambling room shows the King's head (in profile, as he reads from the Bible) briefly superimposed directly to the right (but elevated) of Frederick's (photo 25). This particular composition allows the father to function as a kind of iconographic superego, as the demand of the Other that is "there" even if Frederick refuses to "see" it. The same segment ends with a final affirmation of Father, as well as of the biblical wisdom articulated in the parable (doubling the film's signifiers of the symbolic order), when the camera reveals a fact to which Frederick is oblivious: a French gambling partner is cheating him. A close-up reveals the man's hands shuffling and secretly pulling an ace out of his sleeve. Again here Father possesses an "impossible" power of vision; he seems to see what no diegetic character, except the

7. Foucault, *Discipline and Punish*, 215–16.

25 A dissolve from Frederick's gambling orgy to the palace superimposes Frederick William's head to the right of Frederick's, suggesting the old king's function as superego. **26** The last shot of *The Old and the Young King*: Frederick as bearer of the look.

cheater himself, can. Moreover, as part of Frederick's world the hands are fragmented; they belong to a body lacking the wholeness of a coherent subject. This fragmentation, especially the hands' adornment by long lacy cuffs, recalls classical cinema's fetishization of the female body.[8]

Time intervenes to effect a violent collision of the two spheres and conclude the sequence. As if the clock from the palace were to "invade" Frederick's world of timeless oblivion, a palace messenger bursts in to warn the Crown Prince that he is late for a military drill. Within about eight minutes and with little "happening," every aspect of the film's sociological, ideological, psychoanalytic, gender, and specular regime — in short, its semiotic division — has been laid out. None of the principles stand alone, but are interwoven with the same sets of "qualities" that drive the whole genre: the masculine with "bourgeois values," asceticism, pa-

8. In *Old Fritz* (1927), Otto Gebühr actually cuts off his lacy cuffs with scissors. See Gertrud Koch's discussion of *The Old and the Young King*'s gambling scene in "Der höhere Befehl der Frau ist ihr niederer Instinkt: Frauenhass und Männer-Mythos in Filmen über Preussen," in *Preussen im Film,* ed. Axel Marquardt and Heinz Rathsack (Reinbek bei Hamburg: Rowohlt, 1981), 222. See also feminist film theory's discussion of the fragmentation of women in classical cinema, as in Laura Mulvey's "Visual Pleasure and Narrative Cinema," *Screen* 16.3 (Autumn 1975): 12.

triarchal authority, and "responsibility"; the feminine with courtly decadence, self-indulgence, eroticism, excess.

THE MALE ORNAMENT

I discussed in the preceding chapter how Frederick's status as icon is
dissociated from decorative clothing, or, more precisely, from an orna-
mentalization of his body. This severance of phallic strength from the
ornamental, and, conversely, the decoration of man as an indication of a
deviant feminization is grounded in a historical transition in the semiotics
of clothing from the mid- to the late eighteenth century. During this period
men's clothing became more homogenized than before, thus playing a
decreased role in distinguishing social classes. Clothing played a larger
role, however, in distinguishing the sexes, as women's clothing became
more varied according to style and function: vanity, obsession with, and
frequent changes of clothing—previously signs of aristocratic idleness
attacked by the bourgeoisie—now became associated with the feminine.

Alluding to the work of C. J. Flugel, Kaja Silverman refers to this process as a "revisualization of sexual difference," resulting in a despecularization of the male subject and a concomitant hyperspecularization of
the female subject: "Man abandoned his claim to be considered beautiful.
He henceforth aimed at being only useful"; his clothing comes to symbolize "his devotion to the principles of duty, of renunciation, and of self-
control."[9] This process of despecularization, of a retreat to the "inside" is
part of the transition from premodern, hierarchical societies dependent
upon spectacle to modern, functionally differentiated societies dependent
on internalization of norms and values. As already suggested, it is precisely the transition young Frederick must undergo, albeit in a condensed,
narrative form that invests this change with value: he must cast off orna-
mentalization as a sign of "sickness" and defer to an internalized order
manifested visually in homogenized male clothing—a homogenization
that finds its logical extreme in the uniform (at once an extension and
assurance of body armor): "Male clothing also came increasingly to signify allegiance to the larger social order, and man's privileged position
within that order."[10] One must, then, concede a limited "historical basis"
to the film; its reduction lies in the condensation of a process in one

9. C. J. Flugel, *The Psychology of Clothes* (London: Hogarth Press, 1930), 117–19,
quoted in Kaja Silverman, *The Acoustic Mirror* (Bloomington: Indiana University
Press, 1988), 25.
10. Ibid.

individual; its "pathological" nature in its projection of perversion onto one side of its opposition.

The importance of clothing pervades *The Old and the Young King* and is a key feature distinguishing the film's second oppositional pair: Frederick and his friend Katte. The feminine-masculine contrast that defines Frederick's difference from his father carries over into the distinctly homoerotic relationship with Katte. From the start, Katte represents Frederick's alter ego; he epitomizes the soldierliness that is latent, but not yet manifest in Frederick. Katte's physical appearance is erect and more military than "courtly."[11] In his repeated reference to himself as a "soldier" and tendency to take the father's side, Katte is an extension of Frederick William, more his son than Frederick. The lines both of Katte's body and his clothing are straight, again reiterating the shape of the Garrison Church's bell tower. In nearly every scene showing the two friends together, Frederick appears in a lacy dressing gown whose brocade design repeats swirl patterns of his bedroom wallpaper (linking him not only with the private sphere he must learn to forfeit, but specifically with the bedroom as a place of rest, release, and sexuality); moreover, his hair is long and curly. Like lovers, Frederick and Katte meet clandestinely in Frederick's bedroom, where he plots a kind of elopement.

Not only his attire but his gestures mark Frederick as the feminized, passive figure in the relationship, dependent upon Katte's help in escaping his father. When Katte refuses his help on the grounds of "soldierly" principle and begs Frederick not to "torture" him, Frederick resorts to stereotypic "female" behavior, either acting hysterically, as in his dealings with his father, or needling Katte with classic "female" gibes: "I now know what to think of a Katte's fidelity!" (translatable as "I know you don't really love me!"). The composition of the scene in which Katte, having witnessed Frederick William's brutality toward Frederick, is persuaded to help him escape again strikingly resembles a heterosexual love scene. Frederick, still in his lacy dressing gown, lies prostrate on the ground, looking desperately up at Katte, who has knelt beside him, and whose head looms over Frederick as he promises help.

Not coincidentally, Frederick's fight with his father in the above scene is caused in part by the former's refusal to wear his uniform and by his reference to the uniform as a "shroud"; the King touches Frederick's dress-

11. The actor portraying Katte is the tall, slim Claus Clausen, who also played Steinhoff's symbolically important Hitler Youth leader in *Hitler Youth Quex;* see chapter 8 of this study.

ing gown in disgust with his cane (yet another phallic shape), as if wanting to avoid bodily contact with the feminized object.[12] Numerous times the film equates the uniform with "inner wholeness," as when the King labels Frederick a *Hurenkerl* (literally "whore's guy," suggesting feminization and the Prince's dissolute internal condition) when he appears for a military drill in a disheveled uniform.[13]

The film obsessively thematizes feminized men in episodes that are more or less peripheral to its story,[14] but that confirm impressions of the eighteenth century as a "woman's century" filled with the "perfume of the eternally feminine."[15] The two lavishly attired French fops who encourage Frederick to gamble and later collect his debt take their place among other satires of feminized males in Nazi cinema, along with courtiers in, for example, *Lady von Barnhelm* and *Friedrich Schiller*. Most conspicuous is the comical scene (utterly dispensable to the plot) in which the Hereditary Prince of Bayreuth first enters the palace, hoping to marry Frederick's sister, Princess Wilhelmine. He is overloaded with feminine accouterments: a long wig, outrageously modish clothing, makeup, an artificial beauty mark, perfume, and effeminate gestures. His rudeness and condescension toward the King, whom he mistakes for the "help" in a comedy of errors scenario, corresponds to his "courtly" appearance.

Ironically, Nazi cinema's most extreme compilation of feminine grotesquery proves to be a rare example of pure masquerade in a world where one generally can judge a book by its cover. Anticipating the crucial importance of eyes in Frederick's rehabilitation (and in the process affirming Nazi biologism), the King sees the fortified male hiding beneath the Prince's attire by looking into his eyes, just as, conversely, the trained eye

12. Frederick's reference to the uniform, which he later "never took off," as a shroud is historical. See Thomas Mann, "Friedrich und die grosse Koalition," *Gesammelte Werke* (Berlin: Aufbau Verlag, 1956), 11:68.

13. In a comic interlude just prior to Frederick's appearance, the King has admired a strikingly tall soldier as a "splendid fellow." The King carefully peers up and down at the soldier, reveling in the spectacle of perfect soldierhood, thus enhancing the effect of Frederick's failure to meet his visual standards.

14. Cf. the same motif in a film in which Frederick functions only as a background figure, Karl Ritter's *Cadets* (1941), a film aimed at socialization of youth. Young cadets held hostage by Russians during the Seven Years' War attempt to escape by donning women's clothing as a camouflage. Their commander Tzülow severely chastises them for their transgression against malehood: "Your king should see you like this!"

15. Mann, 82.

recognizes a "Jew": "The eyes are good. They look straight at one. But the rest of this stuff dangling around here, . . . I *don't* like!" As Gertrud Koch has already pointed out, the Prince's "initiation ritual" occurs in the quintessentially "masculine" space of the King's *Tabbagie* or smoking room, whose distance from women ensures "the integration in the conspired male herd."[16] The Prince "masculinizes" himself through verbal fencing, "camaraderie," and the "soldierly" straight talk (masqueraded with feigned drunkenness) with which he confronts the King. The reward the Prince receives is not so much Wilhelmine, but the granting of the desire he expressed earlier, "to be the King of Prussia's son-in-law."

Koch's analysis of this subplot links it with the powerlessness of women, for whom marriage decisions are made through agreements among men (which is readable as a factor of class as well as gender coding, since Frederick's spouse is chosen for him in the film as well). I would, however, reverse Koch's comment: "this man fixed himself up in order to conquer a woman, but finds out instead that he has to conquer the king."[17] In fact, it is symptomatic of the film that the Prince never came to "conquer a woman" in the first place, but the King. As so often, however, when Nazism is most vehement in its flaunting of "ideals," it runs the risk of deconstructing itself. The film's habit of playing off hyperbolic manhood (when the soldiers wake the royal family and the *Tabbagie* men act manly) and hyperbolic femininity against each other threatens to cancel each out or render one as parodistic as the other.

Nonetheless, *The Old and the Young King*'s adolescent "repudiation" of women, to use the term Régine Friedman applies to *Jew Süss,* is far more fundamental than its rendering them powerless (which always has the potential of erupting into its opposite, at least in relation to the spectator). Already the breakfast scene hints at their disruptive presence when Frederick's mother and Wilhelmine appear late, slightly unsettling a family ritual and a sequence that so strongly emphasizes temporality. The mother's very few scenes suffice to heap blame upon her for Frederick's courtly values; in Frederick William's words, she "badly raised" his son. She defends Frederick's gambling as a "thoroughly aristocratic pleasure" and encourages his flight attempt to England, where her brother reigns, rendering Frederick's most cowardly act an attempted flight from his father's space to his mother's. Thus we have an ambivalent depiction of nuclear family, at once affirmed as a source of discipline and indicted as a source of the sickness.

16. Koch, 223.
17. Ibid.

In the final analysis, the only reason this film needs women at all is to legitimate males courting males. Wilhelmine's "romance" with Katte could make even the "women's moments" in other Frederick films seem convincing. Katte expresses his greatest ardor for her when she is present only as a disembodied icon, in the portrait which he fondles before his execution—recalling Theweleit's description of how the fascist man mythicizes absent women who are ethereal, lacking a body and thus a threatening sexuality. Wilhelmine herself is as vacant when on- as off-screen, countering Katte's entreaties with complaints that he is no longer "jovial." Notwithstanding Katte's proclamation he would "rather die" than forfeit Wilhelmine, the film spares its male audience the cinematic indulgence of the romance in favor of its "real" homoerotic love interest.

EYES AS "WINDOWS OF THE SOUL"

We have seen in the film's opening sequence and in the introduction of the Bavarian how Frederick William's eyes penetrate truth even when the physical evidence of this truth is denied him. Eyes function throughout the film as signifiers of phallic strength in the framework outlined by Theweleit.[18] At the same time eyes are crucial to Frederick's transition from external self-display to internalized values. From the very first scene in which Frederick William appears to "see" his son's behavior even when he cannot literally see him, the King subjects Frederick to the power of his gaze—to a constant surveillance anticipating Foucault's panopticism. Frederick William's promise "I'll never let you out of my sight. I'll be your guard—your inexhaustible guard!" personalizes the "conscious and permanent visibility"[19] Foucault describes.

The punishment doled out by Frederick William always involves the specular, whether this punishment consists in looking or not looking, as when the King humiliates his late and disheveled son at military drill by refusing either to look at or speak directly with him. Using a strategy recalling *Jew Süss,* the King then makes a spectacle out of Frederick, forcing him to witness himself as that spectacle. The first spectacle the King engineers is one in which Frederick is forced to act out his own hypocrisy. He asks the Prince to name the sum of his gambling debt from the previous evening, even though he already knows the answer—as if to

18. See *Male Fantasies,* vol. 2, trans. Erica Carter and Chris Turner (Minneapolis: University of Minnesota Press, 1989); "The Eyes," 130–41. See also the preceding chapter herein on the Frederick movies.
19. Foucault, *Discipline and Punish,* 201.

affirm Žižek's point that "totalitarian power is not a dogmatism which has all the answers; it is, on the contrary, the instance which has all the questions."[20] He knows Frederick will lie about the sum of his debt, and intensifies Frederick's humiliation by forcing him to look his father "in the eyes," cajoling him to be honest. (The trap he lays is rendered all the more sadistic by his rare display of "niceness" toward his son). In addition to signaling intimate communication, this gesture forces Frederick to see himself literally *in* his father's eyes, thus beginning a process that will end up with his seeing *with* his father's eyes.

After Frederick indeed lies, the King forces him to look at his own image in a mirror, while the King, with his power of language, provides the *subscriptio* to the *pictura,* giving his son names like "liar," "gambler," and "coward." The mirror functions as a more potent representation of the father's eyes, in which Frederick must again confront himself as spectacle. Most crucially, by employing the mirror, Frederick William shifts the encounter from an exercise exclusively of external reprimand to one in which Frederick must begin to internalize his father's norms, his father's gaze; hence the scene almost literally depicts the mechanisms of modern discipline, and the synthesis of internalized fear and pleasure that National Socialism wants to generate in its subjects. At the risk of caving in to academic fashion, I cannot resist linking Frederick's humiliation at his own mirror image with Lacan's best-known thesis about the role a child's mirror image plays in its recognition of self.[21] The jubilant recognition and acceptance of a mirror image as one's "own" in early childhood is an exemplary situation that determines the future development of the self. It leads, through primary identification, to the formation of an Ideal-I (*"je-idéal,"* Freud's *"Ideal-Ich"*) which is more perfect than the self and hence always retains an element of Otherness. On this basis the I is able to develop secondary identifications (i.e., with others as role models), to objectify itself through the dialectic of identifications with others. Identification does not only mean the identification with another, but *of* another, giving identity to another, including the Ideal-I, which is an imaginary identity determining the actions of the real (nonidentical) I. The more rounded-off or complete the Ideal-I becomes, the more complete the real I is able to present itself.

The soldierly man has to strive for an Ideal I or imaginary identity that

20. *Sublime Object of Ideology,* 179.
21. "The Mirror Phase as Formative of the Function of the I," *Écrits: A Selection,* trans. A. Sheridan (New York: Norton, 1977).

is rounded-off and complete enough to supplement what Theweleit calls his body armor (although in Theweleit's reading this armor substitutes for the impossibility of a nonfragmented identity). Frederick's slumped posture before the mirror testifies to the obvious fact that his I has not yet been formed; the fact that Frederick William still must *force* his son to look attests to the incompletion of Frederick's process of internalizing discipline. Only Katte's death will allow Frederick to complete his Ideal-I by objectifying it through a momentarily established dialectic of identification with his friend. This dialectic, though, exists only for a brief, transitory moment. The death of Katte, that is, the merging of Katte and Frederick's Ideal-I, is the precondition for Frederick to become the King he already "somewhere" always was.

The King's key decision to make a spectacle out of someone else thus becomes the turning point of the film, the execution of Katte "before Frederick's eyes." Frederick is imprisoned in a solid stone fortress, a premodern, metaphoric structure that makes up for the containment he lacks. During the execution, the small window of Frederick's cell functions as the "eyes" of the room, which will become the "window of the soul." For Katte, already "bound" inside, the gaze is pure masochistic pleasure; he refuses to have his eyes bound for the execution, choosing to see himself being seen. His euphoria earlier when learning that Frederick will watch him die recalls the "feminine" dissolution inspired by Frederick's look in the other films, implicitly betraying the erotic relationship the film otherwise tries to disavow through Katte's heterosexual love. (Unlike Frederick's masses, Katte's frisson is grounded in the fact that he *alone* will be the object of the Prince's desiring gaze.) Later the King will order a salvo in Katte's honor when learning that he did not have his eyes bound; with Frederick's remark "first murder, then honor" his last vestige of "sanity" spends itself, to be sublated by the more sublime wisdom of individual perversion and collective insanity.

The execution scene makes explicit the eroticization of the male body, as Katte preens himself for Frederick's look. Again a human body "becomes" the Potsdam bell tower, as the shots just preceding the beheading show Katte from an extreme low angle, stressing his towering, resolute, phallic presence (and contrasting with the hysterical Frederick in his continued refusal to accept a "masculine" interpellation, as he reaches out of the barred window toward Katte). The camera does the work of the sword, cutting in the moment the sword swings toward Katte instead to Frederick screaming from a window. The omission of any direct view of the execution underscores what hardly needs elaboration; what has died is the feminized Frederick, in whose place steps Katte as the Other (masculine, soldierly, Volkish, ascetic) of Frederick (hence the scream emanating from Frederick and not from the silent Katte). Paradoxically, the execution suggests both literal sexual consummation and castration — yet what is "castrated" is femininity, onto which all lack is projected. Through his *Liebestod,* Katte erects Frederick in every sense of the word; the obliteration of Katte's body assures the survival of his subjectivity in the most sublime body of all. From now on, Frederick "sees Katte" when he looks in the mirror, vows full obedience to his father, and is reinstated with his sword (readmitted into the symbolic). He can be liberated from behind literal bars, having assumed the position of what Lacan calls a barred subject, the individual who has given in to the Other.

Another process extending outside of the text is at work here, too, since all of these spectacles have been staged, of course, for the eye of the spectator as well. With the final spectacle Frederick enters our subjectivity, one might say, as definitively as "Katte" penetrates Frederick's. Heretofore, the film has "set us up" more or less to assume the ideological and often (as in the opening scene) even the specular viewpoint of the Father; Frederick has been a wretched object of our gaze for whom we have felt, if anything, embarrassment. Although the Father remains an engaging figure (e.g., the sentimental scenes when he weeps upon receiving Frederick's letter or, dying, is buoyed by his "blue children"), our stance toward Frederick shifts to identification. Ironically, this identification and relation of "real" pathos is indebted, in this most manly of films, to the classically "female" genre of melodrama, in which "tears" occur most frequently when the protagonist's perspective comes to coincide with that of the audience.[22] Until this point, our relation to Frederick is characterized by the irony that separates us from characters in melodrama who lack some crucial information the audience has (he really does love her, she misses the rendezvous because of an accident, etc.). Only when Frederick gains the knowledge we've had all along can he soar far past us, becoming the source of imaginary and symbolic identification and the disavowal of male lack that we crave.

The act delivering Frederick from his hysterical noninterpellation is in a way consistent with Nazism's ideological privileging of the premodern world, since it exemplifies the premodern execution as spectacle. Katte's body, the body of the condemned man, is, in Foucault's words, the "in-

22. See, for example, Steve Neale, "Melodrama and Tears," *Screen* 27.6 (November–December 1986): 7.

verted body of the King," whose task it is to bare "the truth of the crime that he had committed. . . . In him, on him, the sentence had to be legible for all."[23] The spectacle is more terrifying in that Katte is not displaying the truth of his own but of someone else's crime (giving him a messianic quality). On the other hand, we can read Katte as an extension of the King himself: the vehicle who will achieve the King's goal and whose gaze upon Frederick extends and exceeds the power of the King's surveillance. In this final, hyperbolic spectacle an educational process culminates that fully encompasses Lacan's wordplay on *le nom du père:* through his Law and his enforcement of prohibition (the-"no"-of-the-father), Frederick William finally ensures Frederick's internalization of the Name-of-the-Father.[24]

For the rest of the film, Frederick assumes the glazed, resolute "look" Katte had before the execution (of internalized self-surveillance). Just as Katte achieves his apotheosis in his disembodiment, Frederick is now bereft of his earlier excessive physicality, suggesting with Kaja Silverman that "modern male sexuality would thus seem to be defined less by the body than by the negation of the body. This points to the ways in which that sexuality has been sublimated into a relation with the phallus."[25] Frederick's evolution has taken up two-thirds of the film, which, for all practical purposes, is over with the execution of Katte. Essentially in no need of closure, it employs a circular logic, returning to the invocation of bourgeois family that was its starting point. With the family of Prussia secured, the reharmonization of the nuclear family follows suit; "heart" shines through the body armor as the father dies. Yet, it is telling that the film's final indulgence of sentimental family love occurs with a total absence of women.

The Old and the Young King's remaining challenge is the visual rendering of its last crucial shift: from Frederick as a disciplined subject to Frederick as the subject of a quasi-disciplinary gaze on the world. Like *The Great King*, this film ends with a scene leaving cinematic realism and narrative behind, with another attempt to *show* the gaze. Unlike *The Great King*'s coda, however, the scene does not resort to montage or

---

23. Foucault, *Discipline and Punish*, 43.

24. Also called the paternal signifier, the Name-of-the-Father is Lacan's term for the subject's integration into the symbolic language, which is simultaneously an integration into an Oedipal matrix. It is closely connected with the notion of the phallus as the cultural value around which male subjectivity is organized.

25. Silverman, *Acoustic Mirror*, 26.

"celestial" iconography. It consists merely in a close-up slowly tracking in on Frederick's face (photo 26); it is, again, essentially an extradiegetic shot that looks at no one within the narrative, only at the spectator. The break with realism is not in the shot itself but in its length of thirty-seven seconds. As if meant to rivet us to our seats, Frederick just goes on looking at us, condensing in one frame the New Man as armored machine impervious to weakness and devoid of the ornamental, the feminine, the emotional, or the excessive. This Frederick is neither frail, fatherly, nor friendly; he resembles more a (albeit personalized) disciplinary force functioning at once as Ideal I and as big Other demanding the hardening he demands of himself. Ironically, the exorcism of Frederick *qua* feminized spectacle has been the precondition allowing the film to display him proudly as another kind of spectacle whose look one is compelled to return. As a newly born icon, Frederick surpasses his father as master interpellator, as an ego whose "strength" is contagious, but who demands subjection to the violence of discipline. He projects onto one individual what Foucault describes as a "faceless gaze" transforming "the whole social body into a field of perception: thousands of eyes posted everywhere, mobile attentions ever on the alert."[26]

The young Frederick has no more been *trained* to be a King than the mature Frederick of Otto Gebühr; Nazi biologism precludes such training. Rather, the Prussian drill machine has beaten all femininity, weakness, and humanity out of him, unearthing the sublime object within him and rendering him Leader of a new race that was the utopian vision of figures like Ernst Jünger years before the Nazis seized power: "Supple bodies, lean and sinewy, striking features, stone eyes petrified in a thousand terrors beneath their helmets. They were conquerors, men of steel tuned to the most grisly battle. Sweeping across a splintered landscape, they heralded the final triumph of all imagined horror."[27] It is here that the machine of discipline and ideologies of organicism come together — in the moment that the human body is perfected as a disciplinary machine. The violence inflicted upon Frederick's self by his superego has successfully supplanted superficial forms of pleasure with enjoyment. This violence against the self will find its complement in the violence directed against others. Frederick is ready to pursue war "for peace."

26. Foucault, *Discipline and Punish*, 214.
27. Ernst Jünger, *Kampf als inneres Erlebnis*, 32f., quoted in Theweleit, 2:159.

II

AESTHETICIZED

GENIUS

*

FIVE

Duel over the Son: Herbert Maisch's *Friedrich Schiller — Triumph of a Genius*

The following three chapters explore Nazi films resurrecting eighteenth-century German artistic "Genius": Herbert Maisch's *Friedrich Schiller — Triumph of a Genius* (1940), G. W. Pabst's *Komödianten*, and Traugott Müller's *Friedemann Bach* (both 1941). The model of identification I developed with respect to Nazism's "Fridericus" hagiography transfers in many ways to these films, which are, however, preoccupied with Art and not War as a sphere of historical agency. The protagonist of these "artist" movies is never a central subject like Frederick, around whom an entire social network revolves, but rather the bearer of a timeless Culture. Yet the aesthetic terrain on which artist stories are acted out has a curious affinity with that of War as celebrated by Nazism and other twentieth-century movements: both are sites detached from and transcendent to the economic/political, that sphere forever susceptible to "Jewishness" and everything it connotes (a similarity articulated in Benjamin's definition of war as the culmination of *l'art pour l'art*). The total artist, like the total warrior, embodies phallic authority and an imaginary wholeness reflecting back on the film spectator. More precisely, the aesthetic, in the form of the artistic Personality, is *at war* with the instrumentalized world of modernity, politics, and the very discipline that is a paradoxical sine qua non for Nazism. The establishment of a national identity in any collective mirror, whether Art, War, or the King's Body, is inherently political; hence these films exemplify Nazism's aestheticization of politics no less than more obviously "political" films.

The fact that the majority of Nazism's Genius films are clustered in the early forties suggests they were part of a programmatic effort to boost public morale. Film biographies extolling artists like Schiller, Mozart,

Andreas Schlüter, Michelangelo, or Rembrandt, as well as scientists, medical doctors, inventors, and politicians,[1] seem designed as an answer to the growing demands of war, as a form of ideological rearmament. They constituted an important variation on war-affirmative "homefront" films like *Request Concert* and *The Great Love,* which I will discuss in a later chapter; the "management" of desire in both genres is simultaneously negotiation with a war context. "Home" in the Genius film is located, however, not just within a synchronous, geographical spectrum, but across a diachronic spectrum; "home" is a nation's collective narrative. Because the "homefront" films are set in the present and refer directly to their historical juncture (e.g., through conversion narratives in which a character learns to cede personal desire to "Germany"), they necessarily bear a burden in acknowledging—however euphemistically—the social fragmentation of war. The Genius films, on the other hand, evoke the "homefront" film's sense of community while evading the real-life war entirely. Like all historical films, they offer a ready made triumphant closure impossible in films about an ongoing war, but one which simultaneously is *not* closure, since the Culture whose genesis they trace transcends closure and temporality, "living on" forever. The Genius film allows the past to overcome itself and reach into the present and future.

Second, unlike the "homefront" film, which depicts surrogates for the spectator in his/her everyday existence, the Genius film tells stories about figures with whom the spectator is already at "home," thanks to a vast extratextual apparatus disseminating Culture through schools, theaters, museums, monuments, and popular memory. What remains is for the films to provide a (literal and figurative) screen in which Genius and Culture can be reexperienced as the social fantasy they already are. Like Frederick, the Genius is defined according to Lacan's category of "S_2," the chain of knowledge,[2] that is, by the "products" he generates which make up Culture. However, in the process he becomes "more than himself," is retroactively infused with an Otherness (that Thing called "Genius") that always already was within him and no longer needs to be demonstrated by his "products." Not only does he possess, like the King, two bodies, a mortal one and his immortal body of "works"; Genius can indeed be Genius with or without his works, as my reading of Friedemann Bach's

---

1. Other examples are *The Immortal Heart* (1939), *Robert Koch* (1939), *Ohm Krüger* (1941), *Carl Peters* (1941), *Mozart* (1942), *Andreas Schlüter* (1942), *Diesel* (1942), *Secret Files WB1* (1942), *Rembrandt* (1942), *Paracelsus* (1943), *The Unending Path* (1943). I discuss *The Ruler* (1937) and *Diesel* (1943) in chapter 9.
2. See my application of Lacan's matrix with respect to Frederick in chapter 3.

tragic Genius will illustrate.[3] Again in this genre, eighteenth-century narrative paradigms weave themselves into biography, making historical subjects more familiar and, as I will illuminate in individual cases, giving the audience the sense of being an enunciating force along with the Genius.

Although I hope to show that the Genius films are not monolithic in their interpellation, they project into the past a struggle which implicitly affirms the National Socialist present as having surmounted the instrumentalized world with and in which Genius was forced to cope. Affirmation of a supposedly nonalienated present capable of recognizing Personality is implicit in the "master" narrative that runs through all the films: the Genius, whether artist, scientist, or doctor, is a "rebel" constrained by a world that fails to understand him and attempts to subjugate him to "rules," which are inimical to his "nature." As I suggested at the beginning of the chapter, the proximity of this formula to the Frederick movies and to essentially all Nazi Leader stories derives from National Socialism's emphasis on the aesthetic and its fusion of the aesthetic with everything else.

We have seen how the aesthetic in modernity rebels against or retreats from everyday life, from the demands of material needs which (the historical) Schiller referred to as one's "ordinary pursuits, his everyday existence" (*sein Geschäft, sein gemeines Leben*).[4] What matters in the films is not whether the subject is an artist or a doctor, but that the cinematic narrative translates him into a creator of experiences that overcome alienation and that become, by definition, aesthetic. This gives us a clue why whenever the cinematic Frederick flaunts antidisciplinary, "anticentralist" rhetoric, he echoes the fiction of the historical Schiller. Genius movies may be about art, war, or the conquest of disease, but they are pervaded by the same opposition between a centralized social form (planning and calculation as an always already instituted form of alienation) and the "heart" (communal experience),[5] under which lies a more fundamental opposition

3. The notion of "artistry" as an inner quality independent of "product" dates back to the late eighteenth century, with its valorization of the aesthetic as transcending the craftsmanship with which it had heretofore been linked. Cf. the famous speech from Lessing's *Emilia Galotti* (1772; 1.iv) in which the artist Conti laments the loss of artistry as it travels from the eyes to the canvas, and speculates whether Raphael would have been less of an artist had he been born with no hands.

4. Schiller, "On the Uses of the Chorus in Tragedy" (1803–1804), Preface to *The Bride of Messina*, in *The Works of Friedrich Schiller*, trans. Henry G. Bohn (London: Henry G. Bohn, 1854), 3:440.

5. See my discussion of the bourgeois tragedy's rejection of centralism in chapter 2.

between everyday constraints and aesthetic elevation. These are structurally dependent on one another; film offers the pleasure of watching their contestation unfold in a medium that is itself aesthetic and in which the aesthetic can always win out. Nazism's aspiration is that the individual and collective fortification offered by identification with German Genius can be reinvested back into a "real" life organized around an "us" versus a "them," that the aesthetic can translate into activism.

The eighteenth-century setting of the three artist biographies discussed here coincides historically with the evolution of the very ideological presuppositions of all the Genius films — a coincidence which helps elucidate the complex relations between eighteenth-century aesthetics and National Socialism's biologistic celebration of Leader, Genius, or Personality. Not only did the eighteenth century generate a celebrated artistic canon, its loss of faith in art's direct social effect generated the "aesthetic of genius" that even today continues to structure the Western popular mystification of Art and Artist I discussed earlier. These developments constitute in the eyes of many historians a decisive step away from the public sphere aspired to by the Enlightenment.[6] An awareness that an "enlightened" cultural discourse easily became cultural *consumption* led many eighteenth-century thinkers increasingly to vest gifted individuals with authority (an attempt, however misguided, to uphold a culture of "reasoning"); simultaneously much public interest shifted from the contents of the work to the person of the author, allowing a writer like Goethe to become the object of virtual deification.[7]

In addition to reflecting the decay of the Enlightenment project, the "genius aesthetic" further undermined it by providing ego ideals who relieved the public of responsibility for critical textual interaction, functioning instead as narcissistic mirrors (again like Nazi Genius figures).

6. See my excursus in chapter 1. Early Enlightenment thinkers like Gottsched aspired to spread the habit of reading among the public, assuming that a quantitative increase in reading would automatically lead to a qualitative improvement in public morality, that all individuals were equally susceptible to intellectual and moral teaching. Cf. Gottsched's remark: "Bad education is without doubt the most general source of [the public's bad taste]" (*Versuch einer Critischen Dichtkunst* [Leipzig, 1751], 135) or Lessing's remark: "Nature knows nothing of the hated differences that men have determined among themselves," quoted in J. Schulte-Sasse, *Literarische Struktur und historisch-sozialer Kontext: Zum Beispiel Lessings "Emilia Galotti"* [Paderborn: Schöningh, 1975], 35).
7. See Christa Bürger, *Der Ursprung der bürgerlichen Institution Kunst* (Frankfurt: Suhrkamp, 1977), 18.

Adorno indicts the Genius concept as the potential "enemy of works of art": "In the genius concept the idea of the creativity of the transcendental subject is ceded with idealistic hubris to the empirical subject, to the productive artist. This suits bourgeois vulgar-consciousness . . . because it frees the observer [of art] from the effort of dealing with the work: he is fed the personality, in the end the kitsch-biography of the artist."[8] The reactionary potential already inherent in the genius aesthetic was only intensified in the early twentieth century with the social and economic destabilization following the collapse of the Hohenzollern monarchy, metamorphosing a genius aesthetic into what Jochen Schmidt calls an "increasingly reactionary genius-religion." Genius interpellated a society now bereft of an authority it had been socialized to believe in, constituting a "panicky individualistic reaction in the face of the industrial mass society with its leveling tendencies, the hope for a political messiah evolving from misery."[9]

FRIEDRICH SCHILLER

The first Genius movie I will discuss, *Friedrich Schiller — Triumph of a Genius,* fits the model I have just described as well as any film. It tells the story of a rebel hero who is infallible in his affirmation of the fiction of intact manhood and it identifies with late-eighteenth-century aesthetic values to suture its subject into a euphoria in German Genius. Rather than generating a unanimous reaction among film scholars, however, precisely this film has been upheld both as an exemplary Nazi celebration of "a superman . . . the forebear of the writer of *Mein Kampf*"[10] and as a clandestine indictment of National Socialism. For David Stewart Hull, *Friedrich Schiller* "proved difficult to fit into the pattern of the standard pre-Hitler proto-Nazi which the regime demanded," making its producer "hard put to make a propaganda example of his life."[11] Most striking is Rudolf Oertel's reading in the late 1950s: "The most amazing film ever

8. Theodor Adorno, *Ästhetische Theorie,* in *Gesammelte Schriften* (Frankfurt: Suhrkamp, 1970), 7:255–56.

9. Jochen Schmidt, *Die Geschichte des Genie-Gedankens in der deutschen Literatur, Philosophie und Politik 1750–1945,* 2 vols. (Darmstadt: Wissenschaftliche Buchgesellschaft, 1985), 2:202.

10. Erwin Leiser, *Nazi Cinema,* trans. G. Mander and D. Wilson (New York: Macmillan, 1974), 109.

11. Stewart David Hull, *Film in the Third Reich* (Berkeley: University of California Press, 1969), 184–85.

made in the Third Reich. Amazing because from the first to the last scene it was a flaming indictment of the oppression of the spirit by a tyrant and military despot. Surrounded by concentration camps, in the face of a People in uniform marching in unison to the roar of guns and bombs [Nazism's real-life discipline], it sings the high song of freedom with all the fire of genuine passion. . . . One could give this film, too, the motto In Tirannos ['death to the tyrant,' the motto of Schiller's *Robbers*]."[12]

It is easy to dismiss such commentary as a naive apologia that misses the point of a blatantly reactionary film, which few subsequent scholars have hesitated to do.[13] The question driving my analysis is not the correct "choice" between readings of the film as pro- or anti-Nazi. Rather, my questions are what factors make both readings possible, what narrative or cinematic configurations create ruptures in both readings, and what does the film's appropriation of Friedrich Schiller have to do with either of these. In other words, I am interested in internal tensions that render this film more complicated than either reading would allow. I will begin by demonstrating how the film fits Schiller seamlessly into Nazism's antimodern, antidisciplinary ideology. The fact that it thereby preserves its "Schillerian" fervor indeed renders it a cunning example of Nazi cultural exploitation. In the second part, however, I will demonstrate that, although the film's ruptures cannot be found in its citation of Schiller's antidespotism, they can be located if we examine the structural interdependency of Schiller and his Other. The story of the Duke of Württemberg is one of an unrequited desire and a humorous, "lovable" despotism that threatens to deconstruct the tedium of German Genius. In part the film owes its ambivalence to the demands of cinema for relief and entertainment.

WHICH CAME FIRST: THE FICTION OR THE LIFE?

One of the film's main operating principles, and surely a key to its success, is that it echoes the historical Schiller (1759–1805). It organizes a well-known part of Schiller's life as a coherent narrative.

12. Rudolf Oertel, *Macht und Magie des Films: Weltgeschichte einer Massensuggestion* (Vienna, 1959), 418, quoted in Francis Courtade and Pierre Cadars, *Geschichte des Films im dritten Reich,* trans. Florian Hopf (Munich: Carl Hanser, 1975), 98.
13. Cf. Leiser, Courtade and Cadars, Julian Petley, *Capital and Culture: German Cinema, 1933–45* (London: British Film Institute, 1979), or Georg Ruppelt, *Schiller im nationalsozialistischen Deutschland* (Stuttgart: Metzler, 1979).

*

The film depicts Schiller's youthful years in Stuttgart, the so-called "Charles School" Period when he studied medicine at the academy of Duke Karl Eugen of Württemberg. During this time he secretly wrote his first play, *The Robbers (Die Räuber,* 1781), a paragon of Storm and Stress literature with the motto *In Tirannos,* death to the tyrant. The despotic Duke punishes Schiller for questioning empirical science with a prolonged stay in his school, relentlessly pursues the manuscripts he suspects that Schiller is writing, and constantly threatens him with imprisonment in the infamous Hohenasberg, where he already holds the rebellious poet Schubart. Among Schiller's supporters are Duchess Franziska von Hohenheim and Laura, the Duke's daughter from an earlier liaison, who loves Schiller. The film concludes with Schiller's escape from Württemberg in 1782 after the anonymous publication and triumphant performance of *The Robbers* in Mannheim.

*

The film brings Schiller "to life" via a technique that Georg Ruppelt calls "reverse translation,"[14] in which characters from his fiction find their way into his biography. Ruppelt traces a number of these figures to Schiller's early tragedy *Cabal and Love:* Schiller's father is modeled on the musician Miller, a prototypical assertive bourgeois father, Duchess Franziska on Lady Milford, a morally ambiguous figure with redeeming "bourgeois" values. The film's Laura, who is not based on a historical person, materializes the addressee of early Schiller love poems.[15] Most importantly, the film models its cinematic Schiller on Karl Moor, the protagonist of *The Robbers,* which is the play he writes in the movie.[16] Schiller vir-

14. Ruppelt, 128.

15. Some fictitious biographies of Schiller such as Heinrich Laube's play *Die Karls-schüler* (1846), and Hermann Kurz's novel *Schillers Heimatjahre* (1843), however, do include a Laura, and provided inspiration for events in the film, such as the entanglements surrounding Schiller's endangered manuscript. The historical addressee of the Laura poems was probably Schiller's landlady when he was a regiment doctor. See Ruppelt, 128.

16. The character constellations in the film and its counterpart in Schiller's *Robbers* exemplify what National Socialists referred to as "Prussian Socialism": "Some authors discovered in Schiller's dramas the National Socialist version of socialism and its understanding of the community of the Volk. Allegedly Schiller portrayed Karl Moor as a socialist. 'He, the powerful warrior, feels responsible to the highest power. Responsible to his comrades, to all poor and oppressed, to his Volk. But this characterizes him as a

tually lives *The Robbers* while writing it, and sees his creation Karl Moor as an Ideal-I, a more perfect reflection of the self ("My robber Moor is *also* tortured and scorned by a world that does not understand him"). The casting of Horst Caspar as Schiller augments this equation of the writer with his own fictional characters. Caspar was famous for his stage portrayals of early Schiller protagonists in Bochum, especially Ferdinand in *Cabal and Love*. In his appearance and gestures, for instance, when he takes on the pose of Dannecker's famous Schiller bust, he fulfilled the public's image of the young Schiller,[17] The constellation of Schiller vis-à-vis his fellow students is likewise analogous to that of Moor and his gang: the boys "become" the robbers, addressing Schiller as "Captain" and holding clandestine meetings — all of which happens in the play.

Although, as I will elaborate later, Duke Karl Eugen is too ambivalent to be a generic Schillerian villain like *The Robber*'s Franz Moor, *Don Carlos*'s King Philip, or *Cabal and Love*'s President, he does allude to such characters[18] and, most importantly, occupies their semiotic position within the narrative. By this I mean that, although the film's story is guided by Schiller's biography and not by the events of his plays, its thematic configuration between Schiller and Karl Eugen reiterates that of *The Robbers* and other early Schiller plays. The two film characters embody, namely, the opposition of the "heart" to an absolutist machine-state, of "inner freedom" to an external subjugation manifested not only in the Duke's acts, but in his constant talk about "discipline and order" and about training "Subjects." In this opposition lies the key to the film's ideological position and its functionalization of Schiller. With its attack on the discipline the historical Schiller deplored, this film does the opposite of *The Old and the Young King*. If the latter offers a clue to the real violence

---

socialist. He is the classic embodiment of socialistic leadership.'" Ruppelt, 13; he quotes Hans Fabricius, *Schiller als Kampfgenosse Hitlers: Nationalsozialismus in Schillers Dramen* (Bayreuth, 1932), 9. Just as Nazism deprives history of its subversive potential, it deprives socialism of its analytical basis defining conflicting interest groups. Instead it reduces "socialism" to a notion of community which erases inherent class conflict (as we saw in the Frederick genre), as well as the fact that arbitrarily defined groups are excluded from membership in the collective: " 'we' applies only to men recognized as possessors of a German soul" (Klaus Theweleit, *Male Fantasies*, trans. Erica Carter and Chris Turner [Minneapolis: University of Minnesota Press, 1989], 2:82).

17. See Ruppelt, 126 and 240.

18. For example, Karl Eugen's sale of soldiers to foreign sovereigns to finance courtly excess parallels an act of the President in *Cabal and Love,* II.ii.

that is Nazism (legitimated by a "spare the rod . . ." ideology), *Friedrich Schiller* is "pure" ideology; it represents the flight from discipline with which Nazism justifies itself. Nazism's praxis is displaced onto the Duke, who embodies everything that National Socialism is against ideologically and everything it is in reality. Ultimately, the film shrugs off one structure of authority for another that is perceived not as authority but as a joyful sublation of self in the whole.

The film's critique of state planning and of a centralistic social regimentation — in short, its attack on modern discipline — manifests itself most obviously in Karl Eugen's school. The school substitutes for the Duke's family, as indicated by his reference to the cadets as "my sons" and the traditional parental roles of severe patriarch and compassionate mother which he and Franziska assume. He adheres to the rationalistic notion that he can take young men as "raw material" (recall the Goebbels quotation about the nature of political art in chapter 1) and form them according to an abstract social model, or in his own words, show "how a spirit can be tamed!" By depicting the Duke as such an extreme ideologue of enlightened despotism, the film ridicules the Enlightenment idea of progress and the amenability of society to planning. The school appears as an inhuman "machine," a metaphor for a rationalism that cranks out uniform automatons, as the poet Schubart remarks, playing on the proximity of the German verb *züchten* [to breed] to *Zuchtanstalt*, meaning prison or reform house: "Now the Duke is no longer breeding stallions like before, now he's breeding people, too. . . . He calls it an academy, but in truth it's a reform house (*Zuchtanstalt*)."

The equation of school with prison becomes a central verbal and iconic motif throughout the film; indeed, the first shot of the school (which immediately follows Schubart's reference to it as prison) is foregrounded by an iron fence, behind whose bars cadets line up to the call of a bugle. The camera travels to the cadets' sleeping quarters, where a symmetrical shot shows two long rows of beds with the Duke's portrait in the center looming omnipotently over the boys, who likewise have formed two rows (space here is organized in a disciplinary manner and the intrusive camera takes on the panoptical overview which the Duke is determined to command). Like the camera, the institution totalizes the cadets' private sphere to a grotesque degree, as when the tyrannical sergeant models the daily prayer on a military drill, screaming: "One! Two! Pray!" or when the cadets — again homogenized by their identical dress, hairstyles, and stance — sit in symmetrical columns and mechanically braid each other's hair to the rhythm of the sergeant's counting (photo 27). Not only do these

27 The famous braiding scene in *Friedrich Schiller* has been read as a parody of Nazi *Gleichschaltung.*

scenes gain an ironic dimension in light of National Socialist *Gleich-schaltung,* they are diametrically opposed to *The Old and the Young King*'s affirmation of the same grotesque behavior, where such "educa-tion" is not only justified but imperative to Prussia's survival.

The Duke's rage when Schiller's doctoral dissertation deviates from an empirical approach to medicine (instead intermingling medicine with phi-losophy, which is not, in the Duke's words, "your science") likewise un-derscores his role as narrative signifier for a reified, disciplinary form of knowledge and thus for an instrumentalized modernity.[19] Underlying Karl Eugen's objections is the rationalistic assumption that the social welfare depends on the development of narrow expertise (a reference to the divi-sion of labor) based on a hierarchical understanding of scholarship and society. The film's implicit ridicule of his demand that everything be "use-

19. Like the emerging capitalism of which he is a part, the Duke tends to instrumental-ize nature as well. The orchard owned by Schiller's father becomes a metaphor for the human nature the Duke hopes to control. Walking through the orchard, Father Schiller and Karl Eugen discuss Schiller's future. Even while praising Father Schiller's hor-ticultural achievement, the Duke echoes the instrumentality a thinker like Karl Philip Moritz indicts when he writes that "even great, sublime nature is observed only with cameralistic eyes and is considered worth gazing at only as long as the profits to be yielded from her resources can be calculated"; "Das Edleste in der Natur," in *Moritz: Werke in Zwei Bänden,* ed. Jürgen Jahn (Berlin: Aufbau, 1973), 1:236. The Duke can only comprehend the orchard as the result of taming, not indulging nature, a method he extends to the education of men: "With humans and nature, it's always the same. One only has to force one's will on them." Father Schiller, whose nurturance of the orchard already suggests an alignment of the Schiller family on the side of "nature," predictably articulates the film's antirationalist view, protesting that young trees cannot develop without space, without freedom.

ful" recalls the aesthetic culture of German Classicism and Romanticism, which — reacting against a developing capitalistic society — deplored the utilitarian as the antithesis of beauty and creativity. Karl Philip Moritz laments that "the dominant idea of the *utilitarian* has little by little suppressed the noble and beautiful,"[20] and Kant's category of disinterested pleasure posits that artistic judgment should be free from earthly desires. The film's Schiller echoes the same resistance to modernity by decrying the inadequacy of institutions and of a science forcing natural phenomena into neat taxonomies; he categorizes his own work neither as philosophy nor science, but as "what my heart commands." His introduction of "heart" into the discourse not only alludes to the Sentimental devaluation of reason and increased emphasis on emotion (thus implicitly corroborating a late-eighteenth-century antirationalist position), but also valorizes the resistance of the aesthetic to rational constraints, to everyday rules and regulations.

Friedrich Schiller's transplantation of Schiller characters and themes into his biography is doubtless the source for affirmative responses reading these elements as an attack on Nazism, enhanced by the film's incorporation of the villain's death scene from *The Robbers,* about which David Stewart Hull writes: "[The] actors playing Pastor Moser and Franz Moor . . . play their roles with such conviction that the lines would seem almost directed against the Nazi regime."[21] The problem is that "such conviction" can likewise celebrate Nazism's alignment of itself with Schillerian antimodernism, and that, apart from this one scene, which begins a sequence celebrating Genius, what appears in the movie is a functionalized "Robbers" and not the play itself. *Friedrich Schiller* alludes to *The Robbers* as the kind of "rebel" story Nazi hagiography privileged; hence we can as easily read Schiller's identification with Karl Moor as another affirmation of his Leader function. Schiller's cinematic privileging corroborates such a reading: Images of him composing poetry or prose usually show him "feverish" with inspiration in a self-consciously constructed frame whose drama is enhanced by candles or some other light source. Group compositions likewise privilege the tall, lean Schiller as specular object. Shots foregrounding him with his back to the camera, surrounded by jubilant, illuminated faces of fellow cadets, underscore a biologistic, divinely inspired conception of Genius. They suppress what Adorno called

20. Moritz, 1:236.
21. *Film in the Third Reich,* 184.

28·31 The tableau configurations showing Friedrich Schiller (28 and 29) and Friedemann Bach (30 and 31) composing typify the iconography of the Genius film, which erases the *techne* of artistic production.

the *techne,* or "moment of finite doing" of artistic creation, in favor of a notion of art as centered in the "ego" of a Genius masterfully expressing himself (photos 28–31 and 36).

This is not to say that there may not always be a space of ambivalence in this appropriation of Schiller. Moreover, the cinematic privileging I described is likewise indebted to classical movie-hero iconography. As suggested by Stephen Lowry's commentary on the ambivalence in Hans Albers's film persona, the very features that make Schiller a "Nazi" ideal can make him an "anti-Nazi" ideal in the eye of the beholder: "Through identification with the hero these features could be used to bind wishes to ideal images of Leader figures corresponding to Nazi ideology. The same features, if aroused in spectators and not successfully reintegrated, were precisely what Nazis did not wish of their subjects."[22] The points to keep in mind are, I believe, first that Nazism's imagined Leader figure is not just indebted to, but *is* a Schillerian hero and, second, that Nazism's filmic representation of its Leader most often is the same as Hollywood's — hence attempts to unravel the two become a futile game.

Many other features of the film demonstrate the Nazi functionalization of its "Schiller." Its most egregious violation of Schiller is the parading of Nazi biology rhetoric in the scene most often cited by critics, in which the Duke and Schiller dispute the question "Are great minds born or raised/educated (*erzogen*)?":[23]

DUKE: Well, how is it? Are great minds born or raised?
CADETS (*in unison*): Raised, your royal Highness!
SCHILLER: Born, your royal Highness, not raised.
DUKE: Well, look at that! An opponent! (*Opponent*) *Bon!* Let's discuss it![24]

Once again, not only does the film isolate Schiller by his verbal dissent from the mass — intensified by the cadets' mechanical choral response — but privileges him cinematically, as he disrupts the frame's symmetry by

22. *Pathos und Politik: Ideologie in Spielfilmen des Nationalsozialismus* (Tübingen: Niemeyer, 1991), 229.

23. This was in fact a historical lecture by Schiller's professor Abel. See Ruppelt, 129.

24. The relish with which the Duke greets Schiller's dissent also typifies his absolutist enjoyment of a game allowing him to prove his superiority — a demeanor underscored by his usage of French (*Opponent, bon*), associated since Louis XIV with absolutism and a signifier in the bourgeois tragedy of courtly coding.

32-35 Recurrent feminized males in Nazi cinema. 32: Hofmarschall von Silberkalb in *Friedrich Schiller*; 33: French gamblers in *The Old and the Young King*; 34: The Prince of Bayreuth in *The Old and the Young King*; 35: Marchand in *Friedemann Bach*.

jumping "out of line."[25] His response that Genius is "born" and comes to fruition "by its own strength" contradicts the Enlightenment conviction of the potential of all individuals to be educated (as does Frederick's parallel remark in *The Great King:* "One doesn't become a king, one *is* [a king]!"), and allows him to dismiss the Duke's rationalistic argument that "the state directs [the Genius] through its higher institutions on the way to perfection." Underlying Schiller's mystification of Genius is the fantasy of the People as an organic entity analogous to a human being, as suggested by his metaphor of the People giving birth: "The Genius is born not only of his mother, but of his Volk."[26] The birth metaphor implicitly affirms Nazism's usurpation of the role of the family, a function to which I will return.

Another transgression is *Friedrich Schiller*'s xenophobic twist on Hofmarschall von Silberkalb, who corresponds to Hofmarschall von Kalb in Schiller's *Cabal and Love* (photo 32). Silberkalb is a courtier who tries to trick Laura into giving him *The Robbers* so he can ingratiate himself with the Duke. He is "true" to Schiller's model to the extent that he is an effeminate fop whose grotesque vanity satirizes courtly artifice with its imitation of French culture. However, his attempt in the film to ruin Schiller through courtly cabal makes him a more destructive figure than his literary model. Most telling is the fact that Silberkalb (i.e., his equivalences) recurs over and over in Nazi cinema, suggesting a National Socialist obsession with feminized males:[27] we see him as the courtly fops with whom Frederick gambles in *The Old and the Young King* (photos 33–34)

---

25. "Jumping out of line" may seem a strange configuration to the viewer in whose mind images of perfect columns flaunted in Riefenstahl's *Triumph of the Will* are inscribed. It is, however, both a compositional principle and a verbal motif in the film. In his refusal to conform either with the rigid discipline of the Royal Military Academy or with the hierarchical standards of courtly society, Schiller on several occasions literally breaks the symmetry of the frame while other cadets march or stand at attention. Indeed, at his first appearance Schiller leaps out from an inspection line to catch a fainting classmate, thus demonstrating at once altruism and nonconformity; he later leaps out of a marching line in order to bring Laura a poem, etc.

26. Not only does the film portray Genius as driven by fate to pursue art ("He has no choice"), but the acknowledgment of Genius is again based solely upon intuition, illustrated by Franziska's remark, "This person is made out of a different stuff than us. I feel it."

27. This is, of course, found in Hollywood as well. Cf. the juxtaposition of the feminized versus the "natural" male in *The Scarlet Pimpernel,* the Zorro or Superman films, or the scene in George Marshall's *Star Spangled Rhythm* (1942) in which four "virile" Hollywood men imitate a women's bridge party.

and as Riccault in *Lady von Barnhelm,* based on Lessing's *Minna von Barnhelm;* we will also see him in the next chapter as the musician Marchand "from Paris" in *Friedemann Bach* (photo 35). While the historical Schiller and Lessing indeed ridiculed francophile culture and tended to gender it feminine, their critique was informed by the Enlightenment project: an international institutionalization of "bourgeois" ("universally human") virtue in which "inner" values replace self-display, vanity, and agonia. By contrast, *Friedrich Schiller* and other films characterize such courtly fops in nationalistic terms as "un-German." Moreover, when the name of Schiller's literary character Kalb, meaning calf or ninny, becomes Silberkalb, it gains an aura of "Jewishness."

In other, more subtle ways, the film shifts the accent on family and interpersonal relations that is so central to the historical Schiller's aesthetic project. Human relationships give way in *Friedrich Schiller* to the egocentrism of the Genius narrative; the eighteenth-century notion of "Love" as an assurance of social harmony becomes the "Triumph of a Genius," to cite the film's subtitle echoing Nazism's most famous documentary, Riefenstahl's *Triumph of the Will.* Schiller's "loved ones" exist only to be dispensed with, as illustrated by the peripheral role of his biological parents. Schiller's mother, with two brief appearances, is reduced purely to the function Mother, much like mothers in the Frederick films. In her first appearance as a spectator at what is supposed to be Schiller's graduation, she is permitted to see Schiller "perform" with the Duke, and in her other scene she is permitted to say good-bye. Father Schiller, to whom a Schiller play would accord a central role, does little but watch the Genius triumph.

Within the ideological framework of this film and others, Genius has no parents; it always already *is.* This carries on what Walter Benjamin refers to as the Western myth of artistic creation, in which the artist is reborn in the very fulfillment of his creative work: the artist "blissfully surpasses nature, because he will now owe the existence first bestowed upon him by the dark depths of the womb to a brighter realm. His homeland is not where he was born; rather he comes to the world, where his homeland is. *He is the male first-born of the work that he once conceived*" (italics mine).[28] The very same birth metaphor is at the heart of the Nazi Genius aesthetic, with its retroactive nullification of such banalities as "parents." Benjamin's description captures the narcissistic circularity of Schiller's

28. "Nach der Vollendung," in "Denkbilder," in *Gesammelte Schriften,* vol. 4, pt. 1 (Frankfurt: Suhrkamp, 1980), 438.

own rebirth through "giving birth" to his own work. The Genius incorporates the ultimate male fantasy: being born out of one's own will and creation, a circularity sustained in the one poem Schiller "writes" in the film, in which the "creating spirit" creates out of "chaos" to throw an "anchor."[29]

Equally dispensable in the film are women as a site of desire. On the surface, they may fare slightly better than in Frederick films, indulging the female spectator's anticipated erotic investment in Schiller. Especially Franziska is coded as a "strong" woman wielding great influence over her husband. But ultimately Schiller's women are there to give him up for "destiny." The parallel visual coding of Franziska and Laura in their first scene reflects *Friedrich Schiller*'s functionalization of women. Their similarly styled light-colored dresses, their virtually identical wigs, and their exchange of flowers diminish the individuality of each woman, making her appear as a generational counterpart of the other, whose function of nurturing and then relinquishing Schiller is the same. Women cannot have an important role within the Genius narrative because romantic love, though another retreat from the strictures of a rationalized modernity, competes with the Genius's devotion to the public sphere, his "mission," which ultimately means himself. As a classical movie, *Friedrich Schiller* needs to make small concessions to "love interest," but as a Genius story it cannot allow the private sphere to collide with Nazism's attempted fusion of public and private, with its *Entgrenzung* of the whole community. This is why in both Genius and Frederick films the relationship between Leader and People is generally more erotically charged than heterosexual relations. It complements the aestheticization of politics.

Significantly, Schiller's only surviving relationship at the film's conclusion is that with his "sidekick" Andreas Streicher, who ultimately escapes Württemberg with him. As in the Frederick genre, male bonding supersedes the heterosexual relationship, a bonding compatible with Nazism's

---

29. *Die der schaffende Geist einst aus dem Chaos schlug, / Durch die schwebende Welt flieg ich des Windes Flug, / Bis am Strande / Ihrer Wogen ich lande, / Anker werf, wo kein Hauch mehr weht / Und der Markstein der Schöpfung steht.* Cf. Lacoue-Labarthe's and Nancy's discussion of why Nazi ideology posits the Aryan race as *the* Subject: "The soul, or the 'personality,' or the 'genius,' finding itself in itself as its own most proper 'myth,' or, again, the soul engendering itself from its dream, is finally nothing more than the absolute, self-creating Subject, a subject whose essential property is not solely cognitive (Descartes), nor spiritual (Eckehart), nor speculative (Hegel), but somehow transcends all these determinations in an immediate and absolutely 'natural' essence: that of blood and race." "The Nazi Myth," *Critical Inquiry* 16.2 (Winter 1990): 306.

164

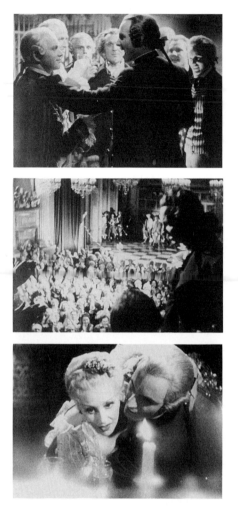

36·37 *Friedrich Schiller*'s iconography of Genius. 36: Typical "genius" iconography foregrounds Schiller as surrogate for the spectator, surrounded by literally and figuratively "illuminated" followers; 37: spatial dynamics and lighting in the Mannheim theater scene underscore Nazi biologism and its cult of the personality. **38** Schiller, forced to imitate the Duke, clowns erotically with Duchess Franziska. The blurred edges suggest the Duke's subjective vision, in which he must confront himself as spectacle, as an impotent buffoon (38).

notion of activism. Streicher's bond to Schiller is merely another narrative configuration symbolizing People and Leader; like Schiller's mother and the film audience, he occupies a spectator role in his first encounter with Schiller, who is literally "on stage" in a public verbal joust with the Duke. Streicher pursues friendship out of admiration, always maintaining a subservient, devotional status, for example, voluntarily giving Schiller the rest of his savings and abandoning his independence to follow him.[30]

30. Streicher himself is performing when he and Schiller first meet; he plays the harpsichord as Schiller enters the room. However, rather than watching another perform,

Streicher's role as surrogate erotic partner is further suggested by his soft voice, the bow he wears in every scene (contrasting with the straight lines of Schiller's clothing), and his curly hair, which gives him a soft, feminized appearance. His status as musician not only enhances his association with the feminine[31] but weaves into the narrative a reciprocity among the arts.

Finally, notwithstanding predictable demonstrations of "caring," Schiller seems virtually indifferent to family and friends who support him throughout the film. Their importance to him seems to lie in the gaze of affirmation they offer, or in their status as contested objects between him and the Duke. Although the film does not make the agonistic dimension in this configuration explicit, it is no coincidence that Schiller forms strong bonds in the film with the Duke's daughter Laura, with his wife Franziska, and with the Sergeant's son George. It would seem that the value of these "friendships" lies in a further intersubjective dynamic between Schiller and his male enemies; "friends" are vehicles by which Genius exerts its power. Schiller's sole fervor belongs to his "work" (even his "love" for Laura expresses itself in more "works" — the poems he recites whenever they meet) and to his drive for approval of the big Other, as he expresses over and over: (to his father) "How can you have me stop when the world has begun to say yes?"; (to the Duke) "Germany admires [my work]," "My work will live on," etc. This allows the metonymic sliding from artistic Genius to political Genius.

Schiller's personal apotheosis (and that of an audience identifying with German Culture) is in the Mannheim Theater premiere of *The Robbers,* the culmination of his desperately sought affirmation; not only does his "work" finally find a mass audience, he himself becomes the happy object of mass spectacle. Analogous to the famous cavalcade at the beginning of *Triumph of the Will* establishing Hitler's interaction with his People, the scene oscillates between shots of a dominantly framed Schiller elevated in a balcony over the jubilant crowd, to the crowd itself, merged visually into one unit. Two shots show Schiller's profile filling out the right-hand portion of the frame, while the masses fill out the left side — signifying in

---

Schiller merely uses the mood created by the music to retreat into his own world. He composes the poem cited earlier — clearly meant to suggest the harmony of two art forms — but also illustrating Schiller's self-absorption.

31. Musicians tend to have an ambivalent status in Nazi cinema, sometimes functioning as spiritual leaders like the sacrificial musicians I will discuss in *Request Concert* (1940) and *The Great Love* (1942), but often tainted by effeminate weakness like the musician Klaus in *Kolberg* (1945) or the protagonist of *Friedemann Bach.*

spatial terms the Personality vis-à-vis his People. The shots depersonalize Schiller, rendering him a mythical icon,[32] as does the comment of a spectator, "a national poet has been bestowed upon Germany" (photo 37). The speaker's use of the passive denies history as active process; it becomes something that always already was. Moreover, the German verb *schenken* translates Schiller literally into a "gift," something conferred upon the People by a higher force. It encapsulates and narrativizes history in a moment that—unlike the dispersed, disorganized process of real historical events—can be watched and enjoyed

Despite all of these elements that we can read as a Nazi perversion of Schiller, I want to stress that the film's total effect depends less on Schiller serving as a Hitler surrogate or on affirmations of "Aryan" racial ideology and more on the same forms of identification we find in other historical films. In addition to identifying with Schiller and his admirers (Metz's "secondary" identification) and with the cinematic apparatus ("primary" identification), we can identify with the "master" narrative of history and literary history—at least if we have the rudimentary background the film anticipates. The fictional story on the screen is, so to speak, "completed" by the spectator who possesses a narrative of history in his or her mind, in which the canonized Schiller's role is fixed. The reception of the film is thus conditioned by a constant slippage between primary and secondary identifications with the filmic text and with the text of history—all of which is complicated by the fact that Schiller is not only the film's fictional *object* but, because of the "reverse translations" from his work, the historical Schiller is in part its *subject* of enunciation. Thus, the spectators' foreknowledge of Schiller's life and work extends their sense of omniscience even beyond the closure of the film narrative. *Friedrich Schiller* disavows the spectators' lack as a cinematic and as a historical subject by allowing them to participate in Schiller's world and know what happens "after the movie"; something impossible in "pure" fiction.

FRIEDRICH SCHILLER'S OTHER STORY

A reading of *Friedrich Schiller* that concentrates on structural interdependencies rather than on narrative oppositions within the text yields a tex-

---

32. One cannot stress enough that this kind of mystification is not unique to Nazi cinema. Just to cite one counter example, one might compare this film with John Ford's *Young Mr. Lincoln,* with its stunning transformation at the end of Lincoln into the stone monument of the Lincoln Memorial in Washington, D.C.

tual complexity which the ideology critique I exercised above does not. If we "look awry"[33] at *Friedrich Schiller,* this seemingly perfect specimen of Nazi ideology displays significant ruptures, starting with its ambivalent critique of disciplinary tyranny, which is not only softened through humor but posited as the condition for Schiller's achievement, as the necessary Other against which he realizes himself. I would go so far as to argue that the very features ensuring the film's commercial success[34] are those that relativize "German Genius" with all its oppressive seriousness. Far from destroying the film's ideological "message" or its celebration of Genius, they give it an "edge," and assure its working as a movie.

While Karl Eugen and his disciplinary world are clearly the foil against which Schiller stands out, they are also what "saves" *Friedrich Schiller* from total predictability and tedium. The film's two most tyrannical figures, Karl Eugen and the Sergeant in his academy — a mirror reflection of the Duke on a lower hierarchical level — not only serve as the film's primary source of humor but as objects of a curious sympathy. The Sergeant borders on the likable due to the impotence of his hyperbolic rage against the world. He is ridiculed by the cadets (illustrated by the scene in which he forces a fellow cadet to call Schiller a "pig's hide," whereupon the cadet carries out the order but looks at the Sergeant himself instead of at Schiller), victimized by superiors who turn the same despotism against him, and betrayed by his own son, who assists Schiller in his deception of authorities. Even more ambivalent is the Duke, whose frustrated desire for the one figure who eludes him, Schiller, drives the narrative at least as much as Schiller's desire to "write" — a desire which becomes a narrative only when it meets resistance. Not coincidentally, two of Germany's best actors were selected for these roles; Paul Dahlke (who in the same year played the humorous servant Just in the Lessing adaptation *Lady von Barnhelm*) is the Sergeant and the superstar Heinrich George (also Duke Karl Alexander in *Jew Süss*) is Karl Eugen. If *Friedrich Schiller* reminisces about a past that did not allow Genius to flourish unimpeded,[35] it is a fond

33. I am borrowing the title of a book by Slavoj Žižek referring to Lacan's principle of anamorphosis; *Looking Awry: An Introduction to Jacques Lacan through Popular Culture* (Cambridge: MIT Press, 1991).

34. See David Welch, *Propaganda and the German Cinema, 1933–1945* (Oxford: Clarendon Press, 1983), 167.

35. Karl Eugen's academy has, for example, been read as a Nazi endorsement of its own schools, advocating greater comradeship among pupils, stressing physical as well as mental health, and integrating practical life and school curriculum. See Petley, 141.

reminiscence, a good-natured and charitable look at a bygone era analogous to a recollection of childhood. The very negativity of Karl Eugen's Württemberg not only drives Schiller "to greatness," as Duchess Franziska remarks, but its nostalgically playful portrayal is part of the film's aestheticization of "Germany."

Amid many superficial affirmations of "friendship" in *Friedrich Schiller,* the film's only two convincing instances of bonding transpire between Schiller and his archenemies. Herein lies the importance of Schiller's fellow cadet, Georg von Scharffenstein, another disciplinary bureaucrat whose sole narrative function is to antagonize Schiller by disparaging his work and assailing his vanity. The persistence with which Schiller seeks Scharffenstein's affirmation betrays his fixation on an external gaze; even after declaring his eternal enmity for Scharffenstein, Schiller meets him months later with a childish declaration that the "general has already read [my work]," as if trying to force Scharffenstein into acquiescence by invoking a higher authority. The happy closure of this relationship is simultaneously the closure of the film, when Scharffenstein, now a border official, surprises Schiller and the audience by letting him escape Württemberg. One of the film's final images shows the copy of *The Robbers* that has finally integrated Scharffenstein into the masses of admirers — again simultaneous with Scharffenstein's "loss" of Schiller.

Schiller's drive to gain the Duke's approval remains unsuccessful (at least on a manifest level), which in turn leaves his relationship with the Duke without an explicit closure. If we rethink the film as the Duke's story, it is as much about his desire for Schiller as it is about Schiller's desire for "freedom" with the various sociohistorical implications described above. Read as the Duke's story, the film thrusts Schiller into a more ambiguous light. In obliterating love and family, the film has obliterated its potential for the emotional involvement of melodrama; it substitutes Schiller's ongoing "family" battle with the Duke for a more common melodramatic structure capable of "involving" the spectator. At least in the Duke the film offers the deficient male typical of melodrama, whose acts are often at odds with his own desire. And as in some expressionist dramas, Schiller commits a form of patricide. While in the film story Schiller abandons the Duke, he kills off Karl Eugen's closest fictional counterpart in the first scene of act V of *The Robbers,* the scene repeatedly quoted and finally staged in the film. This death wish is anticipated by the play's motto, *In Tirannos* or "death to the tyrant,"[36] which the Duke reads with a narcis-

36. Historically, the motto was invented not by Schiller but by his publisher Tobias Löffler as an embellishment of *The Robbers'* third edition.

sism that speaks his desire for Schiller: "I suppose you mean me." (We could, conversely, read this application of Franz Moor to himself as a desire of the Duke to be killed rather than abandoned by Schiller.)

Schiller may be regarded more as a product of Karl Eugen's "planning" than the biologistic "Genius" discussion would allow. While the film assails his school as a symbol of centralistic despotism, it leaves little doubt that as such a symbol the school is hopelessly ineffective. (The hyperbolic discipline in school scenes like the mass braiding have a humorous overtone — much like the militarized breakfast call in *The Old and the Young King*.) The school can easily be read deconstructively as illustrating Karl Eugen's mastery of "reverse psychology," whereby he indeed produces brilliant subjects to "honor his name." What is the school if not an uncannily clever plan of the Duke's to create an institution that couldn't help but breed free thinkers?

While the school unwittingly does "train" the Genius Schiller, it entangles the Duke in a quandary not as easily resolved as the Scharffenstein subplot. Karl Eugen is condemned to an endless frustration of desire stemming from the fact that his love for Schiller is based on the very qualities that will ultimately separate him from Schiller; he wants Schiller to mirror himself in him, yet loves Schiller because he does not. Karl Eugen's constant punishment of Schiller generally involves measures that ensure his contact with him — first one more year in school, and later he permits Schiller a "field trip" to Hohenasberg prison only to have him appear at a "family dinner," as if he were a real son. The Duke wants to be the Other whose gaze Schiller seeks; hence his fury that Schiller finds acknowledgment elsewhere, expressed by recurrent impotent declarations "I am Württemberg"; "I am here in His place" (also readable of course as more indictments of absolutist despotism). His blasphemous declaration, "If I had been God in the moment when He was creating the world, and I had known that Schiller would write his 'Robbers' — I would not have created the world!" is a final expression of desperate desire, a statement meaning its exact opposite, his tragic realization of how far he is from being the object of Schiller's desire.

The source of Karl Eugen's frustration is not only his imminent loss of Schiller, but the dependency of their bonding on adversity or the dependency of their mutual desire on the unsublatable Otherness of the Other. A major source of their obsession with each other is their mutual narcissism, demonstrated in the same verbal debates I subjected earlier to ideology critique. As much as they are loaded with "meaning," the confrontations are agonistic showdowns in which the "issue" at stake pales in contrast to the pleasurable act of the exchange itself. Of their three major verbal battles (the graduation ceremony ending in Schiller's prolonged stay in the school, the dispute on Genius cited earlier, Schiller's final appeal for recognition after the Duke has read *The Robbers*) two occur before a diegetic audience. For both Schiller and Karl Eugen the point of each debate seems to be to defeat the other precisely for the gaze of the Other. The Duke, moreover, appears to possess an insight that easily escapes the spectator lured into identification with Schiller, that Schiller is a narcissist par excellence who circles endlessly in himself and his "work"; even his "Ideal I" Karl Moor is his own creation. Karl Eugen seemingly "knows" that he is a cathected object for Schiller only as long as he refuses to affirm Schiller's work, that acknowledgment would reduce him to the level of the others, rendering him meaningless in Schiller's life.

Another key confrontation between the two illustrates the Duke's imaginary projections onto Schiller. It illustrates his desire to compensate lack on two levels: his desire to possess Schiller as his son (the scene follows close upon one in which he remarks that he "has no son") and his desire to *be* Schiller. Schiller joins Karl Eugen at dinner, whereupon the latter insists that Schiller imitate him — a gesture that both fuses the two temporarily and underscores their difference. Not only does the scene again involve a literal audience, but the Duke, having thus far failed to get his hands on *The Robbers,* makes himself the spectator of another Schiller fiction in which he is himself the spectacle, he himself the subject of Schiller's fiction, which means the center of Schiller's world. Like all of Schiller's works, this gives him more than he bargained for; he is forced to acknowledge himself in the gaze of others, as "a buffoon, a harlequin," to use his own words.

During Schiller's performance the frame becomes blurred at the edges, so that we seem to be seeing with the Duke's subjective look into a new world he has forced himself to enter — a world of fiction that for the first time presents him with Truth. At the same time Schiller's act develops a certain parallel of desire between Schiller and Karl Eugen, through a number of double entendres applying equally to both. When, for example, Franziska asks Schiller/alias Karl Eugen what he "wants," Schiller's "you know!" attests to such a correspondence: Karl Eugen "wants" the son he doesn't have, for whom Schiller serves as an all too perfect stand-in; Schiller "wants" his play (which he believes is in the hands of the court). Both men's desire revolves around different forms of "progeny."

The scene is also rife with sexual overtones that determine the relationship between the two men; Schiller represents the phallus the Duke has been unable to contain (e.g., through mechanistic rituals of cadets wrapping each other's braids), and would doubtless like to be. Schiller appears as a sexual threat in his overt eroticism toward Duchess Franziska (photo 38), which also suggests an Oedipal repudiation of the Duke as father (a constellation then displaced onto a "healthy" relationship with Franziska's youthful counterpart Laura, but in which the transformation to identification with the father does not occur). Schiller's "playing" Karl Eugen also underscores their physical contrast with its sexual implications (which indeed is highlighted throughout the film, either through alternating close-up shots of their faces, or by frames showing them close together): Schiller's literally phallic form contrasts with the Duke's round obesity; Schiller is fertile with his "work" while the Duke, despite the cadets' nickname of "the golden bull," seems unable to produce progeny. Like the ancient régime of which he is a part, the Duke is a dying breed lacking anything to ensure he will "live on" as will Schiller's work.[37] In the final analysis, Schiller's other "staging" of Karl Eugen in which he acts out the motto *In Tirannos* (the death scene of Franz Moor we see in Mannheim) is far milder than the prolonged agony and *agonia* to which he subjects the helpless Duke.

NAZISM'S SELECTIVE AFFINITY WITH LATE-EIGHTEENTH-CENTURY AESTHETICS

Perhaps our odd fondness for Karl Eugen is rooted in the fact that his object of desire is also ours, and in our identification with the "tragic" impasse of his desire. Our knowledge of the deception underlying the cinematic apparatus tells us Schiller is inaccessible to us, too. Hence *Friedrich Schiller* has performed a much more complicated task than would have seemed possible: it indicts "tyranny" while endearing us to the tyrant; it sutures us with the Genius, while implicitly revealing his coldness. What the film does not do is to critique a patriarchal order. It implies that

---

37. I discussed in chapter 3 *Friedrich Schiller*'s invocation of Frederick the Great as the polar opposite of Karl Eugen. Schiller's reference to "the Great King" provokes Karl Eugen's infantile jealousy: "Great King, an exaggeration! He's much too skinny! Take a look at me!" The reference to Frederick's being "skinny" signals Frederick's ascetic, "bourgeois" lifestyle in contrast to Karl Eugen's excess, and the parallel between the "shape" of the body and the state. Ironically, the most corporeal of rulers is the *least* sublime, a connection enhanced by the fact that he eats and drinks throughout the scene (i.e., is obsessed with indulgence of physical needs, in contrast to the cinematic Frederick who, as his soldiers complain, rarely eats, drinks, or sleeps).

had Karl Eugen been a "different" ruler, one severed from the rationalistic philosophy of enlightened absolutism, that is, to exchange value and ultimately to capitalism, Schiller might have accorded him the reverence he does "The Great King," whom, as I discussed in connection with Frederick, he refuses to make fun of (although this would have "killed" the film, robbed it of a story). Most crucially, *Friedrich Schiller* does not repudiate authority at all, but merely exchanges one form of authority with another: the Duke's externally imposed regimentation cedes to the authority of Schiller and his "work," that is, to "German culture" specifically and "Art" generally. It is this authority that permits us a euphoric experience that hides its very nature as authority.

I would like to conclude by turning back to the question of the film's representation of "freedom" and "rebellion" — the concepts that generated Rudolf Oertel's defense of the film and that at times bring Nazi rhetoric so precariously close to a "democratic" discourse. David Stewart Hull tells us that "as originally shown, the movie's last word was Schiller's whispered 'Freiheit' as he escaped the duke's domains, but Goebbels' censors caught the line and cut it."[38] It seems odd that Goebbels would bother to cut the word *Freiheit* in a film in which "freedom" is such a central motif. But what is freedom in this film? It is something subversive only if we read the Duke and his school as a stand-in for Nazism, which, as we have seen, runs up against many features of the text. The notion of freedom left over is not only abstract, typified by phrases like "justice for the world" and "freedom for my spirit," but more importantly it is an aesthetic gesture, an expressive outlet compensating for experiences in other realms that can easily be translated into an activism that is itself aesthetic. This aesthetic gesture of freedom, which the cumulus clouds in the film's final frames echo, becomes what Herbert Marcuse once called a "self-validating hypothesis," a ritualized formula, which, if incessantly repeated, becomes a "hypnotic definition or dictation."[39] The state of euphoria aspired to by the repetition of aesthetic experience is implicitly "free": of external coercion, of occupational or institutional constraints; it is a form of rebellion.

Schiller's early work plays right into this aestheticization of rebellion. His vehement protest against alienation expressed itself in personalized narratives which lent themselves to appropriation, even if in a reductive,

38. Hull, 184.
39. *One Dimensional Man* (Boston: Beacon, 1964), 14.

sentimentalized form, by Nazism's "harmony" rhetoric. Schiller's "The Stage as a Moral Institution" (*Die Schaubühne als eine moralische Anstalt betrachtet*, 1784), for example, describes an impassioned vision of community via aesthetic experience, and invokes a similar narrative opposition as we have seen throughout the films in this study, between "nature" and alienation:

> Effeminate natures are steeled, the raw savage begins to feel for the first time. And then, finally — what a triumph for you, nature! — the nature that has so often been trampled to the ground and has so often arisen again! — when men of all ranks, zones, and conditions, emancipated from the chains of conventionality and fashion, fraternize here in a universal sympathy, forget the world, and come nearer to their heavenly destination. The individual shares in the general ecstasy, and his breast has now only space for an emotion: he is *a man.*[40]

I am, of course, far from equating early Schiller rhetoric with Nazi rhetoric, which would obviously part ways over the term *nature*, over who belongs to "men of all ranks, zones, and conditions." Moreover, while Schiller, like Nazism, equates social health with the stabilization of the male gendered subject, for him this means a *reconciliation* of gender differences: the weakling is "hardened" while the savage, *Unmensch*, is "softened." Nazism's constructed "Schiller" perverts the historical Schiller's aspirations for a community transcending class division and exchange value to fit its notion of a community depending on the definition of and obsession with a "biologically" different Other. Yet, however incompatible the historical Schiller's project was with National Socialism, his emotional vision of a decentered merging of humanity accommodates itself to Nazism's concept of aesthetic wholeness as political experience.

More than "glamour" must have motivated the film's portrayal of the angry young man writing *The Robbers* and not, for example, the more seasoned Schiller of *Maria Stuart.*[41] An increasing awareness of social and

---

40. The German "Mensch" for "man" is, although a "masculine" noun, relatively gender-neutral, distinct from "Mann." Friedrich Schiller, *Essays, Aesthetical and Philosophical* (London: George Bell and Sons, 1875), 339; translation modified.

41. One Nazi film, *Das Herz der Königin* (1940), is a Zarah Leander vehicle dealing with Mary, Queen of Scots, but is not based on Schiller. It reduces the inner conflict between *Sinnlichkeit* and *Sittlichkeit* to a popular narrative determined by external conflict.

artistic commodification undermined Schiller's faith in the ability of literature to have a direct beneficial effect on reality (a notion that is always
prone to a hasty and untimely rupturing of the institutional boundaries
between the aesthetic and the political). Schiller gradually reconceptual-
ized art as the autonomous realm elevated above reality that he articulated
in his *Aesthetic Letters* of 1794. The later Schiller never abandoned the
idea of a relation between art and reality, but developed his concept of art
as an "aesthetic republic" in which the individual could achieve a balance
between the two sides within him/herself, between *Sinnlichkeit* and *Sittlichkeit* (in contrast to the emphasis in his early works on relations between individuals as a political metaphor), and which would be waiting
for a future when society might be "ready" for it. As he emphasized the
autonomy of art, Schiller increasingly stressed the importance of vehicles
that distance the reader from the work of art, such as the chorus:

> For the mind of the spectator ought to maintain its freedom through
> the most impassioned scenes; it should not be the mere prey of im
> pressions, but calmly and severely detach itself from the emotions
> which it suffers. The commonplace objection made to the Chorus,
> that it disturbs the illusion, and blunts the edge of the feelings, is what
> constitutes its highest recommendation; for it is this blind force of the
> affections which the true artist deprecates—this illusion is what he
> disdains to excite.[42]

The later Schiller's quasi-Brechtian insistence on the separation of "reflection" from "incidents,"[43] his dramatic focus on the contradictions
within the individual rather than on external enemies, and especially his
pessimistic, critical view of political reality were still enmeshed in the
aesthetic ideology I discussed at the beginning of this study, and consequently vulnerable to the kind of critique exercised by Paul de Man (see
chapter 1). However one might deconstruct his aesthetic of distance, his
endorsement of reflection and rupture made the later Schiller a less appealing subject for National Socialism, especially for a biographic narrative aiming at a subject effect of euphoric wholeness and indebted to the
"clear-cut" constellations of early Schiller (among others).

I hope to have demonstrated how even without transparent concessions
to Nazi ideology like the biologist rhetoric *Friedrich Schiller* puts in Schiller's mouth, it would have generated a sense of community by aestheticiz-

42. Schiller, "On the Use of Chorus in Tragedy," *Works*, 3:443.
43. Ibid.

ing Genius and history, by conflating the imaginary of the aesthetic state with reality. With all its ruptures and with what one might call a touch of self-irony, the film affirms everybody's favorite fantasy, the self as counter-hegemonic rebel. The next two films will carry on this aestheticization, only in very different terms: in one case the film's "true" Genius will only be a peripheral narrative figure, and in the other he will be a "true" but dysfunctional Genius.

SIX

Anomaly or "Fascist Delusion of Female Autonomy"?

Pabst's Neuberin Film *Komödianten*

Strictly speaking, Pabst's *Komödianten*[1] (1941) is not a Genius film.[2] It is a biography of actress Caroline Neuber (1697–1760), known as *die Neuberin,* who by no accident is never referred to as a "genius." I have chosen to include the film here because it follows the master narrative of the Genius film in celebrating Neuber's historical efforts to institutionalize theater as a serious medium. Neuber, too, is a visionary who prevails against a hostile environment; she is, like Schiller, "the way I *have* to be." More importantly, the film generates the same euphoria in German culture as does *Friedrich Schiller,* aligning itself with the late eighteenth century's aesthetic of the "heart." It, too, blends biographical events with stories from canonized literature, this time dramas by Gotthold Ephraim Lessing, who is also integrated into the film's plot (as is the early Enlight-

The title refers to an article by Heide Schlüpmann, "Faschistische Trugbilder weiblicher Autonomie," *Frauen und Film* 44/45 (October 1988): 44–66.

1. I am using the German title since it is essentially untranslatable, meaning a traveling artist troupe.

2. Nazi Germany seemed an unlikely place for G. W. Pabst, the co-founder of the leftist Popular League for Film Art in 1928, who was often labeled "the red Pabst" because of pacifist and socially critical films like *Westfront 1918, The Threepenny Opera* and *Kamaradschaft.* Pabst had been living in France when Hitler came to power and resolutely refused work in Germany. The war broke out while he was visiting his mother in Styria, then part of the German Reich, and he claims to have been effectively a prisoner, although many interpreted his film work under the Nazis as opportunistic. See Hans-Michael Bock, "Georg Wilhelm Pabst: Documenting a Life and a Career," in *The Films of G. W. Pabst: An Extraterritorial Cinema,* ed. Eric Rentschler (New Brunswick, N.J.: Rutgers University Press, 1990), 217–35.

enment writer with whom Neuber collaborated, Johann Christoph Gott-sched). In short, *Komödianten* operates in the same space as the Genius film, that of an imaginary collective history molded by the struggle of an individual for artistic autonomy, for the uniquely "German."

Having argued thus far that Nazism's construction of its imagined com-munity and its imaginary narrative of history is organized around a body politic, I want to explore what happens when that body is female. Can a woman be a sublime, fetishized object that is "more than herself"? Can she function as a site of reconciliation in the mode of Frederick or Schiller? If a woman serves, even rarely, as a subject and object of history, must we not conclude that the functionalization of gender in Nazi cinema is more complex than the usual arguments about woman's "colonization" would suggest? Finally, how does the inscription of gender in *Komödianten* fig-ure in its identification with late-eighteenth-century aesthetics?

My answer will be an ambivalent, maybe even confusing one. *Komö-dianten* is indeed something of an anomaly in letting Caroline Neuber play the role of historical agent with all its narrative manifestations in the Genius film, in particular, the exorcism of the private sphere. Neuber does provide a site in which social fragmentation cedes to imaginary reconcilia-tion in the aesthetic realm. The crucial feature separating *Komödianten* from a "real" Genius film is, however, that Neuber *provides* this recon-ciliation, while Frederick or Schiller *are* it, *embody* it in themselves. This difference will emerge from a reading of how the narrative and the camera represent Neuber, in contrast to Nazi cinema's representation of male Genius. Precisely the "techne" or effort Adorno laments as repressed by the genius aesthetic (see chapter 5) is omnipresent in *Komödianten*'s por-trayal of Neuber. However forcefully the film celebrates her achievements, it makes us aware of cultural history *as process*, not as the mystery that simply happens in Genius films. *Komödianten* thus covertly reconciles discipline with "antimodern" ideology; the internalization of discipline manifested in Neuber's "hard work" helps her deliver us into the timeless world of noninstrumentalized values (Schiller's work, by contrast, never seems like "work"). Neuber is neither fetishized as the film's object of desire, nor accorded the same enunciating role as Genius figures. In other words, while *Komödianten* illuminates Nazism's ambivalence with re-spect to the women in the forties, it does not constitute a radical reassess-ment of the feminine, either as body or abstract principle.

The limitation of Neuber's historical role vis-à-vis "real" Genius is al-ready implicit in the film's preoccupation with the institutionalization of art, rather than with Great Works, which remain the underlying presupposition of Genius, even if it is ultimately the Genius himself who becomes the filmic object. As the film's fictionalized Gottsched remarks, theater is "a forcefully effective instrument" — no less and no more. This focus on the instrument of art is also present in the film's title, which refers to seventeenth- and eighteenth-century traveling artists' troupes, the historical successors of the commedia dell'arte who were excluded from respectable society. Historically, Neuber was part of a new institutionalization of bourgeois theater that had a fixed social place — both literally and figuratively. Achieving this place meant freeing German theater from the buffoon tradition of Hanswurst, the German version of commedia dell'arte's Harlequin, whom Neuber (both historically and in the film) burned in effigy. Social status gains leitmotif character in *Komödianten,* as when Lessing praises Gottsched for even mentioning theater in the university or when Neuber calls actresses "more disdained than bums and thieves." Moreover, the film constantly juxtaposes (often French) terms associated with the older institution of theater, *Komödiant* or *Actrice/Acteur,* with authoritative terms like *artist* (Künstler) and *poet* (Dichter).

*

The film begins with a dispute between Caroline Neuber and Hanswurst after the latter disrupts Neuber's performance of *Medea* with his vulgar jokes, which, however, are popular with the public. Humiliated, Neuber vows to create "decent German theater." Her theater troupe travels to Leipzig, where they perform Gottsched's *Dying Cato,* but after an argument with Gottsched on the direction theater should take, Neuber and her troupe leave. On the way to Leipzig they pick up a young orphan, Philine Schröder, who has run away after her guardian tried to force her into an affair with Privy Councilor Klupsch in exchange for business favors. The playboy and theater buff Baron Armin Perckhammer falls in love with Philine and wants to marry her against the wishes of his aunt, Duchess Amalia of Weissenfels. Philine is separated from Armin through the intrigue of his relatives, and Neuber's troupe loses the support of the Duchess following an argument. Neuber is attracted to the Duke of Courland (the "secret ruler" of Russia), who invites her to make a guest appearance in St. Petersburg. The troupe becomes involved in an orgy in St. Petersburg and Neuber realizes that she must return to Germany. Here she burns Hanswurst in effigy, but Hanswurst and his supporters burn her stage and costumes in revenge. When the troupe runs out of money, Neuber's actors abandon her. The Duchess is distressed when Philine informs her of Neuber's plight; moreover, she finally recognizes the sincerity of Philine's love for Armin. Neuber dies in a remote forest, whereupon the Duchess builds the German National Theater in her honor.

*

I've structured my analysis around two triadic character groups in the film text, which, in a way, is several films in one. The first, partially fictional triad is made up of its three women, each of whom is encoded in a different patriarchal narrative paradigm: Neuber in a Genius/Leader narrative; Philine in the bourgeois tragedy; the Duchess both in the latter and, at least semiotically, in a soldierly paradigm. In each case the woman occupies (or comes to occupy) what is usually a male narrative position, which forces her to oscillate between a positioning as subject and as object of desire (with all their cinematic implications). Since, however, women dominate all three of these narratives, to a degree gender is displaced as the film's thematic focal point. The second, historical triad (Neuber-Gottsched-Lessing), which I defer to the end of the chapter, restores gender as a principle of stratification. This configuration again valorizes the feminine as crucial to German cultural history, but maintains a hierarchy of historical agency in which the masculine dominates. Finally, in fictionalizing history while feigning authenticity, it supports Nazism's aestheticization of politics.

"AN DER IST EIN MANN VERLOREN GEGANGEN": NEUBERIN

Caroline Neuber (Käthe Dorsch) "breaks the rules" of gender coding, particularly within the Genius paradigm with its standard dismissal of women as what Teresa de Lauretis would call "obstacles."[3] The whole point of the film is Neuber's part in constructing the narrative of German cultural history — a narrative heavily determined by a temporal dimension of forward movement, suggested by her motto "further! further!" (although this forward movement is *retroactively* "written" into the past), and by establishing Culture within "German" space. Neuber's narrative requires not only a rare display of autonomy (as when she disparages women's dependency on men, insisting, "If I had ever had to, I would always have chosen the theater over love") but the adoption of a "mythical subject" status, to maintain de Lauretis's terminology (following Jurij Lotman), a subject who traverses boundaries.

3. *Alice Doesn't: Feminism, Semiotics, Cinema* (Bloomington: Indiana University Press, 1984), 103–57.

To the extent she has any private life at all, Neuber is the center of a love triangle that again reverses "normal" gender constellations. While classical narrative commonly juxtaposes two women (i.e., male projections of women) competing over a male figure, *Komödianten* juxtaposes two examples of what one might, in an ironic reversal of Silvia Bovenschen's model, call "imagined masculinity."[4] On the one hand is Neuber's husband Johannes, whose main function is to demonstrate her subjugation of the private to the public: Johannes *is the wife*,[5] the one who sacrifices personal needs for Neuber's "higher" cause. On the other hand is the sexualized Duke of Courland, who attempts to drive Neuber back into the private sphere. The Duke (Gustav Diessl) might have stepped off of the set of Joseph von Sternberg's *The Scarlet Empress* (1934), so strikingly does he resemble the Russian Duke in that film played by John Lodge, who arouses and betrays Marlene Dietrich. The interlude with the Duke is important to the film on a variety of levels consistent with its temporal and spatial dimensions: first, he is a sexual "obstacle" impeding the forward trajectory of Neuber's "mission"; second, he embodies the courtly culture that must be overcome by a "bourgeois" culture effacing class difference; and, third, he represents the geographical Otherness that must be contained in order for German culture to exist as community.

The Duke assumes his first function on a manifest level, providing a "love interest" that at once titillates the viewer and imperils "history." Neuber's scenes with the Duke are the only in the film in which she is treated as a sexual object, an incongruity that provokes Anke Gleber to label the scenes "visually improbable."[6] As so often in classical cinema, the Duke encounters Neuber literally as a spectacle: she is the center of a gala theater performance at the Duchess of Weissenfels's court, which is followed by an even more stirring "performance" she delivers arguing with the Duchess over the social status of actors. In this and other scenes

4. *Die imaginierte Weiblichkeit: Exemplarische Untersuchungen zu kulturgeschichtlichen und literarischen Präsentationsformen des Weiblichen* (Frankfurt: Suhrkamp, 1979).

5. In his sociological study of Nazi film, Gerd Albrecht discusses the relative infrequency with which the marital status of the male protagonist is even disclosed in what he calls "P-films" (films with a political function), while the marital status of females is always a central issue, reflecting woman's confinement to the private sphere. *Nationalsozialistische Filmpolitik* (Stuttgart: Ferdinand Enke, 1969), 147–54.

6. "Masochism and Wartime Melodrama: *Komödianten*," in *The Films of G. W. Pabst: An Extraterritorial Cinema*, ed. Eric Rentschler (New Brunswick, N.J.: Rutgers University Press, 1990), 178.

with the Duke, Neuber not only appears in lavish dresses underscoring her womanly figure, but is eroticized through framing and lighting. Elsewhere her clothing has a vaguely military aura, such as the travel suit whose buttons recall an officer's jacket or her rehearsal dress, which has a criss-cross pattern reminiscent of a soldier draped by an ammunition belt. The temporary shift in her clothing style reflects Neuber's status vis-à-vis the Duke as *desired object,* culturally coded as female, while her more func-tional clothing during most of the film accords with her role as *desiring subject,* a prerequisite for historical agency of any kind. "Functional" dress suggests a renunciation of specularity that, as Kaja Silverman has argued, is more accurately readable as a *disavowal* of specularity essential to the illusion of mastery; the male subject wants to "see himself (and thus be seen) as 'the one who looks at women.' "[7]

The Duke's eroticism can be read allegorically, allowing him to repre-sent the eroticization of the arts (as *divertissement*) as it functioned histor-ically in courtly culture through the eighteenth century. The opposition between the Duke and Neuber is thus in effect that between an art sub-jected to class-specific interests and one which functions autonomously. Like *Friedrich Schiller, Komödianten* champions autonomous art by link-ing the Duke's notion of art as power with the courtly, the political, the erotic, and the alien: "You evoke passions, I tame them; you free feelings, I use them. Art and politics are related; both want to rule man."[8] In this sense he is not only a personal but a historical obstacle retarding the development of a powerful (autonomous) artistic culture in Germany — one complicated by the film's semiotic play with geography.

Friedrich Schiller also involves a geography, culminating as it does in Schiller's flight into aesthetic "freedom" from a space controlled by tyr-anny and coded as a "prison." Even this space is, however, subsumed under a larger "German" space which is retroactively unified in the mind of the film viewer; hence Karl Eugen's Württemberg is recuperable, subject

7. "Fashions of a Fashionable Discourse," in *Studies in Entertainment: Critical Ap-proaches to Mass Culture,* ed. Tania Modleski (Bloomington: Indiana University Press, 1986), 143.
8. Note the similarity between the Duke's juxtaposition of art and politics with the Goebbels letter I discussed in the introduction, citing politics as an art with which "a solid, well-wrought structure of a *Volk*" can be forged out of raw material. Gleber likewise remarks on affinities between the Duke's comment and "ideological assump-tions behind Nazi film," 181. The Duke is in this and other aspects a stand-in for the "Jew," onto whom Nazism's "real" self is displaced.

to correction over time. *Komödianten*'s Eastern space is, by contrast, irreducibly Other, nonrecuperable, and thus capable of impeding the progress on which the narrative depends. The East with its "subhuman" inhabitants is here linked with a Dionysian abandonment of boundaries, a pursuit of (sexual) pleasure, and with the amorality of courtly culture, standing since the eighteenth century in opposition to bourgeois "virtue." Much like Nazism's fantasy of the "Jew," the xenophobic portrayal of the East as the site of dissolution is structurally necessary as a negative social fantasy (complemented by the "organic" unity of the German People as its *positive* form). As the Other of the Nation, it helps embody that very Nation as a geographic space securing individuals in a collective. Moreover, by linking the Duke with courtly art as the sphere of the erotic, excessive, and dissolute, *Komödianten* displaces the historical opposition between the courtly and bourgeois institutions of art onto an *ahistorical* opposition between power and creativity, between "lust" and "virtue," in which lust is a degenerative force eroding biological and spiritual strength. The film implies that both art and the erotic must be contained as threats to internal autonomy; the spheres of the self and of art appear homologous (hence the Duke's double function as erotic and artistic threat).

Neuber's trip to St. Petersburg, essentially a mise-en-scène of Spengler's theory of Eastern depravity not uncommon in Nazi cinema (cf. *Fridericus,* Karl Ritter's *Cadets,* 1941), equates abandonment of *Heimat* with loss of self. The monumentality of the mainly interior sets in the St. Petersburg sequence underscores the overpowering effect of this "wild and alien" environment on the characters.[9] (They also recall the stylized sets of Sternberg's *The Scarlet Empress,* reflecting the "gift for sensualizing the sordid" that Raymond Durgnat ascribes to Sternberg and Pabst.)[10] Neuber's in-

9. Cf. the visual relief to the massive, overpowering studio sets of the Russian sequence provided by Germany's "fresh air" in the subsequent sequence when the troupe returns home and is forced to perform outside. This contrast may seem contradictory to Nazism's well-known endorsement of monumentalism in art and architecture. Grand-scale interiors tend in Nazi films to characterize the lifestyle of the self-aggrandizing and materialistic (indeed, the huge chest opened in *Komödianten*'s Russian sequence to reveal lavish costumes recalls the chest in which Süss Oppenheimer hides his wealth in *Jew Süss;* in both cases the chests suggest excess and materialistic values). The grandiosity of Nazi art by contrast celebrates either the alleged apotheosis of the Germanic "race" or an embodiment of the Nazi state (which is by definition seen as a pure expression of the People), but remains confined to an exterior, public sphere. The collision of interiority and monumentality in Nazi cinema tends to disrupt the nurturance of the private sphere, ensured by a feminine presence.

10. "Six Films of Joseph von Sternberg," in *Movies and Methods,* ed. Bill Nichols, vol. 1

toxication with the Duke's eroticism culminates in a room dominated by a massive fireplace that dwarfs the figures near it, while the fire itself—its flickering shadow reflected on the floor—acts as a metaphoric extension of the "fire" within the figures, as the Duke orders Neuber to "finally become a woman . . . burn your life!"

Because of the film's homology between art and eroticism, Neuber's ultimate rejection of the Duke, her disciplinary fortification of "inner self" is as important an achievement as her historical feat itself; indeed, the former is the prerequisite for the latter. The source of her "inner strength" is her orientation toward a Thing external to herself; a desired object (German Art) which, if the film "works," should be transferred onto the film viewer. The object Neuber pursues is, however, future-oriented (albeit a future permeated by *timeless* Art), while the status she herself gains as a source of identification for the spectator is oriented toward the collective past. As an icon of the past sustaining the present, Neuber plays a role structurally analogous to the future vision that sustains her in the fiction. Through this process history is robbed of its temporality.

Paradoxically, the process of exorcising desire from the self that Theweleit describes for the fascist male applies to a public female like Caroline Neuber as well. Just as the fascist male violently annihilates the feminine within himself, retrieval of self for Neuber means doing violence against her own female Otherness. Gleber convincingly argues that Neuber's violent rejection of desire is part of a misogynist, masochistic scenario determining a film which only "pretends" to celebrate woman. Neuber's gender-specific enjoyment in sacrifice[11] is, however, part of a broader interpellation within Nazism to experience the superego's violence against the self as sublime enjoyment, as we saw in connection with *The Old and the Young King*. Consequently, "suffering," "sacrifice," and martyrdom run not only throughout the Genius films but through all Nazi Leader narratives (which does not, though, make suffering women "equal" to suffering men).

In charting the ideological configuration underlying the Russian episode, I do not want to overlook its ambivalence. Although the narrative

---

(Berkeley: University of California Press, 1976), 269. Sternberg likewise renders "Russia" a space of enigma, but of a more playful sort in which eroticism, far from being suppressed as in *Komödianten,* becomes a power tool with which Dietrich masters the Russian "system," becoming "a female Sade." Durgnat, 267.

11. This is a common feature in Nazi films. See Stephen Lowry's reading of *Mother's Love* (*Mutterliebe*, 1939) in *Pathos und Politik: Ideologie in Spielfilmen des Nationalsozialismus* (Tübingen: Niemeyer, 1991), 205–10.

retardation occasioned by Neuber's romantic interlude needs to be read on a manifest level as designating "threat," it simultaneously affords vicarious pleasure and a certain release from the relentless ideological correctness of the Genius narrative. It represents a detour into a more familiar narrative pattern in which woman can narcissistically identify with her own specularized body but which also specularizes a male fantasy object, as did *The Scarlet Empress*. The eroticization of actor Ferdinand Marian I discussed in connection with *Jew Süss* transfers to *Komödiunten's* Duke as well: a special titillation precisely in male types who contradicted Nazism's "Aryan" ideal. Much like the ambivalence of Duke Karl Eugen in *Friedrich Schiller,* the Russian episode keeps the film going *because* it retards the "mission's" tedious linearity. The resumption of this linearity when Neuber "finds" herself likely evokes as much disappointment as relief in the female spectator at whom the film is presumably aimed.

If, as I have argued, *Komödianten* does not treat Neuber like the specular object "woman" and also not like the fetishized object "Genius," how does it treat her as body and narrative figure? In nuce, Neuber is the Mother of all Geniuses. She serves throughout the film as a spiritual mother to her "family" of actors, who are repeatedly described as "a herd" in need of "a shepherd,"[12] to the orphan Philine, the budding poet Lessing, and ultimately to the film audience. Her earliest scenes exhibit salient features of motherhood: discipline (in the everyday sense, as when she hurls packing instructions to her troupe), nurturance (as she picks up the runaway Philine), education (rehearsal scenes), moral policing (frequent references to her "cloister" methods), and, throughout the film, "sacrifice." In contrast to Schiller, who essentially operates alone and to whom others mean no more than a (albeit necessary) gaze of affirmation, Neuber depends on and is indispensable to others. She is a far cry from the Schiller inscribed in elaborately composed frames mystifying artistic creation. Cinematically, Neuber evokes "gumption," toughness, and a corporeality defined not as specular beauty but physical effort: she often appears exhausted, hair disheveled, yelling in exasperation; she is defined not by her Otherness but by her humanness. Her cinematic Otherness in the Russian episodes to which I alluded is that of woman, not that of Genius.

12. In the very first scene of the film Neuber appears on stage as "Raging Medea." As Gleber points out, no documentable drama of the period marks Medea with the epithet "raging," which links motherhood with irrationality ("Masochism and Wartime Melodrama," 176 and 261, n. 6).

The text opening the film prefigures the role that her narrative and cinematic treatment will sustain: "Caroline Neuber liberated the theater from the cheap obscenities of Hanswurst. Through hard labor she raised actors and spectators [and now, via film, all of us]. Without Neuber our classic writers like Lessing, Schiller, and Goethe would have found no theater to provide a worthy forum for their works." *Komödianten* reverses the trajectory of *Jew Süss* with its social destabilization wrought by the "wandering Jew," and that of *Friedrich Schiller,* whose self-extrication from an oppressive space at the end is personal liberation *and* a first step toward creating the community that will ultimately resurrect that space as well. Neuber's vagabond existence is, by contrast, collective liberation at the price of self-destruction; she takes exhaustion and uncertainty upon herself to provide Germany's evolving (male) culture with a *Heimat,* as articulated in Philine's initiation of the theater: "Caroline Neuberin! You were homeless, here is your home. You were without peace; here your bold spirit can rest." Neuber's feat, then, is to embody on the level of history and of the public sphere precisely the metaphoric status Nazi cinema generally ascribes to woman: roots and nurturance.

Neuber's death scene visually underscores this metaphor: she dies leaning against the wheel of a cart, oblivious to the legacy she leaves behind. The camera travels down to focus on Johannes's brightly illuminated hand grasping hers, which dissolves to a long shot of the newly founded German Theater. Chiaroscuro effects highlight Neuber's matronly bosom, and the subsequent dissolve virtually allows the building to evolve from her womb as her consummate "child," with the windows of the building radiating the same bright light as her breast (i.e., "heart"). She spends herself giving birth, paying with her life for her "labor" quite in opposition to Schiller's giving birth to himself in an eternal narcissistic spiral. At the same time, the shot of her death is centered by the clasping hands, suggesting that a historical "mission" requires not only the enshrinement of the historical figure as a secular saint, but the unwavering fidelity of the follower (in this case Johannes symbolizing the People). Neuber fills in for the female spectator also slowly forced out of the private sphere in the early forties, and the film's historical images provide a site of "rest" for all of the People.

PHILINE AND THE RECONCILIATION OF PRIVATE AND PUBLIC

As Neuber's functional double, Philine (Hilde Krahl) brings a different kind of temporal dimension to the film. Neuber is, in the film's present time, what Philine is to become at the end; Philine is what Neuber used to be, as Neuber herself remarks. Through this configuration we see then on a synchronic level the trajectory of woman's historical agency, which will live on past the end of the movie into Philine's future and the film viewer's present.

Throughout most of the film Philine plays a very different role from Neuber's; she is embedded in a bourgeois tragedy scenario in which she functions as woman does in that literature: largely as desired object. The coexistence of this story alongside Neuber's is important in a number of ways: it complements the latter by alluding to and valorizing the autonomous art whose dissemination is the goal of Neuber's "mission"; it gives the content and structure of the bourgeois tragedy an authenticity by acting as if such stories were "history"; in short, it helps to construct German Culture as cathected object. At the same time it provides (like Neuber's Russian episode) a more familiar space of identification for male and female spectators as theorized by feminist film theory, in which the male possesses an authoritative gaze and the female can enjoy her own specular image. The film "treats" Philine with strategies typical of classical cinema, in which the heroine serves as erotic object both for the fictional characters and for the spectator.

The ideological configuration determining the Philine subplot, borrowed from the "high" Enlightenment motif of the heart's triumph over class division (which permits a reconciliation of class difference via gender difference), complements in the private sphere Neuber's public struggle for the social valorization of autonomous art. In the name of the "family of man" (*das Allgemeinmenschliche*), Philine's love story elides class difference, but allows woman to represent the private sphere, compensating for the alienation of public (male-centered) life. As in Schiller's *Cabal and Love,* hostile forces stand in the way of this transcendence of class, typically in the form of aristocratic intrigue.[13] These impediments include Armin himself, whose social class determines his cocky, patronizing attitude toward women.[14] Yet in the course of the narrative, Armin, like

13. Concrete barriers visualize class division, such as the gate (marked by a conspicuous "X" design) to the prison in which Philine is held due to aristocratic intrigue, the gate that confines the homely cousin whom Armin refuses to marry in her aristocratic "prison," and the massive gate to the Russian court.

14. Again as in eighteenth-century dramas, *Komödianten* thematizes trust, especially when Armin's uncle persuades Philine that Armin is engaged to a woman of his own class. Philine possesses the absolute security of feeling characteristic of such figures as

Mellefont in Lessing's *Miss Sara Sampson,* acquires bourgeois virtue, discovers his "true" love for Philine, and abandons his lust for *divertissement,* becoming an "aristocrat of the heart." As in the bourgeois tragedy, there need be no "explanation" for his conversion to virtue; he is merely persuaded by the force of the "heart."

While the story insists upon Philine's innocence, the camera titillates the viewer by cinematically exhibiting her eroticism. Philine's passivity is suggested by the frequency with which she is viewed sitting, allowing the camera to "leer" down at her décolleté and voluptuous bosom. We are trapped in an ambivalent position of sympathizing with Philine as victim, yet enjoying her suffering and her softly illuminated body and sensuous voice. When Armin first encounters Philine, she provides a striking contrast to the promiscuous actress Viktorine, who disrobes in his presence. The first shot of Philine in the scene is preceded by her shocked off-screen voice ("Viktorine!"), which permits us to discover her with Armin as she sews — a domestic activity reminiscent of Gretchen's spinning.[15] Corresponding to Laura Mulvey's original paradigm, in which "the gaze of the spectator and that of the male characters in the film are neatly combined without breaking narrative verisimilitude,"[16] over-the-shoulder shots enable the spectator to share Armin's look (photo 39). These shots alternate with "objective," unclaimed shots of them both; nowhere at this point is Philine granted a subjectivity of her own from a cinematic perspective; only Armin possesses authoritative vision. When Philine makes her debut on Neuber's stage (and simultaneously her debut as spectacle for Armin), G. E. Lessing, a student and friend of Armin, raves about Neuber's artistic greatness, while Armin can only think of Philine's legs, exposed by her

---

Schiller's Luise Miller (*Cabal and Love*), thus initially refusing to believe Armin capable of leaving her. Yet like *Cabal and Love*'s Ferdinand, whose aristocratic socialization permits him to more readily believe the falsified letter portraying Luise as promiscuous, Armin "falls" readily for the intrigue. Both male figures have grown accustomed to hypocrisy and promiscuity through their aristocratic context.

15. Philine recalls Goethe's Gretchen in *Faust,* when a maid addresses her as "noble miss" (*gnädiges Fräulein,* recalling Faust's address to Gretchen) and she responds that she is not of nobility. See Miriam Hansen's discussion of the importance of the male hero initiating the gaze in classical cinema, and of how being looked at (versus looking) serves as an indicator of a female's virtue. Miriam Hansen, "Pleasure, Ambivalence, Identification: Valentino and Female Spectatorship," *Cinema Journal* 25. 4 (Summer 1986): 11–12. See also Mary-Ann Doane's *The Desire to Desire: The Woman's Film of the 1940s* (Bloomington: Indiana University Press, 1987).

16. "Visual Pleasure and Narrative Cinema," *Screen* 16.3 (Autumn 1975): 19.

39-40 Philine shifts from the object of the gaze early in *Komödianten* to the subject of an authoritative gaze. 39: Through over-the-shoulder shots early in the film, we share Armin's look at Philine 40: At the end of the film, Philine serves as surrogate viewer for the film audience, contemplating Neuber's achievements. The two women are historically framed multiple times: Philine by the door frame, the disembodied Neuber by the picture frame.

page costume. The comments not only highlight the difference between the two men, but capture the contrast with which both camera and narrative will treat the two women. The words also link the artists Neuber and Lessing as transcending the physical, with Lessing always remaining observer of — never participant in — human interaction.

In its quest for "community" *Komödianten* thus champions the valorization of feeling in Sentimentality, which is associated with the feminine and placed in narrative opposition to the dry rationalism represented by Gottsched and the vulgar un-Culture represented by Hanswurst. Neuber is the public spokeswoman for the "heart"; in the private sphere, Philine adopts this role. Philine's understanding through the "heart" transcends the discursive language of rationality, as Armin articulates: "You have a fine ear; you hear things that one has not even said," or: "Heaven made you more courageous than me and made your heart clearer than my understanding." Furthermore, in keeping with the role of both woman and art since the mid-eighteenth century as forces compensating for the alienation of a rationalized existence, Philine seems to possess an intuitive reverence for Genius. Despite her cultural naiveté, she not only "feels" (like Schiller's Franziska) that Neuber "serves a great cause" but seems likewise to sense Lessing's greatness. When Armin introduces Lessing to the troupe as a budding writer, Philine alone is privileged with a close-up as she, captured by a high-angle shot and veritably glowing through lighting effects, bursts out in awe: "Oh, you're a *Dichter!*" (i.e., poet, with all implications of the genius aesthetic).

Komödianten's exploitation of canonized literature reflects, like *Friedrich Schiller,* the "achieved" establishment or "containment" of the aesthetic as a quasi-autonomous sphere in modern societies, which compensates for the agonistic struggles and alienation of everyday life. However, the film's (along with Western culture's) mythification of autonomous art as value disguises this compensatory function. As the Other of the modern experience, the beautiful, which aesthetic ideology values over the sublime, connotes the feminine and provides a site for decentering experiences. Yet as such, the beautiful has to be contained because a victory of this (feminine) principle in society would undermine the balance between real-life delimitations and imaginary dissolution on which modern societies rely. Philine comes to symbolize the establishment of a contained realm of autonomous art when toward the end of the film she begins to adopt the unfeminine attitudes of her surrogate mother, Neuber. Like Neuber, Philine transcends both social class and the private sphere through "art": Armin becomes administrative director; Philine, artistic director of the theater that realizes Neuber's dream. In both art and the private, the feminine principle remains institutionally contained.

Reflecting the film's subtext of 1941, the domesticated woman plays a game of narrative musical chairs, displacing Neuber in the public sphere. Philine's transition is not a reversal of her role in the bourgeois tragedy paradigm but an escape and a mastering of it (she is about to direct a play based on her life). This transition, to which I will return, is the condition for the film's imaginary reconciliation not only between bourgeoisie and aristocracy, between the private and the public, but between the "feminine" principle contained in art and the "masculine" principle of rational delimitation — a coalition which provides the basis for the organization of society.

DUCHESS AMALIA AS ARMORED WOMAN

To the extent any woman has a male subject position with respect to *Komödianten's* bourgeois tragedy story, it is Duchess Amalia of Weissenfels (Henny Porten), Armin's aunt and Neuber's patron. The Duchess consciously adopts an enunciating role, designing the intrigue that will separate Philine from Armin, which she refers to as staging "a drama." As an embodiment of class order resisting all transgressions of that order (whether in the public or private sphere), the Duchess is another obstacle both Neuber and Philine must surmount. She demands that the actors stay within their "boundaries" and resists Neuber's claims to be the equal of any aristocrat through her art. She likewise resists Sentimentality's attempt to close the gap between the private and public, literally speaking of marriage as an institution of *Staatsraison* rather than "love": "Persons of standing are not asked whether they *like* their marriage partner." The camera's frequent presentation of the Duchess within or next to frames intensifies her narrative symbolization of barriers as well as her own confinement[17] within them: we see a framed portrait of the Duchess before we see her; next we see her approaching in a mirror (again framed) before the camera cuts to show the Duchess herself. Her own chambers are surrounded by large portraits of Weissenfels ancestors, which provide a formidable backdrop against which figures like Neuber and Philine fight for recognition.

"Order" for the Duchess takes on a phallic dimension in her soldier coding. In a performance so overstated as to border on caricature, she appears in military style clothing as the commander of a retinue in which Armin is a lieutenant, and displays hyperbolically masculine behavior; she pinches snuff and speaks like a Prussian officer. In keeping with this least comfortable "fit" between gender and narrative paradigm (and with the impotence of either her soldierly or class authority to vanquish "true love"), the film most quickly abandons the Duchess's "body armor," especially her soldier role, which seems little but a gratuitous subtextual allusion to women on the homefront (another function of Neuber's "military" clothing). Duchess Amalia's extreme masculinity unveils itself, with no more "explanation" than Armin's change, as a facade beneath which is another "aristocrat of the heart." She merely "hears" truth when she meets Philine, whose words sentimentalize the soldier: "In your words a pure heart beats."

The film concludes with each woman progressing past the narrative paradigm in which she has been encoded: Neuber is canonized, the Duchess feminized; Philine shifts into a "male" subject position. The chiasmic relation between the Duchess and Philine (the only two women "left over" as the film reduces its surplus of characters) manifests itself visually in their clothing when they finally meet toward the end of the film. For the

17. Cf. the Duchess's response to Armin's presumption that she, too, was allowed to marry and be happy: "And if it wasn't so?"

first time the Duchess wears a strikingly low-cut dress, while Philine appears in a "professional" ensemble with a black jacket and a lace jabot, not unlike men's clothing at the time and clearly in contrast to the décolleté of her earlier dresses. Moreover, Armin, the male who heretofore commanded such cinematic authority, is from now on bereft of any authority at all, either bodily or narrative. In a reversal of classical cinema's predilection for confining woman as framed icon, Philine briefly fondles a miniature portrait of Armin. When we see Armin himself, he has undergone a form of symbolic "castration": his arm is in a sling from a "Turkish bullet" indicative of his abdication of narrative power. For the rest of the film Armin takes orders from others: Lessing chastises his class condescension, the Duchess permits him to marry Philine, and she in turn refuses, echoing Neuber's frequent analogy of theater to lover: "I have already chosen the stage and must remain faithful to it." Philine dominates the closing dialogue and frames, which position her in the center of the image from an authoritative low angle (with Armin at the periphery in soft focus) as she appropriates Neuber's motto "further, further!"

Only in her absence and simultaneous petrification in an engraved relief of her head does Neuber gain an iconic status in some way commensurate with that of male Genius in other films. As Philine dedicates the theater to Neuber, her back faces the camera, allowing her to become a surrogate viewer for the spectator (photo 40). The frame surrounding the relief which we see in the distance echoes the frame of the door through which we see Philine. The containment of each figure by frames suggests less confinement than the historical inscription of their achievements in the world of 1941. Philine, dressed in a scintillating white gown, remains a spectacle while simultaneously gaining the subject status she was earlier denied; we see with her, as she brings Neuber figuratively back to life. Inside the theater, Philine continues speaking to Neuber, who likewise has "become" the theater that, in the Duchess's words, is "pervaded by Neuberin's creative breath." Though never able to master space in life, she is now atomized, diffused in the space by which she transcends herself. A long shot of Philine glowing from a balcony that elevates her as on a pedestal seems to look from an "impossible" midair position, from some imagined location inhabited by Neuber, who has become pure gaze, albeit a nurturing one.

The scene recalls the Mannheim premiere in *Friedrich Schiller,* in which theater serves as a receptacle or "womb" nurturing German culture and allowing the spectator, here occupying the space of an absent public, to revel in his or her cultural identity. Again the difference must be emphasized: Schiller is the Art nurtured by the theater and Neuber is the theater itself; moreover, the presence of both Schiller and a diegetic audience in the latter film is significant in illustrating the treatment of male Genius as special body, as Germany's "gift." Nonetheless, *Komödianten* has reached a point in which gender has been overshadowed by a Leader/mass distinction in which either gender is capable of assuming the role of Leader. Gender has not been replaced but displaced, a displacement made possible by the immediate demands of war, and more generally by modernity's institutionalization of the aesthetic as a stand-in for lack. Here the film structurally slips between the traditionally separate spheres of the aesthetic and political, as Neuber is infused both with the power of the aesthetic and with the implicitly political power of a Leader.

THE SUBTEXT OF FEMALE MOBILIZATION

Rather than reading into *Komödianten* fundamental change in Nazism's phallocentrism or an unmitigated affirmation of it, I propose that the film be taken as evidence of inevitable shifting, slippage, contradiction in the gender discourses and social realities in any society and particularly one at war. Many historians have pointed out the inconsistencies in the position of women in Nazi Germany.[18] Early social policies were aimed at removal of women from the work force and at promoting motherhood, which was rewarded by social benefits as well as by a hierarchy of medals bestowed upon prolific child-bearing women. Nevertheless, the Nazis were never able to stop the trend either toward small families (and a high illegal abortion rate) or toward the participation of women in the workplace. Even between 1933 and 1938 the number of working women rose from 4.24 to 5.2 million.[19]

As the war progressed economic demands opened up new employment opportunities and generated changing attitudes toward women, who increasingly worked in heavy labor. In 1941 Hitler spoke of the "additional contribution" women can make: "Millions of German women are in the

---

18. See, for example, Renate Wiggershaus, *Frauen unterm Nationalsozialismus* (Wuppertal: Peter Hammer, 1984); Annette Kuhn and Valentine Rothe, *Frauen im deutschen Faschismus* (Düsseldorf: Schwann, 1983), 2 vols.; Claudia Koonz, *Mothers in the Fatherland: Women, the Family, and Nazi Politics* (New York: St. Martin's, 1987); David Schoenbaum, *Hitler's Social Revolution: Class and Status in Nazi Germany, 1933–39* (New York: Norton, 1980), esp. "The Third Reich and Women," 178–92.
19. Schoenbaum, 185.

country on the fields, and need to replace men in the most laborious work. Millions of German women and girls are working in factories, workshops and offices, and measure up to men there, too (*stellen auch dort ihren Mann*)."[20] These were to serve as a "model" to other women. By 1943, Goebbels went so far as to state his conviction that "the German woman is determined to fill out *not only partly*, but *totally* the space left by the man who has gone to the front."[21] Goebbels cautiously reassures in his speech that Germany "need not rely on the bolshevist example," thus implying the limitations in the changed status of women. While it called upon women to sacrifice glamour and leisure to the war economy, Nazi Germany would never "hide behind women's skirts" (see p. 117).

Komödianten reflects the anticipation that women would necessarily assume an ever larger public role due to the involvement of the male population in the war.[22] The visual codification of the "public" woman, that is, her masculine features, ensures that the public service of a female is the exception in times of need, for example, during war. The film's mirror image of existing social relations, in which the various roles played by men are usurped by women, also undermines a nostalgic reading of the film as feminist. All components of social organization in *Komödianten* are represented by women: the Duchess as upholder of class hierarchy, Neuber as embodiment of cultural progress, Philine of private harmony. Because the forces of community, alienation, and class boundaries are all embodied by females, the issue of gender in the film recedes, as suggested earlier, in favor of other concerns. This elision of gender by no means suggests that the film "speaks" woman's experience any more than male genres "speak" men's experience. So-called male genres compensate for that experience (which is one of lack) with ego ideals no less contrived than those aimed at female mobilization. In the words of the film's Lessing, cinema provides

20. Speech of May 4, 1941, to Reichstag, reprinted in Kuhn and Rothe, 1:117.
21. Goebbels's speech February 18, 1943, at NSDAP rally in Berlin Sport Palace, quoted in Wiggershaus, 27.
22. Karen Ellwanger's and Eva-Maria Warth's excellent reading of *The Woman of My Dreams* (1943) regards the film protagonist's manipulation of her own image through clothing as a sign of emancipation, warning against the "ahistorical" tendency of some feminist scholarship to regard all Nazi films under a one-dimensional perspective of the image of woman propagated in the thirties, thus ignoring "changed social reality of the forties with its modified role expectations for women." "*Die Frau meiner Träume.* Weiblichkeit und Maskerade: eine Untersuchung zu Form und Funktion von Kleidung als Zeichensystem im Film," *Frauen und Film* 38 (May 1985): 67.

shadows "more glowing than the live person," images "more blooming than the source."

Mary Ann Doane has argued that within the parameters of dominant cinema the "woman's film" "den[ies] woman the space of a reading" by virtue of a dual maneuver: it transplants a woman into the space of action usually reserved for males (thus offering the female spectator an identification that does not force her to accept the "transvestite" role of identifying with male action), but simultaneously robs woman of visual enjoyment of her own body.[23] With its synthesis of "male" narrative roles inhabited by women and "old-fashioned" stories from the "school of feminine literature,"[24] *Komödianten* may have mitigated resistance to those positions which seemed to violate gender boundaries (among female as well as male viewers). This same synthesis may, however, have also contributed to the film's "overloaded" feeling that led one reviewer to complain that there's "much too much material there, and thus much too little that can be worked through."[25] Perhaps even more than in most women's films, then, *Komödianten* leaves woman "stranded between incommensurable entities,"[26] caught in a gridlock of conflicting genres in an effort to harmonize "female" fantasies with ideology.

GENDERIZING EIGHTEENTH-CENTURY AESTHETICS: THE TRIAD NEUBER-LESSING-GOTTSCHED

I want to conclude by elaborating the second, historical character configuration I mentioned at the beginning of the chapter, Gottsched-Neuber-Lessing. This configuration is crucial to *Komödianten*'s location of itself within a cultural-historical framework and to its ultimate phallocentrism. I should preface this section with a brief explanation that all three are important figures in the development of autonomous art in Germany. Lessing (1729–1782), whose drama *Emilia Galotti* I incorporated in my discussion of *Jew Süss,* not only wrote some of the most important bourgeois tragedies, but was a key theorist of bourgeois literature. J. C. Gott-

---

23. *The Desire to Desire*, 19.
24. Tania Modleski, quoting Hitchcock on his own *Rebecca*, in *The Women Who Knew Too Much: Hitchcock and Feminist Theory* (New York: Methuen, 1988), 43–55.
25. Review in *Der Filmberater*, Luzern, Nr. 12a (December 1941), quoted in Boguslaw Drewniak, *Der deutsche Film 1938–45: Ein Gesamtüberblick* (Düsseldorf: Droste, 1987), 450.
26. De Lauretis, 7.

sched (1700–1766) was less important as a fiction writer (he "borrowed" French classics, which he adapted for the German stage), but was one of the earliest bourgeois theoreticians (with his *Critical Theory* of 1730) and a tireless proponent of the Enlightenment morality project (for example, through the publication of Moral Weeklies).

Parallel to Neuber's fight for the theater is another story in *Komödianten,* that of Germany's developing drama culture. The film reshuffles eighteenth-century cultural history, transforming the early Enlightenment's struggle for bourgeois aesthetic forms (with Gottsched in the 1730s) into a "high" Enlightenment debate between rationality and the "heart" (with figures like Lessing from the 1750s to the 1780s). Besides displacing this debate from the second to the first half of the century, the film condenses it in the narrative constellation between Neuber and Gottsched, collaborators who parted ways at one point. The film translates their historical coalition for the institutionalization of a genre into an ahistorical, personal conflict, in which Neuber represents the position Schiller takes in Maisch's film (as Gottsched's contemporary, Neuber predated such a stress of affective art). By allowing a woman to serve as its central defender of a "heart" that surmounts Gottsched's male rationalism, *Komödianten* valorizes the feminine as a principle encompassing the affective, the intuitive, and a space of dissolution in the "dark" realm of the aesthetic. This celebration of the feminine is equivocated by the film's integration of the third member of the triad, as I will elaborate.

In its strategy of transforming the diachronic into a synchronic, gender-based constellation, *Komödianten* resorts to several historical distortions. First, it lends a xenophobic dimension to the respective aesthetic positions, articulating the Gottsched/Neuber debate as a competition between French and German drama. Just as it associates courtly art with the East, the film projects onto autonomous art a containment within a defined geographic "German" space. The presupposition in the fact that the two figures standing for "heart," Neuber and Lessing, fight for the "German" over the "French" is an equation of the "German" with the "universally human," analogous to Sentimentality's equation of the bourgeois with the universally human. The film's fictional coalition of the "German"/Neuber/Lessing (whose mother/son relationship also suggests "family") against the "French"/Gottsched (who appears childless, effectively impotent) is all the more remarkable in that the historical Lessing rejected Gottsched's French (aristocratic) dramatic model in favor of an English (bourgeois) rather than a German model.

Komödianten reinstates a bogus temporal dimension in the age configuration of the figures vis-à-vis their aesthetic position. Although Gott-sched, born in 1700, was three years younger than Neuber (1697), he appears as a bald old man, definitely "beyond" sexuality. The age differ-ence between the two stands metaphorically for the old being superseded by the new; in this case early Enlightenment, the logocentric, by Senti-mentality — albeit twenty or thirty years too early and using (partially) the wrong figures. Not only does the film render Gottsched old and outdated with his adaptation of a foreign drama, *Dying Cato* (1730), which indeed had the reputation of being the product of "scissors and paste"; it depicts his attitude toward the public as one of arrogance toward "dull, stolid masses," whereas historically his condemnation of the masses' lack of "taste" was based on a (for its time) progressive faith in education to improve that taste.[27]

Neuber's defense of the People's intuitive appreciation of art inter-mingles the discourse of late-eighteenth-century aestheticians with Nazi *Volk* rhetoric — insinuating, like *Friedrich Schiller,* that aesthetic instinct need not, indeed cannot, be taught rationally. Neuber imagines her art as the People's "voice": "They sit down there and wait for their dark feeling to be illuminated, their dull thoughts to be sharpened, their silent mouth to speak the words it couldn't form until then. . . . I want the mute Ger-many to begin to speak." Sentimentality's valorization of intuition rever-berates in Neuber's implication that "speaking" is not achieved merely discursively but through the "heart," through that which is always already present outside of discourse as "dark feeling." Her defense of the elision of class distinctions through art echoes thinkers like J. M. von Loen, who wrote that "no one can express nobility who is not noble himself or por-tray the sublime if he has not the sublime within him. . . . The great artist is himself a high aristocrat."[28] From a historical perspective, these ideas

27. Gottsched's remark in the film — "Theater is not the mirror of life. Life is filthy, only art is pure" — is at odds with the historical Gottsched's vision of art as a medium that could directly influence "life" for the better. Art as an autonomous sphere in itself would have had no legitimation for Gottsched; the words this film puts in his mouth would better suit a Novalis or a Schlegel.

28. Cf. von Loen's *Aristocracy:* "[Virtue] alone is of noble birth, because it stems from heaven. . . . This nobility is possessed by all pious and wise people" (Ulm, 1752), quoted in Jochen Schulte-Sasse, *Literarische Struktur und historisch-sozialer Kontext: Zum Beispiel Lessings "Emilia Galotti"* (Paderborn: Schöningh, 1975), 23. Neuber's insistence against the Duchess that being "chosen" for art supersedes being born to nobility recalls structurally and in its biologistic dimension Schiller's argument with the Duke over the nature of Genius.

should go hand in hand with Lessing's theorization of art as a medium for "practicing" the disposition of sympathy and virtue, rather than as one that could be dispensed with once society had received its (rational) message — as implied by early Enlightenment.

Before discussing Lessing's role in *Komödianten,* I want to turn briefly to a fourth figure I left out of my historical configuration, Hanswurst, in part because he is a historical theatrical figure but not a (single) historical individual (although the film's Hanswurst has a historical basis in an actor named Müller who became the director of a troupe rivaling Neuber's). Hanswurst, more allegory than real person, is important as the principle against which Neuber (and implicitly Gottsched and Lessing) fights. Hanswurst, too, has a temporal dimension, existing as a leftover from an early, primitive art form before art became Art, symbolized by his vulgarity, which is another manifestation (complementing the Eastern Duke's more refined eroticism) of the sensuality threatening autonomous art. He literally embodies primitivity, as illustrated by his (and the camera's) constant foregrounding of his buttocks. A small heart is sewn into the seat of his costume, a mockery of Sentimentality's "heart."

His existence as surplus from an era predating the autonomy of the aesthetic puts Hanswurst right off the "map" on which I have charted the Neuber-Gottsched-Lessing configuration. More important for Neuber than his vulgarity is his singular lack: he lacks a future orientation toward an external Thing that is to become German Culture. Not only is he not oriented toward a Thing, but he lacks the thing that drives Neuber and the narrative forward: *Sehnsucht* or "yearning," to reiterate Neuber's condemnation of him. Hanswurst coexists, however uncomfortably, with Neuber-Gottsched-Lessing on a synchronic level as another institution of art and as a carnivalesque aesthetic principle that ruptures aesthetic boundaries, and hence must be contained (and never is).

If one departs from the manifest level and again considers the subtextual, one might, very cautiously, consider elements of subversion in the carnivalesque Hanswurst figure, analogous to a segment which Régine Friedman refers to as a "zone of disturbance"[29] in Pabst's other existent Nazi film, *Paracelsus* (1943), a biography of the sixteenth-century physician Theophrastus Bombastus von Hohenheim. Narrative movement is arrested in this segment. It begins with a dance of death orchestrated by Paracelsus's doppelgänger Fliegenbein, in which townspeople dance

---

29. "*Ecce Ingenium Teutonicum: Paracelsus,*" in *The Films of G. W. Pabst,* ed. Eric Rentschler, 184.

41 *Komödianten:* Hanswurst's head resembles an obscene baby whose physicality may be read as a deconstruction of Neuber's immaculate conception.

themselves into a convulsive state, and ends with a procession of flagellants. Friedman theorizes these episodes as a *mise-en-abyme* that repeats and condenses the narrative while reflecting on it, that consequently "at once reveals and subverts the textual workings of the film," in which bodies display the conflicting desire "to be liberated, but also to be disciplined and punished."[30] Similarly, Sheila Johnson grounds her reading of *Paracelsus*'s "ideological ambiguity" in Bakhtin's notion of the carnivalesque, citing Fliegenbein as a "Menippean" figure, a double explicitly undermining the authority of the film's dominant ideology, particularly if one reads the episodes as a metaphor for Nazism as mass psychosis.[31]

Keeping in mind all the risks involved in subtextual readings (above all, one's own participation in a Genius aesthetic in which we aspire to make the filmic Genius Pabst "say it ain't so"), I want to point to structural parallels in Hanswurst's carnivalesque presence that might render him a "figure of disturbance." Like Fliegenbein, Hanswurst is an inverted doppelgänger for Neuber, as corporeal as she is violent in her rejection of the corporeal; note his response to her insistence that theater should "elevate" — taking the term literally in reference to the sexualizing effect of his humor. He is outside of social authority (especially "decency"), observing and persistently mocking the "seriousness" of Neuber's Führer qualities. As with Fliegenbein, the film equates his art with all that is natural, spontaneous, and funny, symbolized by the "magic" fool's costume, confiscated by Neuber, full of "jokes and buffoonery."

Hanswurst's disruption of Neuber's awkward histrionics at the begin-

---

30. Ibid., 196.
31. "Ideological Ambiguity in Pabst's *Paracelsus*," *Monatshefte* 83.2 (Summer 1991): 104–26.

ning of the film exhibits a misogyny which Gleber rightly critiques,[32] but also a deconstruction of everything the film "stands for": historical Personality, deification, and sublimation of the physical (the "great Columbus" yields to his "needs" and "shits on the God Neptune"). His gesture of thrusting his round, bald head through the stage curtain like an obscene baby being born deconstructs Neuber's immaculate conception of legitimate theater (photo 41). Finally, like Fliegenbein, Hanswurst possesses an aura of immortality, of a being outside normal rhythms of life and death. He proclaims this immortality in the moment Neuber tries to burn him (in effigy); significant for a subtextual reading is Neuber's military costume as Diana. His comments that laughter and Hanswurst "cannot be extinguished by a flame" might allude to Nazism's infamous book burnings[33] (and Neuber's comment in the same scene, "Oh Muse of German Drama, you lie dishonored and violated on the ground," might likewise be read allegorically). Although *Komödianten* does not offer as consistent a basis for theorizing subversion as *Paracelsus,* it seems possible that more than one viewer was tempted to read against the grain of the film, hoping Hanswurst (if not the Duke) might "win" over both Neuber and Goebbels with his proclamation, "We must . . . drive out the Hanswurst."[34]

As decidedly as Neuber prevails when juxtaposed with two men in the private sphere (her husband and the Russian Duke), she is submerged by one of the figures in the second oppositional pair in the public domain, Lessing. In Lessing at least the film includes a historical representative of the Sentimentality Neuber predates — though not this early in his career, when he was roughly four or five years of age. This collapsing of decades underlies the film's most important anachronism: after Neuber's death, Lessing appears with a new drama written for her, *Emilia Galotti.* Since Neuber stopped performing in 1750 and died in 1760, it gives pause that a

32. Gleber, "Masochism and Wartime Melodrama," 176.

33. Pabst had built in such a reference before; see Eric Rentschler, "An *Auteur* Directed by History," in *The Films of G. W. Pabst,* 17. Hans Bock speculates that "Pabst played a tactical game with Goebbels, trying to avoid tendentious film projects by repeatedly revising scripts and thus slowing down preproduction work so that shooting never started" (Bock, 232). During Pabst's work on *Paracelsus,* Reichsfilmintendant Fritz Hippler wrote on October 5, 1942: "The behavior of the director G. W. Pabst with Bavaria is not in keeping with what we expect today of a film artist. . . . Production firms are emphatically requested not to have any dealings with Pabst until he has come to terms with Bavaria" (Drewniak, 92; translation from Bock, 232).

34. Quoted in Albrecht, *Nationalsozialistische Filmpolitik,* 500.

drama published in 1772 makes its way onto her stage soon after her death. Yet, if it is off-balance chronologically, *Emilia Galotti* fits in ideologically, epitomizing the "high" Enlightenment position with which the film as a whole aligns itself.

The sudden appearance in the film of *Emilia Galotti* is most amazing because in the Philine narrative we have in effect just seen parts of *Emilia,* which may have led a reviewer to remark that the film really boils down to "a series of memories from High School German classes."[35] Not only does Lessing tell Philine that *Emilia* has much of her "tragic destiny," but we hear familiar motifs from the play like that of "calmness." When Neuber remarks to Philine that she is "so unnaturally calm," Philine responds by directly quoting *Emilia:* "You call this being calm? . . . Suffering what one should not suffer? Bearing what one should not have to bear?" (V.vii). Lessing "overhears" Philine's quotation of Emilia's intuitive prophesy: "Pearls mean tears" (when the Duchess offers pearls as a bribe to Philine for leaving Armin; see *Emilia* II.vii).[36] The film then transforms its quotation of Lessing's famous line into the *source* of the phrase that reappears in *Emilia Galotti.*

Not only does *Komödianten* thus blend "life" and canonized fiction to create a nostalgic pleasure in "recognizing" a history that never was — analogous to *Friedrich Schiller* — it launches the same narcissistic spiral of artistic creation decisive in Maisch's film. A woman who "really lives" in the diegesis is canonized by Lessing in a literary text (which also shows up in the diegesis), yet the woman's semantic properties in the film are indebted in the first place to that canonized text. Philine's "life" is at once Lessing's source and his "product." Consequently, although his role within the narrative is peripheral, his presence gains immensely in significance with regard to the film's hierarchical ordering of "achievement." He retroactively becomes, in the moment he announces his play *Emilia Galotti,* the enunciator Neuber never can be, the point of textual origin both inside and outside of the film text itself.

Where does this leave woman and the historical agency I have outlined? It leaves her immersed in history as process, as "techne," as implemen-

---

35. Review in *Der Filmberater,* Luzern, Nr. 12a (December 1941), quoted in Drewniak, 450. The reviewer goes on to recommend *Komödianten* more to "educated lay people than to the film connoisseur."

36. Armin's declaration, believing himself abandoned by Philine, that he will join a military campaign "down in Turkey," quotes from another Lessing play, *Minna von Barnhelm.*

tation. I have tried to show how to some degree all of *Komödianten*'s women transgress beyond the interior of the narrative, or what Kaja Silverman has referred to as a "recessed" area within the story to which women are usually confined (and thus excluded from outside elements of the story that seem to frame that recessed space).[37] The Duchess "writes" a drama of intrigue, provides its central prop (the pearls that "mean tears"), and ultimately changes its ending. Although Philine remains on a level of "fiction" both in the film's story and in Lessing's drama, she seems about to adopt an enunciating role (again on a diegetic level) *after* the movie, as co-director of the first performance of *Emilia*. Neuber, too, straddles the inside and outside of the textual space. At times she is thrust "inside," as in the Russian episode, but the whole raison d'être of the film is her escaping to the outside, her "historical importance." Not even Neuber, however, competes with Lessing as textual enunciator. The "Lessing" that exists in the film viewer's head remains so firmly "outside" the story that the film's Lessing never seems real. He is, like Schiller, incapable of "love" except of his own disembodied creation; he loves a "shadow" of Philine who, if she "really" escapes narrative interiority, will do so on his shoulders: "If I am successful, her destiny will become eternal destiny!"

With all her speeches articulating the "needs" of the People and her acts which allow her to "live on" as an "inspiration to all women," Neuber remains spokesperson, coach, mediator, nurturer, never enunciator. As an actress, she represents Sentimentality's valorization of the aesthetic, of feeling, all of which require "feminine" qualities of emotion and sensitivity, corroborating Alfred Rosenberg's remark that woman is "lyrical" by contrast to man who is "inventive, forming (*gestaltend, architektonisch*) and synthetic (*zusammenfassend, synthetisch*)."[38] As Andreas Huyssen reminds us, within bourgeois society theater was one of the few spaces that permitted women a primary artistic role, "precisely because acting was seen as imitative and reproductive, rather than original and productive."[39]

37. *The Acoustic Mirror: The Female Voice in Psychoanalysis and Cinema* (Bloomington: University of Indiana Press, 1988), 54.

38. Alfred Rosenberg, *Der Mythos des 20. Jahrhunderts* (Munich: Hoheneichen Verlag, 1930), 508. Nazi cinema's portrayals of such "inventive" spirits focus on male biographies, as in *Andreas Schlüter* (architecture), *The Immortal Heart* (craftsmanship), or *Paracelsus, Robert Koch, The Heart Must Be Silent,* and *Enemy of the People* (medicine).

39. "Mass Culture as Woman: Modernism's Other," in *After the Great Divide* (Bloomington: Indiana University Press, 1986), 51.

It is Lessing who provides the "sperm," the written word of *creative* genius that "immaculately" fertilizes Neuber's merely *reproductive* and ultimately *replaceable* womb, just as the film's opening text promises. This deification of his creative Genius is playfully suggested by Armin's word-play rendering Lessing's first name (Gotthold) an adjective: when Lessing rejects the supremacy of French drama as a typically "Gottschedian" idea, Armin quips back, "and how would a Gott-holdian idea look?" playing on the combination of *Gott* (god) and *hold* (loving or attached to). Finally, only Lessing is privileged, albeit seldom in keeping with his small diegetic role, by Nazi cinema's stylized framing of the inspirational act, as when he appears at a desk discussing his attempts to capture Philine in fiction. The frame is foregrounded by the diagonal line of the room's wall, and light streams through the window behind him as if to illuminate his creative impetus.

For all its role reversals, *Komödianten*'s tribute to a woman's historical role exemplifies Hitler's comment, "When I acknowledge Treitschke's statement that men make history, I'm not forgetting that it's women who raise our boys to be men."[40] While conceding that — under certain conditions — women may assume a public role, the film affirms at once the Führer principle and the predominance of male creativity, leaving Neuber something of a "fascist delusion of female autonomy."

40. Hitler's speech opening the exhibit "Die Frau" on March 18, 1933, quoted in Wiggershaus, 15.

SEVEN

Tribulations of a Genius: Traugott
Müller's *Friedemann Bach*

Friedemann Bach (1941), the only film directed by acclaimed set designer Traugott Müller, who worked with Erwin Piscator and Gustav Gründgens,[1] is one of Nazi cinema's most unusual Genius movies. It again fetishizes creative male Genius, this time the musical genius of Johann Sebastian Bach's eldest son Friedemann (1710–1784), whose life story was less well known than that of Neuber and especially Schiller. It tells the usual Genius story about a rebel misunderstood by an instrumentalized world, but with a crucial difference: Friedemann Bach fails as a Genius. This chapter will examine how it is possible for Genius to fail within Nazi cinema, focusing on three elements that also structured the preceding films: mastery of space, of interpersonal relations, and of time. I will read *Friedemann Bach* against *Friedrich Schiller* and *Komödianten,* demonstrating how Friedemann's failure to master these spheres culminates in his inability to embody "home" like Schiller or to provide it like Neuber.

Though usually categorized as a Genius film, *Friedemann Bach* turns the genre upside down, offering in place of authority an impaired masculinity that is exposed by a series of spectacles in the film. In other Genius films, the specularization of Genius is concomitant with his triumph, even and especially when that spectacle was designed to humiliate him, as when Duke Karl Eugen orchestrates public arguments with Schiller in *Friedrich Schiller.* Spectacles like Schiller's Mannheim theater premiere remind us that the movie is about the Schiller we've read in school, thus allowing him to transgress the boundaries of the film text. In *Friedemann Bach,* by

---

1. See Alfred Mühr, *Mephisto ohne Maske: Gustaf Gründgens Leben und Wahrheit* (Munich: Müller Verlag, 1981), 24 and 33.

contrast, putting the Genius on display reveals his lack as Personality and as historical text. He is repeatedly subjected to the gaze both in the sense that he becomes an object of others' desire, and in the sense Lacan talks about of being looked at from a place from where we can never see ourselves.[2] This gaze looking at Friedemann is, like the "Jew's" look in *Jew Süss*, a force of irreducible alterity, ultimately of "castration."

It makes sense that a film using spectacle as a form of humiliation will generate a subject position vastly different from that evoked by the preceding films, including *Komödianten*, with its gender limitations. Despite *Friedemann Bach*'s cinematic indulgence of its protagonist, Friedemann does not transfer the same illusory wholeness onto the audience as the other Genius figures. Consequently, critics have tended to read the film as a didactic "warning." Not being able to identify with a character as an authority figure does not, however, preclude other forms of identification; hence I will argue at the end of the chapter that the film's didacticism is at least partially overridden by a different appeal that seems to anticipate a female audience. In its very denial of euphoria in German Genius as triumph, *Friedemann Bach* offers its own kind of pleasure, allowing its watcher to identify with a feminized, "hysterical" figure and to assume the role of vicarious nurturer.

*

The film begins as Friedemann returns to the Bach home in Leipzig, having quit his position as organist in the city of Halle. A royal courier from the court of Saxony invites J. S. Bach for a guest performance in Dresden, but the elder Bach sends Friedemann in his place. Friedemann is a success at court with his innovative musical style. He has an affair with the court ballerina Mariella Fiorini, who convinces him to compose a ballet for her. The ballet is again a success, but Friedemann realizes he has "lost himself" in courtly life, and with the support of Countess Antonia Kollowrat, whom he plans to marry, decides to pursue his "own" music. He leaves the court and attempts to secure another position as organist, yet no church will have him. His last hope is a vacant position in Brunswick, but here again he is rejected, as the style of his music is considered too temperamental. Given a second chance in Brunswick, Friedemann attempts to pass off a composition of his father's as his own. A competitor exposes

2. See Lacan's *Four Fundamental Concepts of Psychoanalysis*, ed. Jacques-Alain Miller, trans. Alan Sheridan (New York: W. W. Norton, 1973): "Of the Gaze as Objet Petit a," 65–119, esp. 89f. and 103.

Friedemann's deceit. Friedemann disappears, ultimately ending up with a traveling theater troupe and making fraudulent copies of his father's music. The film concludes as Friedemann attempts to sell a manuscript of his father's, but is mortally wounded in a dispute with an aristocrat who insults the Bach name.

*

THE RELATIONS OF AN "IMMORTAL REJECT"

Friedemann's lack is not locatable in his biological "stuff," which the film takes for granted and again codes in terms of ideological configurations appropriated from eighteenth-century literature: a volatile, uncompromising music that gives free expression to the "heart" combats a rationalistic, centralized order offering only prescribed routes for "success." Although the historical Friedemann Bach's music combined as many "old" as "new" musical traditions, the film plays on his reputation for a "highly personal style of emotive expression," which has caused "some scholars to classify [him] as a proto-Romantic composer," and on his personal reputation as an unstable individual who, like the film protagonist, ended up jobless and hawking his father's forged manuscripts — although much later in life than in the film.[3] Much like *Komödianten,* then, with its chronological maneuvers, *Friedemann Bach* transplants Storm and Stress from the last decades of the eighteenth century into the 1730s and translates its elliptical, volatile style into musical "revolution."[4]

What precludes Friedemann from transferring a sense of "wholeness" onto his audience is his own split subjectivity, which is externalized in the narrative via a number of characters (Fiorini and Antonia), spaces (home

3. See *The New Grove Dictionary of Music and Musicians,* 20 vols., ed. Stanley Sadie (London: Macmillan, 1980), 246.
4. A further indication that the film attempts to lend Friedemann's music an emotive character "ahead of its time" is the fact that he consistently plays a pianoforte, rather than a harpsichord. Experimentation on the pianoforte had only just begun in Germany in the 1730s, when the instrument was not perfected. It found widespread use (e.g., at the court of Frederick the Great, where it was approved by J. S. Bach) only at midcentury (see *The New Grove,* 14:682–91). Friedemann's access to the pianoforte at this juncture is clearly anachronistic (indeed, most of the historical Friedemann Bach's keyboard works were composed for harpsichord), yet it enhances his portrayal as a "revolutionary" musician. The instrument is capable of greater dynamic expression than the harpsichord, which can neither produce significant changes in volume in response to touch nor sustain notes for a "dramatic" effect.

and outside "world," subdivided into church and court), and "themes" (rebel vs. coward). Despite National Socialism's rejection of Freudian psychoanalysis as incorporating the "dangers of the Jewish spirit,"[5] *Friedemann Bach* follows something of a "Freudian" methodology, tracing the roots of Friedemann's "psychological problems" to his family constellation, probing family structures like paternal favoritism and sibling rivalry. Friedemann is subjected to the gaze of a big Other, a world that annihilates him by holding up his father as a mirror. He seeks to maintain an Ideal-I, an *imaginary* identification with a pleasing image of his "own," rather than being submerged in an ego-ideal, a *symbolic* identification with the place *from where* he is observed.[6] In Friedemann's case this place of the symbolic is defined literally and figuratively by the Name-of-the-Father. He is most literally trapped by the signifier "Bach," with which he is incessantly bombarded, and by the demand that he "recognize" himself in the configuration accepted by other males, who feel "so small next to [J. S. Bach]." Like the young Frederick in *The Old and the Young King,* Friedemann resists the symbolic mandate bequeathed to him, with a gesture akin to the Lacanian "hysterical" question "Why am I what you're telling me that I am?" His failure to leap the chasm separating imaginary from symbolic identification, to escape the Bach name, renders him a permanent, dependent child figure who keeps returning home, literally at the film's beginning, figuratively at its conclusion.

Herein lies the film's fundamental rupture of a genre in which Genius knows no split subjectivity, no childhood, no "real" sons, regardless of how often it depicts father-son relations. With all his "youthful fire," Schiller never has to "grow up" or "develop" as a character; he surpasses in every respect his would-be father Karl Eugen, while his biological parents are expropriated. Similarly, the moment Katte dies in *The Old and the Young King,* Frederick essentially ceases to be a son (notwithstanding the film's ideological exploitation of filial sentimentality). He becomes essen-

---

5. Kurt Gauger, "Psychotherapy and Political World View" (1934), in *Nazi Culture: Intellectual, Cultural, and Social Life in the Third Reich,* ed. George Mosse, trans. Salvator Attanasio et al. (New York: Grosset & Dunlap, 1966), 224.

6. Slavoj Žižek, *The Sublime Object of Ideology* (London: Verso, 1989), 105. Following Jacques-Alain Miller, Žižek distinguishes imaginary and symbolic identification or ideal ego (Ideal-I) versus ego ideal as follows: "Imaginary identification is identification with the image in which we appear likable to ourselves, with the image representing 'what we would like to be,'" and symbolic identification is "the very place *from where* we are being observed, *from where* we look at ourselves so that we appear to ourselves likable, worthy of love."

tially parentless, like Schiller, totally centered in himself. Later chapters will illustrate how Genius Rudolph Diesel and Nazi martyr Heini in *Hitler Youth Quex* are essentially born grown up. Friedemann's status as son to the bitter end, his psychic dependency (indeed, the fact that he has "meaningful" interpersonal relations at all) precludes his "triumph" as a Genius, one of whose preconditions is the narcissistic spiral described earlier, often manifest in the narratives as the Genius/Leader's "loneliness." Ironically then, the narcissistic weakling Friedemann is not sufficiently narcissistic; he needs the one thing the Schillers and Lessings do not: other people. This latter form of narcissism is equatable in National Socialism with intact masculinity.

The film's gender configuration is more strongly indebted to the Weimar Republic's "street" films than to Nazism's Genius films, which often rob women even of their status as specularized objects. Film historiography usually reads the street film as an expression of male subjectivity in crisis, reflected in stories of a repressed bourgeois male who wanders into a dangerous, exotic realm and is juxtaposed by malevolent or benevolent females, often mother figures.[7] Throughout the film Friedemann likewise wanders into unfamiliar spaces, constantly in search of a symbiosis with nurturing mother figures to compensate for his lack and his loss of *Heimat* (his biological mother is effectively negated by his superdimensional father; she is a female lacking will, responding merely to male commands). Paradoxically then, Antonia Kollowrat and Mariella Fiorini owe their narrative existence utterly to their function vis-à-vis male Genius (as good and bad mothers, as projections of his "heart" and vanity), but they simultaneously wield considerable diegetic power — the condition of which is Friedemann's impaired masculinity.

The women's function as allegories of the two sides that will battle over Friedemann's "self" is already suggested by their physical coding. Antonia appears predestined for motherhood, for the private sanctuary of family. Her full, white dresses connote bride or mother (vs. Fiorini's feathered dressing gown and other erotic clothing), as do her soft, round facial features, which contrast with Fiorini's angular face. Antonia's hair is "contained," bound up on her head, whereas Fiorini's often flows loose, suggesting sensuality, abandonment, unleashed "instincts." Antonia's sparse physical movement suggests a rootedness and constancy recalling the

7. See Kracauer's definition and discussion of the genre, *From Caligari to Hitler* (Princeton: Princeton University Press, 1971), 157f., and Tom Plummer et al., eds., *Film and Politics in the Weimar Republic* (New York: Holmes & Meier, 1982), 61–68.

42·43 The recurrent composition of subservient malehood recalling Weimar cinema undermines *Friedemann Bach*'s overt opposition between Antonia (*above*) as the "good" and Fiorini (*below*) as the "bad" mother.

Bach home (marked by slow camera movement) and opposing Fiorini's restless dance movements. Fiorini's dancing further links her to Friedemann's aimless wandering, on which I will elaborate. Finally, each woman is linked metonymically with telling objects: Fiorini with mirrors, Antonia with a harpsichord — an iconography connoting domesticity and "race," as I discussed in connection with *Jew Süss*. Fiorini once violates the instrument, leaping upon it to kiss Friedemann.

The same two women are also readable as very much *outside* of Friedemann, as agents of the gaze that cripples him. Ironically, it is Friedemann's search for nurturance, for a site of decentering in the private sphere beyond the gaze of the big Other, that leads him right to its most imperious representatives. The first shot of each woman shows her as an enthralled spectator of Friedemann's performance; editing continues to alternate between one woman and the other placing demands upon him. Although the film clearly rejects Fiorini's demands while affirming Antonia's as "for his own good," recurring iconic and verbal configurations link them in their quest for power: several times we see Friedemann bow down before Fiorini, most strikingly when he kneels with his head on her knee upon agreeing to compose her ballet — a configuration which, as Kracauer points out, is rampant in Weimar film (photo 42).[8] He similarly bows to Antonia when agreeing to give up courtly art (i.e., artifice) (photo 43). Both women use virtually the same words in articulating their demands, Friedemann has to "just want to." Finally, female desire underlies Friedemann's most disastrous performances, in court ("for" Fiorini) and in church ("for" Antonia).

Finally, Friedemann's women function allegorically as anchors of the film's late-eighteenth-century aesthetic position: Fiorini stands for courtly art and Antonia for autonomous, bourgeois art, much like the allegorical positioning of the Russian Duke and Neuber in *Komödianten*. As *Friedemann Bach*'s main stand-in for courtly art, ballerina Fiorini commodifies her body and her art, which are inextricably linked. The equation of ballet with both literal and figurative prostitution recalls the diegetic function of ballet in *Jew Süss,* with its famous shot of coins that dissolve into spinning ballerinas. Both films associate ballet with capitulation — with a ceding to the Other's desire that propels an irreversible downward trajectory.

Although Antonia is not an artist at all — indeed, her one attempt to produce music sets her in awkward contrast to Friedemann — she intuitively "understands" real art, although she is only able to retard, not hinder, Friedemann's descent. Her intuition helps the film valorize, like *Komödianten,* a late-eighteenth-century emphasis on nondiscursive cognition or *anschauende Erkenntnis.* Just as Philine "understands" what is not said, Antonia speaks what Friedemann knows "inside." The fact that a nonartist woman stands allegorically for autonomous art reflects another equation of art and woman as sanctuaries from the strictures of modernity. Moreover, *Friedemann Bach* repeats *Komödianten*'s homology between an art and a private sphere that wants to transcend class divisions; Antonia's love story with Friedemann reverses *Komödianten*'s Philine narrative, in that here an aristocratic *woman* wants to transcend class boundaries by marrying a commoner. In Antonia, then, the film effectively collapses mother, womb, *Heimat,* and the aesthetic.

Music serves as a metaphor for the Sentimental community of hearts for which Friedemann and Antonia's love is also a metaphor. Friedemann tells Antonia the story of a lonely note that one day hears an answer from

8. See Kracauer, *From Caligari to Hitler,* 99, 99n, 157–58, 171. Cf. also the contrast to the similar configuration in *Friedrich Schiller,* in which Schiller bows down before his mother just as he leaves her. The frame at once renders Schiller a messianic figure and functions as a ritual upon which he abandons the private sphere.

another note, whereupon the two discover harmony together. His story recalls the early (historical) Schiller, who frequently used music as a metaphor for interpersonal and ultimately for social harmony. Famous lines from Schiller's tragedy *Cabal and Love* are paradigmatic for this equation of music with humanity: "Who can tear asunder the bond of two hearts or rip apart the tones of a chord?" (I.iv) or "How can broken chords bring forth such harmony?" (V.vii). As in these Schiller texts, Friedemann's anecdote parallels the search for a relation free from social constraints with a noncourtly (i.e., "real," autonomous, "bourgeois") music. Within the context of Nazi Genius movies, Friedemann's failure to attain more than a momentary state of aesthetic decentering—indeed his need of another "note" to do so—prevents him from becoming an authoritative creator of liberating aesthetic experiences like Schiller and Lessing, or even the provider of a space for such experiences, like Neuber.

Crucial to Friedemann Bach's allegorical gender constellation is also Fiorini's patron and Antonia's future husband, Count Brühl. In keeping with the film's homology between the private sphere and the public sphere of art, Brühl is at once Friedemann's sexual competitor and the most blatant opponent of his art. Like *Komödianten*'s Duchess, Brühl embodies a courtly culture determined to contain a culturally unscripted music, to keep artists where they belong, "in the class of comedians (*Komödianten*) after all!" Antonia and Art are parallel as the terrain over which the men's battle is waged; Brühl successfully counters Friedemann's threat to appropriate Antonia as he counters the threat Friedemann poses to the world of courtly musical *amusement*. Yet as much as Brühl is Friedemann's narrative opposite, his hatred of Friedemann is motivated in part by the sense of lack he shares with Friedemann, which he hints at in several conversations (with Antonia's mother and with a servant). To compensate, Brühl takes on the role of textual enunciator that again recalls *Komödianten*'s Duchess: he engineers a number of the spectacles that will humiliate Friedemann and his art, the ballet and his final spectacle of self-debasement before Antonia at the end of the film. I will return to Brühl's function as orchestrater later.

"EIN HERGELAUFENER MUSIKER": NARRATIVE SPACES IN *FRIEDEMANN BACH*

Much of the film's energy results from its use of space and a traveling camera whose eye penetrates further than that of any diegetic figure. Friedemann is, like Pabst's Neuberin or Paracelsus, a nomadic figure, with the difference that wandering in the latter films ultimately unites a dispersed "German" space, transforming it into "home," no matter how forcefully wandering connotes "suffering." The first shot of Friedemann we see shows his feet walking into the Bach home, a cloak hanging by his side, a highlighting of legs and feet that will recur. The fragmentation of his legs in these shots suggests Friedemann's victimization by space, the film's resurrection of an old wandering motif in which the protagonist is a circulating object suffering self-denigration and alienation (see my discussion of *Jew Süss*). Far from representing "home," embodied in the film by Johann Sebastian Bach, Friedemann desperately pursues it, as already suggested.

Moreover, Friedemann's wandering is not directed toward defined ends; it is as much a running from as a running to. He oscillates between different spaces that have little to do with the geography important in other films. In *Friedrich Schiller,* the partial space "Württemberg" is encased in a vise from which Schiller must extricate himself in order to retroactively resurrect that very space; *Komödianten* juxtaposes an essentially "whole" German space with one of Eastern Otherness. In *Friedemann Bach,* these different spaces are displaced into semiotically charged social contexts, many of which are present in other Genius films (courtly vs. bourgeois culture), but assume a vastly diminished role there. "Social Context" is hostile in the Genius films, but is always already superseded by the historical narrative the film audience has internalized; the hostile context is only "there" to get its comeuppance (even though it might, as in the case of Neuber and the Eastern Duke, temporarily threaten history). Audience pleasure is derived from this "past tense" of antagonism; we look *back* on the struggles that led to today's Great Culture. Suddenly, in *Friedemann Bach* we have a Genius film where context "matters," opening the way for a "psychologizing" focus on the dynamics between the individual and social forces. The reason each negative context becomes a "problem" is that it is not confined to an "outside" struggle (like Schiller's with the Duke), but exists "inside" the central figure (more like the feminized world of young Frederick).

Before proceeding to the relevance of the film's public spaces, I want to examine the comfortable, contained space of the Bach home from which Friedemann emerges. The film begins with J. S. Bach giving a music lesson in which he and two others are playing harpsichords, surrounded by a group of standing men listening with rapt attention. A slow camera travels past vacant harpsichords as if lured by the music, tracing the room whose open feeling echoes a music that is unbounded but ordered, pervaded by piety and humility (again reconciling discipline with timeless liberation). The camera finally rests upon J. S. Bach, whose dominant framing and illuminated whiteness (white wig, lace jabot and cuffs) sets him apart from the others. Crosscutting juxtaposes the open space of the music room with a small, separate room in which Bach's wife and daughter do domestic chores. The women's room "next door" is permeated by the music, which, however, remains at a distance, visually and spatially separate (only Friedemann will pass from one room to the other). The two rooms' contrast at once enhances the otherworldliness of Bach's music and Nazism's positioning of women vis-à-vis Genius: "Father lives in such a great world." Friedemann's unexpected entrance into the music lesson fails to disrupt its flow. His father merely rises so Friedemann may take his place at the instrument, a metaphoric gesture signaling the latter's status as privileged son, which is further suggested by visual parallels between the two men; Friedemann wears the same white cuffs and jabot, his blonde curls repeating his father's white.

Except for a love song Mother Bach sings, the music lesson is the only performance occurring in the Bach home throughout the film, a performance that is at once communal, and, as a lesson, more nurturing than competitive. Never again is J. S. Bach thus specularized, seen performing or composing; he possesses a mythical, "always already" stature that needs no demonstration. His cinematic privileging in this scene speaks of a hierarchy, but a harmonious hierarchy in which each figure is interpellated by his or her place in the symbolic. The exception is of course Friedemann, who immediately brings an agonistic dimension into the house, sparking rivalry with his brother.

Friedemann's failure to be interpellated by the place assigned to him determines his encounters with the film's two dominant spaces of Otherness, the extravagant Saxon court and the restrictive world of the church. Ironically, their status as strangulating social forces manifests itself in the spatial vastness they have in common — a vastness that renders Friedemann a small figure lost in space. The two institutions function thus as a crippling gaze, for whom Friedemann is part of the picture, a performer trying to live up to his Ideal-I. He is answered with an ego-ideal, with each context's determination to mold him as epigone or spin-off of his father; note the King of Saxony's remark: "Always stick to your father. There's none greater than he." The trajectory of the whole film is one of descent inverting the Genius story, proceeding from the communal performance that begins the film to a series of agonistic ones, each of which is a step in Friedemann's self-alienation. The performances have a symmetrical structure: in each context he appears twice, with the second constituting a downturn, a catastrophe (his ballet performance at court, his second try-out as Brunswick organist when he passes off his father's music as his own).

Friedemann's first performance at the Dresden court is thoroughly marked by the crippling demand of self-abnegation. This demand begins with the fact that he is replacing his father, about which the King expresses disappointment and proceeds to ask which composition of his father's he intends to play. Following the tradition of courtly art in the service of *representation* and *divertissement,* the court stages a degrading "musical contest" in which Friedemann is allowed to play his own music against that of court musician Marchand, whose clownish, effeminate gestures and appearance (makeup, beauty mark, extravagant clothing) render him yet another rendition of the grotesquely feminized courtly male like *Friedrich Schiller*'s Silberkalb or *The Old and the Young King*'s gamblers. The film seizes the opportunity to "blame" aristocratic culture for indulging the same exhibitionistic "contests" Nazi cinema relishes in all Genius films.

On the surface the performance is a triumph, the one time Friedemann appears to master space and with it his audience. The scene begins with a set of large doors that swing open, revealing a long, intimidating aisle through the concert hall. At this moment the "objective" shot of the alien milieu is subjectivized, as Friedemann enters the room, his back to the camera. He becomes a surrogate for the film audience, which experiences the overpowering opulent setting with him, augmented by the hollow sound of his steps traversing the threatening space (photo 44). The dynamics change, however, once Friedemann begins playing. He increasingly dominates the frame, "taking over" the room with his music. The camera, traveling at a much greater speed than in the Bach home, circles his head, centering the film world around him, and finally turns toward the diegetic audience now viewed from his perspective in an over-the-shoulder shot that literally "photographs" the courtiers, making them as much objects as they are subjects of spectacle. While remaining inside of spectacle himself, Friedemann returns the gaze, becoming a disruptive stain in their field of vision, a "subversive" (*Umstürzler*), as the Saxon King puts it.

Through a Genius "born" and not "trained," Friedemann turns what is intended to be courtly *amusement* into autonomous art, into something that, like Schiller's prose, not only rebels against aristocratic hegemony but bursts all social boundaries. A dramatic traveling shot to the empty

44·45 Though seeming opposites, the two spaces of court and church, in which Friedemann must compete, mirror each other. The symmetrical composition of each is foregrounded by a large aisle; the massive size of each dwarfs the individual.

chair of Friedemann's competitor Marchand signals this triumph; Marchand has fled in recognition that he cannot match Friedemann's genius. Yet the deviant trajectory of this "Genius" film is signaled by the timing of the triumph, which is not late in the film like Schiller's Mannheim spectacle, but "too early," launching Friedemann into a precipitous downward movement in which he can never "grow up." He is, moreover, thrust from the overwhelmingly male world of Bach music into a "feminized" space in which he is not only object of spectacle but has to compete with another as object, much as in a beauty pageant. The cowardly Marchand "from Paris" is at once Friedemann's antithesis and a doppelgänger making a travesty of the Ideal-I he holds before himself.

If Friedemann has "won" the contest, he has won it on courtly terms, and his disruption of courtly equilibrium subjects him to ever more scrutiny; numerous reaction shots before and after he plays document a spectrum of gazes that "want something" from him. The foregrounding of watching spectators in the scene is striking in its contrast with the opening scene in the Bach home, where eyes look two places: downward, in reverence (the listening young men) and into a space beyond this world (J. S. Bach and Friedemann). No one looks at another in scrutiny; indeed J. S. Bach implies the superfluity of eyes in his world of music for its own sake.

In his music lesson, he does not need "eyes; only ears." Ironically, the more Friedemann vows not to go "through life with closed eyes," the more resolutely he runs into disaster.

The film generates a series of metaphors locating the court on the semiotic map of National Socialist historiography: the labeling of the court as a "foreign" world transfers the geographic dimension of other Genius films to an institutional subcontext; the reference to Friedemann's courtly music as an "intoxication" (vs. his father's music as a "prayer") suggests it is pervaded by an Otherness associated in *Komödianten* with Eastern nonculture. Consistent with its "psychologizing" focus, *Friedemann Bach* also invokes metaphors of health and wellness: Once Friedemann has "found himself" with Antonia's help, he composes "as if in a fever," through which he paradoxically becomes "well." (Schiller similarly works in a "fever" of poetic inspiration, but "sickness" is foreign to a figure whose only conflicts are with external "prisons").[9] Significantly, Friedemann's momentary state of wellness is the only time we see him composing and playing without a fictional audience. Even this moment is compromised, however, by a dependency on Antonia for his redemption, signaled by cross-cutting to her. He fails to ever find a center in himself, needing something, someone external to himself: "I now know what I'm working for."

Opposing the court as the film's major space of heterosexual relations is a celibate space of institutionalized religion by which Friedemann is never "intoxicated." Although the film endeavors to portray the Bach home as "loving," the church is the ideological state apparatus underlying his "roots," the cruelty of which only becomes manifest in this institutional, public setting. Consequently, even before the film begins, Friedemann has had infantile conflicts with church authorities in Halle, pulling out all the stops in the organ and "drowning out the prattler," a clergyman objecting to his music.[10] The monumental Brunswick cathedral in which he tries out as organist mirrors, with its long aisle leading to the organ, the intimidating Saxon court (photo 45). While Friedemann plays, the camera explores the surrounding hollow space as in his first court performance. However,

9. Sickness takes on an important metaphoric dimension in a number of Nazi films celebrating medical breakthroughs like *Robert Koch, Paracelsus, Germanin,* and *La Habanera.*

10. Either Friedemann exhibits infantile behavior or protests against National Socialism with its prophets "spouting junk" (see John Heartfield's famous photomontage "Alfred the Superman") from their pulpits.

the terms of the church are different, with no room for (at least an overt) narcissism. Rather than swirling about Friedemann's head, the camera sweeps down the pipes of a massive organ that dwarfs him (this film's "answer" to The Old and the Young King's Potsdam bell tower). The gaze to which Friedemann is subjected here is less an interpersonal one, as in the court with its various reaction shots, but more institutional. It resides in the massive building itself, which is largely empty but for a group of stern clergymen, uniform in their somber attire and wigs. They appear as bereft of individuality as the masses of Saxon courtiers, whose opulent dress and wigs render them likewise homogeneous. The same music of "revolution" — a word repeated in both settings — that the court commodified meets in the church with a resistance as hard as its stone walls: "We are not looking for a genius, but an organist."

THE FILM'S TEMPORALITY, OR "EARTH TO DAD!"

Friedemann's inner split results in his forfeiting of both the forward, as-cendant trajectory that other Genius figures have and, more importantly, the timelessness in which Nazism's historical Personality (whether artistic or otherwise) exists. The only embodiment of timelessness in this film is J. S. Bach, suggested by the camera's farewell sweep after his death through the Bach family space, in which music resounds despite harpsi-chords without players. The camera comes to rest upon his portrait, which, as in so many films of the forties, "becomes the signifier of repeti-tion itself."[11] The elder Bach's death makes little difference in the film, however (except to the dependent Friedemann), since he always was, to use a Žižek phrase, one of the "living dead." His oblivion to earth-bound desire borders on caricature, especially when this man who only "needs ears" fails for years to see that his daughter wants to marry. Her "I'm alive too" in response to her mother's remark about the "great world" in which Bach lives has a vitalistic ring that overshadows its obvious function as one more relegation of woman to the "small" world of the private sphere.

Precisely because he is so benevolent and removed from human tem-perament, Bach is ultimately a far crueler superego than The Old and the Young King's Frederick William with all his external violence. One might read Friedemann's hysteria not only as a response to the demands of the world around him, but to the affective coldness that underlies his father's

11. Mary-Ann Doane, The Desire to Desire: The Woman's Film of the 1940s (Bloom-ington: Indiana University Press, 1987), 143.

perfection, to his father's disaffectedness by the world around him (an attitude grotesquely magnified in the Brunswick church). The scene in which Bach is invited to the Saxon court is telling: not only does he fully negate his son Emmanuel (responding to his anxious query, "Who will represent you, father?" by looking away at "Friedemann!"), but bestows a far worse fate upon Friedemann himself, whom he thus propels into the annihilating world of the gaze.

The series of tests that, as Count Brühl cogently remarks, Friedemann consistently fails ultimately have their origins in his father, as if aimed at containing Friedemann as a "too weak son of too strong a father." Friedemann's annihilation by and in the Name-of-the-Father displaces the Thing that might have sustained him as a Nazi historical personality (i.e., an external projection like "German Art" internalized in the self); in its place steps another Thing one might call "me." Friedemann becomes entrapped in a narcissistic spiral different from Schiller's, one of a self-pity that makes him unable to reach beyond himself and give "birth" to Culture as a clone of himself.

As out of step temporally as he is lost spatially, Friedemann fails to transcend either the negativity of his own diegetic time or the text itself (as do Schiller and Lessing through their place as sources of textual origin). Indeed, his self-reflexivity is in inverse proportion to his "achievement" inside and beyond the text; refusal to "recognize" himself as do the other Bach men launches him instead into a constant misrecognition and miscalculation typical of figures in melodrama. His failure to transcend temporality, for example, is an effect of his own obsession with a forward trajectory in the sense of "career": one of his crucial "wrong" choices (composing the ballet) is precipitated by Fiorini's repeated assurance that it will help him "get ahead." Never is Friedemann more subjugated than after his court debut when he echoes the Duke of Courland's remarks in *Komödianten* about art as a form of power over others. The more resolutely he promises never to "go peddling with music" (*mit meiner Musik hausieren gehen*), the closer he is to doing so. His own variation on Genius's narcissistic spiral ultimately propels Friedemann not forward in time or outward beyond it, but backward into the space of his origins — to a prodigal son status satisfying the sadistic desire of every male in the film, regardless of whether this sadism is overt (Count Brühl) or couched under the mantel of altruistic "concern" (brother Emmanuel, who becomes progressively "nicer" in proportion to Friedemann's failure; brother-in-law Altnikol, who subjects Friedemann to his last church debacle; and, by extension, figures absent at the end of the film: the ominously silent servant Franz, with his castrating gaze of moral rectitude, and father-Bach, secure in his omnipotence).

Friedemann's simple death does not suffice to satisfy the sadism of the film's enunciation; he suffers what Lacan might refer to as two deaths. Rather than dying physically and then being put to rest symbolically (through funeral ceremonies, etc.), he undergoes a symbolic death constituting an exclusion from the symbolic order (marked incrementally by the spectacles), and only later a biological one, eased by his eventual embracing of the symbolic. The first of his two church recitals constitutes his last attempt to celebrate himself, suggested by the camera's only encounter with his body. As it closes in on him, he watches himself intensely in a mirror that hangs over the organ, as if anticipating Lacan's mirror stage in the formation of the "Function of the I." The configuration invites comparison with *The Old and the Young King*'s striking mirror scene, in which Frederick William forcibly confronts young Frederick with his deficient image, with the difference that Frederick's encounter with the mirror signals an externally imposed self-introspection (indeed, his father stands next to him in the mirror). While young Frederick avoids his image, lacking a gaze "of his own" with all its phallic implications, Friedemann seeks to evade the symbolic imposition of Father, to make the image in the mirror fit an imaginary ideal he can enjoy.

This "last stand" is followed by the film's irreversible turning point in which Friedemann "betrays" everyone and everything by performing his father's music as his own — a "betrayal" which, as Friedemann remarks, is more "honest" in its satisfaction of the Other's demand than their feigned concern for him. Yet the camera punishes him more sadistically for meeting the Other's desire than for defying it: it responds by avoiding him completely, roaming restlessly through the church interior. It neither takes on Friedemann's subjective perspective (as in the court performance) nor privileges him with a close-up shot (as in the first Brunswick audition) but travels instead to a decorative iron fence behind which Altnikol and Antonia sit.[12] As Friedemann allows himself to be negated, the camera avoids looking him "in the eyes" and focuses instead on a symbol of the barriers separating him from the others and the Other he desires.

---

12. There is a parallel to Friedemann's second court "performance," his conducting the "nymph ballet" he composes for Fiorini. Again the camera restricts itself largely to impersonal long shots of the stage and audience, losing interest in Friedemann amid the spectacle. The few medium shots of Friedemann conducting never permit us to "share" the experience with him.

The second fragmented shot of Friedemann's legs, once he has left the symbolic map on which his various textual spaces were charted and has joined a traveling "Komödianten" troupe, marks his definitive state of "second," symbolic death; as if wandering in a void, he has landed back where he started in the film. His extrication from all the film's spaces is again externalized in a woman, his Gypsy girlfriend who "doesn't even know who Johann Sebastian Bach is." Friedemann regains his place *in* the symbolic only when he acquiesces *to* the symbolic, "recognizes" himself as "so small" next to his father, which is also the moment of his death. He dies not only *of* the Name-of-the-Father, but *for* it, his last request being that Emmanuel play a work by their father.

His impossibility of mastering time also precludes Friedemann's functioning as textual enunciator. He remains more the object than the subject of history, confined, like women in Kaja Silverman's analysis, to the interior of the narrative.[13] I have already discussed how both *Friedrich Schiller* and *Komödianten* are pervaded with a textuality clearly marked as outside the diegesis. In addition to its fictional play with Lessing's *Emilia Galotti, Komödianten* begins with an extradiegetic inscription celebrating Neuber's feat and ends with a verbal text doing so. *Friedrich Schiller* lacks such a framing device but is determined by the presence of another text that belongs as much "outside" as "inside" the film: *The Robbers.* Although it draws on similar literary paradigms (like early Schiller with his music metaphors), *Friedemann Bach* is not pervaded with such a textuality on a musical level — at least not a music marked and recognized as Friedemann's. The film works rather on a semiotic level, rendering Friedemann's music "revolutionary" via mise-en-scène and a "tempestuous" performance style. Yet to the extent that a familiar extradiegetic textuality pervades the film, it is that of J. S. Bach, whose music begins the story (his Concerto for Three Pianos in D minor) and often recurs. Ironically, once even "temperamental" music passed off as Friedemann's is in fact that of J. S. Bach. During his first Brunswick audition the music the clerics reject as "too" radical is J. S. Bach's Fantasia and Fugue in G minor, further confusing the question of "ownership" so crucial to the film.

In the course of the film, Friedemann becomes more, not less, subjected to interiority as the eternal diegetic performer, a role Silverman cites as one of the most prominent textual operations confining women to textual "interiority" in classical cinema. The performing woman is not only an object

13. *The Acoustic Mirror: The Female Voice in Psychoanalysis and Cinema* (Bloomington: University of Indiana Press, 1988), 54. See chapter 6 herein on *Komödianten*.

of spectacle, but her voice is "doubly diegeticized," overheard by the fictional and cinematic audience (a double-effect transferable to Friedemann's music).[14] The first time Friedemann performs, the film "acts" like a Genius film indulging the symbolic transference from father to son (Friedemann slipping literally into Father's chair at the harpsichord) of the right to perform for God, whose position the spectator inhabits. This, however, is where the Genius film should *end*, as does *The Old and the Young King*. Instead *Friedemann Bach* wanders, like its protagonist, from a Genius narrative into a street film marked by the definitively "woman's" genre of melodrama, to a biblical saga of a prodigal son. His father has, in every respect, the last word.

THE FILM'S SUBJECT POSITION(S)

The very last diegetic spectacle to which Friedemann is subjected is emblematic of his failure as historical Personality; it is indebted rather to the "too late" meeting characteristic of melodrama.[15] He arrives with his traveling "Komödianten" in Dresden, where Antonia is married to Count Brühl, but obviously has "never forgotten" Friedemann. Brühl permits Antonia to pay him a visit, during which Friedemann becomes rude and defiant. With his usual precision, Brühl calculates the encounter's effect; Antonia severs "herself from a man who no longer resembles his own image." The Count's analysis goes far beyond its commonplace juxtaposition of "the man" and "his myth"; the point is that what Friedemann has been stripped of is exactly "his own" image, an Ideal-I that belonged to him alone. With this final, castrating spectacle, Brühl sadistically stages the "undignified comedy" he purports to "prevent": that of Friedemann's definitive humiliation on the terrain of his greatest triumph, complete with an audience spanning the history of his descent from his "highest" (Antonia) to his "lowest" (the traveling players) point. Friedemann's second, transcendent body is as easily exorcised as his mortal body soon thereafter, since it exists only in Antonia's head and barely exists outside the text. For Antonia and the spectator alike, Friedemann fails as a narcissistic mirror affirming the dominant fiction that covers up male lack.[16]

14. Ibid., 56.

15. See, for example, Steve Neale, "Melodrama and Tears," *Screen* 27.6 (November–December 1986): 8.

16. I am borrowing the term *dominant fiction* from Kaja Silverman, who, following Jacques Rancière, describes the central agency of social consensus with which subjects

The question remains where authority rests in the film if not with its protagonist. Although a number of figures serve as "spokespersons" diagnosing Friedemann's split and controlling his fate, authority does not generally rest with the characters, especially not with those who win out in the film's various social contexts, to each of whom the film ascribes his own form of kow-towing emasculation — from Friedemann's dutiful and jealous brother Emmanuel, to court musician Marchand, to the obsequious, "squealing" organist Herr Länne who gets Friedemann's position, as much a doppelgänger for Marchand as the latter is for Friedemann. (Ironically, the film's best "diagnostician" is at once Friedemann's most hostile critic, Count Brühl). Clearly, authority does rest with J. S. Bach, whom the film privileges as much by what it does not show as what it does (e.g., subjection to specularization). Nonetheless, its "treatment" of the elder Bach as more deity than "real" human being precludes the identification I have referred to as a narcissistic mirror. His importance lies in his embodiment of the symbolic order, his agency of interpellation, of obscene superego.

Another answer regarding the film's authority lies in the institution lacking in its world and only implicitly, subtextually anticipated. The Nazis' self-image as the supporter of the arts, as representative of "community" and timeless values, suggests itself here as it does in *Komödianten* and *Friedrich Schiller*, which invites a comparison of Karl Eugen's academy with Nazi education. *Friedemann Bach* intermingles its critique of Friedemann with that of a social order offering only two institutions of art, both of which inhibit an autonomous art dictated "by the heart." Nazism's function as religion permits its denigration of institutionalized religion, supplemented by a critique of exchange value. In its disparagement of a courtly culture that pursues the "new" for its own sake, making Friedemann "*la mode,*" the film pretends to revive late-eighteenth-century polemics against the development of art as a market commodity, rather than a force of enlightenment. Eighteenth-century contemporaries moralized the problem, condemning the *Neuigkeitsjägerei* ("hunting the new," Wieland) of a self-indulgent public, as well as its tendency to "enjoy one's

---

are asked to identify as a fiction. The dominant fiction is the representational system or reserve of images and stories through which the subject is accommodated to the Name-of-the-Father. Silverman shifts the focus of much feminist film theory from the castration anxiety aroused in the male by the female body to a displacement of male lack onto woman. See *Male Subjectivity at the Margins* (New York: Routledge, 1992), 42, and *The Acoustic Mirror*, 1–41.

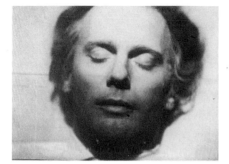

46 Friedemann Bach's soft, feminized appearance may open up a space of identification for the female spectator.

self" (Hoche, 1794).[17] The critique of the court as agency of commodification is again less a historical than an ahistorical one involving an unarticulated series of equivalences (alienation, exchange value, materialism, "Jew," capitalism) — the perceived forces of modernity against which National Socialism finds its identity.

Finally, a certain authority also rests with the spectator, not one experienced via identification with authority as in the other films, but by an advantage over Friedemann connected with his child status: the film audience "knows better." Critics have responded to this advantage by reading the film as an authoritarian indictment of lack and excess resembling *The Old and the Young King.* "Moral" character is at the root of the film,[18] which shows "what happens when the rebel does not submit to any kind of discipline and is not strong enough to combat the decadence or the short-sightedness of the world that surrounds him."[19]

This reading foregrounds the enunciatory sadism to which I alluded, one which affirms the side of Nazism stressing discipline (which Friedemann lacks, no matter how it is defined). It assumes a *schadenfreude* on the part of the spectator which the film may elicit, a sadistic enjoyment of Friedemann's humiliation analogous to the pleasure offered by Neuber's or Philine's tribulations. I believe, however, that the film's more dominant subject effect works in an opposite direction, evoking an imaginary "interactive" relationship with Friedemann as the film's cathected child-object;

17. J. G. Hoche, *Vertraute Briefe über die jetzige abentheurliche Lesesucht* (Hannover, 1794), 76.
18. Francis Courtade and Pierre Cadars, *Geschichte des Films im dritten Reich,* trans. Florian Hopf (Munich: Carl Hanser, 1975), 100.
19. Julian Petley, *Capital and Culture: German Cinema 1933–45* (London: British Film Institute, 1979), 146.

consider that scholarship invariably refers to "Friedemann" by his first name — a habit explained only in part by the need to distinguish him from his father. This "parent-child" relationship between audience and protagonist is where the many similarities to *The Old and Young King* end; the feminized young Frederick is an alienated from the spectator as he is from his father and himself. Our suturing into a relation with Frederick progresses in accordance with his phallic authority, culminating in the final close-up in which he meets but far exceeds our gaze. The affective and the ideological coincide as we "know" and "feel" that father knew best. The final close-up of Friedemann is diametrically opposed; he lies before us as a death mask, stripped of any gaze but also liberated of the alterity of the gaze, having retreated to the father's world where one doesn't need eyes (photo 46). Far from being alienated from Friedemann in the knowledge that his father, too, knew best, we are all the more "affected." The shot "speaks" a different language and experience than *The Old and the Young King,* opening up a space of reception that is indifferent to discipline and has been theorized as "feminine."

As Heide Schlüpmann has pointed out, Friedemann is in many respects a feminized figure who "stands for the woman in front of the screen."[20] The constant state of "being watched" that makes him paranoiac is that state described by Mary Ann Doane as a "hyperbolization of the 'normal' female function of exhibitionism in its attachment to the affect of fear."[21] Friedemann is specularized, however, not only by the annihilating gaze of ideological state apparatuses, but by a camera that consciously celebrates the male beauty aptly summarized by Schlüpmann: "Gründgens is the object of numerous close-ups in the film, usually from a frontal perspective and frequently in soft focus. The illumination of his forehead, eyes, and cheeks emphasizes the evenness of the face, framed by the curly hair like a halo. The lips appear sensuously full, are slightly opened. The strangely vacant eyes complete the impression of marble beauty."[22]

To Schlüpmann's description one might add other "feminizing" cinematic techniques: the fragmentation of Friedemann's body, his framing by

---

20. "Faschistische Trugbilder weiblicher Autonomie," *Frauen und Film* 44/45 (October 1988): 47.

21. Doane, 126.

22. Ibid. Despite Gründgens's enormous stature as actor and director, he never became an idol of the public as did figures like Hans Albers or Emil Jannings. See Friedrich Luft, "Gründgens und der Film," in Henning Rischbieler, ed., *Gründgens: Schauspieler, Regisseur, Theaterleiter* (Velber bei Hannover: Erhard Friedrich Verlag, 1963), 32.

a window, or his positioning in cinematic tableaus conceding his deficiency (as when he leans his head on an organ in despair) or indulging his Sentimental feeling, most strikingly in the long montage sequence in which he composes "real" music to candlelight. More than other Genius figures, even celebrated male bodies, the film "constructs his image as an image," one of the features Patrice Petro argues is typical of Weimar cinema's feminized males.[23] Finally, the film links Friedemann with women from the start, when he first speaks with the family women and ensures his sister's engagement, to the end where the Gypsy girl reflects his state as Antonia and Fiorini had earlier. If, as Schlüpmann argues, the film displaces women's desire for the "great wide world" into their libidinous relation to a male protagonist, this desire must remain frustrated, since Friedemann's subjectivity, like that of women, is wiped out by that very "great wide world." Like women, he remains "stuck inside" the narrative and, like women, is forced to adopt a "masquerade," "becoming" whatever is necessary to fulfill the demand of the big Other.[24]

Schlüpmann reads Friedemann's surrogate suffering woman role as the source of masochistic pleasure, drawing on the third phrase uncovered by analysis in Freud's *A Child Is Being Beaten,* in which the female analysand is positioned as a spectator to the beating of some boys (standing in for the woman's self) by a father figure.[25] Friedemann's body and his suffering stands in, then, for the female's own; the pleasure she derives in watching is masochistic. Moreover, her identification with the male body is built up in Schlüpmann's reading only to be negated along with that body in favor of the "symbolization of the phallus."

23. *Joyless Streets: Women and Melodramatic Representation in Weimar Germany* (Princeton, N.J.: Princeton University Press, 1989), 195. See in particular Petro's discussion of *Zuflucht* (189–99).

24. Joan Riviere originally theorized femininity, in 1929, as a "masquerade" in which it is impossible to separate "real" feminine behavior from that adopted to prop up the male ego. See "Womanliness as a Masquerade," in *Formations of Fantasy,* ed. Victor Burgin et al. (New York: Methuen, 1986), 35–44; also Mary-Ann Doane, "Film and the Masquerade: Theorising the Female Spectator," *Screen* 23.3–4 (September/October 1982): 74–87.

25. Phase one, in which a child is being beaten, may have its roots in family or school memories; later it becomes clear that the beater is the father beating a child "whom I hate." Phase two is where masochism enters in, with the woman herself substituting for the beaten child. Phase three combines masochism with sadism (the "probably watching" woman). See "A Child Is Being Beaten," in *Sexuality and the Psychology of Love,* ed. Phillip Rieff (New York: Collier Books, 1963).

Doubtless the "message" of the film affirms the phallus or the Name-of-the-Father with its discipline, showing "what happens" when one defies it. The question is the degree to which this ideological level permeates the subjective, affective "working" of the film. Is its "dominant ideology" sufficient to negate a desire tied to Friedemann, or might the film affirm — against its ideological closure — an affective relation to what Silverman might call a masculinity "at the margins"? One might even question how dominant the film's "dominant ideology" is, given features which render its affirmation of the phallus ambivalent: in particular the transcendental disaffectedness of the father and the wimpiness of Antonia, who at two junctures in the film all too quickly retreats into the ease of courtly decorum (her off screen marriage to Brühl and her last meeting with Friedemann, where she does nothing but again hold up the Bach family name, effectively driving in the "last nail" his coffin).[26] Not only is Friedemann the only figure with a certain authenticity, he is increasingly alone at the end — an "aloneness" that, as in other cases I've discussed, effects its opposite, "community" with the film audience. It invites a particularly "female" response of nurturance and mourning, a desire to step in where Antonia with her self-pitying "It was so terrible . . . " gave up. In this sense, too, the Genius narrative gives way to melodrama, which constructs a place for the spectator, from which, in Steve Neale's words, "we are led to wish 'if only.' "[27]

In our endeavor to locate *Friedemann Bach* as a "Nazi film" with a "Nazi message," we might overlook the fact that its source of frustration is also that of its narrative pleasure, which, as in "pure" melodrama, is tied to what does not happen, to what Tania Modleski calls taking up "the challenge of loss."[28] The failed career, missed wedding, and flawed communication at once frustrate the spectator, who is powerless to change the narrative events, and indulge the fantasy of intervening where the charac-

26. A feature of Nazi cinema's essentialism with respect to women is its privileging of courageous, gutsy women fighting exactly where Antonia does not, "for their men."

27. Neale, "Melodrama and Tears," 12. Thomas Elsaesser, too, emphasizes the superior knowledge of the spectator as crucial to audience participation in melodrama. He distinguishes irony, which privileges the spectator vis-à-vis the protagonist and elicits a "desire to make up the emotional deficiency, to impart a different awareness," from pathos, which is elicited by noncommunication. "Tales of Sound and Fury: Observations on the Family Melodrama," *Movies and Methods: Volume II,* ed. Bill Nichols (Berkeley: University of California Press, 1985), 186–87.

28. "Time and Desire in the Woman's Film," *Cinema Journal* 23.3 (Spring 1984): 28.

ters failed. As virtually all recent theories of melodrama conclude, its process of articulation is not to be sought in the intellectual but in other registers, particularly in mise-en-scène, which as we've seen is crucial to *Friedemann Bach*: "In the melodrama the *rhythm* of experience often establishes itself against its value (moral, intellectual)"; "lighting, composition, decor increase their semantic and syntactic contribution to the aesthetic effect. They become functional and integral elements in the construction of meaning."[29]

The way *Friedemann Bach* fetishizes its protagonist sustains the privileging of the feminized male that Patrice Petro has argued was crucial to Weimar cinema's anticipation of a female spectator. Challenging the usual readings of that cinema as a story of male subjectivity in crisis, Petro insists that the destabilization of (both male and female) gender boundaries and specifically the privileging of the feminized male mobilizes female desire, constituting a certain resistance to patriarchy. *Friedemann Bach* certainly does nothing to destabilize female gender boundaries nor can it escape a reading in terms of male subjectivity in crisis (especially within the Genius context), but it does indulge a "passive, eroticized male" of the type described by Petro as offering a space for female desire in Weimar cinema. Particularly important here are the contemplative tableau configurations in which he is framed and the wandering of this Genius narrative into the melodrama of the Street film. Petro ascribes a liberating effect to the aesthetic underlying Weimar cinema's melodramatic conventions, one "indebted less to stability . . . than to instability, theatricality, and an expressive play of mourning and pathos."[30] Drawing on theories of melodrama that reevaluate this disparaged genre as one often appropriated by and for social outgroups like the working class and women,[31] Petro addresses aesthetic features of melodrama (excessive visual and narrative repetition, nonverbal expression via character types, gesture, and cinematic tableau) as vehicles encouraging a less goal-oriented form of looking that combine with the melodramatic convention of a destabilized male identity as outlets for a repressed female voice. This is not to exclude the possibility of strong male identification with *Friedemann Bach*, which

29. Elsaesser, 167 and 173 f.
30. Petro, xxiii.
31. Especially Peter Brooks's *The Melodramatic Imagination: Balzac, Henry James, Melodrama, and the Mode of Excess* (New Haven: Yale University Press, 1976) and Tania Modleski's "Time and Desire in the Woman's Film," *Cinema Journal* 23.3 (Spring 1984): 19–30.

offers the male "a vicarious, hysterical, experience of femininity, which can be more definitively laid to rest for having been 'worked through.' "[32]

Precisely in its failure to evoke a collective identity based on "timeless Genius," *Friedemann Bach* succeeds in creating a "personal" space with which an audience can identify and another space of imaginary agency outside of the text. Neither space subjects the female spectator to the awkward reversals of subject position, to the oscillations and contortions she undergoes in *Komödianten*. Nor is either aimed directly at homefront mobilization; rather, both are familiar, affective spaces colored by "real" experience (even if masochistically enjoyed) of subjective annihilation by an Other. Although few would argue that making a female spectator feel "motherly" is to liberate her, there may be a small liberating moment in the film's rupturing the dominant fiction of intact Nazi Genius Malehood, and in a fetishization that succeeds in defiance of the Name-of-the-Father.

My intention has not been to redeem *Friedemann Bach*, but to demonstrate the possibility of competing imperatives within all three Genius films, even given the restrictive apparatus of Nazi cinema. In claiming that *Friedemann Bach* does not aestheticize history in the same way as the previous two films (by presenting its spectator with the artist as narcissistic mirror), I am not suggesting that it does not aestheticize history at all. Despite all of the psychic strictures that separate Friedemann from Schiller and Neuber, the cinematic celebration and mourning of his Genius is based on the same biologism that informs the other films of this genre. If the narrative displays an ambivalence toward Friedemann's failed resistance to the Name-of-the-Father, it nonetheless inspires pride in the "stuff Germans are made of." In its very lament for what "could have been," it, too, compensates for the shortcomings of everyday life. Like other films from the early forties, *Friedemann Bach* responds to a need for psychic "rearmament" during the war, affirming Adorno's linkage between the experience of "real unfreedom" and the compensatory functionalization of Genius as a space in which freedom could be preserved: "The less the world is a human(e) world and the more neutralized the mind, i.e., the consciousness of the world becomes, the more [the genius] becomes an ideology."[33]

Second, *Friedemann Bach* reiterates the other films' dependence on eighteenth-century German aesthetic culture in defining its narrative

32. Ibid., 25.
33. Theodor W. Adorno, *Gesammelte Schriften*, ed. Rolf Tiedemann, 20 vols. (Frankfurt am Main: Suhrkamp, 1970), 7:256.

terms and subject effect, lending historic events a quotational fictional structure. In co-opting the German cultural heritage and blurring the demarcation between aesthetic culture and political culture, all three Genius films I discussed, even *Friedemann Bach* as the least affirmative, contribute to Nazism's destruction of a textual culture that emphasizes the necessity of reflection. The textual culture that evolved in the eighteenth century entails processes of reasoning and thus of distanciation which, however problematic, were at odds with Nazism's dependency on aestheticization.[34] Nazism needed to undermine the hermeneutic culture that developed in an eighteenth-century reading culture, but simultaneously to portray itself as the culmination of that very same Great Culture, which meant celebrating and imitating that culture. It is this paradox that yields texts as ruptured as the three I have examined.

34. The frequent pejorative portrayals in Nazi film of parliamentary democracies as chaotic assemblies testify to the threat Nazism perceived in processes of even marginally "reasoned" discussion. See, for example, *Enemy of the People* (1937), *Robert Koch* (1939), *Carl Peters* (1941), *Bismarck* (1940), or *The Dismissal* (1942).

III

BEYOND

THE EIGHTEENTH

CENTURY

*

EIGHT

Vicious Circulation: Money and

Foreignness in Nazi Film

In juxtaposing a series of Nazi film "translations" of eighteenth-century history, it has not been my intention to elucidate the influence of the eighteenth century on Nazism, but rather to situate Nazi film aesthetics within a large cultural apparatus that is grounded in the eighteenth century, and that reflects the normative narrative models, disciplined subjectivity, and functional differentiation of society that emerged in early modernity. The eighteenth-century settings and historical protagonists we've encountered had the advantage of rendering transparent the relationship between Nazism's social fantasies and the period that generated the ideological configurations underlying those fantasies as well as the narrative framework giving expression to them. For every distortion and "biologization" of a tradition that was historically "emancipatory," we have found more uncomfortable affinities.

In the late seventies, Jürgen Link traced the evolution from eighteenth-century drama through modern popular literature, from *Cabal and Love* to *Love Story*. Link demonstrates via paradigmatic examples from the eighteenth, nineteenth, and twentieth centuries how modern popular narratives tend to preserve the structure of bourgeois tragedies like Schiller's, only that they deprive the latter of their political critique and assume a more socially affirmative function than did the bourgeois tragedy.[1] Seen from this evolutionary perspective, the affinities between a "high" Enlightenment tradition and Nazi (and other forms of) kitsch are no more an

1. "Von 'Kabale und Liebe' zur 'Love Story' — Zur Evolutionsgesetzlichkeit eines bürgerlichen Geschichtentyps," in *Literarischer Kitsch,* ed. Jochen Schulte-Sasse (Tübingen: Niemeyer, 1979), 121–55.

anomaly than National Socialism is a historical aberration. What I want to do in the following chapters is to demonstrate, using textual examples, what should be obvious: that a specific setting or historical configuration is irrelevant to the fundamental textual operations at work in Nazi cinema. Eighteenth-century literature erected a narrative, ideological, social-psychological apparatus that remains in place today in modern narratives, and that seems especially "transparent" in popular narratives (although their simple-mindedness may be somewhat deceptive once we look for internal ruptures). If nothing else, the fact that the first five minutes of any Nazi feature film generally tells us where our emotional alignment belongs (even if today, with our twenty-twenty hindsight, we may refuse to cooperate) should tell us we're in familiar territory. This does not render these texts less instructive or interesting, however.

This chapter and the next will parallel the beginning of the book, focusing on a fantasy structure that is not unique to National Socialism but takes a particularly pathological form in it. By now familiar elements of this structure include Nazism's perception of a delimited social body, its juxtaposition of an "inside" constituting community and an "outside" marked by Otherness (which in Nazi narratives is generally an irreducible Otherness), its imaginary mastery of the Other, and its projections of social antagonism or harmony onto certain individuals or groups. In short, both Nazism's "positive" social fantasy of the Leader/People symbiosis and its "negative" counterpart are subject to endless narrative variation. This chapter explores further discursive representations of social negativity, while the next does the opposite, examining Nazism's peculiar relation to machines as vehicles securing community.

The "body politic" common to the very diverse films covered in this chapter is the fantasy of "Germany" itself as an organic, vulnerable body. The threats to that body take the form of abstractions: the first is money, whose danger as an abstract and abstracting force I began elaborating in connection with *Jew Süss;* the second is "foreign contamination" or the fear of the "international," in which the source of dissolution is often not specified. The two are inextricably connected; both involve a circulation permitting the penetration of the social body — a penetration in many cases perpetrated by the same groups (the "Jew" is both international and obsessed with money; the British, whom Nazism equates with capitalism, are "foreigners," etc.). Moreover, each narrative renders the abstract comprehensible by condensing it in a concrete body, an individual or group who embodies abstract forces.

All of these narrative configurations are equivalences whose identity is marked by the metaphoric surplus of the others. They aim at constructing a unified subject position that is based on an artificial linkage of contingent elements. There is, in other words, no essential connection between Jews and money or "foreigners" and capitalism, but Nazism naturalizes contingent elements into a relatively cohesive Weltanschauung that conceals the fact that the identity of National Socialism's "community" is blocked by itself. This process is the same one that condenses contradictory negative features in Nazism's "Jew" (wealth and filth, communism and capitalism, impotence and licentiousness, etc.). Each "threat" to Nazism's imagined social body is a positive embodiment of social negation that amounts to *negation of negation.* It is driven by the desire to make possible the "impossible" "organic," racially and ideologically harmonious society.

MOVIES ABOUT MONEY: HANS ZERLETT'S *ROBERT AND BERTRAM* and KARL HARTL'S *GOLD*

The cultural fascination with money lies in its sublime status as something "more than itself." As Žižek reminds us, our attitude toward money is part of the "I know but just the same" mechanism of psychoanalysis. We know that money is merely a materially worthless thing whose authority depends on its role in a network of social relations. Nevertheless, in what Žižek calls a "fetishistic inversion," we act is if we did not know it; in our social relations we act as if the material object called money were the immediate embodiment of wealth as such.[2] Money, like the fetishized King in Kantorowicz's theory of "two bodies," possesses an indestructible and immutable body: "this other body of money is like the corpse of the sadeian victim which endures all torments and survives with its beauty immaculate."[3]

Although money becomes an increasingly important narrative element in the nineteenth-century "petty bourgeois anticapitalism" that culminated in National Socialism, its symbolic function as a material embodiment of alienation dates back to the eighteenth century. Since Storm and Stress and Romanticism, alienation in modern societies has been connected with the power of money to disperse substance, essence, and human value. Whereas the Marxist tradition analyzed money in terms of value, as representing the structure of social relations in modernity, so-

2. *The Sublime Object of Ideology* (New York: Verso, 1989), 31.
3. Ibid., 18–19.

called "conservative" movements persisted in mythicizing money as an inimical force. This mythification is indebted to the rejection of economic categories in these movements, which restrict themselves to moral terms and designate money or gold as at once demonic and enigmatic. Conceived in this way, money underlies binary figures of thought and can be mobilized ideologically.[4]

As an abstract sign, money is implicated in the abstracting process of modernization so suspicious to National Socialism with its privileging of the "thingly," of production and not finance capitalism. Obviously, the development from a barter economy to one based on gold and later to paper money entailed ever-increasing levels of abstraction. Brian Rotman demonstrates, in his *Signifying Nothing,* how as money became detached from its material value it entered into a "relation with itself and became a commodity," thus disrupting an old, product-based economy and introducing the "code of commodities engendered by mercantile capitalism."[5] In adopting such a function, money became a metasign, one whose development Rotman equates with that of zero in arithmetic and the vanishing point in perspective art. Like the latter, money became a sign about signs "whose meaning is to indicate the absence of certain other signs" (the absence not only of a commodity "equal to" another commodity as in the barter system, but also of gold with its intrinsic value, which long served as the standard against which the value of goods was measured).[6] As a metasign, money became autonomous, reversing "the original movement from object to sign";[7] not only do prices describe real transactions existing prior to money, but money is able to conceptualize transactions

4. This subversion of economic terms explains why "conservative" movements could so vehemently reject Marxism as representing the destruction of all "German" values, while some like the left-wing of the NSDAP embraced the concept of "socialism." Just as the Nazi critique of capitalism, as an emotional reaction to social upheaval and insecurity, has no basis in economics, Volkish "socialism" did not propose an economic system but a romanticized solution to the problem of greed. "Socialism" would somehow prohibit such greed and force economic interests to serve the community (*Gemeinschaft*), which in itself was of course a vague category. To the extent that it meant more than a vehicle for counter-propaganda against the German left, the "socialist" component of National Socialism must be seen in this light.

5. *Signifying Nothing* (New York: St. Martin's Press, 1987), 24.

6. Ibid., 1. Rotman concentrates on imaginary money, which involved promissory notes issued to a certain bearer at a certain time. It was developed to counteract the instabilities of a currency whose value depended on its own materiality. Imaginary money emerged in Venice and Amsterdam, where the importance of international trade made the economy vulnerable to the physical debasement of money.

7. Ibid., 28.

that could never be achieved (just as mathematics works with numbers beyond a conceivable process of human counting and pictures can be painted of what does not exist). The development of money as an autonomous force was a precondition for the internationalization Nazism equates with a loss of *Heimat,* and with the disciplinary social organization against which it aligned itself ideologically. Money permitted infinite circulation, manipulation, the traversing of foreign boundaries.

The fantasy of anonymous manipulators "pulling strings" with the help of money underlies one of the least known anti-Semitic films produced in the Third Reich, Hans Heinz Zerlett's musical comedy *Robert and Bertram* (1939).[8] Although its attempt to couch anti-Semitism in humor entangles the film in a number of narrative contradictions, it is unique in the narrative strategies with which it literally presents not only Jews but money as "abstract." *Robert and Bertram* is, indeed, all about the circulation of money, yet in the course of the action no money passes between the hands of the central characters.

*

The film is set in 1839 in the Biedermeier period. Robert and Bertram are two vagabond friends who are accidentally reunited in prison. After escaping together, they are befriended by Lenchen, the daughter of a village restaurant owner, Mr. Lips. Mr. Lips has debts with a man named Biedermeier (the allegorical representation of a period famous for its materialism), who threatens to destroy the business unless Lenchen marries him. Hoping to save the family who has fed them, Robert and Bertram steal Biedermeier's wallet, whereupon they discover that Biedermeier himself has debts with the Jewish banker Nathan Ipelmeyer in Berlin. They gain access to Ipelmeyer's house in Berlin, disguised as the "Count of Monte Cristo" and a famous music professor. They steal numerous jewels from the Jew and his family, with which they liberate Lips and his daughter. Robert and Bertram escape the law in a hot air balloon, which transports them to heaven.

*

8. Allegedly Hitler disapproved of *Robert and Bertram* because it did not show Germans in a good light. It was based on a farce of 1856 by Gustav Raeder (1810–1868), which had been successfully performed in the theater in 1865 with Jewish actors. Zerlett used only episodes from Raeder, but added an anti-Semitic perspective lacking in the original. None of the actors in Zerlett's films are Jewish. See Dorothea Hollstein, *"Jud Süss" und die Deutschen: Antisemitische Vorurteile im nationalsozialistischen Spielfilm* (Frankfurt am Main: Ullstein, 1971), 48–53.

The only scene actually showing money in *Robert and Bertram* is connected precisely to the figures most indifferent to it, the two vagabonds (who have sold horses to buy clothing with which they fool Ipelmeyer). Otherwise, money exists only in transactions prior to the film's narration; like anti-Semitism's fantasy of the "Jewish" international conspiracy, it stands *behind* phenomena. The intricate, coercive connection between the German family and the Jew is, within the film itself, manifested on paper; it is linked to a system of credit in which money exists only "in theory." Intimidation through money and possession of money are not necessarily synonymous, as Bertram remarks: "By no means does somebody who *spends* a lot of money need to *have* a lot of money!"

Significantly, the vagabonds constantly steal, but never money. The wallet they steal from Biedermeier contains no money, only a threatening letter from Ipelmeyer. The credit letter is part of the culture of writing that *The Old and the Young King*'s Frederick William assails and that helps maintain disciplinary power relations, as Ipelmeyer himself remarks: "If you want to hurt someone, don't take a sword, take ink and feather!" The other written text in the film, the invitation to Ipelmeyer's soirée, fulfills a similar function by maintaining class distinctions. Both of these contrast with the more "natural" text of the Aryan, a heart carved into a tree by Lenchen's boyfriend Michel.

The final act with which Robert and Bertram achieve justice again involves a theft not of the Jew's money, but his jewels. On the one hand, jewels belong to the world of aristocratic decadence (recall, for example, their role in *Jew Süss*); yet as real, palpable, intrinsically valuable objects (derived, no less, from "nature"), their employment in the liberation of the German family from the strangulation of credit is a semiotic gesture consistent with Nazism's privileging of the "thingly." In the long run, not only do Robert and Bertram avoid transactions with money, they purchase the Lipses' freedom with nothing at all, merely with the circulation of goods: Lips can use the jewels to pay Biedermeier, who can in turn pass them back to Ipelmeyer, who is then "paid back" with what was his in the first place; a gesture justified by the assumption that "Jewish" possessions are always already stolen (note a guest's response to Bertram's remark that Ipelmeyer's house must have cost a fortune: "Indeed, it cost several fortunes, but not those of Ipelmeyer, rather of those he swindled!").

Perhaps most striking about *Robert and Bertram* is its achievement of rendering Jews literally an "abstract" force of modern capitalism, creatures whose very identity is counterfeit. Although they embody Rotman's "meta-subject" par excellence, they need at the same time to be rendered visible *as* a "hidden" power. Two strategies enable this seemingly para-doxical execution. The first lies in the discrepancy between the film's story (which, if told chronologically, would introduce the "Jew" much earlier) and its plot, which introduces him late and devotes roughly a half-hour to him. In other words, although he is indispensable to the story, the film gives the "Jew" minimum presence in its plot (or narration), preferring instead to concentrate on the disorder created by an "invisible" Jew be-hind the scenes. It firmly establishes a narrative configuration (indebted to the comedies of Plautus, Gryphius, and Molière) aligning the spectator with or against certain characters only to reveal that this configuration is incomplete: we are worried about the Lipses' fate at the hands of Bieder-meier, not suspecting that there are more narrative figures to come.

As implied by the homophonic quality in the names "-meier" and "-meyer," Biedermeier and Ipelmeyer are gentile-Jewish counterparts in their representation of exploitation.[9] Not only is "meyer" the more com-mon spelling for Jewish names, but "Ipel" is a South-German variation of *übel,* meaning "evil." Yet a narrative constellation that mirrors the projec-tion of the "Jew" as the abstraction of capitalism renders the homology superficial: Like an unseen marionetteer behind the set, the Jew controls the fate of the whole community, villain and hero alike (during the credits, Robert and Bertram even appear as dancing marionettes). Moreover, the Jew's power is as self-perpetuating as it is anonymous: as Robert remarks, if Biedermeier is unable to pay his debt, "he'll just go to another Jew and pay higher interest" and Mr. Lips "will be the loser."

The second strategy rendering the Jew abstract is standard anti-Semitic fare and pervades both *Jew Süss* and *The Rothschilds:* the indictment of Jews as thieves of "Aryan" culture. The disguises selected by the Ipelmeyer family when they host a masked ball imitate "old world" absolutist power structures: Ipelmeyer dresses as Louis XIV, the absolutist par excellence (referred to by a servant as "Louis Quatorze the fifteenth"); his wife is Madame Pompadour; his daughter, Cleopatra, redubbed "Queen Klep-

9. In her filmography Hollstein states that Biedermeier's name in the script is to be spelled Biedermeyer; Hollstein, 249. The departure from the usual spelling of the name could be an effort to "Jewify" the man. The merchant or "businessman" is of course a staple of Nazi cinema not necessarily linked to either Jews or foreigners; cf. the wealthy sixteenth-century merchant Pfefferkorn in Pabst's *Paracelsus* (1943), whose lust for profit leads him to unwittingly let the plague into Basel; the merchants who drive Rembrandt to destitution in Steinhoff's *Rembrandt* (1942); or the wealthy businessmen in *Kolberg* concerned that resistance against Napoleon will disturb "peace, order, and prosperity."

tomania." The only things actually "belonging" to Jews are bound to the body; their Yiddish accent (Ipelmeyer admonishes his servant to get rid of his accent and not to use "so many foreign words," which do not befit "a lackey"), their gait (Mrs. Ipelmeyer recognizes another Jew by his "feet," to which I will return), and the imagined physical markings that maintain the distinctions on which the social health depends (Bertram recognizes Ipelmeyer on the street: "That must be him, judging by his profile!"). In fact, these "Jews" are no more "real" Jews than Ferdinand Marian's Süss Oppenheimer; hence their "Jewish" body traits cannot be anything other than those of "Aryan" actors (actress Tatjana Sals, who played Ipelmeyer's daughter, confessed that it was "a rather touchy feeling to be thought of by the public as a Jewish girl"[10]). In other words, again this film has to rely on its own "Aryan" badness to conjure up its fantasmatic "Jew."

From the moment the invisible "Jew" acquires a body at Berlin's famous Café Kranzler, he tries, like Süss Oppenheimer and Nathan Rothschild, to blend into German society and erase his Otherness.[11] The real effect is that he casts himself as a parody of an "Aryan" parvenu, which the film satirizes by juxtaposing his internationalized with Bertram's national tastes. When Ipelmeyer requests a copy of the *Berliner Börsenblatt,* a liberal "Jewish" newspaper focusing on financial issues, Bertram (sitting across from him disguised as a "gentleman") requests the conservative, monarchical *Königlich Privilegierte Zeitung.* While Ipelmeyer orders a glass of sherry and a caviar bread, Bertram orders a sandwich and beer (*eine richtige Stulle mit Schleppe and Berliner Weisse*). Even Ipelmeyer's title of councilor is one that was historically purchased by the upwardly mobile.

We have here, then, a somewhat different temporal, spatial, and specular configuration than in other films so far: the before, far away, and hidden affect negatively the here and now which we see. *Robert and Bertram* has in common with *Jew Süss* that what is hidden from us must be rendered visible — we must in both see the Jew "as he really is." The difference is that while Süss infiltrates "Aryan" space in a bodily way and

---

10. Quoted in Hollstein, 51.

11. Cf. Nathan Rothschild's unsuccessful attempts to gain admittance into the upper echelons of British society in *The Rothschilds.* In one scene Nathan sits alone with his secretary Bronstein at a massive, sumptuously set banquet table, while crosscutting shows the invited guests at another affair, ridiculing Nathan's attempts to join their ranks: "They [the Jews] may have to deal with us, but they can't join us!" (Translation from Welch, 266.)

renders himself a captivating spectacle as well as master of the specular, the "Jew" in *Robert and Bertram* need not invade "Aryan" space in order to disturb it. On the contrary, in keeping with the film's more advanced historical stage, his power lies in *maintaining* this distance and invisibility, that is, in an abstractness, anonymity, and panoptical "overview" of financial connections that again links him with the "bad" side of discipline. The "fun" of *Robert and Bertram* lies in the fantasy of reversing *Jew Süss,* allowing "Aryan" figures to invade "Jewish" space and make the Jew laughably visible. Robert and Bertram beat the Jew at his own game, not only by moving in on him and causing upheaval, but by satirizing "Jewish" masquerade themselves. Only the two vagabonds, as undisciplined and nondisciplinary outsiders liberated from the power of money and social functionalization, are able to invade his space unscathed.

The film's ridicule of Jewish masquerade threatens, however, to turn against itself in the case of Samuel, the bookkeeper in love with Ipelmeyer's daughter. Zerlett minimized Samuel's role vis-à-vis Raeder's farce to that of a spurned lover grappling awkwardly with a suit of armor at the ball, with which he can neither dance nor make love. By outdoing itself in its effort to render a Jew ludicrous (and by displaying the impossibility of a Jewish "armored" man), the film unwittingly makes Samuel a poignant, at least potentially likable figure, with whose frustration the spectator can identify. In short, while *Jew Süss* risks rendering its antagonist appealing through his superiority, *Robert and Bertram* runs the same risk through its humor. The Jews creatively distort, for example, the French terms with which they want to "impress": they pronounce *Overture* as *Ofen Türe,* meaning oven door, and confuse the French *faché* (= angry) with chopped beef (*Hackepeter,* also called *Faschiertes*), etc. Not only might these very features endear them to a film audience, but they suggest a precarious resemblance to the Jews' supposed opposite, the uncultured Bertram with his confusion of *au revoir* with *au troittoir,* etc.

The social organism restored by Robert and Bertram's circular transaction with the jewels is an essentially premodern order beyond the machinations of absent capital. Where transactions occur in this "premodern" world, they are a simple, direct, and fair exchange of goods and services: Lips's restaurant prospers presumably because of "quality service"; Robert and Bertram eat at the restaurant in exchange for washing dishes (which a policeman labels "honest work"). On a visual level as well, the film intensifies its exposé of Jewish culture as fake by juxtaposing the latter with German folk culture, which is indulged in long spectacles arresting the narrative; an enormously disproportionate amount of screen time is devoted to "cultural" events, considering their minimal diegetic importance. For once, "Aryan" culture "spills over" onto Jewish noncul-ture in a bodily way (through Robert and Bertram's "invasion") and a syntactic way.

The Berlin "Jewish" sequence with Ipelmeyer is framed on either side by lengthy exhibitions, not only of Robert and Bertram's musical "numbers" but of cultural ceremonies bordering on the documentary. Prior to the "Jewish" episode, Mr. Lips hosts a wedding reception, a celebration that not only anticipates the trajectory of the narrative (Lenchen's imminent marriage), but that becomes a sumptuous display of traditional folk cos-tumes, dance, and merriment. Subsequent to the "Jewish" episode is a carnival scene, again exhibiting German traditions like the *Moritas* song. The substance, genuineness, and "heart" (literally suggested by the heart Michel carves) of "German" culture veritably submerges "Jewish" par-venuism. At the same time the scenes slow the film down, giving it a feeling of tedium that might have contributed to its only modest public success.

Finally, the film displays German culture as "substance" in its formal reference to a number of German cultural and literary traditions embod-ied in the figures of Robert and Bertram. The figures capitalize on a popu-larized Romantic tradition celebrating the "artistic" individual as outside of bourgeois constraints — a tradition that resisted discipline and the in-strumentalization that accompanied it. Bertram describes Robert as a "run-down genius" and himself as a "runaway bourgeois" who would rather be a "tramp" than a "petty bourgeois" (*Spiesser*). With his decrepit umbrella, Bertram might have stepped right out of Carl Spitzweg's famous painting *The Poor Poet,* painted in 1839, in the same year in which the film is set. Their itinerant lifestyle recalls the valorization of wandering as a pursuit of freedom from the eighteenth-century bildungsroman through Romanticism, and is implicitly juxtaposed to the rootless "wandering Jew" circulating exchange value I discussed in connection with *Jew Süss*.[12] Bertram's repeated references to himself and his umbrella as having "no purpose" invoke the Romantic tradition of the "Good for Nothing," epit-omized by Eichendorff's novella *Aus dem Leben eines Taugenichts* (The Good-for-nothing) with its rejection of the utilitarian and its celebration of life as a form of art. When taken for "wandering artists," Robert retorts they are "artistically wandering." This resistance to discipline is, as al-

---

12. In one of many musical medleys celebrating "German" musical culture, Robert and Bertram even sing the same lines from Schiller's *Robbers* set to music in *Friedrich Schiller:* "A merry life we lead and free, a life of endless bliss."

ready stressed, the precondition for their slapstick disruption of "Jewish" machinations.

Robert and Bertram repeatedly highlights its setting in 1839 — a century prior to its release — through verbal references and close-ups of calendars. This temporal dimension, combined with the film's allegorical figures (Biedermeier, Dr. Kaftan, and German Michel), has the effect of generalizing from the screen events into a larger "German" context. Again hindsight becomes a form of pleasure in a film looking back into an era at once idealized and benevolently ironized. Indeed, this "look back" is to be understood in the most literal sense, as an empowerment of the spectator to look, see, and understand. Ironically, the "silliest" figures, Robert and Bertram, become agents of comprehension, enabling the film audience and diegetic figures alike to "understand" the power of Jewish capital. Bertram serves as a comic counterpart to Faber in *Jew Süss,* with the penetrating gaze that strips the Jew of his enigma and relegates "Jewishness" to a bodily level: When Ipelmeyer reveals to Bertram a "big secret — I'm an Israelite" — the overweight vagabond confides another "big secret": "I have a belly!"

Empowerment through vision operates throughout *Robert and Bertram* on a formal level as well. Frequently throughout the film, the camera is poised so as to look through a window, foregrounding the inscription of a frame into the movie frame itself.[13] We first see Lenchen wrapping a ham through the frame of a window; we first see Robert through a prison window; we see caricatures of police officials commiserating over the vagabonds behind a window, and so on. The camera plays with the boundary between inside and outside, not to restrict our vision but to call attention to the ubiquity we gain with its help; it shows us a fragment through the window frame, only to take us wherever it "wants." More powerfully than calendars or dialogue references, the camera becomes our eyes penetrating history.

A curious exception to this sense of ubiquity is the scene immediately preceding Ipelmeyer's masked ball, when the camera passes by a series of windows behind which each figure is preparing his or her costume. The diegetic figures refer playfully to the spectator's voyeurism; in each case someone pulls the curtain shut, blocking our view. Though the scene is readable as a further highlighting of Jewish masquerade, of their attempt

13. The credits also begin with a curtain rising, again foregrounding demarcated boundaries; Hollstein remarks that Zerlett consciously "offered this story as theater in film." Hollstein, 48.

to hide the crucial element of "Jewishness" that eludes us, it again runs the risk of rendering the Jewish characters sympathetic, as our partners in play. Only in this scene do diegetic characters directly acknowledge the presence of the film audience, whose voyeurism they frustrate. The scene thus not only ruptures the conventions of classical cinema (in which characters do not generally look into the camera or acknowledge the film audience), it implicitly calls into question our right to look "innocently," playfully chastising our inquiring minds and eyes.

Running parallel to the film's main plot is the story of Michel, the peasant boy sent off to military service, where he undergoes a metamorphosis from wimp to soldierly man fit to marry Lenchen. The film's Michel literalizes the allegorical figure "German Michel" with his sleeping cap, who since the sixteenth-century peasant wars has symbolized Germany's good-natured but sleepy People unable to forge a successful revolution ("German Michel" played an especially important role in the public discourse surrounding Germany's failed 1848 revolution, just subsequent to the film's time). Michel is the humorous counterpart of the deserters made "men" by the King in the Frederick films. Like young Frederick, he is subjected to a Theweleitian "drill machine" (again the paradoxical affirmation of extreme discipline) with which he casts off femininity. The uniform and drill transform not only his appearance but his speech and gestures; it is as if the uniform becomes fused with his body. Michel's lack of internal discipline is compensated by a symbolic order ready and able to fit him with a new identity; the military barber jovially refuses his request to see a mirror while his hair is being cut: "*We'll* decide how you're to look!" Michel's Ideal-I is to be found in the military world around him, not in vain self-reflection. The film's militarization of Michel gains a particular significance in light of this film's anti-Semitism. Sander Gilman discusses in *The Jew's Body* how in nineteenth-century Germany and Austria the Jewish body was regarded as "inherently unfit for military service,"[14] and military service was, in turn a prerequisite for full participation in the body politic. In particular the notion of the Jew's unhealthy, flat feet, which was sustained by the dominant medical discourse, allegedly precluded the Jew's military serviceability. Not only does *Robert and Bertram* make reference to Jewish feet; it invites a juxtaposition of Michel *qua* New Man with the hapless Samuel struggling in his armor and with Jews in general as exhibiting bodily deficiency.

14. (New York: Routledge, 1991), 42; see his entire chapter on "The Jewish Foot: A Foot-Note to the Jewish Body" (38–59).

The masculinization of Michel is seemingly just another episode in a rambling narrative full of contingent encounters. Yet the concurrence of the restoration of a healthy family (read: social organism) by Robert and Bertram and the affirmation of phallic authority in the figure of Michel is anything but accidental. Not only does the narrative anticipate the mating of German woman with a militarized Michel over a gentrified civilian, it awakens "German Michel" to manhood while quite literally putting the "Jew" to sleep: the last time we see Ipelmeyer he has been drugged by his own physician, with the telling name Dr. Kaftan, in a rivalry over a ballerina (whose movement is again linked with "wandering" Jews). A final allegorical dimension inheres in Michel's realization that he possesses a heretofore undiscovered superhuman strength — the strength German males one hundred years hence should find as they undergo a real-life metamorphosis into soldiers.

Precisely where it celebrates Germany's reborn manhood, the film exposes more of its own contradictions; Lenchen's allegorical "choice" of the "right" man is merely an exchange of one kind of oppression for another. Although dialogue repeatedly insists upon Lenchen's desire, it effectively renders her a thing to be possessed by the man displaying the most effective authority. A hint of misogyny lies already in Lenchen's first appearance: the carved heart that bears her name dissolves into a close-up of a large ham she is packing; just as the shot links her metonymically to the ham, the story will link her metaphorically to it. The "new" Michel's courtship is, if taken literally, no less coercive than that of the blackmailing Biedermeier; Michel teases Lenchen sadistically, abruptly kisses her, thrusts a ring on her finger and announces publicly that they are engaged. While clearly the film intends his decisive gestures to be read as the fulfillment of Lenchen's own desire, the proximity of the two men's methods of wooing is striking. Biedermeier's courtship is tainted less, it seems, because he uses duress (he, indeed, is the one who repeatedly *asks* Lenchen to marry him), than because of its entanglement in capital and Jewry. Not only does the soldierly Michel render Lenchen's desire superfluous, he displaces her as the film's specularized object. Henceforth he magnetically attracts all eyes to himself; Lenchen's identity will be constituted by mirroring herself in him. (When he first appears in the fetishized uniform, she begs, "Will you go to the carnival with me tomorrow *like that?*")

In another contradictory move, it is as if, notwithstanding its efforts to celebrate Michel, the film "really knows" that in Michel it has generated nothing but an ineffectual specimen of narcissistic bravado. Like Lenchen, Michel is but the passive recipient not only of a disciplinary socialization process but of the circumstances enabling him to appropriate his woman. While the "real" story of the Lipses' salvation is happening, Michel appears only sporadically at military drills, Nazism's counterpart to today's aerobic classes. Michel builds Self while the undisciplined Robert and Bertram build community; he plays no role in the reappropriation of Lenchen, and his agency in getting rid of Biedermeier is restricted to a pointless macho threat, "Can I talk to you later?" which follows more narcissistic exhibitions of strength at the carnival.

The triumph of machismo has been prepared, ironically, by the film's least macho figures, Robert and Bertram, who repeatedly adopt feminized positions (washing dishes, donning women's clothing, in which they flirt with men). The unproblematic nature of this feminization stems not only from the film's comic genre but from the men's status as part of another world outside the normal rhythms of human life. With respect to heterosexual relations, they are more like those figures in a fairy tale that Vladimir Propp labeled "helpers" than like "real" people participating in the action. Above all, they are able to transgress normally prohibited borders, as suggested by their transgression of gender boundaries and their access to heaven while still alive.[15] This detachment enables them to stand in for the contemporary spectator, who shares their insight into social contradictions and derives pleasure from their disruption of an order that worldly authority in the film, like the king, can only intuitively sense: "The situation is such that these two small swindlers, if caught, would be locked up for years, even though they didn't carry out their swindle for their own advantage. Something's wrong here!"

Although the king serves as enunciator of the film's "message," the narrative's resort to divine intervention is a testament to the ineffectuality of his words at this historical juncture, in which Right can be restored only through transgression of Law (unlike in the Nazi present of 1939). At the end, Robert and Bertram literalize the "gaze from above," with which such films view the People, in the form of a bird's-eye shot gazing down upon a world marked by antagonism.[16] The film's gesture of "looking

15. Another indication for their ambivalent relation to the symbolic order is the frequency with which they are photographed through bars; once we see Bertram "behind bars," when the camera tracks out to reveal he is merely standing beside a park fence. The quintessential "jail birds" cannot be contained by Law.

16. The vagabonds are forcibly reintegrated into the social order in 1942, when the film's ending was changed to show them entering military service under the command of Michel—a move justified by the need to sustain the public's military morale. See Hollstein, 52.

back" subtly reverses itself into a forward trajectory toward a present in which anonymous forces of capital are contained on a worldly level; nostalgia turns into interpellation.

The narrative fetishization of gold in a number of Nazi films is a gesture of regression to a more primeval sign standing for the same dispersal and alienation later associated with money. While playing an analogous narrative role to money in films like *Robert and Bertram,* gold is clearly a different kind of sign: it is not merely a sign whose value derives only from a social contract, but an object in itself possessing beauty and material value — for years the anterior object lending legitimacy to printed money. The reintroduction of gold as currency in medieval Europe constituted an intermediary step toward a capitalist economy. It replaced the existent barter economy with a universal pricing system, and its use was part of a process abstracting currency, since a given ware was designated "equal to" a certain amount of gold. Despite this step, there was, as Rotman argues, "nothing intrinsically capitalist in the sort of metallic economy brought about by gold; transactions it made possible were essentially transposed acts of barter."[17] The precondition for the crucial shift to "capitalism" was the loss of money's material value, its transformation into a commodity relating not only to material goods but to itself.

Its intrinsic value and ancient roots destined gold for an even greater narrative mystification than money; it is not surprising to find narratives investing gold with the same enigmatic Otherness projected onto woman and nature. Within Nazi cinema, a title like *The Golden City* (1943), referring metaphorically to Prague as the locus of materialism, destruction, and foreignness, suggests this status. Inevitable social calamity accompanies the discovery of gold in Nazi film narratives. In *Ohm Krüger* (1941), Boer leader Krüger tries, even as a small boy, to keep his discovery of gold on Boer territory a secret; in Luis Trenker's *Kaiser of California* (1936), the California gold rush destroys Johann August Suter's dream of transforming desert land into a garden.

Nowhere is the mystification of gold more central than in Karl Hartl's *Gold* (1934), a box-office success whose narrative amounts to a kind of reverse science fiction, invoking the potential of future technology (nuclear energy) to realize an ancient desire, alchemy. *Gold* is one of the few films of a fantastic genre produced under National Socialism, which, as Eric Rentschler writes, generally eschewed a genre "rife with subversive

17. Rotman, 23.

potential, encompassing alternative worlds, flights of imagination, expressions of intoxication and exhilaration, the realms of the irrational, inexplicable, and uncontrollable."[18] Like some Weimar films — in particular Fritz Lang's *Metropolis* (1927) — *Gold* savors the titillation of the fantastic, while simultaneously harnessing it in an exemplary "anticapitalist" narrative moralizing the destructive properties of gold, which "brings no blessing."

*

A German scientist, Professor Achenbach, has built an atomic reactor with which he attempts to transform lead into gold.[19] Achenbach is killed in a sabotaged experiment arranged by the wealthy Scotsman John Wills, which his assistant Holk (Hans Albers)[20] barely survives. Months later Wills hires Holk to continue the research in his laboratory below the ocean floor off the Scottish coast. Holk complies in the hope of proving the sabotage was instigated by Wills, who harbors fantasies of omnipotence and whose reactor is suspiciously similar to Achenbach's. Holk succeeds in producing gold, but destroys the machine before Wills can begin mass production. A deranged Wills jams the doors protecting his workers from the explosion, which submerges the laboratory under the ocean. Holk manages to close the doors and all but Wills escape.

*

The film opens with a written text setting up its anticapitalist framework by recalling the timeless destruction wrought by gold: "For centuries people have longed to create gold artificially — because gold is both fortune and curse of this world — For gold clans, tribes, and peoples battle each other — For gold people betray, persecute, kill each other —." The hyphens punctuating the phrases create a sense of ellipsis, suggesting a circular, self-perpetuating process; the fading in and out of each line of the text intensifies its aura as a voice of truth from nowhere.

18. "The Triumph of Male Will: *Münchhausen*," *Film Quarterly* 43.3 (Winter 1990): 17.
19. David Stewart Hull, who garbles his synopsis of the film's plot, claims that the machine was such a convincing portrayal of a real atomic reactor that the Allied censorship board viewing the film after the war seized all available prints of it, which they had examined by American scientists to see if the Germans had invented a reactor. It was decided the machine was "simply the product of the set designer's imagination." *Film in the Third Reich* (Berkeley: University of California Press, 1969), 57 f.
20. See Stephen Lowry's description of Albers's screen persona in *Pathos und Politik: Ideologie in Spielfilmen des Nationalsozialismus* (Tübingen: Niemeyer, 1991), 229–30.

Notwithstanding this invocation of gold as a temptation both universal and timeless, the film's xenophobic figure constellation links the abuse of gold with the foreign: indeed, *Gold* is one of the earliest Nazi films to embody "exchange value" in the British — an equation that becomes much more explicit in the early forties after Great Britain entered the war. An excerpt of dialogue from *Ohm Krüger* testifies to the equation of the Englishman with capitalism. Leading up to the scene, gold has been discovered on Boer land, which Cecil Rhodes (Ferdinand Marian, who three years later played Süss Oppenheimer) intends to appropriate:

DR. JAMESON: I am an Englishman.
RHODES: Do you want to say that I'm *not* an Englishman?
JAMESON: You are a capitalist!
RHODES: That's the same thing![21]

Gold's historical function at the crossroads between a feudal and a capitalist economy is apparent in its narrative function as desired object in Hartl's film: The desire driving the narrative figures is an ancient one, to create gold as a means of mastering nature, whether in order to instrumentalize it (Wills) or for pure narcissism (Holk, concealed in the motif of "serving science"). Yet *Gold* implicates this "timeless" and "universal" drive in the most modern of capitalist dynamics, devaluation. Once it becomes a mass product, gold stands to forfeit its material value, even the symbolic authority possessed by paper money, and to unleash endless destruction.

Rotman recounts the historical scandal which the mass production of money initially created. Mass production amounted to the final assurance that money was to be a sign rather than a "thing," that it was increasingly abstracted from its connection to "real" goods. Money appealed to the "anterior existence of gold at the same time as it deconstruct[ed], via its capacity to manufacture money, the very possibility of this anteriority."[22] A different process is of course involved in *Gold*'s alchemist fantasy; the Thing itself (in a literal and Lacanian sense) becomes ubiquitous, with the

21. Equivalent figures are rampant in Nazi films of the early forties: *Titanic* (1943) ascribes responsibility for the shipwreck to British capitalists playing stock market games; in *Germanin* (1943) the British obstruct for years a German professor's development of an antidote to African sleeping sickness. *The Rothschilds* (1940) assails the British for their alliance with Jews and their fusion of capitalism and religion; where God is "a business partner," there is "no harmonium in your money-church."
22. Rotman, 53.

effect that it ceases to be the Thing it was. As in the historical evolution of money, gold would undergo a transformation from substance to function. Only unlike in the case of mass-produced money, which facilitated, indeed was necessary to, the increased complexity of societies, mass-produced gold becomes a body "too much" threatening an existing economic equilibrium. It becomes another of Frankenstein's monsters.

Although only one tiny piece of gold appears in *Gold*, the film ascribes to it a social-psychological power, a sublime essence independent of its real presence. The infusion of limitless gold into the world never really happens in the film — always remaining something that *potentially will* happen — yet even this potential inflicts major disaster; seeing and foreseeing are fused so that the actual can no longer be distinguished from the potential. The film encapsulates the downward spiral effected by the specter of mass-produced gold in a brief montage sequence which, though presented in documentary style (dates, then newspaper headlines are framed by grainy images of panic-stricken crowds), consists of a narrative within the narrative — a six-day sequence seemingly replicating the labor of biblical creation:

> 5.10.: The Golden Age To Come! . . . Major Economic Leaders Predict General Prosperity.
>
> 6.10.: Mass Production of Artificial Gold . . . Presumably a Significant Stimulation of the Economy.
>
> 7.10.: Inflation of Gold! . . . Large Banks Warn of Inflation . . . Feverish Preparations for Gold Production.
>
> 8.10.: Stock Market Panic as a Result of Imminent Gold! . . . Serious Unemployment Riots in South African Gold Districts.
>
> 9.10.: World Catastrophe! . . . Deaths and Injuries at Protests against the "Wills Gold."
>
> 10.10.: The Golden Plague Forging its Path of Annihilation! . . . John Wills Remarks Unscrupulously, "Every Invention Demands Sacrifices!"

The press discourse symbolizes Germany as a body vulnerable to assault by "injury" and "annihilation," by an anthropomorphized "plague forging its path." (While the chaos inflicted by gold affects the whole world, the film's restriction to German headlines, in combination with its semiotic opposition between Germany as *Heimat* and foreignness, implicitly equates "Germany" with the civilized world.) Unleashed capitalism literally induces a crisis of vision suggested by the appearance on screen of two separate images shifting frenetically back and forth and at points overlapping with each other. The subsequent appearance of John Wills's face superimposed over the headlines "answers" the popular confusion: the anonymous force of capitalism has a face; Wills literally embodies the "bacillus" impeding the health of the social organism.

Despite its own "feverish" efforts to be the anticapitalist narrative it is on the surface, *Gold* betrays a profound ambivalence. It owes much of its narrative and erotic tension to the allure of the very object it seeks to condemn.[23] While *Robert and Bertram*'s allegorical perspective and temporal allusions take an inductive approach broadening from the microcosm within the narrative to the social whole (and even beyond the text), *Gold* belies its surface moralism and seems to be more interested in the desire of the two protagonists as a personal showdown. As much as Holk and Wills are oppositional figures, the obsession with gold production they share lends them a commonality that Holk in particular disavows (while justifying his obsession with the desire to prove that the discredited Achenbach was on the right path, to resurrect Achenbach's good name and with it, "science"). What threatens Holk and gives life to the narrative is not Wills's gangster method or the social repercussions of gold, but Holk's struggle between a symbolic father and Wills as the "shadowy double of the Name of the Father"—the kind of father Žižek analyzes, following Lacan, as a constitutive element of film noir (which, like *Gold*, in indebted to German expressionist film).[24] However much the film eulogizes Achenbach, it is the obscene, excessively present father Wills who captivates Holk and toward whom his actions are directed; he is the "other" father, a "master of enjoyment" who penetrates Holk's desire, who essentially "knows" Holk is there to destroy him.

How else is one to explain the fact that Holk turns his first act of gold production into a spectacle presented for the gaze of Wills and his men? As Holk steps forth with gold in his hand, the men stand behind the massive doors to the laboratory, which slide open like curtains opening onto a

23. A contrasting example is Trenker's *Kaiser of California,* whose narrative structure and cinematography more consistently sustain its anticapitalist "message." The film lives off the semiotic opposition between the use value and aesthetic value of land versus gold, whereby land becomes the film's central source of visual pleasure. Indeed, the camera fetishizes Suter's "garden" in the desert much like the mountains in the mountain films. The film's music, moreover, is by Giuseppe Becce, whose sound became synonymous with mountain films (he composed for Trenker's *The Mountain Calls, The Son of the White Mountains,* Leni Riefenstahl's *The Blue Light,* etc.).

24. See Žižek's *Enjoy Your Symptom! Jacques Lacan in Hollywood and Out* (New York: Routledge, 1992), 158–59.

stage. (The doors play an important diegetic and symbolic role in the story; they serve as a symbolic barrier between a contained life of anti-materialist values and an uncontained world of indulgence and decentering on which Holk must "close the door"; their dysfunction at the end nearly kills masses.) The machine itself becomes another form of stage, from whose heights Holk triumphs. Holk's first act is to hand Wills the gold, a gesture which proves to be an act of bonding (however disavowed), a bonding most clearly represented by the intense close-up of Holk and Wills together, both perspiring with exhilaration. Wills, of whom we hear that Holk is the "first man he seems to respect," later reciprocates, handing a piece of gold back to Holk, completing the gesture of bonding, from which Holk violently extricates himself.

The film is marked by a structuring absence, that of gold itself. The narrative compensates for gold's necessary absence by displacing it onto two fetishized objects, the reactor itself and woman's body. With its large protruding valves, the machine resembles a superdimensional heart housed in a cavity buried deep in a large organism (suggested by Wills's subterranean laboratory), one whose giant dimensions render humans Lilliputian — a symbolization further sustaining the film's predilection for bodily metaphors. Wills refers to the machine as "the heart of the world," a mechanized "heart," which, like *Metropolis*'s robot "Maria," disguises itself to gain control over the human "heart." Via the machine, gold takes on an allegorical function as the core of civilization, the destructive force of modernity. The machine gains an almost anthropomorphic dimension; much crucial action occurs literally on its surface, such as the climactic showdown between Holk and Wills. Accordingly, in key scenes the film gives form to its intersubjective dynamics by alternating between long shots from an extreme low angle (of figures on the machine) and high angle shots of figures far below. For example, Wills announces his intention to mass-produce gold from atop a platform on the machine, where he towers over his workers, who are symmetrically grouped around the illuminated Holk. This (by contrast to a more conventional shot/reverse-shot technique) dramatic formal strategy simultaneously visualizes Nazism's distinction between an authority externally imposed (from above) and one fused with the People, as well as the domination of capital over the People.

Gold extends its "heart" metaphor even further. Via the figure of Wills's daughter Florence, the narrative introduces an erotic desire subtly intermingled with the lure of gold. As a figure who defies gender boundaries, Florence appears a leftover of Weimar culture. She is erotically attractive;

the scene in which she first meets Holk is framed by shots of her standing by a large fire. At the same time, her tall, slim, angular figure borders on the masculine; her independence likewise transgresses the feminine (she smokes, drives, defies her father, travels alone). She is played by Brigitte Helm, whose role as the robot Maria inciting chaos via sexualized dance in *Metropolis* predestined her for another linkage of woman and destructive machine.

The mutual attraction between Florence and Holk serves little function in the narrative except as an undercurrent running parallel to the erotic temptation of gold, that is, as a displacement of gold's erotic allure onto woman. Though nothing implicates her in Wills's machinations (on the contrary, she attempts to "protect" Holk), Florence nonetheless represents a threat to Holk's anticapitalist agenda and his symbolic mandate; the threat not of Wills but of Holk's own desire. This threat — which, like that of gold, remains potential — is articulated in the story of Willy, the old friend Holk encounters working on Wills's yacht, whose involvement with a woman years ago cost him his career and his honor.

Although the desire for Florence and for gold are separate in narrative terms, the film's syntax persistently links them. Holk decides to destroy Wills's reactor the moment Florence makes clear her desire for him; hence his decision appears more a form of self-defense against his own desire than a defense of the social welfare. His ultimate acquiescence to desire, though for gold, not Florence, is also syntactically linked with Florence, whose own desire remains unfulfilled (she waits for him in vain at a party, during which time he secretly visits the machine). However, in order to produce gold, he turns the machine's voltage up to dangerous limits, as if to displace erotic tension. Finally, his encounter with Florence after producing gold seems almost a form of consummation; Holk appears drained and exhausted as she drives off with him in her car.

Accordingly, Holk's ultimate act of containing the machine is simultaneous with his renunciation of Florence, yet it is the former renunciation which the film chooses to exploit. The machine's destruction becomes its climax — a literal explosion again displacing the erotic — while Florence is merely banished from the film, which displays no tearful farewell, no cross-cutting revealing her reaction. It is as if the narrative is suggesting that, just as gold would become defetishized, lose its status as Thing by being omnipresent, the same banalization would occur with Florence. Were Holk to pursue his desire for her, she would become another everyday object. Above all, her importance lay not in herself, but in the link she represented to gold and to Wills, and "the default of the paternal metaphor" as described by Žižek with reference to film noir: "As long as the obscene-knowing father is still present, the woman is not yet fatal, she remains an *object of exchange* between father and son — father *qua* 'master of Enjoyment' disposes of the woman."[25] With Holk's forced reinstatement of the paternal metaphor embodied in Achenbach's "memory," Florence's narrative and screen role is spent.

The flood at the film's conclusion suggests both apocalyptic biblical retribution and the unleashing of uncontained, erotic Otherness linked to gold and to Florence. Simultaneously, water acts as a form of baptism purging the social body of Wills's evil and purging Holk of his guilt (of desire) by his sacrificial redemption of the People (a motif recurring in other films like Herbert Selpin's *Water for Canitoga*, 1939, in which the Albers hero likewise nearly drowns). Yet even this is ambivalent; in his suicide Wills exhibits a consistency, if not an ethos. As "master of enjoyment," he enjoys to the end, refusing to capitulate to Holk's renunciation on behalf of the symbolic order. In a film that from the first moment associated gold with specular pleasure, Wills is last seen with his eye illuminated as he peers into the machine, satisfying his scopophilic drive, ultimately relinquishing the distance of vision and becoming one with his creation.

Also parallel to Holk's renunciation of gold in favor of moralizing platitudes is his renunciation of the erotic woman for "little Margit," a literal embodiment of Theweleit's white nurse, whose round, "soft" features render her "maternal" (in blatant contrast to Florence), and who, like the white nurse, is absent throughout most of the story, waiting in the *Heimat* she embodies. Margit's linkage with Holk via blood — she donated her blood to save him after the first explosion — affirms his choice as one in favor of "nature" (vs. bonding with a "foreign" element), as well as sustaining the film's "heart" metaphor.

Ironically, Holk, precisely the narrative opponent of "exchange value," is the figure who in the course of the story completes a circular series of exchanges: he exchanges Margit for Florence and back; he exchanges Achenbach as symbolic father for Wills and back — all linked to the circulating object of a tiny piece of gold. In fact, Holk does not renounce Florence as much for Margit (whom he "almost forgot"), but for various forms of male bonding: with his spiritual father Achenbach, who in death is imbued with a mythical geniality and godlike creativity (he is "substance" in opposition to the dissolving and dispersing effect generated by

25. Ibid., 160.

money),[26] and with Wills's workers, with whom Holk develops a characteristic Leader/Volk relationship, attested to by a worker's comment: "As
long as Holk is there, we don't have to concern ourselves [with the perils
of gold production]." In many ways the film's resolution with its quasi-
biblical flood again recalls Lang's *Metropolis*,[27] with the difference that
Holk empowers the People to destroy the machine about to bring "pov-
erty and misery upon the world," while in *Metropolis* they remain an
uncontrollable mob. This difference is, however, deceptive; while *Metropolis* is open in its disdain for the People, *Gold* disguises its disdain under
an idyllic gaze that likewise assumes the People's dependency on a
"higher" agency of Leadership.

FOREIGN CONTAMINATION: *HITLER YOUTH QUEX, HANS WESTMAR,*
    S.A. MAN BRAND, FOR HUMAN RIGHTS, POUR LE MÉRITE

Although each of the preceding films also involved the fantasy of foreign
penetration threatening the "German" organism, I would like to turn my
discussion to some films that respond in a most literal sense to the fear of
penetration by an unspecified "outside," to *Überfremdung.* The notion of
foreign penetration takes a number of predictable narrative forms in Nazi
cinema. The popular topos in Nazi cinema of returning "home" (cf. the
title of *Heimkehr,* literally "Returning Home," 1941), for example, illustrates the parallel between the need for spatial, geographical containment
and personal containment: A spatially contained, homogeneous "German" environment provides a context in which the individual can avoid
contamination and in which community can come to fruition. Hans Albers's return home in *Gold* and *Refugees* (1933), Zarah Leander's return
to her village in *Heimat* (1938), Luis Trenker's and Willy Birgel's return
from America in *The Prodigal Son* (1934) and *America — A Man Wants to
Go to Germany* (1934), and so on. A variation on this narrative addresses
the necessity of spatial armament or containment, the protection of the
German organism at the geographical fringes. This story line takes on a
biological dimension in *The Golden City,* in which the heroine Maria is
the product of a German father and a (deceased) Czech mother, whose

26. In addition to recalling Nazi Genius narratives, he embodies Nazism's martyr fantasy (cf. the Horst Wessel legend).
27. It is well known that the scriptwriter for *Metropolis,* Thea von Harbou, went on to
become a prominent Nazi, writing the script for many films, among them *The Old and
the Young King, The Ruler,* and *The Broken Jug* (after Kleist).

basic character flaw — fascination with city life — Maria inherits. All these narratives invest geography with an imaginary quality that is, as I will elucidate, internalized within the individual and yet never ceases to exist as a psychic value outside of him/her.

Another narrative variation is the contamination of an individual body within an otherwise healthy organism. In *Ohm Krüger,* Krüger's son studies in England and returns home defending "internationalism," a view brutally corrected by the film's trajectory, in which he and his family are murdered by British colonialists. *Kolberg* embodies the dangers of internationalism in the form of the feminized musician Klaus, who has studied in Strasbourg (a French city in the historical context of the film) with the same effect as in *Ohm Krüger.* The restoration of *Kolberg*'s narrative equilibrium depends on the social body purging itself of an individual body "poisoned" by the foreign; hence Klaus (like Maria in *The Golden City*) drowns as Kolberg is flooded (a flood again rife with Theweleitian implications). He is attempting to save his violin, the metaphoric representation for corrupt, soft "civilization."

Three programmatic films made the year the Nazis seized power, *S.A. Man Brand, Hans Westmar,* and *Hitler Youth Quex,* all 1933, reverse the above configuration, depicting "contained" individuals struggling within a geographical space of contamination. The old "propaganda" oriented scholarship I criticized early on is perhaps most valid in the case of these films, which more than even most films commissioned by the Nazi state bear the stamp of a movement using "entertainment" to consolidate its power and consequently producing, with the exception of *Hitler Youth Quex,* box office failures of whose "sledgehammer" effect even the Nazis themselves were skeptical. The films essentially fill out and personalize the right's crucial post–World War I narrative, that of the "stab-in-the-back" (alleging that the democrats in power in the Weimar years had "sold Germany out" during World War I). On the other hand, these early films illustrate in an exemplary way the role imagined geography played in Nazism's narrativization of its own evolution. Their structural similarity alone attests to their programmatic value; consequently, I will outline their structure rather than attempt plot synopses of each (I will discuss *Hitler Youth Quex* in more detail below). All are variations on the Horst Wessel myth,[28] on whose name Hans Westmar is a fictional variation: in

28. *Hitler Youth Quex* was based on a 1932 novel by Karl Aloys Schenzinger about the (historical) murder of a Nazi youth named Herbert Norkus, who was subsequently much celebrated by the NSDAP. The Wessel myth, however, provided National Socialism with its master narrative of martyrdom.

all three a paradigmatic hero dies for "the cause"; all assail "communism" as a false solution to capitalist corruption; all feature young communist women who develop sympathy for the Nazi hero; all juxtapose the ubiquitous "Internationale" with music connoting Nation. These films appropriate history no less than the eighteenth-century paradigms discussed earlier, with the difference that they look back at a recent history marked by trauma, reviving the retroactive discursive construction "Weimar" in which nothing less than "Germany" itself is the infested space needing purgation by Nazism's "armored" male. In the words of a figure in *Hitler Youth Quex,* "Germany lies in slave-chains which we must break."

Nazi films set in Weimar tend to associate its dissolution with the masses that grew with the urbanization accompanying Germany's swift, late industrialization. Weimar's "mass" takes essentially two forms: the sexualized, degenerate, parasitic "capitalist" classes and the destructive, aggressive, likewise sexualized proletarian masses — both urban phenomena viewed in Nazi discourse as feminized. Already Gustave Le Bon's *Psychologie des foules* of 1895, which was an important source for Hitler's analysis of mass behavior, links the masses to woman; both are unpredictable and capable of going to "extremes." Given the increasing power of both the industrialized classes and the proletariat in modernity, subjugation of "mass" behavior became synonymous with preservation of the dominant fiction of phallic authority, indeed with self-preservation for the fascist male.

While the three films from 1933 depict (in however primitive a way) their imaginary "communism" as a political-economic threat, Weimar "capitalism" manifests itself almost exclusively as a violation and disfigurement of Germany's social body. A sequence from *Hans Westmar* shows Berlin to be disfigured beyond recognition, as a character remarks: "This is Berlin? This is Germany's capital? I don't recognize it." As Westmar leads a German émigré to the United States and his American daughter on a tour of the city, they are flooded with signifiers of the alien and incomprehensible. Neon signs cut diagonally across the screen from all directions: "On parle français," "English spoken," names of international restaurants intersect with each other, rendering the otherwise familiar topography of Berlin a disorienting twilight zone.[29] The older man's Stammkneipe, his favorite pub from his youth, now bears the name Chez

---

29. Cf. the portrayal in *Togger* of a conference at the ruthless, monopolistic Reuter corporation, which tries to secure domination of the international market. The scene consists of a long series of corporate board members holding speeches, each in a different language.

Ninette, which is emblematic of the encroachment upon Berlin of the foreign and feminine (especially given the phallic overtones of *Stamm* as stem, trunk, or male genetic line). Not only is Berlin's general topography thus disfigured, but individual bodies as well. Chez Ninette's clientele consists of bald, obese, cigar-smoking, boisterous men, marked throughout Nazi cinema as "capitalists." The scene further illustrates the violation of the social body as it foregrounds racial impurity, nakedness, and degradation. In the bar the group is greeted by a black coat boy, and everyone speaks French. To the older man's question, "Can one speak German here too?" the uncomprehending coat boy answers: "*Naturellement!*" and gestures toward the men's toilet, to which the camera pans, showing theater posters advertising "A Jew Goes through the World" and "Berlin without a Shirt." The German language is polluted in this world by excrement.

The slang term the films use for nightclub, *Bumslokal,* suggests its status as a stain on the health of the social organism, a status invoked in many Nazi films set in the Weimar era which feature variations on Chez Ninette (*Pour le Mérite,* 1938; *For Human Rights,* 1934; *Togger,* 1940). *Bumslokal* comes from *bumsen* (literally bang, bump, or bounce), which refers to the atavistic beat of jazz and is also a slang word for sexual intercourse. Nightclub scenes are among the few in Nazi cinema to specifically thematize blacks as a race wrestled from its "natural" context by imperialist forces antagonistic to Germany, and as a sexual threat or what one might call in Theweleitian terms a black — as equivalent to red — "flood." (This contrasts with their benevolent portrayal in *Ohm Krüger* and *Germanin,* where, however, they are contained by a white "father" and have not penetrated Germany's space.[30]) Whether represented naked on wall

30. *Germanin* pits the life of its German medical hero against that of a British colonel who has destroyed all but one vial of the life-saving vaccination Germanin. Although the German doctor sacrifices his own life to save Africans, the film never narrativizes the widespread suffering of the black population from sleeping sickness as it does the two Europeans' — even the villainous British colonel. While the film's narration follows the course of each man's sickness on a personal level, the suffering of the Africans is consistently portrayed via a documentary discourse (using nondiegetic voice-overs, newsreel-style photography of anonymous victims whose emaciated state ironically recalls Nazism's camp victims) that emphasizes the gravity of the epidemic but in detached, abstract terms. While the film portrays blacks as "good-natured," nowhere does it personalize black suffering or suture the spectator into an identification with a black. See Sander Gilman's fascinating analogy of Nazism's linkage of blacks with sickness in Africa (healed by German doctors) and of Jews with sickness infesting Europe. Gilman, 221.

murals or as striptease dancers, blacks in the nightclub threaten the containment of sexuality essential for the armored man's self-preservation. *Togger* even shows a black man dancing with a white woman, an "obscenity" (*Schweinerei*) that provokes near-nausea in the protagonist. Such transgressions are not without their titillating dimension; they permit the spectator an imaginary decentering experience, while never threatening his or her real-life containment within a "moral" identity.

Social dislocation occurs in nightclub scenes on the level of sound as well as of the visual. Once Chez Ninette is established in *Hans Westmar* as a space of confusing, incomprehensible foreign phrases, it continues to veritably rape "Germany" through music. A drunken man requests the orchestra to play "The Guard at the Rhine," a song heavily invested with national sentiment. The orchestra plays a jazzed up version of the song, and drunkards begin dancing. Overwhelmed, Westmar protests loudly and, near tears, stalks out of the bar. It is significant that what pushes Westmar "over the edge" is not just the disfigurement of Germany's physical space but the disturbance of his aesthetic enjoyment, via the song, of the Thing "Germany." "The Guard at the Rhine" helps make "Germany" the emotional space Westmar hopes to recover in geographical terms, as implied by his remark to the American girl: "Germany — is somewhere completely different" (*ganz wo anders*). No matter where "Germany" is at any given time, it is a community that must always remain imaginary, and hence be experienced aesthetically.

The nightclub as an "international" phenomenon points to another dimension affecting the social body: the penetration of "German" space by capitalism, by exchange value, homogenizes the culture — the specific of Germany gives way to the abstractness of international capitalism.[31] National Socialism counters this abstractness not with a specific, but with another form of abstractness: emotional collectivism. Westmar's remark that "Germany" is somewhere else suggests that it exists at this point only within him, the Volkish, soldierly man (calling to mind Klaus Theweleit's

31. The same film links the "international" with intellectuals. A liberal university professor defends Germany's humiliation in World War I with "world citizenship": "The treaty of Versailles, which brought us the peace we yearned for, drew the political borders of Germany even tighter. But . . . with narrower borders we became border-*less.* We have become Europeans, world citizens. We have been taken up as equals into the great cultural nations. . . . Down with weapons!" As if to affirm the spectator's anticipated response, the camera cuts to a shot of two raised fencing swords — a typically phallic image declaring war on the professor's pacifism.

definition of the Nation as existing in the individual or in the male group). Berlin, which in its present state provides a spatial metaphor for the threat of capitalism, is important not as a specific location but as a representative element of the greater whole, Germany. Yet within the film's discourse Berlin and even "Germany" cease to be spatial categories, but rather emotional ones: Germany is "inside" — at this point only inside an individual, but it must begin penetrating everyone. The "Germany" *inside* of Westmar is also an imaginary body *outside* of him, a Thing that must remain inaccessible, experienced through various substitutes (flags and other symbols, songs and narratives) that are never entirely "it" (see my discussion of Lacan's Thing in chapter 3). Still, the narrative assumes that once "Germany" as an abstract emotional force has been internalized by the masses, its spatial boundaries can likewise be secured. The very notion of a "German" identity is dependent upon such bodily and psychological containment, since identity always already means containment and the demarcation of boundaries (and at the same time it reconciles the individual's containment in an armored identity and the pleasurable release in merging with a whole).

The best known of the three films, Hans Steinhoff's *Hitler Youth Quex,* similarly invokes Germany's space as an imaginary value that is at once "inside" its protagonist and projected by him onto something outside of himself. The film is set in the Berlin working-class neighborhood Beuselkiez during the Weimar years when National Socialism was a fledgling movement. It tells the story of Heini Völker (= of the *Volk*), a boy of about fourteen and son of a communist, who is drawn against his father's will to the Hitler Youth. Despite initial distrust by his new Hitler Youth friends, Heini repeatedly proves his fidelity by warning them of communist ambush plans and by printing pro-Nazi leaflets at the print shop where he works. He survives asphyxiation when his destitute and anxiety-ridden mother commits suicide, but increasingly incurs the wrath of the communists. At the end of the film a communist with the telling name Wilde (= the wild one) murders Heini, who dies with the words of the Hitler Youth song on his lips.

As many have remarked, this film often "feels" like films from the Weimar era.[32] Yet while much Weimar film and literature celebrates the uniqueness and local color of urban settings, the specific in *Hitler Youth Quex* again exists only to be surrendered to the general. Beuselkiez,

32. See, for example, Francis Courtade and Pierre Cadars, *Geschichte des Films im dritten Reich*, trans. Florian Hopf (Munich: Carl Hanser, 1975), 43.

Berlin, the river Spree all gain significance in the film as specific entities that need to be reincorporated into the large, abstract community "Germany," which is less a place than an "armored" mentality embedded in discursive representations. This valorization of the general over the specific is most clearly articulated in the film's discussion between the communist Father Völker and a Hitler Youth leader when Heini is hospitalized after his mother's suicide. Below is a transcription of the scene's dialogue, which is often reproduced in studies of *Hitler Youth Quex* (often, unfortunately, at the expense of other registers of meaning in the film). On a level of ideology no scene better captures *Hitler Youth Quex*'s project: valorizing National Socialism as community. But it also condenses the film's main narrative dynamic of movement within an imagined space; it anticipates a subject's trajectory from an inadequate mode of family to a bigger, more nurturing one; from physical to emotional space. We cannot reduce the film to this "talky" propaganda lesson, but we can use it as a point of departure whose words become translated into pictures, sounds, and a story:

> YOUTH LEADER: Hello, Heini. The doctor says you can leave the hospital now.
>
> HEINI: But where am I to go?
>
> FATHER: What sort of question is that? With your father, of course, where you belong.
>
> YOUTH LEADER: But that's precisely the question. Where does the boy belong today? My parents were well-meaning, but when I was fifteen, I ran away . . . many boys did the same . . .
>
> FATHER: Rascals, that's what they were, all of them.
>
> YOUTH LEADER: Ah, but that is their nature, and it always has been. Once they reach a certain age they all want to roam. Where then does a boy belong? Why don't you ask your son?
>
> FATHER: Well then, what have you to say for yourself? (*Heini starts to answer*)
>
> YOUTH LEADER: Tell me, were you in the war?
>
> FATHER: Why, of course I was . . .
>
> YOUTH LEADER: Well then, over two million boys volunteered for action. All of them had families, fathers, and mothers. Tell me, where did they belong?
>
> FATHER: I am a simple man of the people, a proletarian [*ein Prolet*].
>
> YOUTH LEADER: You've heard of the Movement, haven't you?
>
> FATHER: (*gesticulating*) Movement! Up one, two, — Up one, two — that's the movement I understood. Until I was hit by a bullet and then

the movement stopped. From then on I had to limp to the labor exchange. Week in, week out, year after year. It drove me crazy. Do you think that I got fat through eating too much? Of course not, it was because I was out of a job. Sitting around made me fat. So where do I belong? I belong with my friends, from my own class. And where I belong, my son belongs too.

YOUTH LEADER: With your own class? By that, I take you to mean the Internationale?

FATHER: Yes, of course, the Internationale.

YOUTH LEADER: (*pauses*) Where were you born?

FATHER: Why, in Berlin.

YOUTH LEADER: Yes, but where is Berlin?

FATHER: Why, on the Spree.

YOUTH LEADER: Yes, I know that. But in what country?

FATHER: (*impatient*) In Germany, of course.

YOUTH LEADER: Yes, of course, in Germany — in *our* Germany. Now I want you to think about that.[33]

Most obviously, the scene illustrates Nazism's early courting of the working class by means of an idyllic construction it calls "the worker" (analogous to the invention of the King, Genius, or People we've seen in other films). Heretofore we have seen Father Völker largely as a drunkard and a bully and in relation to son and family; that is, we have seen him as a failed father. Here he is in relation to no one but himself, he becomes a subject whom "society" has failed.[34] This is the precondition for our emerging identification with him, which is in turn the precondition for his beginning conversion to Nazism. The World War I injury Völker mentions is another important signifier of his "inner" value, especially because it is dispensable to the plot; he is capable of soldierly "sacrifice." Moreover, a contemporary German audience would have recognized in Völker one of Weimar culture's best-known proletarian victims, Franz Biberkopf of Piel

---

33. English translation with some modifications from Welch, *Propaganda and the German Cinema* (Oxford: Clarendon Press, 1983), 69.

34. Such martyrdom is not uncommon in Nazi cinema, illustrated by the portrayal of a worker as a Christ figure in *The Dismissal* (1942). Nazi films always distinguish, however, between the misguided leftist worker and "communist" leadership. The latter often consists literally of foreign bodies: inhuman Russians and/or Jews who treat their followers "like children" and have no time for "silly sentimentalities" (*Gefühlsduseleien*). When a German communist objects in *S.A. Man Brand* to cold-blooded murder, his Soviet colleague responds sarcastically: "Still so German?"

Jutzi's *Berlin Alexanderplatz* (1931, based on Alfred Döblin's novel), which starred the actor playing Father Völker, Heinrich George (also Duke Karl Alexander and Karl Eugen in *Jew Süss* and *Friedrich Schiller,* respectively).

After the discussion with the Youth Leader, we never again see Father Völker as anything but the victim/subject he becomes in the scene. His eventual repetition of the Youth Leader's phrases about "our" Germany becomes paradigmatic for the worker's recuperability. Significantly, however, his conversion also signals his dispensability to the film; his narrative "job" is to demonstrate Nazism's appeal and not to be a parent, which, we will see below, Nazism can do more effectively. The repetition of the communist's conversion in other films attests to its programmatic importance as Nazism consolidated its power: the protagonist's father in *S.A. Man Brand* undergoes a similar trajectory, remarking at the end of the film "I belong to the 'we' now, too!" "Communism," the father implies, is false community; the only way out of isolation is Nazism.

More important for my focus on imaginary space is the fact that *Hitler Youth Quex* "answers" communist ideology by ceding the specific to the general. Despite all its predictable coding of "communists" as disorderly drunks, to a degree the film refers to communism on a manifest political level. Völker's discourse is articulated throughout the film around the notion of class difference and conflict (which was, of course, central to Marx's notion of social relations). The Youth Leader uses the idea of a German *Volk* united by blood, by common origin, as an antidote to Völker's Marxist concept of society as a struggle among different classes for hegemony. The idea of "one" (that is, "our") Germany that begins to "grow" on Völker serves merely to undermine this rudimentary political basis. "Community," like the Volkish concept of socialism, aspired to efface social differences, yet it was accompanied historically by few changes in the real social structure, especially after 1934. Unlike Berlin and the Spree, for which Völker feels no ideological fervor, "our" Germany again begins to transcend the geographical as an emotionally charged locale. Precisely such a displacement of political discourse (class consciousness) by cathexis ("ours") is the precondition for aestheticized politics. The sequence of questions posed by the Youth Leader nonetheless disguises his discourse of invocation as one of rational argumentation.

Hans Westmar's romantic, "true" socialism has the same aestheticizing function. Westmar, a university student, gives up his studies to become a worker and begins successfully converting other workers to National Socialism: "We [the educated] must fight side by side with the workers. . . .

There must not be classes any more! We, too, are workers! We work with our heads—and our place is next to our brother who works with his hands." Westmar's comment once again recalls the much maligned solution to social conflict in Lang's *Metropolis,* with its call for the "heart" to mediate between the "head" (management) and the "hand" (labor)—to avoid any real confrontation of social problems by proposing what Axel Eggebrecht called an "unscientific sympathy-socialism." The film's most famous shot shows close up a clenched "communist" fist, which slowly opens up to assume the Hitler salute.

What makes *Hitler Youth Quex* more interesting than the other early films is its skill in mobilizing many levels (spatial, bodily, familial, specular, acoustic-musical) to displace the political onto the aesthetic, to realize aesthetically the ideology in the "conversion" scene quoted above. Ideology critique can easily uncover the film's tension between "communism" as chaos (unbridled drive and violence) versus National Socialism as order (containment and "inner peace"). This binarism determines the juxtaposition of spaces (the Völker family's cramped flat vs. his Nazi friends' spacious, bourgeois apartment), of women (the sexually aggressive communist girl Gerda vs. the deeroticized, boyish League of German Girls member Ulla), of modes of behavior (the neat columns of Hitler Youth vs. the boisterous disorder of communist youth on the train platform), and of music styles (the buoyant enthusiasm of the Hitler Youth song vs. the drunken slurring with which Heini's father belts out the "Internationale"—literally belting his son in the process for having sung the Nazi song). Moreover, even within the confines of its Berlin setting, the film interweaves a broad, "antimodern" spatial opposition between the urban and rural with its chaos/order opposition. It links "communism" with a local carnival[35] pervaded by a visual/acoustic confusion similar to that I discussed with respect to nightclub scenes; hence communism appears as a decidedly urban phenomenon typical of "Weimar." Heini's first encounter with National Socialism, by contrast, occurs in a forest outside Berlin, and the above-quoted scene sparking Father Völker's conversion is located in a natural enclave within the city, a parklike area surrounding Heini's hospital. Throughout the film National Socialism thus represents a return of the

---

35. See Thomas Elsaesser's discussion of carnivals as ironic parallelism in melodrama; "Tales of Sound and Fury: Observations on the Family Melodrama," in *Movies and Methods,* ed. Bill Nichols (Berkeley: University of California Press, 1985), 2:167.

city to the principles of nature, to what Hanno Möbius refers to as an intended "re-naturalization" of the urban environment.[36]

To this spatial regime one might add a bodily-spatial critique. Iconically, *Hitler Youth Quex* links "communism" with a circular movement that not only is dizzying, but goes nowhere; Heini is lured into frustration by a spinning wheel at the carnival, where he tries unsuccessfully to win the knife that eventually kills him; the communist Stoppel (literally "stubble," as in an unkempt beard) coaxes Heini to join his peers in front of a swiftly revolving carousel, on which the sexualized Gerda constantly rides and onto which Stoppel hops (photo 47). National Socialism, by contrast, is linked with close-ups of walking legs that clearly symbolize agency, community, bodily discipline, a straight line into the future (photo 48). The often repeated first line of the Hitler Youth song, with its suggestion of marching, sustains this forward movement: "Our flag flutters on before us." This leg iconography is one of the film's debts to Jutzi's leftist film *Mother Krause's Journey to Happiness* (1929), which concludes with legs marching symbolically toward a proletarian order (exemplifying not only the ironic fact that Nazism "borrowed" many propaganda tools from its archenemies, but the fact that leftist movements are also predisposed to aestheticized politics).

The nickname Heini's Nazi friends give him and that finds its way into the film's title, Quex or quicksilver, suggests not only constant movement but speed. Heini is forever on the move, distributing warnings and leaflets, all of which move Nazism *ahead*. But his narrative function is also to run *between* Nazism and communism, to provide a mediating bridge between the two that, at least in the case of his father, begins to take hold (this mediation is, of course, intended as a usurpation of the political "movement" deemed illegitimate). Even the last shot of Heini before he falls to his death shows a close-up of his child's legs in shorts inching forward despite his mortal wound.[37] The few shots of "communist" legs in the film generally show Gerda's, which either hinder Nazism's forward trajectory (e.g., when her foot covers a Nazi campaign leaflet or her legs, shot close-up, mislead the one Hitler youth who is vulnerable to her sexual ad-

36. Hanno Möbius, "Heimat im nationalsozialistischen Film," *Augen-Blick 5: Heimat,* Marburger Hefte zur Medienwissenschaft (1988): 35.

37. Leni Riefenstahl includes a similar shot of a boy's legs in the Hitler Youth scene of *Triumph of the Will*—presumably both shots inspire parental feelings of protection in the spectator.

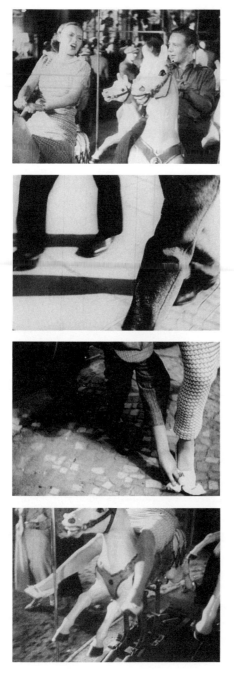

47·50 While *Hitler Youth Quex* links "communism" with dizzying, circular movement and female sexuality, it links National Socialism with resolute, forward movement. 47: "Communist" woman Gerda and a morally vulnerable Hitler Youth ride the carousel; 48: the camera focuses on legs as Heini and his newfound Nazi friend walk; 49: Gerda's foot stops a Nazi leaflet; 50: the camera dwells on the sexual, rocking movement of Gerda's close-up legs.

vances), or move in a masturbatory, aimless way (her sexual rocking on the carousel horse) (photos 49–50).

This bodily dimension of movement echoes the central verbal motif of movement in the confrontation between Father Völker and the Youth Leader. For the Youth Leader, Nazism is a "movement" with all its connotations of progress and "spiritual" transcendence. For Father Völker, a victim both of class oppression and class ideology, "movement" remains on a level that not only is grotesquely literal but which, like "communism" itself in the film's discourse, leads, if anywhere, to a quagmire. The "movement" Völker describes proceeds from one which is rhythmical and repetitive ("Up one, two, — Up one, two," recalling other "communist" legs in the film), to one which is impaired ("I had to limp to the labor exchange"), and finally to stasis ("The movement stopped. . . . Sitting around made me fat"). Until he can displace material oppression (and with it his materialist philosophy) onto the psychic, ultimately aesthetic "movement" offered by the Youth Leader, Völker will continue to feel "crazy," a state evoking the spiral movement of "communism."

Another important level on which *Hitler Youth Quex* replaces the need for political "explanation" for Heini's conversion is, as already suggested, the familial. Many have pointed out how the film eliminates the nuclear family in favor of Nazism, which is also prepared by the Youth Leader's story of having left his own family, and by his mythical invocation of this as the "natural" trajectory of boys: "Ah, but that is their nature, and it always has been." What was only implicit in the "eighteenth-century" movies is here explicit: Nazism increasingly takes over the family's function; it becomes a totalizing force pervading all aspects of the private and the public sphere.

One might refine this argument a bit by stressing that Nazism doesn't as much eliminate the nuclear family in *Hitler Youth Quex* as it does step in for an aberrant family structure in which the father/son constellation is from the start reversed. As Gregory Bateson's early commentary on the film (edited into prints still in circulation) points out, Father Völker is far more infantile than his son. Unable to control either his impulses (like alcoholism) or his temper, he alternates between begging his wife (whom he calls "Mother") for money to buy beer and destructively pillaging for it. At the beginning of the film he comes home wounded like a child from the playground, while the first shot of Heini shows him working at his (diegetically important) printing press (photos 51–52). To complete the role reversal, breadwinner Heini arrives in time to give his mother a coin to give the father in order to curb his tantrum. Although we have seen that

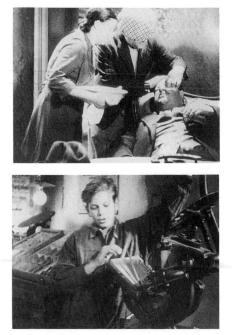

51·52 *Hitler Youth Quex:* Editing juxtaposes the infantilized father (*above*) home from a "playground fight" with son Heini (*below*) always already an adult and "bread-winner."

the film's characterization of Father Völker develops in complexity, this display of family dysfunction and the default of the paternal suffices to naturalize Nazism's friendly takeover. It also serves as preparation for the child/pupil role Father Völker readily assumes vis-à-vis the Youth Leader. (A more deconstructively inclined viewer might read the ease with which Father Völker "buys" the Youth Leader's "message" as a sure sign of infantility.)

Familial dysfunction reaches its culmination, however, in Mother Völker, notwithstanding her surface portrayal as "pure" Mother *qua* victim. She is burdened with the guilt of abandoning Heini — more importantly, of trying to kill him — through a murder/suicide plot also borrowed from *Mother Krause's Journey to Happiness* (Mother Völker turns on the gas when Heini is asleep, convinced that communists will kill him anyway). Mother's abdication as giver-of-life again naturalizes Heini's relocation in Nazism's superior family, this time as a form of rebirth, which is also evoked by the suicide scene's stylized cinematic technique. When Mother Völker turns on the deadly gas, the frame begins to "swim," transporting Heini into a space beyond reality, erasing time and the existing symbolic order. When he reawakens he is helpless in a bed (a womb or crib), needing outside help to orient himself. His question "Is Mother coming?" is answered by the arrival of his (essentially parentless) Hitler Youth friends. Indeed, despite the maternal presence of the nurse and Ulla, Heini is essentially left without a mother — only with a *paternal* figure of symbolic identification in the Youth Leader whose blond, slim erectness not only fits the "Aryan" ideal more than the corpulent father, but who looks literally more like Heini's father. It is Nazism itself that takes on the nurturing, enveloping function of Mother. The gift the Hitler Youth brings Heini also suggests rebirth and an enveloping nurturance: his new uniform, complete with mirror, will fuse with his body to form a new identity. He immediately puts on the hat, finding, like Lacan's famous infant, enjoyment (*jouissance*) in his Ideal-I. He can also mirror himself in the photo of his Hitler Youth friends that he finds in the uniform pocket.

Finally, *Hitler Youth Quex* unabashedly confesses the secret of Nazism as theater. Heini's "discovery" of Nazism when coaxed to go on a camping trip with his communist "friends" synthesizes the specular and acoustic with other elements discussed so far. This discovery begins with forward movement as Heini walks *away* from the communist camp, drawn *toward* the Hitler Youth camp. The walk is the film's first encoding of birth or passage into a new world — like a child in the womb, Heini hears before he sees. March music wafting from beyond the frame overlaps briefly with the communists' accordion music, only to become louder, eventually drowning out communism musically as it will in narrative terms. The magnetic promise of the music is fulfilled by the spectacle Heini (at times framed by foliage) witnesses perched on a hill, as if in a Greek amphitheater (photos 53–54). The entire spectacle has an aura of the elemental — it progresses from night into day as Heini is "enlightened," its alternation between ritual and sport encompassing air, earth, fire, and water.

As long as Nazism is pure spectacle to Heini, however, it remains the elusive object of his desire. He is excluded by distance, restricted to a desiring gaze, and must be content with a bodily simulation of Nazism's forward trajectory, as when he marches in place to the music, vicariously accompanying the marching boys below. Heini's subsequent reference to the Nazis as the "Others" suggests the simultaneous joy and pain this relation elicits. Here Otherness connotes a sphere of beauty and transcendence suggested by projections from the eighteenth century on of woman and nature as Other. The appeal of Nazism as desired Other depends again on its aestheticization, its promise of a perpetual state of euphoria, as well as its promise to serve as a benevolent, nurturing big Other.

Nazism never entirely loses its quality of Otherness for Heini; indeed, it cannot, given its dialectical relationship to its subject. Like all imagined

53·54 National Socialism is presented as theater, as an inaccessible object of desire linked with nature in *Hitler Youth Quex*. Heini is framed by foliage (*above*) as he secretly watches the Hitler Youth camp (*below*).

communities, "Nazism" is at once incorporated into its subject and embodied in external projections. Nonetheless, the trajectory of *Hitler Youth Quex* is to allow Heini to diminish this distance, to allow Nazism to become the "home" he always already feels it to be. On one level, his story is the tragedy of a misplaced subject sucked into communism's deadly spiral, as suggested by the Moritas singer's preordained story of death arresting the subject's path ("but the train, it can derail . . . "). On another, it is the story of a subject who finds his "natural" place in two stages, a bodily stage of fusion with the uniform and a transcendent stage of death, which is his third and final stage of "rebirth." The film's final montage sequence that follows Heini's death is again of feet, this time masses of feet multiplying Heini's spirit hundredfold, marching forward toward the spectator, as if to march right off the screen and into life (and death!), depicting retroactively the geographical and spiritual reappropriation of "home," not only for an individual but for a collective.

Whereas these three 1933 Nazi martyr film narratives depict a man or boy combating a contaminated German space while the spirit of Nazism is always already within him, another paradigm exhibits the same structure with a more historical trajectory, that of the World War I soldier thrust into the feminized world of "Weimar." The resistance of males returning from the war to civilian assimilation likewise pervades films set in Weimar, especially *For Human Rights* and *Pour le Mérite*. Both follow multiple plot lines depicting the trials of soldiers forcibly confronted with civil society. They recall postwar Americans films like King Vidor's *The Big Parade* (1925), Louis Milestone's *All Quiet on the Western Front* (1930), or William Wyler's post–World War II epic *The Best Years of Our Lives* (1946). Kaja Silverman has analyzed *Best Years of Our Lives* as unusual in its acknowledgment of male lack, at least at a particular historical juncture.[38] In all of these films, history functions not as the collective mirror it is in most Nazi and, indeed, most Hollywood films, but as a force of dislocation generating trauma within an established system of representation, one which profoundly affects subjects depending on those systems for their sense of identity. Milestone's *All Quiet on the Western Front,* based on Erich Maria Remarque's pacifist novel, does the unthinkable in this respect, allowing its American viewers to occupy the fictional space of their World War I "enemy"; it tells the story of a group of naive German schoolboys persuaded by an ideologue school teacher to enlist. Like the ex-GIs in *The Big Parade* and *Best Years of Our Lives,* or the soldier on leave in *All Quiet on the Western Front,* the German soldiers returning from World War I in *For Human Rights* and *Pour le Mérite* are displaced; Weimar offers "no place for our kind." Characters in the German films are unable to readjust easily to married life, and self-serving employers are unwilling to acknowledge their service; like Fred in *Best Years of Our Lives,* they are unable to find lucrative employment and are traumatized by memories of the war (while Fred has nightmares, a figure in *For Human Rights* is unable to dance with his wife, feeling he's dancing on the corpses of dead comrades).

Despite these similarities, a fundamental difference separates Nazi films of this genre from at least those American films that, as Silverman argues, do not attempt to align male subjectivity with phallic values. The films I mentioned all took chances commercially by acknowledging war as a deadly, castrating force, symbolized by the many stumps of legs we see in *The Big Parade* and *All Quiet on the Western Front,* and most brutally of all, by the amputated hands of the ex-GI Homer in *Best Years of Our Lives.* The Nazi films, by contrast, unequivocally equate war with the fulfillment of manhood; in war men are intact and bonded together, in war even "half children" are "whole men" (*Pour le Mérite*). While Silverman illustrates how in *The Best Years of Our Lives* Fred's erotic appeal for his

38. *Male Subjectivity at the Margins* (New York: Routledge, 1992), 52–121.

wife depends on his uniform — a fact which magnifies Fred's postwar humiliation (a motif we find in *The Big Parade* as well), *Pour le Mérite* not only equates military decoration with phallic power in a hyperbolic way, but affirms it. During the first section of the film, set before the war's end, a young soldier is awarded the prestigious medal Pour le Mérite, which, the film tells us, was an honor institutionalized by Frederick the Great (in itself evoking associations of phallic authority). The boy disrupts his girlfriend's banal chatter by removing his hand, which has been covering the medal, as if exposing himself in some intimate act which elicits squeals of delight from the girl. His own pleasure derives from rendering himself an object of erotic spectacle, from letting the thrilled girl *see* the medal, rather than telling her about it in words. The scene implicitly restages Freud's narrative of penis envy; the little girl sees it, she immediately wants to have it.

In part this denial of male castration in *Pour le Mérite* and *For Human Rights* can be explained by a historical difference between these films and their American counterparts: while American postwar films worked through the trauma of an ultimately victorious war, my German examples were the product of a state attempting to rewrite the collective loss of World War I as the personal victory of soldierly men, to celebrate itself as the restitution of the wholeness these men seek in the films, and finally to anticipate (at least in the case of *Pour le Mérite,* made the year of Austria's annexation) another war that would negate World War I and "Weimar" through victory. It is as if the "America" of *The Big Parade, All Quiet,* and *Best Years* could afford to lick its collective wounds, while the "Germany" of the thirties had a frenetic need to constitute itself as an imaginary whole, which included depicting the social fragmentation of "Weimar" as a temporary, aberrant phenomenon surmountable by the reemergence of the German "essence."

The divergent role of women in *The Big Parade* and *Best Years of Our Lives* and the German films illustrates the latter's need to uphold an imaginary phallic authority. While in the American films women are ultimately the salvation of the fragmented male egos, they generally function as a threat in the German films. Men return from war, like the artist in *For Human Rights,* to find women occupying their living space; worse yet, the entire culture is "soft": "*men* needed everywhere; only not here" (*Pour le Mérite*). Rather than war, it is peace which traumatizes the narrative figures, especially a peace equated with humiliation and betrayal. These films insistently disavow a destabilized male identity; they project it onto external phenomena. The counterpart to amputated legs and hands symboliz-

ing war's bodily inscription on the male in the American films is the repeated appearance onscreen in *For Human Rights* of a dead comrade's
face looking into the camera (a subjective vision of one of the protagonists). Unlike the stumps, which graphically and traumatically attest to
male castration, the subjective shots of the soldier act more as an ego ideal,
a force of interpellation for the ex-soldier and the film audience remembering the war. They evoke Nazism's kitsch and death aesthetic (Saul
Friedländer), interrupting the seamless flow of continuity editing as a
memory of messianic sacrifice and whole malehood, one mandating that
"Weimar" be surmounted, a masculine subject position restored.[39]

While *The Big Parade* and *The Best Years of Our Lives* focus on each
protagonist's reassimilation into a love and ultimately family relationship[40] — thus affirming heterosexual bonding and integration into a civilian order — the Nazi films equate such a reassimilation with a capitulation
to a feminized Weimar. The only narrative solution offered the protagonists in both films is a continuation of the sociality dictated by war, a
sociality centered on male bonding. *Pour le Mérite,* for example, chooses
not to foreground Captain Prank's relationship with his young wife, but
with his World War I airplane. The film does not even exploit the wife's
(offscreen) death in either cinematic or narrative terms; Prank reports it
with indifference. His reconciliation with his World War I plane, mirac-
ulously saved from surrender to the French by a faithful comrade, is, by
contrast, an emotional high point of the film. Although the war is over and
the plane thus functionally obsolete, Prank exclaims, "My machine! My
Focker! [*sic!*] Now life has meaning once more!" Again the object embodying phallic wholeness is presented as spectacle; the moment Prank's
comrades unveil the hidden plane, he covers his eyes, overwhelmed by the
sight of the fetishized object. The scene strikingly affirms Theweleit's analysis of how in fascist and prefascist literature erotic descriptions are reserved not for women but for horses and other animals and objects (guns,
the hunt, the uniform, the hometown). To the extent the soldier loves

39. Cf. the invocation of "fallen comrades" in *Hans Westmar.* Westmar's remark that
Germany is "elsewhere" is followed by a montage sequence of dancing couples seen
through distorted lenses and in blurred focus, which dissolves into a sequence of battle
scenes from World War I, and finally to a shot of military graves. Westmar exclaims:
"Three million had to die. And they (gesturing toward the club) — they are dancing . . .
boozing . . . howling!"

40. *All Quiet on the Western Front* most radically equates closure with death; the
protagonist's abrupt death is rendered all the more pointless by its coincidence with life
symbolized by a butterfly toward which the protagonist reaches out as he is shot.

humans, they are male: the "men" or the Leader — never females, who pose the threat of Self dissolution, of penetration.[41]

Accordingly, Captain Prank sustains himself with his former World War I squadron as well as his airplane, in an attempt to fuse the military and civilian codes. Two proletarian soldiers beg to stay with "their" Captain Prank during peacetime, and the three perpetuate the male bonding of wartime as well as the same hierarchical order of military bureaucracy, with the educated bourgeois Prank clearly functioning as Leader.[42] Male bonding functions unimpaired; male failure and male lack are displaced onto the context of Weimar corruption (the men's "soldierly" integrity dooms them in civilian occupations; they're "too honest" to succeed as auto mechanics, too scrupulous to work in nightclubs, etc.).

The oppositional closure achieved by *The Big Parade* and *The Best Years of Our Lives* and the German films is not surprising given their different historical junctures. Closure in the American films is synonymous with marriage (i.e., social assimilation). *For Human Rights* and *Pour le Mérite* achieve closure in an opposite manner: a retreat into a state of "war," this time a more metaphoric war against Weimar culture. Unlike in narratives culminating in the protagonist's "return home," that is, in the assurance of personal containment via stable geographical boundaries, "Weimar" protagonists are forced to retrieve their geographical space as their own. Purgation of the foreign and the feminine can only be achieved by protagonists who carry the "front" with them. The films directly equate restoration of phallic authority with National Socialism. Although Goebbels later banned explicit political allusions in film, a number of early films end with the triumph of the Nazis in 1933 or at least in anticipation of that moment — as when one figure in *For Human Rights* remarks just before 1923: "The party I am thinking of doesn't exist yet."

S.A. Man Brand, the third programmatic film the Nazis produced in 1933, most literally gives credit to the Nazi takeover for the restitution of phallic authority in a comical mini-narrative involving hero Brand's middle-aged Nazi landlord Anton and his wife, Genoveva. Genoveva re-

---

41. *Male Fantasies,* vol. 1, trans. Stephen Conway (Minneapolis: University of Minnesota Press, 1987), "A Soldier's Love," 52–53 and 57–63.

42. Despite rhetoric to the contrary, Nazi film portrays class differences, only it ceases to refer to them as such. Paradoxically, "community" depends on hierarchy; social differences appear as "natural" as they do in eighteenth-century drama. As in the eighteenth century, the lower classes display unwavering solidarity with their superiors, as well as providing comic relief.

peatedly forces the henpecked Anton into a feminine position by making him don an apron and wash dishes while she attends meetings. Anton generously lends back to a destitute war-widow the money she pays him in rent, but the greedy Genoveva insists on trying to squeeze money out of renters whether they can pay or not. Anton is thus forced to hide money in a box disguised to resemble a copy of *Mein Kampf,* which presumably Genoveva, as a member of the anti-Nazi Catholic Women's League, will never touch. The news that Hitler has been appointed chancellor provokes a transformation in Anton:

ANTON: Germany Awake!
GENOVEVA: (*shrill*) Anton! That gets on my nerves!
ANTON: Genoveva, in the Third Reich we can't be concerned with your nerves!
GENOVEVA: Anton!
ANTON: (*interrupting*) — Quiet! Anton has awakened!

In one of Nazi cinema's most blatant politicizations of gender, secondary identification with Hitler restores Anton's potency and Ideal-I, which in turn enables him to cast off all traces of femininity and "handle" his astonished wife. This transformation, although couched in a humorous vignette, is the ultimate paradigm for the containment of Otherness, the restoration of male cultural authority necessary for reinstating Germany as *Heimat.*

NINE

Nazism and Machines

This chapter will amount to a final commentary on the epistemological impasse in which Nazism entangles itself; namely, how it reconciles its contradictory affirmation of the "antimodern" and the modern, of a Schillerian "freedom" rooted in eighteenth-century anticentralism and a Foucauldian discipline, of society as an "organic" body and as a machine run by men of steel. How, to arrive at my specific focus, does Nazi cinema come to terms with real machines?

From a narratological standpoint, any given motif is always subordinated to a "greater" narrative and ideological project. Since the eighteenth century, this project has been centered upon the fundamental opposition between "alienation" and "community," between the fragmented and the whole, rootlessness and a sense of place. A configuration like the one I discussed in the preceding chapter, *Gold*'s opposition between machine and man, is merely a contingent narrative manifestation that can as easily be reversed, as it is in the films that follow, in which machines are man's ally. The fundamental opposition of modern narrative may be defined by an endless variety of terms, for example, by juxtaposing industrialized with agrarian culture (as in "blood and soil" literature),[1] the "German" with the "foreign" or "Jewish"; it may also foreground tensions *within* any one of these cultures. Machines, when depicted at all, may represent the threat of modernity *or* a force of collectivity that needs to be secured

---

1. Stephen Lowry presents a very differentiated argument how *The Golden City,* famous for its antiurban "blood and soil" ideology (as well as its xenophobia and misogyny), is much more ambivalent than critics generally acknowledge. *Pathos und Politik: Ideologie in Spielfilmen des Nationalsozialismus* (Tübingen: Niemeyer, 1991), 65–115.

and protected. In short, National Socialism targets the dispersing, alienating, and fragmenting effect of modern life but does not necessarily identify industrialized society as evil in itself.

The privileging of machines is not irrelevant, however, to Nazism's so often disavowed affirmation of a disciplinary world. The films in this chapter retain vestiges of ideological antimodernism while paradoxically championing machines, these most modern of Things, as essential to "Germany's" corporatist "spirit." They work around their aporia by, in one way or the other, allowing their machines to be "reborn" as organic, if not exactly human, bodies. They may fetishize the male body or Personality that runs a society of machines, as in *The Ruler,* which exhibits a fascinating chiasmic reversal: man becomes machine while the machine world becomes organicized. They may, as in *Diesel,* anthropomorphize the machine. Finally, they may celebrate machines (more exactly, technology) as something in and on "the air" that transcends the physicality of the body. *Request Concert* is a celebration of the radio, which, in Alice Kaplan's words, transformed the 1930s into "a veritable festival of oral gratification."[2] While all of Nazism's "good" machines work to oppose the alienation wrought by exchange value and *Überfremdung* highlighted in the last chapter, radio and, by implicit extension, film represent the apex of a technology rendering whole the fragmented body of "Germany." Science and technology here constitute another "positive" social fantasy forcing Nazism to negotiate the "backwards-looking utopia" Ernst Bloch spoke of with another ideological vision of a "forward-looking technocracy."

INDUSTRY: VEIT HARLAN'S *THE RULER*
AND GERHARD LAMPRECHT'S *DIESEL*

The Ruler (1937) and *Diesel* are essentially industrial variations on the Genius film. *Diesel* (1942) follows, as will become apparent, the genre's master narrative, with the difference that it fetishizes Diesel's "product" rather than the man himself; his machine is the real star of the show. In the contrasting case of *The Ruler,* which is "loosely" based on Gerhard Hauptmann's *Before Sundown* (*Vor Sonnenuntergang,* 1932), we never learn what specifically the "ruler" produces, so absorbed is the film in the protagonist as Personality. Although German steel manufacturer Alfred Krupp was the historical model for the film's industrial magnate Matthias

---

2. *Reproductions of Banality: Fascism, Literature, and French Intellectual Life* (Minneapolis: University of Minnesota Press, 1986), 23.

Clausen (Emil Jannings),[3] it chooses not to identify Krupp directly. At stake is Clausen's "ruling" itself, making him more of a Hitler surrogate than other Genius figures. Like Hitler, Clausen constantly gives speeches in the film, including a concluding exhortation essentially directed at the film audience. During one of these a photo of Hitler is placed dominantly above him — rendering the two men metonymic complements of each other. A reference to Clausen as "the first worker of our firm" furthermore likens him with the "first servant of the state," Frederick.

The film begins with the funeral of Clausen's wife. His egotistical children take the opportunity to gain greater control over his life. When their desire for short-term profit interferes with his ambition to invest company earnings in research, he collapses in what seems to be a nervous breakdown. Clausen is helped in his exhaustion by his new stenographer Inken Peters, with whom he falls in love. His family fears that his possible remarriage will threaten their inheritance, ultimately they attempt to have their father declared mentally incompetent in order to gain control of his fortune. He is declared competent in a trial.

*

On an ideology-critical, subtextual level, we can understand *The Ruler* as a legitimation of the NSDAP's eradication of its left wing in the 1934 Röhm Putsch, as an attempt to bring together an "impossible" coalition of "community" and capitalism. Clausen's speech to his board of directors echoes the film's "white socialist"[4] fantasy of a capitalism pervaded by the "spirit" of socialism: "Gentlemen, we are here to provide work and bread for millions of people. We are here to work for the community of the nation. The aim of every industrial leader conscious of his responsibility must be to serve this community. This will of mine is the supreme law which governs my work. All else must be subordinated to this will, without opposition, even if in doing this I lead the firm into ruin."[5]

3. Harlan contended that he and Jannings studied newsreels of the Krupp family in order to produce their mannerisms on the screen. See David Welch, *Propaganda and the German Cinema: 1933–45* (Oxford: Clarendon Press, 1983), 160.
4. The term refers to early-twentieth-century conservative notions of a socialism "from above" depending on the altruistic motivation of economically powerful classes to use their assets for the good of the community, much like late-twentieth-century "trickle down" theories. See Helmut Lethen, *Die Neue Sachlichkeit 1924–32: Studien zum "Weissen Sozialismus"* (Stuttgart: Metzler, 1970).
5. Translation from Welch, 161.

With such speeches, *The Ruler* essentially disavows capitalism *as capitalism,* which National Socialism projects onto an abstract, immaterial process executed by "middlemen" working in finance capital (see my discussion of *Jew Süss*). A capitalism producing goods, like Clausen's, becomes in this discourse not really capitalism at all, but creative activity, suggested by the double entendre of the Clausen "Works" (*Werke*) and by a statement echoing *Friedrich Schiller*'s Genius discussion: "The born Leader needs no training — only his own Genius." *The Ruler* prefers to recast its capitalism as a socialism driven by Personality, lending it a curious mixture of the abstract (our ignorance of Clausen's "product") and the thingly (he obviously produces "something"). Clearly the abstract dimension of Clausen's "works," which risks rendering him an Aryanized "Jew," intends to foreground the Volkish "spirit" of industry, one which can transfer to any "product." However, the film accommodates Nazism's hypostatization of the thingly in the form of a model of Clausen's original factory presented to him by loyal employees on the fortieth anniversary of the Clausen Works. In the model the film offers us a thingly version not of some individual product but of a working relationship; Clausen can virtually hold in his hands the symbiosis of Leader and People. The model is a concretization of the Thing, the "positive" social fantasy driving National Socialism, rendering graspable "community."

The Ruler's contemporary setting in the Nazi state threatens to rob it of a story. As a film predating World War II, it cannot act like the "home-front" films to which I'll turn at the end of the chapter. More seriously, the Genius/Leader/Rebel narrative in which it is embedded depends on an equation of "state" with instrumentality, exchange value, tyranny. In short, its contemporary German setting leaves *The Ruler* no choice but to turn the tables on the Genius film, since a "hostile environment" is a sine qua non of the Genius master narrative. *The Ruler* resolves its problem by treating the state as it does capitalism, essentially denying the state as a "state" at all. Like Nazism itself, the film fantasizes the "state" as an organic body besieged by a bacillus left over from another time, by a surplus of "Weimar" that wants to turn it into "a charity organization for suffering stockholders." In place of the inhuman machine of "state" steps a nonstate symbolized by Clausen's anthropomorphized industry of Volkish machines, recalling Hitler's line in *Triumph of the Will,* "We don't belong to the state; the state belongs to us."

Of all the films so far that "wipe out" the nuclear family, *The Ruler* does it most overtly, dispensing with the usual concessions to bourgeois family ideology. Clausen's nuclear family embodies the disease assailing the social body and consequently provides the film with a story; indeed, the synchronic configuration of this family vis-à-vis Clausen stands in for a diachronic development from "Weimar's" bumbling, feminized "state" to Nazism's nonstate. Yet if other Leader figures possess two bodies, Clausen possesses two families, the only "real" one being that of his employees, who embody the solidarity he is denied in the private sphere. His home is even located right next to the factory, symbolizing the unity of home and workplace fantasized by one of the nineteenth century's most celebrated "antimodernists," Wilhelm Heinrich Riehl.[6] Riehl's model for the ideal family structure was the *oikos* or *das ganze Haus,* the preindustrial household in which the nuclear family lived together with servants and apprentices, bonded by a natural chain of authority and mutual responsibility. In his ideal of a harmonious hierarchy among sexes, classes, and peoples, of a "natural" community no longer disrupted by the "leveling" tendencies of modernity, Riehl was an ideological forerunner of National Socialism and its "Volkish-national" relatives.[7] Specifically, Riehl's collapsing of the private and public spheres into one overarching family anticipates Nazism's symbiosis of Leader and People embodied in figures like Clausen or Frederick.

Here "story" does not happen only on the private level: indeed, since the fusion of Clausen's private and public lives is all but total (reflecting Nazism's totalizing system, his fortune merely circulates to further his industry), his children's greed penetrates the latter sphere as well, rendering his "real home" *unheimlich* or uncanny. His children and their spouses infiltrate his board of directors, refusing to fund the firm's research division with which Clausen hopes to "create the new" and gain independence from foreign industry. (Via *The Ruler*'s "research" theme, it gains a curious intertextual relation to *Diesel,* in which Krupp is the only industrialist willing to give Diesel indispensable support in developing his engine.)

6. See *Die Familie,* vol. 3 of *Die Naturgeschichte des deutschen Volkes* (Stuttgart: Cotta, 1859). Riehl was so popular that he gave countless lectures propagating his ideas around Germany, and excerpts from his books as well as his poems were often printed in journals such as *Die Gartenlaube.*
7. "The more the voluntary acknowledgment of a natural authority in all realms of our bourgeois life became outmoded, the more later generations were sure to become politically unstable and lacking in social masters." Riehl, 156. The similar notions espoused by other "antimodern" thinkers like Paul Anton Lagarde, Julius Langbehn, and Moeller van den Bruck indicate the symptomatic status of Riehl's thought. See Hans Rosenberg, *Grosse Depression und Bismarckzeit: Wirtschaftsablauf, Gesellschaft und Politik in Mitteleuropa* (Berlin: de Gruyter, 1967).

I have already hinted at the film's forceful thematization of temporality. Rather than adhere to the Genius film's obsession with a forward temporality (against stasis) that ultimately transcends itself in timelessness, *The Ruler* opts for a more complex dynamic involving several notions of time running parallel to each other; it narrativizes the simultaneity of the nonsimultaneous. The two temporalities are linked with the characters and "values" that the narrative pits against each other. Ironically, both formulate themselves as espousing the "new," as progressing forward beyond something. For Clausen's family the "new" represents an accelerated, instrumentalized "progress," a capitalization of time transparently equivalent to "Weimar" and, in turn, to "modernity." The "old" makes way for exchange value, egotism, and a threatening destabilization of gender boundaries. Consequently, their physical coding, like that of Florence in *Gold*, suggests gender reversal: the women smoke, wear masculine-styled haute couture, and behave in an independent, manipulative way. The men are accordingly modish and subjugated to their castrating wives. For Clausen the "new" means the utopian perspective of a community transcending the egotism of modernity, which, however, paradoxically involves a return to "old" values of extended family and Riehl's *oikos*. He thus embodies National Socialism's project of *re*-newing an imaginary "old" with the help of the most modern of technological forms, film.

Clausen's family is terrorized by Clausen's inversion of their concept of the "new," in which they see an uncanny ghost from an undead past, articulated in their obsessive repetition of the phrase "You can't turn back the clock." Recurrent variations on the line in Nazi film suggest the significance of this notion within Nazism's historical-philosophical framework, as when Napoleon uses the exact same words in *Kolberg,* complaining that the population of Kolberg is so naive as to believe they can halt "progress," which in this context means the centralization of the state in the hands of foreign domination and "liberal" ideas. Similarly, in *Bismarck,* the liberal parliamentarian Virchow accuses Bismarck of wanting Germany to return to the "Middle Ages."[8]

This linkage of time metaphors with figures standing in for a hostile modernity sustains Nazism's ideological orientation toward the past,

8. In his analysis of National Socialism, Daniel Guérin uses the related metaphor of the wheel to illustrate, from a critical standpoint, the same idea: "National Socialism wants to stop the automatic movement of the capitalist wheel, put a brake on it, then make it turn back to its starting point and stabilize it there." *Fascism and Big Business* (New York: Monad Press, 1973), 86.

however relativized this stance was in theory and practice. As Donald Lowe points out in his *History of Bourgeois Perception,* clocks and watches are among the most consistent symbols of modernity, of which the systematization of time was one of the most dramatic innovations.[9] Foucault similarly theorizes the seriation of time as a fundamental step in the process of modernization, only he links it more closely to the body, speaking of an "anatomo-chronological schema of behavior" in which "time penetrates the body and with it all the meticulous controls of power."[10] National Socialism, of course, drives the disciplining of the body in its temporal and spatial dimensions to a logical extreme, just as it in fact mechanizes the state to a heretofore unprecedented degree, as suggested by its own favorite metaphor of *Gleichschaltung.* Yet with its insistence upon reviving a premodern "past" onto which it retroactively projects "harmony," National Socialism again disavows — this time its own, very modern — exercise of disciplinary time.

Paradoxically, the ideological subject position Nazism deals itself vis-à-vis its modernized enemies is that of a corpse rising up out of a grave, keeping alive what modernity thought was dead and buried. This corpse (preferring to think of itself as a New Man "reborn") is rendered invincible by the very modernity on which it seeks to avenge itself: by a technology that carries the corpse beyond restraints of time and space (diegetically present in Clausen's "Works" and extradiegetically in the film medium itself). Even on the level of plot, Clausen undergoes a spiritual death (something like *Hitler Youth Quex*'s Heini Völker), from which he emerges invincible, like "steel." Exasperated at the "boundless egotism" of his family, Clausen falls unconscious, only to awaken into a world of desire in which ordinary time and space are suspended.

Desire takes its narrative form in Clausen's young stenographer Inken Peters, who leans over Clausen in a blurred, subjective shot coming slowly into focus. Though he wakes up to her nurturant gaze, film audience and Clausen share the first desiring look at her. As a creature not "of this world," Inken is seemingly timeless, a youth embodying a dead world of preindustrial harmony, having grown up in her mother's orchard (referred to pejoratively as a *Grünkramladen* — literally "green stuff store" — by Clausen's avaricious daughter-in-law). Just as the valorization of Nazism's community of "Germany" in *Hitler Youth Quex* occurs in a park within

---

9. *History of Bourgeois Perception* (Chicago: University of Chicago Press, 1982), 35.
10. *Discipline and Punish: The Birth of the Prison,* trans. Alan Sheridan (New York: Vintage, 1979), 152.

the city of Berlin, Inken's semiotic linkage with nature equips her to redeem an urban organism infected by modernity. She revivifies Clausen, sexualizing him to the rage of his family, transforming him into Nazism's New Man. The improbable, almost embarrassing age difference of the lovers mirrors itself in their vacation, in which the twentieth century meets an antiquity that, like Clausen's "new," is both dead and timeless. They visit Greece and the Parthenon, literally returning to a premodern era, to Hitler's "ideal of culture" that should remain "preserved for us in its exemplary beauty. . . . A culture combining millenniums and embracing Hellenism and Germanism is fighting for its existence."[11]

Clausen's modernist adversaries are not without their Undead. The film begins with the funeral of Clausen's first wife, to whom the moral and biological decay of Clausen's children is ascribed, and with a literal and figurative storm to be superseded by sunshine. In another reversal, Clausen hopes to bury the modernist past with the wife's corpse. That corpse refuses to stay dead, however, and haunts him in the form of his corpse-daughter Bettina, who literally throws herself on her mother's grave at the funeral and relentlessly inhibits her father's pursuit of a new life.

Although he is virtually indestructible once he has entered Inken's world, the film finalizes the process by exorcising Clausen's humanness, rendering his organic body a machine "of steel," in a chiasmic reversal of its endeavor to render the "machine" of state an organic body.[12] This metamorphosis is suggested by a visual metonymy that comes, on the level of the symbolic, to serve as metaphor: In one of the film's final scenes, Clausen walks past a superdimensional furnace spouting fire in the background and comments: "One must undergo a process of refinement to push forward for final victory. Only then does one become steel—though one must not be afraid of the furnace."[13] *The Ruler* is singular in its cathecting of an audience to "something" both thingly and nonthingly, without ever alluding to any specific "product." It fuses its subtext of Krupp to a Jüngerian fantasy fusing flesh with steel, life with death, pretending that "capitalism" and "state" can be spheres of Otherness and timeless desire. "Ruling" itself becomes aesthetic experience.

---

11. *Mein Kampf*, trans. Ralph Manheim (Boston: Houghton Mifflin, 1943), 423. See Philippe Lacoue-Labarthe and Jean-Luc Nancy's discussion of the importance of Greek culture within German tradition in "The Nazi Myth," trans. Brian Holmes, *Critical Inquiry* 2.16 (Winter 1990): 291–312.
12. In Hauptmann's play, Clausen commits suicide.
13. Translation from Welch, 162.

Lamprecht's *Diesel* is a biography of Rudolf Diesel (1858–1913), the inventor of the internal combustion engine that bears his name.

*

The child Diesel comes to live with his uncle, since his father is unable to support him. Diesel, a model pupil and surrogate son, pursues his passion for engineering and spends years developing his engine. He gives up not only his private life, to the frustration of his wife, but opportunities for lucrative employment. Eventually the Krupp firm supports his experiments until his engine runs efficiently. A disgruntled professor attempts to sue him for the patent, but fails.

*

Like *The Ruler* with its suggestion of Clausen's "Works" as artistic creation, *Diesel* rhetorically equates technological with aesthetic creativity by repeatedly referring to its protagonist as "a Raphael." Unlike *The Ruler* with its more general emphasis on the "spirit" of industry, *Diesel* fetishizes a specific technological apparatus. By paying more attention to the machine than the man, however, it diverges slightly from the "artistic" Genius narrative infatuated with the artist as body and Personality. In his role as hard, unsexy worker, Diesel might be productively compared with Neuber, who likewise "gives birth" to the real Thing. Diesel's engine acquires its fetishized status through a number of means: in the narrative the machine is a desired object endlessly inaccessible to Diesel; the camera privileges it with an indulgent gaze; finally, the verbal metaphors describing it all involve the notion of metamorphosis.

The film consistently anthropomorphizes Diesel's fledgling engine, although there is considerable slippage in its assignment of gender or character traits. Generally speaking, it oscillates between representing the machine as a child and woman.[14] In most explicit terms the engine is represented as Diesel's offspring: it is christened with his name, and he trains it until it attains the grace and sophistication of a learned adult,

14. Another field of metaphors revolves around the notion of hell and heaven, devil and angel. In the film's opening scene, the machine room of a ship into which the child Diesel descends is described as a "hell" in which a little boy doesn't belong; Diesel himself is described as a figure metamorphosing from devil to angel when, as a small boy, he crawls into a bath and is told "Climb in as a devil and emerge as an angel." The spectrum of possible readings of the metaphor all accord with the hagiographical tendencies of the Genius genre and a trajectory of ascension as well as "progress": the reference to Diesel's lightening the burden of workers shoveling coal and to the literal weight of heavy, cumbersome machines; the reference to the "hell" suffered by every historical personality, and to the "hell" the genius causes his "loved ones."

developing from a "child with rickets" to a "child learning to walk," to one who will someday go "out into the world." Diesel attempts to compensate decades of indifference to his wife Martha by according her the status of mother, epitomized by the scene in which he presents the finally perfected engine to her. The two stand before the engine like proud parents before a cradle; Martha comments on her surprise that it isn't larger, whereupon Diesel ridicules her expectation that it should have grown in four years "like a child":

> MARTHA (*to the engine*): My God, how you worried us!
> DIESEL: We really ought to be angry at him; he stole the best part of our lives — yours especially!

Although Diesel permits Martha to name the machine and constantly alludes to her indispensable role in sustaining him, the film as a whole essentially dismisses her as excess baggage, as a transparent concession to family ideology. Rather than being the product of a "real" heterosexual union, the machine appears to have sprung from Diesel himself, from an act of masturbation or sexual interaction with an inorganic world — much like Nazi cinema's Schiller with his narcissistic cycle of giving birth and being reborn. As much as it superficially espouses her motherhood, Diesel's "introduction" of Martha to the machine attests to his "single parenthood" (photo 55); when Diesel teaches Martha how to make it run, she displays a timidity and awkwardness recalling the classic husband fumbling for the first time with diapers (photo 56). As if to signal a disavowed comprehension of her exclusion from the machine's creation, Martha faints at the conclusion of the preceding scene, referring to her "heart." The fainting is a singular occurrence in the film, which makes no further reference to any sickness on her part; on the contrary it is Diesel who experiences a kind of "postpartum depression" (he collapses and is hospitalized with a nervous breakdown).

Finally, the film presents the creation of the machine visually as a sexual act, beginning as "experimentation" or foreplay in Diesel's youth (photo 57). Early in the film, Diesel's uncle rewards his academic excellence by offering him the gift of his choice. Diesel chooses a compression igniter (*Kompressionsfeuerzeug*) — an obvious reference to his biological predestination to develop an engine of the future. We see a close-up of the boy's hand rhythmically pushing the igniter into the floor, foregrounding a pumping action prefiguring the future Diesel engine, but simultaneously laden with sexual connotations. Equally ambiguous is Diesel's repeated description of the machine's action: "When the cob is thrust forward the

55-56 Diesel portrays Diesel's motor alternately as a mistress and as his offspring; in either case, his wife is excluded. Wife Martha confronts Diesel's "black mistress" (*above*); Martha awkwardly pulls the machine's lever, like an inept husband changing diapers (*middle*). **57** Young Diesel's experimental foreplay.

air becomes so hot that the fuse begins to glow." (A more technologically accurate translation for cob would be "piston," which, however, diminishes the ambiguity of the original German *Kolben* [= "cob," "spike," "piston"].) Like Hans Albers's erotically invested reactor in *Gold,* Diesel's engine needs constantly to achieve new heights of tension; Diesel's first words as an adult after an ellipsis of nineteen years are "we have to go higher."

The analogy of Diesel's engine to a tempestuous woman needing to be contained and subordinated sustains both the representation of its creation as a sexual act and the exclusion of wife Martha from this creation. Like woman, the machine is unpredictable, even dangerous, as exemplified by a small explosion in one scene. Diesel couches his struggle with the machine in the discourse of taming or mastering a spirited woman, a "black lover,"[15] a "demon" permitting Diesel to defer endlessly a family relationship (note the contrast between Diesel's early promise to Martha he will be "all hers" the minute the machine is complete with his declaration after it's done that the "real" work has only begun). Although references to the machine as "she" is a function of the German language (hence the pronoun referring to the *die Maschine* is feminine, *sie*),[16] a number of scenes make the analogy explicit, as when a worker proclaims Diesel's promise to give up experimentation to be as illusory as his own promise never to look at another woman, or when another worker imagines the machine as transsexual, and accordingly ascribes its vexing qualities to its female side: "When he looks at me so frankly, one could think he had character, that he were a man like you and me!" At other times the machine acts like a woman, "lets herself be admired, and when you've come to the point where you're ready and want to, she just says 'nah!' " Looking up at the machine with territorial pride, Diesel insists, "But today she has to say 'yes!' " In time Diesel masters the machine, insisting he has her "firmly in hand; she's not going to get her way; I'm going to get mine."

Diesel's displacement of desire onto machines has a likely source in his failed interpellation by his father. During the first section of the film depicting Diesel's childhood, crosscutting links Diesel with his biological family, with whom he is never actually seen together, except for a brief encounter with his father. The paternal legacy left to Diesel is impoverished, hindering his formation of an identification with his father, who is a failure both in the public and the private sphere; he tinkers with unsuccessful inventions that earn no money and appears unable to assert authority over a wife who perpetually humiliates him. Father Diesel is a syntactic as well as thematic obstacle in Diesel's life; he arrives to enroll Diesel as an apprentice precisely in the moment Diesel experiments with the igniter, that is, anticipates the activity that will ensure his historical legacy. The interruption of Diesel's pleasurable activity is readable with the same ambiguity that characterizes his play with the instrument: as a

15. The term "black lover" (*schwarze Geliebte*) would in German most likely be a reference to hair color than a racial designation.
16. At other times the engine is masculine as *der Motor*.

disruption of "destiny" (father wants to reduce Diesel to his own mediocrity), and as a disruption of pure, libidinous pleasure — family as *coitus interruptus*.

Indeed, *Diesel* rewrites the Oedipal narrative to fit the Genius narrative. Since Diesel is effectively motherless (his mother's rare appearances make no reference to her feelings for him; she merely berates his father for his failure to meet her externally driven needs), he displaces desire onto cold, inorganic machines rather than to "real" women substituting for the mother. Freud's mother-father-son triangle becomes here a machine-father-son triangle, implied by his father's helpless query: "Don't you love your father any more? Do you only love your machines?" If anything, Diesel appears to have been born "grown up" — somehow recalling medieval portraits of the baby Christ with an adult face. The single scene with his father reverses, like *Hitler Youth Quex,* the roles of father and child, forcing his father into the subject position of a child unable to gain acquiescence from a firm father; Diesel's "I cannot!" in response to his father's request that he rejoin the family and undertake an apprenticeship already harbors the complete sacrificial structure of his historical myth.[17]

The camera upholds the analogy between woman and machine by presenting the perfected engine as specularized object unveiled much like classical cinema exhibits woman. Significantly, the spectacle is presented only for the male gaze, as it is inspected by the company managers supporting Diesel, followed by workers, who request a look (only much later, seemingly as an afterthought, is Martha allowed to see it).[18] Like the massive laboratory doors serving as stage curtain in *Gold,* the boards of a large temporary wall are carefully laid flat to permit the workers an unobstructed view of the engine. The camera oscillates from a long shot of the awestruck men, illuminated as if by the light of Genius, to the pulsating

17. Again here an analogy with *Friedrich Schiller* is unavoidable, particularly with the scene in which Schiller refuses his father's wish that he stop infuriating the Duke with his writing. Another potential father figure in *Diesel* is the uncle who supports Diesel's ambition and gives him the important gift of the compression igniter. Yet within the film's discourse the uncle seems less a figure of imaginary identification than an early witness to the Genius always already within Diesel.

18. The successful unveiling of the motor is anticipated by the empty space it leaves at a Paris exhibition earlier in the film. Though Diesel has refused to exhibit the still imperfect motor, Martha begs to see the spot where it would have stood. The void itself becomes a kind of spectacle determined by the motor's absence; Martha masochistically savors the space, much like a parent at what would have been the graduation of a sick or dead child.

engine, from which management steps aside to permit her full command of the "stage." The workers begin waving hats and shouting, like men aroused by the view of a dancing woman.

If the film credits anyone with co-partnership, however subordinate, in Diesel's progeny, it is not his family or his marginalized wife, but his workers, once again portrayed as an imaginary People with a healthy "instinct for greatness." The name "Diesel" that Martha "chooses" has already been chosen by the workers, who all along have called the engine "the Diesel, his motor" (*der Diesel, sein Motor* — a common proletarian substitution of article and possessive adjective for a "correct" possessive form). As in other films, the workers/People are the "hands" indispensable to Genius.[19]

Fetishized technological apparatuses like the Diesel engine serve, like Clausen's empire, as both symbols and interpellators of community. Although Diesel patented his engine in 1892, the film opens in the year 1870, which flashes across the screen before the narrative unfolds. The choice of this specific year directly preceding German unification appears to be motivated not by Diesel's biography but by its equivalence with "Germany" as a unit, a community. The end of the film, which lapses into a documentary discourse, underscores the noncoincidental choice of the year as a signifier for "nation." A montage sequence traces the development of the Diesel engine through the Third Reich, always superimposing a specific year over the stage of the engine at that period.[20] As in *Germanin* and other films that intermittently use a documentary style, *Diesel* thus allows the narrative to extend beyond its textual boundaries, to establish a direct relationship to the spectator's reality and fortify a sense of "German" identity.

---

19. Volkish ideologies functionally collapse the notions of People, soldier, and worker. Ernst Jünger's novel *The Worker: Domination and Form* (*Der Arbeiter: Herrschaft und Gestalt*, 1932), in which the worker appears as a heroic warrior on the production landscape, invokes the analogy between the latter two. This equivalence also common within Nazi cinema recalls the liturgical chant of the Labor Service in *Triumph of the Will*: "We did not stand in the trenches, nor did we stand under the drumfire of the grenades, and, nevertheless, we are soldiers, with our hammers, axes, shovels, hoes, and spades — we are the young troops of the Reich!"

20. The video version of the film circulating in the United States and Germany has been "updated" to include a shot of a Diesel locomotive in the fifties. The addition, intended no doubt to depict the linear evolution from Diesel's first engine to "today," attests equally to continuities in film from the Third Reich to "today," when the film still enjoys circulation.

RADIO AND THE "HOMEFRONT": EDUARD VON BORSODY'S
REQUEST CONCERT AND ROLF HANSEN'S *THE GREAT LOVE*

Nazi cinema celebrates radio neither as a fetishized Thing like Diesel's engine nor as the product of a fetishized Personality like *The Ruler*'s Clausen. It is, rather, a vehicle that allows space and time to be transcended and that thus compensates for real-life fragmentation with imaginary wholeness.[21] In the "homefront" films of the early forties dealing with wartime separation, radio becomes diegetically important as a means of disavowing separation as separation, and above all, of disavowing war as war. My primary example for this functionalization of radio is Eduard von Borsody's *Request Concert* (1940), the second most popular film in the years 1940–1942 following another "homefront" film, *The Great Love* (1942).[22] *Request Concert* frames its story around two "shows" that at once reach multitudes and seemingly suspend time: the first is located in one place, the 1936 Olympics in Berlin; the second is projected from one place to "everywhere," the popular historical Sunday afternoon radio program "Request Concert" broadcast from Berlin, which played songs requested by soldiers, collected donations for the war, and conveyed per-

---

21. Given their reliance on voice and speeches, it is not surprising that Nazi films generally valorize radio over the press. Journalists, whom Hitler referred to as "rascals on principle," often appear as little runts wearing glasses. Besides being one more agent of capitalism, the press represents a print culture, especially Weimar print culture, when many large publishing houses were owned by Jews. Cf. Hitler's rhetorical questions: "Did [the press] not help to teach our people a miserable immorality? Did it not ridicule morality and ethics as backward and petty-bourgeois, until our people finally became "modern"?" (*Mein Kampf*, 243). *Ohm Krüger* (1941), for example, opens with reporters swarming in the hospital lobby, little moved by doctors' refusal to admit them to interview the dying Boer leader Krüger. A reporter from the *Berliner Tageblatt*, a well-known "Jewish" newspaper, barges into the room and snaps a flash photo of Krüger, whose eyes are already damaged. A "white nurse" reads a distorted newspaper account about the "narrow-minded" Boers, provoking Krüger to tell his story. Oral history becomes a vehicle of Truth juxtaposed with the distorted truth propagated by the press as a "machine" of capitalism. Like all machines in National Socialism, however, the press can be infused with the spirit of community. An example is Jürgen von Alten's *Togger* (1940), in which the last newspaper in Berlin to take a stand against the conspiracy of international capital, *Der neue Weg* (The New Way), is saved from financial ruin by a journalist from the provincial *Siebenbürger Bote* (the Siebenburg Herald).

22. *Request Concert*, which was commissioned by the state, drew 26.5 million viewers in its first year and grossed 7.6 million Reichsmark (as compared to 8 million for *The Great Love*).

sonal messages to soldiers at the front. The two shows have in common an aesthetic experience of unity, but only the second allows unity to be experienced despite spatial separation. The film's narrative trajectory is thus characterized by a process of abstraction, a progression from "real" to ever more imaginary experience.

*

Inge Wagner goes to the 1936 Berlin Olympics with her aunt, who must run home to get the tickets she put in the wrong purse. Lieutenant Herbert Koch, a stranger, offers a hesitant Inge the extra ticket left him by a soldier called to duty. Only when Hitler arrives at the games does Inge abandon caution and enter the stadium with Koch. They quickly fall in love and decide to marry, but after three days Koch is suddenly called away to the top secret mission *Legion Condor* aiding the fascists fighting in Spain, from where all correspondence is prohibited. The couple is separated without a word for three years. While listening one night to "Request Concert," Inge's hopes are answered. Koch calls into the program and requests the music of the 1936 Olympics, signaling that he has never forgotten her. The war and misunderstandings keep hindering their reunion: Helmut, an infatuated young lieutenant from Inge's hometown, carries her picture, which his commanding officer, now Captain Koch, sees, leading him to believe that Inge is engaged to Helmut. The confusion is resolved only when Helmut is injured and all three meet in the hospital.

*

The above plot synopsis is somewhat deceptive in its concentration on the "main" characters in a film which foregrounds shows that are virtually impossible to summarize and includes multiple peripheral stories of civilians turned soldiers: a schoolteacher, a butcher, a baker, and a musician, the only figure who dies. (Only Koch, as the film's central male, seems to have no profession except that of officer, less a "job" than membership in a Theweleitian warrior caste that permeates his whole being.) Typically for homefront or what Heide Schlüpmann calls "everyday life in the Reich" films,[23] *Request Concert*'s plot strands bring together a social microcosm encompassing several social classes (and several state and ideological state apparatuses: school, the arts, the media, the military). All of these transcend difference for the war effort; all of the characters act as

23. "Faschistische Trugbilder weiblicher Autonomie," *Frauen und Film* 44/45 (October 1988): 60. Other examples are *Two in a Big City* (1942), *Six Days of Vacation at Home* (1941), *A Small Summer Melody* (1944).

surrogates for spectators experiencing real separation by the war. The synchronic configuration spanning the social spectrum is complemented by a diachronic one spanning a human lifetime, from birth (the teacher's wife has a baby) to (the musician's) death.

What ties all the plots and all the homefront films together is a thematization of desire vis-à-vis collective need characteristic of what Dana Polan calls "war-affirmative" narratives.[24] More strongly than, for example, the Genius films, homefront films acknowledge desire, while subordinating it to the need for "commitment." Indeed, they attempt to recast commitment as another, more sublime form of desire, in part by constantly interweaving the story of "the individual" with that of Nation, "writing them all," to use Polan's expression, as "one story." In the first minutes of *Request Concert,* a soldier's phrase "I want to for sure, but . . . " (*wollen schon, aber*), which means that he has to miss the Olympics because he's on duty, establishes itself as a leitmotif repeated when the same subordination of desire is demanded on various, private and public, levels. Only during the film's fleeting "moment of happiness" at the beginning does it permit a reversal: While kissing Inge in a boat, Koch nearly collides with another, remarking, "We can for sure, but don't *want to*" when asked whether he can't watch where he's going.[25]

In a sense, *Request Concert* is several different movies written as one movie. It wanders back and forth from a monumental, "overt" narration that "feels" like propaganda, to the "covert" narration of the personalized story lines, to the show at the end which sublates the story, at once incorporating diegetic characters and submerging their stories *in* show. Finally, not only are the subplots different, drawing on family and war stories, but even the central love story itself has trouble "deciding" whether it is melodrama or comedy of errors. Holding all the different narratives and cinematographic styles together is the metaphor of a magnet, which draws Inge to Koch, both of them to Hitler and the Olympics, and all of "Germany" to music, radio, spectacle, and ultimately, film.

Most strikingly detached from the rest of the film is its beginning at the Olympics, which functions much like a prologue preceding, and in a way *exceeding,* the "real" movie. Indeed, the entire scene functions for the film audience and diegetic characters like a dream which the rest of the film

24. *Power and Paranoia: History, Narrative, and the American Cinema, 1940–1950* (New York: Columbia University Press, 1986).
25. *Request Concert*'s "I want to for sure, but . . . " is a more domesticated version of the cinematic Frederick's phrase "Life is ruled by the Must."

will work toward reliving. The "dream" is framed by close-up shots of the Olympic bell, whose slow, resonating ring suggests the narrative's principle of a repetition that sublates time. The dreamlike quality of the opening shots is indebted to the aestheticizing cinematography of Leni Riefenstahl, from whose *Olympia* (1938) the footage is taken: a montage sequence begins with the bell close-up, superimposed with the Olympic insignia, followed by close-ups of flags set against a sky with cumulus clouds. It makes the most of our "primary" identification with film itself, allowing us to participate in a stunning historical moment, particularly when the camera sweeps dramatically from the elevated flags down the poles to the city below, or suggests the enveloping nature of the event by traveling in a panoramic, circular motion around the decorated poles. An aerial shot travels into the stadium, capturing its concave shape as container of the popular euphoria, and then on to the crowd outside flocking toward it (photo 58). The images are underscored by music, beginning with the dramatic Olympia fanfare, which will play an important diegetic role by later reuniting the lovers who first bond here.

The kernel of story that gets under way amid the Olympic spectacle anticipates the contingency, the duty-bound separation and "spiritual" reunion determining the narrative: a soldier's sudden call to duty spurs the chance meeting of lovers. Once inaugurated, the film story has an awkward time competing with the show of the Olympics, which keeps intruding into Inge's and Koch's flirtatious banter, as if determined to keep the upper hand. The first disruption is Hitler's arrival at the games, which proves to be a corrective force that overturns Inge's social decorum, propelling the couple still outside the vessel of the stadium to its inside. The second disruption is the arrival of "the Germans" amid parading national teams. After giving way to *Führer,* personal exchange gives way to a *Volk* aesthetically fused into a mass ornament: "the Germans" consist of a perfect column of white, undulating figures crosscut with shots of the frenetic crowd saluting and cheering. Hitler's appearance echoes Polan's description of Roosevelt's function in American wartime films: "Roosevelt as figure seems to hover over many films while remaining just beyond full representation. . . . He is a godlike figure, not representable but merely alluded to — a mediation between earthly and higher meanings."[26] As a desired object beyond narrative representation, Hitler does not play a diegetic role in any Nazi feature film (see chapter 3). Here he appears only from a vast distance, and for a brief moment. Nevertheless, he indeed

26. Polan, 67.

58·60 Popular unity shifts from the physical to the abstract via technology in *Request Concert*. 58: As *Request Concert* begins, the Olympic stadium serves as a concrete vessel containing public euphoria. 59: As the camera sweeps past the dead Schwarzkopf's empty piano during the Request Concert, it catches the radio speaker and Beethoven together, as if to harmonize tradition and modernity, the "real" production of music and its technological diffusion. 60: As *Request Concert* concludes, recurrent shots of radio speakers suggest how technology compensates for lost physical unity.

"hovers over" the narrative (and literally on the walls of Koch's military headquarters, where his photograph hangs). His presence has a magnetic effect like that of the Olympic festival, both of which combine to act as a catalyst for the magnetic attraction of the couple: Inge's decision to plunge into a community with Koch coincides with the community experience of the crowd, which also literally converges upon the stadium when he arrives.

Throughout the rest of the film, which leaps ahead three years to the 1939 "present," the Olympic segment stands on the level of memory or dream for a *Gleichschaltung* of person and collective, in which everyday life merges with aesthetic plenitude. The icon of the Olympic Stadium provides a transcendent anchorage of collectivity in which the masses subjugate themselves to the all-encompassing gaze of a benevolent big Other, while the film spectator soaring with Riefenstahl's camera has the illusion of possessing that gaze. It is only in the medium of film that this experience of masses watching themselves from the position of the Other, which Kracauer theorized as crucial to fascist propaganda, is possible. With its solidity and concave shape, the stadium symbolizes a seemingly paradoxical containment *and* ecstatic dissolution (*Entgrenzung*) within contained boundaries, thus allowing each individual to merge "safely" with the whole. This literal and figurative containment is a precondition for the defusing of the "international" in this setting, where the parading of the Other (various national teams) serves only to underscore the racial health of "Germany."

The privileging of a particular location as a site of collectivity is a commonplace in "homefront" films. In Karl Ritter's *Holiday on Word of Honor* (*Urlaub auf Ehrenwort*, 1937) a platform at the Potsdam train station comes to exercise the magnetic draw of community. When a World War I regiment stops briefly in Berlin on its way to the front, their young captain risks a court-martial by allowing his men (again a microcosm of society) a few hours' vacation before their departure. While the train platform appears to be a location marked by dispersal, by absence throughout the film, the conclusion reverses it into a locale of unity, when in the nick of time three missing men return. The dispersal of and in space proves not to be threatening in itself as long as it is contained, or balanced by "inner strength" — again the specificity of location is transcended by an imagined community; moreover, the spatial anchor "train station" increasingly gains a spatial-temporal dimension of forward movement (forward in space and time into the community of war).

Rolf Hansen's *The Great Love* (*Die grosse Liebe*), which was seen by more Germans during and after the war than any other German film, locates collective experience in the Berlin Revue hall dominated by Nazi cinema's premiere vamp, Zarah Leander. The film repeats the public-private dichotomy of other homefront films, in which collective need is coded male and desire, female: The singer Hanna Holberg (Leander) loves a fighter pilot who is constantly forced to the front until their romance breaks down for her lack of patience. Yet the film complicates this configuration by splitting Hanna Holberg into a public and private person in competition with each other. Her public person stands for the collectivity her private person must painstakingly learn: with her performance she effortlessly buoys the spirits of civilians and soldiers, reminding the latter in one song that "the world will not go under" because of a mere war. Such scenes, like similar ones in *Request Concert,* enhance community feeling through the interaction of shots and countershots allowing the film audience to watch its surrogate, the fictional audience, watching the unifying spectacle. Imaginary bonding occurs, then, not only between Leander and her audience but between the film audience and its self-reflection. Referring to the derivation of the revue from "review" or military inspection, Karsten Witte reads the revue as an anticipation of war in the realm of entertainment: "The fact that 'girls' are on parade in these uniforms may heighten the erotic appeal, but actually degrades it through the very massive deindividualization of those girls. The director . . . inspects the revue girls as representatives of the female reserve army, who hold up the home-front even as the warfront of male armies is collapsing."[27]

The film's trajectory is aimed at allowing the private woman to catch up with the star, which occurs in her final performance conflating public and private affirmation in what became Nazi cinema's most famous song, "I Know Someday a Miracle Will Happen." In its assurance that a "thousand fairy tales will come true," the song text promises happy closure at once to the war, to the waiting, and to Hanna's career. Ironically, in other words, her catching up with her star self has the effect of voiding her star status as she becomes "his" alone. Stephen Lowry has analyzed Leander's/Holberg's redemption in this scene as a simultaneous visual deeroticization, especially vis-à-vis earlier, vampish performances. She appears in celestial white, immobilized and veritably pinned to the stage set.[28] Indeed, by the time she rushes to her wounded lover's side at the film's end, the film has utterly abandoned its precarious straddling of private and public need in one female figure, restoring the dominance of the male-female, public-private homology — albeit with a penitent Hanna. Not only does she subordinate desire, but she relinquishes her active orchestration of community for a purely passive standing by her man.

The post-Olympic segments of *Request Concert* go further than either of the above films, synthesizing the timeless interpellation of music with a timely mystification of radio's transcendence of time and space. The "Request Concert" broadcast acts as another kind of magnet, restoring the

27. "Visual Pleasure Inhibited: Aspects of the German Revue Film," *New German Critique* 24–25 (Fall/Winter 1981–82), 238.
28. Lowry, 184–91.

unity of a wide spectrum of dispersed figures, beginning and ending with the microcosmic world of Inge and Koch. Not only does the radio literally bring the lovers back together over space when Inge overhears Koch's request for the Olympic music, it brings closure to a personal trial (caused by the Spanish Civil War) that anticipates the ongoing trials of the nation on- and offscreen. It substitutes the closure of a past public episode (Legion Condor) and a fictional private episode (the lovers' separation) for the closure it cannot deliver, to the war. The minor historical moment of Legion Condor, though barely present in the film's narration, takes on a similar functionalization as history in other films, only on a level of everyday people. Although the film takes pains to foreground time (Inge's discussion with her aunt over whether the lovers have "so much time" or "no time at all") and "realistically" juxtaposes three days of "happiness" with three years of waiting, its narration undermines such honesty, indulging the lovers' brief "moments of happiness" and erasing in ellipsis both Koch's fighting (and an injury he sustains in Spain) and Inge's waiting. The ellipsis is complete as the Olympic music transports, in a gesture recalling *The Ruler,* the narrative forward toward harmony by transporting Inge *backwards* into an earlier harmony. The aestheticized, backlit shot of her euphoric face hearing the radio suggests her transportation into "another" space where time no longer matters. This closure will, however, merely begin a new, sadistic cycle of waiting and confusion, calling for a second, "final" closure to which I will return.

During the last, long segment of the film, the musical spectacle of the "Request Concert" almost completely puts narrative resolution on hold. Like many wartime American films built around star-studded USO shows (cf., *This Is the Army, Star Spangled Rhythm, Follow Those Boys, For Me and My Gal*), this segment avoids an "impossible" resolution by dispensing almost altogether with story. It also, of course, avoids the war, which, rather than being leapt over as in the case of Legion Condor, is literally drowned out by music, acoustic and visual plenitude, stars "everyone" knows, and wholeness. The "Request Concert" takes over the project of vicariously reuniting the whole nation, as if the film were acknowledging that it doesn't have time or energy to take care of all the bodies it has generated. Technologically dispersed music stands in for "real" community and supposedly "speaks" the People's experience for them — even tracing the cycles of life built into the character configuration: the names of new babies born to soldiers at the front are announced, followed by a montage of children and a lullaby sung by a children's chorus. Among the images are the teacher's wife and baby, shown by crosscut images denied either diegetic parent. Finally, the death of another character is remembered, the musician-soldier Schwarzkopf.

Every successful artist/Genius figure we have encountered, from Schiller to Neuber to Diesel, has been discursively cast as a soldier as well. This fusion reaches its extreme in the subplot involving Schwarzkopf, whose dispensability to the main story suggests his ideological significance. He provides the rather confusing narrative with a symmetry, surfacing three times near the beginning, middle, and end (a trinity in keeping with his messianic role), each of which mobilizes music to fuse dispersed people. He first appears at home playing Beethoven's *Pathétique* (second movement) on the piano. Various characters living in the same apartment building burst into the room talking and are admonished to reverent silence for the music. Although the figures' reactions differ in accordance with their social class (the comical baker is much more ill-at-ease in the presence of Culture than the educated teacher), the mere utterance of the word "Beethoven" transports them all into a state of epiphanous ecstasy—recalling Werther's sentimental reaction to Lotte's exclamation "Klopstock!" in Goethe's *The Sorrows of Young Werther* 150 years earlier. In the midst of war, diverse individuals are made one by their common German cultural heritage, as they are elsewhere in the film by the Olympics and the radio. Again "high" Culture becomes a collective mirror, although the film unwittingly reveals this Culture as ideology; the characters' obligatory metamorphosis follows not from the music itself but from the Naming of Genius to which they are "supposed" to react. "Beethoven" freezes time in a tableau of listeners with their heads dutifully cocked in attention, as if to ironize the "contemplative" reception of art.

The conclusion of the "Beethoven" scene anticipates Schwarzkopf's second, parallel scene, which provides the film's only significant acknowledgment of war. The camera cuts from the tableau in which Beethoven reigns to an outside window, from where it seems magnetically pulled toward the street. Here a perfect column of soldiers ("today's" counterpart to the Olympic "Germans"), shot from a Riefenstahlesque bird's-eye view, drowns Beethoven and the private sphere out with a literal interpellation, a fusion of male voices in a marching song. We next see Schwarzkopf on the Polish front, in a church, awaiting the return of his comrades from battle. When the men are unable to find the meeting place due to intense fog, Schwarzkopf begins playing Max Reger's "A Mighty Fortress" (*Ein feste Burg*) on the organ to guide them, exposing himself as an easy target for enemy fire. Martin Luther's text "A Mighty Fortress" invokes salvation through "Jesus Christ," just as the scene crosscuts between the doomed Schwarzkopf and a statue of the crucified Christ in the church. This time the magnet of German Culture ensures at once literal survival and a masturbatory enjoyment of "sacrifice," suggested by Schwarzkopf's euphoric gaze into nowhere as he plays.[29]

With each appearance, Schwarzkopf becomes incrementally "more than himself," acting first as musician, then as musician-soldier-savior, and finally undergoing a transmutation into music itself. In his final scene at the sentimental conclusion of the radio concert, the absent Schwarzkopf is "spiritually" reunited with his mother as the orchestra fulfills her request to play his favorite song. The film complements its displacement from the particular (the individual Schwarzkopf) to the general (he stands for "all soldiers") with another displacement from the symbolic to the imaginary. The camera tracks, to the sounds of a male voice singing "Good Night, Mother," from the ubiquitous radio speaker past Schwarzkopf's empty piano to a photograph of him (photo 59), and finally to the mother sitting at the same table and with the same stance as in the "Beethoven" scene. Schwarzkopf is doing what he's always done (draw "Germany" together), only now the film dispenses with "high" Culture and owns up to the kitsch it really enjoys, a kitsch that complements the death the film can now disavow as death. By retracing its steps, the camera pretends nothing has changed; indeed, the enjoyment of Schwarzkopf's playing gives way to the greater enjoyment of pain, just as the obligatory "enjoyment" of Culture gives way to an unabashed enjoyment of kitsch. Art-kitsch-death-sacrifice-memory fuse with each other in the Schwarzkopf story and with other visually mediated "embodiments" in the film like geography or collective and individual history to nostalgically culminate in a vague notion of "unity."

29. The appearance of Luther's "A Mighty Fortress" in a scene aestheticizing and sentimentalizing death is no accident. The metaphor of the "mighty fortress" suggests the ideal and fortified ego-substitute Theweleit describes in his notion of the "armored" individual impervious to weakness. The song, which Heinrich Heine referred to as a "battle song," had been recited during military actions since the seventeenth century, with its reference to God as "a good defense and weapon" or the final line "the empire must remain ours" finding a new, more literal meaning. During World War I nationalistic leaders suggested that soldiers recite it as a form of "spiritual rearmament." Lothar Schmidt, " 'Und wenn die Welt voll Teufel wär': Zu Martin Luthers 'Ein feste burg ist unser Gott,' " in *Gedichte und Interpretationen: Renaissance und Barock*, ed. Volker Meid (Stuttgart: Reclam, 1982), 66.

Just as Schwarzkopf has become an abstract "idea" of wholeness, so the "Request Concert" has gained in abstractness over the Olympics, whose concreteness is rendered inaccessible by their status as memory and better-than-life dream. Radio compensates by allowing an imagined community to transgress beyond a physical location; technology allows the emotional value of Berlin, the focal point of community, to bring together disparate spaces like the living room of the dead musician's mother, Helmut's hospital room, the air force headquarters. While on the diegetic level music displaces geographical space into an imaginary realm in which city and country, center and periphery are reconciled, the film audience experiences a *specular* unity denied the diegetic characters. Montage sequences accompany each musical piece, composed of images marked by an absence that enhances their sense of togetherness, as in the case of Schwarzkopf's commemoration. A militaristic march, for example, accompanies images of industriously working civilians linked by the conspicuous absence of young men, as when the camera dwells on a young woman sewing with her children, or when it tracks out from a radio speaker to reveal a woman writing a letter next to a soldier's photograph. These images are constantly juxtaposed with those of the front, where the soldiers are minus their "loved ones." Tools tap to the beat of the music (something like Verdi's Anvil Chorus in *Il Trovatore*), whose time is likewise kept by whirring sewing machines, all of which most literally synchronize (*gleichschalten*) a dispersed society. An aestheticized feeling of unity informs each of these vignettes, even and especially when its contents depict an act of "sacrifice," which is transformed into pleasure.

One last time public spectacle intervenes as a corrective measure in the lives of the film's main lovers, as the narrative's sadistic-playful cycle of deferral continues. Inge's reunion with Koch is disrupted by his sudden call to battle, where Inge's young neighbor Helmut is injured in an air attack that forces their plane down (an "acknowledgment" of war that ends up affording the soldier a vacation in which private need can be indulged, much like in *The Great Love*, where the lover's injury finally gives the lovers time to marry). "War" here is staged for the sole purpose of allowing Koch to find Inge's picture among Helmut's things, propelling further confusion as to whose fiancée Inge is. The inevitable unraveling of Truth in the hospital room is permeated by "Request Concert's" broadcast of the overture to Mozart's *Marriage of Figaro* (with Eugen Jochum as guest conductor). Like Hitler at the film's beginning, the *Lustspiel* opera, with its confusion and marital end-point mirroring the film's tangled romance, "hovers over" the story to assure that the "right" people find each other, dispelling a false love triangle stranding Inge between two more "incommensurate entities," a Herbert and a Helmut. Again Culture acts as a magnet with which war as reality can be abjured, with which a brooding Beethoven is submerged by a light-hearted Mozart. Missing in Mozart is the resolution of an Oedipalized rivalry (between the childlike Helmut and the fatherly Koch) that allows male bonding to supersede heterosexual desire; each man attempts to "renounce" Inge for the sake of the other.

The film's frequent close-up shots of radios attest to the overt level on which it celebrates radio technology as a conscious means of transcending space (photo 60). On a more covert level (even though the spectator, like Freud's subject, "knows it all the time") *Request Concert* celebrates film technology's powerful potential for forging community. To the film's dual structure, real-life event (staged, like *Triumph of the Will*'s rally, for media reproduction) and simultaneous dissemination via radio, one must add the third, though extradiegetic, element of cinema, the latter achieving not a mere dissemination but a lavish restaging of "events," enhanced by a visual plenitude lacking in radio. It is film itself that provides the culminating god's-eye perspective of community; the film image thus stands in for the cathected imaginary object "Germany" that is both internalized by the subject of Nazism and a Thing external to him or her.

A brief but key scene in *The Great Love* also suggests the enhanced "reality effect" of cinema's realm of the imaginary, as Hanna Holberg (Zarah Leander) sits in a movie theater watching a newsreel showing fighter pilots, which she relates to the current, "real-life" mission of her absent lover: "He's a pilot, too!" Noteworthy is the manner in which *The Great Love* introduces its film clip: it cuts from a shot of the two lovers together to one of planes battling in the sky, initially deluding us into assuming we have experienced an ellipsis and are seeing the lover on duty. Only when the camera pulls away, revealing the dimensions of the frame, do we realize we are seeing a film within a film, of which Hanna is, like us and those around her, a passive spectator. The scene confuses a number of crucial boundaries: it is momentarily unclear what is "real" within the movie and what is "only a movie." Yet ironically, as a newsreel, the movie-within-the-movie has a status of extratextual "reality" exceeding anything in the movie itself. Second, the usual object of our gaze, Zarah Leander, becomes the subject of a desiring gaze, although this occurs only retroactively when we realize that we saw the clip "through her eyes" and the "objective" view of the war became subjectivized, invested with feeling. The brief specularization of the lover at war (more precisely, of airplanes, of war itself) gives way again to the spectacle of a nostalgic Zarah, located in her gender-appropriate site of the private sphere, of passivity, anticipating the role she will assume "after" the movie when she is married and no longer on stage as a star.[30] Although the newsreel scene is not "necessary" to the story itself, it is important as one of the few occasions in which the Nazi film apparatus articulates its own crucial role in Nazism's aestheti cization of politics and "life": working on the level of the imaginary, the newsreel seems to make real to Hanna what her lover's verbal explanations (i.e., the level of the symbolic) could not.

Whether or not these homefront films celebrate technology explicitly, as does *Request Concert* with its radio show, all allow cinema technology effectively to deny real, everyday lack by purporting to serve a "greater" end, the transformation of actual experience into imaginary, and thus aestheticized, experience. The latter by definition displaces need fulfillment into the imaginary, providing compensatory satisfaction. Within these movies, the Olympics, the radio concert, and Leander singing are "real," but their importance lies in their imaginary value, which can be experienced by technological mediation as well as by physical presence (and by a film audience as well as a diegetic audience). These imaginary experiences need to be reinforced, however, by the narratives that surround them—specifically, by the temporal dimension the narratives offer. Most obviously, the films' happy conclusions, with their anticipatory function, assist Nazism's reconciliation of imaginary and real. *The Great Love* concludes with a famous shot in which the reunited lovers look up toward distant planes in anticipation of the "miracle" Leander's famous song promises. The shot of planes recalls the newsreel we saw Leander watching earlier, enhancing the sense of empowerment and fusion of the imaginary and reality through film. But the shot also is a kind of iconic question mark complementing the lovers' verbal question "And then?" (What will happen after we get married?). The very last shot of their close-up faces evades the question but doesn't quite erase it.

We have seen how *Request Concert* similarly allows one, reunited couple to stand in for the reunification of real individuals separated by a real

30. The fact that Hanna's musician friend, composer Rudnitzky (Paul Hörbiger), shares this feminized location in the movie theater attests, along with many other factors, to the "impossibility" of his love for her. He must content himself with an enunciating role—as composer of her songs, most importantly the song initiating the "miracle" fusing private and collective love. Though propelled by desire, he remains, like the film viewer, utterly excluded from any sexual reciprocity.

war. Its temporal structure is, however, more complex. While *The Great Love* consists of a linear set of deferrals which can be expected to continue beyond the end, notwithstanding its happy closure, *Request Concert* is more circular, essentially ending where it began (at the beginning of a war in 1939–40). In other words, *Request Concert* anticipates the real-life separation to come by showing an earlier, fictional separation (1936–1940) whose happy end is premature for the population as a whole, whose trials are only beginning. It couches its ending, moreover, in comedy, making no reference to any further separation of the diegetic lovers. Any glimmer of the kind of question mark with which *The Great Love* ends is purely extratextual, informed by what a contemporary audience knew.

Finally, *Request Concert*'s temporality is further complicated by the relationship it posits between its Olympic and radio time, which recalls *The Ruler* with its odd synthesis of Hellenic symbolism and cutting-edge industry. The Olympics, being confined to a fixed place, represent an earlier stage of aestheticization over which radio constitutes a distinct advancement and advantage; at the same time, they represent a timeless, unsurpassable experience of wholeness, of life as a dream or work of art that National Socialism constantly aspires to retrieve. Of the aestheticizing strategies I have identified in this chapter, only the last has a peculiarly "Nazi" resonance. The others, like community invoked through musical spectacle or narrative closure, we would find in any American films of the same period and contending with the same war, as Dana Polan's *Power and Paranoia* demonstrates so well. However, their lack of specificity by no means diminishes the lessons these strategies hold for understanding National Socialism's management of desire. The key to this management lies not in uniqueness, but in the kind of symptomatic displacement suggested by the very word *aestheticization*.

TEN

Of Lies and Life: *Münchhausen*'s

Narrative Arabesque

I am going to conclude the study in the spirit of contradiction with which it began: by glancing at a film constituting at once an affirmation and upheaval of everything that preceded it. If Josef von Baky's *Münchhausen* (1943) is not propaganda, it most definitely is an early form of media hype. Commissioned as a twenty-fifth anniversary celebration of Ufa, Germany's most powerful commercial film studio since the Weimar Republic, the film was one of the era's premier extravaganzas. It stunned the public with its advanced technology, including Agfacolor and trick photography, and with its outrageous narrative based on the tales of Karl Friedrich Hieronymus Freiherr von Münchhausen (1720–1797), the famous "lying Baron," whose stories were given literary form by, among others, Rudolf Erich Raspe and G. A. Bürger. No costs were to be spared in the production, which featured the absolute superstar of Nazi cinema, Hans Albers, as well as many other well-known actors.

The interest of *Münchhausen* for this study is that it brings together crucial themes pervading the films we've examined — history, social body, Personality, "Jew" — yet these receive a most unusual treatment that threatens to overturn the whole ideological "system" of Nazi cinema. The film drives many tendencies we've seen to an extreme: it is extreme in its display of internal tension, both unleashing and containing fantastic elements that have a potentially subversive effect. Since *Münchhausen*'s raison d'être is to celebrate cinema, it drives to an extreme the celebration of machines we saw in the last chapter. More important than its genesis as an homage to Ufa, however, is its self-conscious, allegorical reflection on its own medium. Finally, *Münchhausen* drives to an extreme the "collision" of the two times around which my study has revolved, eighteenth- and twentieth-century Germany. It does so by including both times in its diegesis, yet also by confusing the two and pitting them against each other

*

The film begins in the twentieth century. Baron Münchhausen hosts a rococo ball, at which a young woman attempts unsuccessfully to seduce him. Later the Baron recounts the exploits of the legendary Baron Münchhausen to the woman and her fiancé. The setting changes in an extended flashback to the eighteenth century, as Münchhausen arrives at his home in Bodenwerder with his longtime servant Christian. Prince Carl of Brunswick summons Münchhausen to accompany him to St. Petersburg, where he will be allied with Catherine the Great against the Turks. In St. Petersburg Münchhausen has an affair with Catherine, fights a duel with the jealous Prince Potemkin, and receives the gift of immortality and a magic ring from the sorcerer Cagliostro. Prince Potemkin lights a cannon on which Münchhausen is sitting, propelling him through space until he lands in Sultan Abdul-Hamid's palace in Constantinople. Münchhausen gains his freedom by betting the Sultan that he can procure him a bottle of the world's best Tokay in an hour. He then flees with the captive Princess Isabella d'Este by making himself invisible with the magic ring. They return to her home in Venice, where her brother has her kidnapped and put in a cloister. After dueling with the brother, Münchhausen escapes Venice with Christian in a hot air balloon, which lands on the moon, where people's heads can separate from their bodies and one day is the equivalent of one year on earth. Christian dies and the story returns to the present time. The Baron admits to the couple that he himself is Münchhausen. He renounces the gift of immortality.

*

As most readings of the film have emphasized, *Münchhausen* is an extraordinary film for its time and its context. Its screenplay was written by Erich Kästner, who was, with this one exception, prohibited from publishing in Nazi Germany. *Münchhausen* is unusual in its self-reflexivity, its indulgence of sexual desire and unleashing of fantasy.[1] Once again, this film renders a machine organic, only in a most curious way;

---

1. Eric Rentschler discusses these three peculiarities, though his general conclusions differ considerably from mine. See "The Triumph of Male Will: *Münchhausen* (1943)," *Film Quarterly* 43.3 (Spring 1990): 14–23. Rentschler draws convincing analogies between the weapons of film and the weapons of war.

namely, Münchhausen himself is an allegory for cinema. He embodies cinema's power over time and space, as well as its power of captivation. Like the cinematic image, Münchhausen remains untouched by the ravages of time and emerges unscathed from the most perilous adventures. He shares with film editing the ability to leap not only continents but centuries, enjoying a ubiquity akin to film's "primary" identification. He controls whether his image is seen or not, and has weapons that double as lenses allowing the eye to transcend vast distances.

In many other ways, too, *Münchhausen* displays a self-consciousness alien to classical cinema. It contemplates, for example, cinema's simultaneous dependency on and transcendence of other media. Already in its first image preceding the credits it brings a static painting "to life." A large portrait of Münchhausen suddenly winks at the spectator, breaking with conventions of classical cinema not only by acknowledging the presence of an off-screen audience, but by establishing a kind of pact with it: we know very well it's just a movie, but just the same we'll pretend we don't. As it foregrounds the act of telling, the film imitates earlier narrative forms: it adopts an oral tradition as Münchhausen narrates his story to a collective diegetic audience and when he adopts the discourse of a fairy tale at the end ("and if he isn't dead, he's still alive today" — the German equivalent of "and he lived happily ever after"). It imitates the private medium of print, showing close-up a book of Münchhausen stories as he begins telling, and it conjures violin music out of nowhere. In its very homage to earlier media lies the film's covert self-aggrandizement; it appears to take satisfaction in its infinitely greater ability to tantalize in living color and with living bodies.

Like the "homefront" films I've just examined, *Münchhausen* answers a contemporary situation, only its answer differs sharply. While the homefront films provide a reassuring stability, *Münchhausen* offers a pleasurable instability of, as we shall see, time, space, narrative, and body. While other films cover over a lack of historical closure with a narrative closure securing heterosexual monogamy, *Münchhausen* indulges fantasies of an irresponsible, amoral polygamy. It counters the spectacle of war with one of special effects, the call of the collective with a narcissistic individualism, want with plenitude. In short, it comes to terms with a crazy world by offering an even crazier one of eroticism, excess, and surrealism. *Münchhausen* is a trip, in every sense of the word.

But what kind of a trip does the film represent? In the course of this study we have encountered many travelers: the "Jew" traveling to violate community, a few aimless travelers (like Friedemann Bach or *The Golden*

City's Maria) who have lost community, and many figures traveling with the aim of securing or restoring community (*Komödianten, Paracelsus, Friedrich Schiller, Robert and Bertram, Gold,* etc.). Despite many variations on the status of travel, each of the films so far has privileged the social body as *Heimat,* as the place to which you return. And on an ideological level, *Münchhausen* is no exception. It interjects into its dialogue platitudes about *Heimat* and mother; moreover, its entire frame device is a concession to this master narrative of *Heimat.* Each end of the frame is marked by moral edification. On one side, Münchhausen rejects the girl's advances with a patronizing benevolence almost recalling Frederick; on the other side, he definitively renounces both travel and immortality, choosing to resubject himself to time so he may die with his matronly wife: "I voluntarily lay the great gifts back in the hands of destiny. Eternal youth makes for half a god and half a human being. I demand it all—I want the rest as well." His moralization is anticipated by a close-up of an owl, with its suggestion of wisdom, night, and sleep for the man who "loved restlessness" (*die Unruhe*). *Münchhausen*'s frame seems as much a literal as it is a narrative frame, since it functions to harness the excess, to tame the narcissism, the reckless adventure and sheer purposelessness of an extended flashback that plays down the Faustian implications of the Münchhausen persona and plays up its hedonism. It even traps Münchhausen himself, restraining in a huge portrait this Personality who nonetheless hovers over twentieth-century happenings.

Finally, besides *containing* the unruly forces the film unleashes, the frame with its petty bourgeois moralism offers a means of *ending* an otherwise unendable narrative: Münchhausen's cycle of propulsion into new spaces with new women could perpetuate itself endlessly. As in *1001 Nights,* whose arabesque narrative style *Münchhausen* echoes (complete with frame story and the theme of chopped off heads, as I will discuss later), narrative in *Münchhausen* is synonymous with life, and is thus inseparable from Münchhausen's eternal youth. Like Scheherazade in *1001 Nights* as described by Sandra Naddaff, Münchhausen is "the sterling example of the narrator who succeeds in staving off and ultimately avoiding death by telling stories."[2] He even literally saves himself from beheading by telling the Sultan stories of European life, just as Scheherazade keeps herself alive on a day-by-day basis. *Münchhausen*'s artificial ending, then, is a form of death in which Münchhausen not only faces

2. *Arabesque: Narrative Structure and the Aesthetics of Repetition in 1001 Nights* (Evanston, Ill.: Northwestern University Press, 1991), 40.

mortality but, more importantly, stops telling stories: "the absence of narrative . . . promises certain death."[3] (In this sense the film is allegorical in another way, prefiguring the death of National Socialism two years after the film.) Thus, although the frame story permits Nazi cinema to align Münchhausen with the ranks of its many travelers magnetically drawn back to *Heimat,* the question remains whether this "politically correct" ending is enough to sublate the real energy from which the film lives. To use a familiar analogy, *The Wizard of Oz* is, much more than *Münchhausen,* driven by the protagonist's desire to return home. Yet what makes the film compelling is not "there's no place like home," but the vibrant colors of Oz, the wicked witch with her monkey servants, Glenda's bubble and the vindictive apple trees. Dorothy's return home is as much a letdown as it is soothing; in more than one sense it represents a return to black and white. The same, I would argue, holds for *Münchhausen.*

We might even go further in suggesting that the flashback constituting the main part of *Münchhausen* contradicts its frame. One of them is lying and I'm inclined to think it's the Lying Baron *telling* the story and not the one *in* the story. The frame's Münchhausen belies the very essence of "Münchhausenism" by embracing the demands of a social community so alien to everything he stands for. What drives the other ("real") Münchhausen is narcissistic omnipotence, an eternal adolescence evading, at all costs, "commitment," as when he tells his father he "already has a respectable number of grandchildren, but unfortunately none of the brats is named Münchhausen," or when he dismisses the aging Casanova's remarks that "the eyes become satiated but the heart remains empty." (It is because of Münchhausen's itinerance, moreover, that his servant Christian barely knows his own children.) Suddenly we are to believe Münchhausen's happy entry into a world where one is a kid only once a year (a *Geburtstagskind*). We are to believe his double encoding in a hierarchy of family, where he becomes at once a prodigal son, renouncing eternal promiscuity for one who, as Rentschler puts it, is "more a mother than a wife,"[4] *and* a father figure founding the family that never interested him before: the flirtatious young woman is frightened by Münchhausen's Faustian dalliance with nature and subjects herself remorsefully to the fiancé whom she had earlier scorned.

What separates the "real" Münchhausen of Nazi cinema's imagination

3. Ibid.
4. Rentschler, 21. He likens the resolution to Weimar's "street" film genre.

from protagonists of other films is that he is driven by no "mission" greater than himself, no Thing demands to be retrieved by him. He lives, rather, in a sphere that remains purely private even when he becomes involved in (most literally) affairs of state, where the "meaning of life" is a bottle of Tokay. His rhetoric notwithstanding, the social body is for him one place among others, a springboard from which to explore more exotic locales that gratify, even defy, the imagination. Münchhausen's language is at times almost, in a Bakhtinian sense, in dialogue with itself; his predictable "blood and soil" remark to the Sultan, "everyone has only one homeland just as he has only one mother," is directly preceded by another that much more adequately accords with the film itself: "Who can decide what is better if hardly anybody knows what's good?"

Looking back at the films compiled here with their various ilks of travelers, Münchhausen bears the greatest resemblance — perhaps not so surprisingly — to the "Jew" with his transgression of spatial boundaries. Mastery of space defines his character ("the earth was too small for him") and propels the narrative forward. Not only is Münchhausen, like Süss Oppenheimer, consistently linked with women; he effortlessly conquers each space by taking its most desirable woman — a feature almost totally missing from the Münchhausen stories. His relations with women are sexually free and unserious; he exchanges women as freely as he exchanges spaces. His entrance into spaces of Otherness is sometimes violent, as with his arrival on the cannon ball, and always disruptive to "family" (in one way or the other) and a patriarchal community. What could, after all, be more inimical to Nazism than the supreme individualism both Münchhausen and Süss Oppenheimer represent?

I have already argued that the cinematic Frederick the Great mirrors Nazism's "Jew" as a "positive" social fantasy, a vessel into whom reconciliation could be projected. I want to suggest here that, in a very different way, Münchhausen also mirrors the "Jew." If Frederick, like other historical models and Hitler himself, represents an anchor offering an imaginary reconciliation, Münchhausen is a more apocalyptic figure acknowledging its impossibility. Certainly we have, as Rentschler argues, to see *Münchhausen* as part of a cynical apparatus that "trades in illusions," as a work that reflects "at once the operations of cynical reason and those of male fantasy production."[5] On another level, however, more than cynicism and misogyny are at work here. It is as if in *Münchhausen* Nazi cinema allows the fantasies of ubiquity and omnipotence, of psychic and

5. Ibid., 16 f., 15.

bodily liberation it disavows through projection onto the "Jew," to be released, lived out. Once it seeks out its own desire at this crucial juncture so close to its own closure, it lands right in the fictional space of its Other, the "Jew." "Germany" can finally admit it really wants to be the "Jew"; it wants, with impunity, to do the things he does.

If anti-Semitism fantasizes the "Jew" as the master of an all-seeing, malevolent gaze, as a force controlling otherwise anonymous structures, he remains a mystery; we can't fathom the "Jew," can't quite know what he wants. Although Münchhausen likewise controls the story as well as, to a great extent, the image, rendering the film something akin to a first-person narrative, he, too, remains something of a mystery. He begins the Münchhausen legend with the words: "Everybody knows of him and nobody knows him. Nobody can answer the question: what kind of person was Münchhausen?" His attractiveness lies precisely in the impossibility of pinning him down; in one of the film's many sublations of clear boundaries, we are not even sure of his identity. Only at the end, when the film returns to the present and Münchhausen reveals his identity, can we be sure that he is himself — though ironically it is at the very point when he *ceases* to be "himself" and breaks with the narrative logic.

As textual enunciator, Münchhausen is, like the "Jew," a master of the gaze, allowing us to transgress with our eyes forbidden spaces, as when he enters the Sultan's harem full of naked or half-naked women. In a trick shot he turns his eyeballs outward in opposite directions, giving himself an "impossible" 180-degree breadth of vision. Conversely, he can visually disorient his enemies, blinding them with metal and making them see double. Also like the "Jew," he controls his own image, adapting his clothing to each culture and retaining his youth, leading Casanova to wonder if he is "in league with the devil" — another reference in common with Süss Oppenheimer as well as Frederick. The piercing blue eyes for which Albers was so famous function, something like Frederick's, as subject and object of the gaze. From the very beginning Münchhausen is the object of fascinated watching and listening, by the young woman at the ball, by his wife, by the listeners of his tales. Females are constantly looking in through or out of windows to watch him, as when he rides into eighteenth-century Bodenwerder at the beginning of the flashback. At times his clothing surpasses women's in its flashiness, especially the glitzy jacket he dons for his audience with Catherine. He is, moreover, conscious of himself as a spectacle: In the film's most famous image, when he is literally and figuratively "shot" through the air on a cannon ball, he almost loses the ball when he removes his hand to tip his hat to the film audience (photos 61–62).

Again like Süss, Münchhausen has no narrative antagonist; more precisely, the narrative antagonists he does have are merely there in order to be as effectively "castrated" by him as the eunuchs in the Sultan's domain. He humiliates Prince Potemkin, who loses an eye—linked by Freud to castration—in jealous fighting with another man. He manipulates the Turkish sultan, finally abducting his most privileged possession, Princess Isabella. When Münchhausen duels with her possessive brother, subjective shots show a multitude of blades dancing before the latter's face (rather than kill the brother, Münchhausen strips the clothes from his body, making public his "castration"). Moreover, the affection Münchhausen displays during Christian's death scene merely underscores that he indeed has no friends, *can* have none since everyone either serves him, is humiliated by him, or finally succumbs to aging and death. (Although Süss Oppenheimer supposedly acts on behalf of world Jewry, he, too, is effectively alone; all other Jews seem merely tools in his quest for individual power.) Nor is Münchhausen, any more than Süss, subservient to his social superiors, all of whom either depend on him (the Prince of Brunswick), are seduced (Catherine), or outmaneuvered (the Sultan) by him. Münchhausen even outdoes the "Jew" by conquering the most abstract of antagonistic forces, time.

The ambiguity between hatred and fascination with the "Jew" displayed by the film is most evident in Münchhausen's curious relationship with the one formidable antagonist he appears to have, Count Cagliostro. Even before Cagliostro actually meets Münchhausen, the film links him via association with the "Jew." The actor playing him is Ferdinand Marian, who played Süss Oppenheimer, as well as *Ohm Krüger*'s "Aryan" Jew, Cecil Rhodes (see chapter 8). As Münchhausen comments, "He lends [foolish people] his daydreams, but at a usurious interest rate" (another allusion to cinema as well). Like the "Jew," Cagliostro is the subject who "knows"; he "hears" what he cannot, such as pejorative comments made in his absence (Münchhausen's remark "he's just not a gentleman" aligns Cagliostro outside of "Aryan" Culture). He makes two appearances, each of which intervenes in the narrative flow, coming "out of the blue." Neither seems to have much connection with the other or with the flashback narrative, which, although composed of a series of barely related vignettes, does follow a certain logic: the relationship with a woman causes the humiliation of a male, forcing Münchhausen to leave one space for the next. Cagliostro's narrative function, then, stands apart, rendering him an agent or helper along the way. He first meets Münchhausen on his way from Bodenwerder to St. Petersburg; Cagliostro, like the "Jew," is "in-between" places. In the first meeting Cagliostro tries to persuade

61·62 The narcissistic Münchhausen, while greeting the film audience, nearly loses control of his famous cannon ball. **63** Cagliostro, linked semiotically with Jewry, comments that Münchhausen's profile is more "suitable" for the pursuit of power.

Münchhausen to join forces with him in conquering Poland via a strategic marriage:

> MÜNCHHAUSEN: The two of us will never agree on one thing — the main thing. You want to rule — I want to live. Adventure, war, foreign lands, beautiful women! I need them. But you abuse them.[6]
> CAGLIOSTRO: Mitau, Courland, Poland . . .
> MÜNCHHAUSEN (*as if finishing his sentence*): Petersburg!

6. In the original German the two words play off against each other; *ich brauche / Sie missbrauchen.*

Münchhausen's moral rejection of Cagliostro's megalomania, combined with the different meaning each gives the sequence "Mitau, Courland, Poland," seemingly casts the two men as opposite poles. For Cagliostro the sequence signifies the "Jewish" accumulation of spaces, the intensification of power; for Münchhausen, it is mere travel, pleasurably irresponsible movement from one space to another. In keeping with his role as textual enunciator, the camera obeys Münchhausen's cue "Petersburg!" by abruptly cutting to the carnivalesque city without resolving the discussion.

Curiously, however, the second time the two meet, in Russia, their earlier animosity has disappeared and they are inexplicably transformed into allies. The scene is in every respect a reversal of the earlier encounter; this time it is Münchhausen who seeks out Cagliostro to convey a political message, while Cagliostro indulges Münchhausen in "life's pleasures" (he magically conjures music, brings a nude painting to life). This time it is Münchhausen who is "in between" spaces and women; he is still in Russia but effectively "done" with it, signaled by Catherine's disappearance without a trace from the film. The ensuing bond between the two men is sealed by the most "Jewish" of acts: exchange. Münchhausen warns Cagliostro that Russian authorities are after him, enabling him to escape. In return Cagliostro grants Münchhausen one wish "beyond all conceivable wishes," which for Münchhausen is eternal youth, and also gives him a ring with which he can become temporarily invisible (recalling the preponderance of rings as signs of bonding in *Jew Süss*). In other words, the transcendence of time and control of vision that endow Münchhausen (and, vicariously, the audience) with his superhuman status are gifts of none other than the "Jew," the irritating, nontotalizable element threatening "society."

If we look retroactively at their earlier encounter, Cagliostro's proposal for collaboration seems to have a logic that escapes us at first: In Cagliostro's plan, Münchhausen was to be the facade of power, Cagliostro the truth lurking beneath: "*We* will be king." Cagliostro subtly suggests his own "Jewishness" when he explains his need to remain behind the scenes because "warrants of arrest have made my face so popular throughout Europe that no one would dare print it on coins. *Your* profile is decidedly more suitable" (photo 63). Unwittingly the film owns up to its disavowed pleasures by allowing Cagliostro / the "Jew" to emerge as a kind of doppelgänger for Münchhausen. What seems to be a quirk of the plot, the sudden "unmotivated" reversal to "more than . . . friendship," in fact reveals the film's crucial dialectic: carefree "living" and "power" (the apolitical and the political) emerge as one and the same thing: both master not only other people but nature itself. It is with good reason that servant Christian (when complaining that Cagliostro keeps "crossing our path") calls the magician "uncanny," if we recall Freud's analysis of the uncanny (un-*heim*-lich) as the return of that which is familiar, some repressed part of the self. It seems Münchhausen and the "Jew" agree, after all, on the "main thing."

Many features of *Münchhausen* are potentially readable as subversive subtextual references; Cagliostro's aspirations for Poland in particular have been seen as a critique of Hitler's imperialist Eastern policies;[7] the Venetian inquisition's "ten-thousand eyes and arms" as well as the Sultan's arbitrary murders could refer to Nazi terror; the frequent references to time and death suggest war. The potential of subversion may be a reason why Nazi cinema produced so few films of the fantastic genre.[8] What we can determine with more clarity is that, as I suggested earlier, the hedonistic abandon *Münchhausen* offers is predicated on an almost apocalyptic vision of a world out of whack, marked by chaos. The film presents time, space, the social and human body as disoriented, as having lost order (perhaps it even deconstructs the notion that there ever was an order). Most obvious is the film's temporal instability. At first it confuses us as to what century we're in (more on this later). It plays with the temporality of music, when music becomes "frozen" inside a hunting horn. When the horn thaws, the music of its hunting call comes tumbling out, getting out of control until the instrument is trampled to bits (as if interpellation has gone berserk). On Münchhausen's last diegetic trip, to the moon, where trumpets and contrabasses grow on trees, time is most literally "broken." One day there is a year on the earth, drastically shortening the life span of its inhabitants and rendering "this star" an ungodly place (*ein Unstern*). The history Nazi cinema so exalts elsewhere is reduced here to pure contingency, as when Münchhausen relates how Vienna was saved from the Turks in the Battle of Kahlenberg, 1683, only because the Viennese commander had drunk too much Tokay and saw his five thousand troops double, thus doubling his courage.

Spatially *Münchhausen*'s world seems hardly more normal; every space he enters is a boisterous carnival, one more outrageous than the next (again recalling Bakhtin's notion of the carnivalesque as subversive). In every space, either the organic becomes confused with the inorganic, or

7. See, for example, Kraft Wetzel and Peter Hagemann, *Liebe, Tod und Technik: Kino des Phantastischen, 1933–45* (Berlin: Verlag Volker Spiess, 1977), 33.
8. See ibid., 7; also Rentschler, 17–18.

the human with plants and animals: In Münchhausen's home in Boden-werder rabies-infested clothes dance frenetically after being exposed to a crazed German shepherd (another possible reference to the contagion of fascist insanity); in St. Petersburg men are paraded like caged animals and the court serves giant jewels as dessert; in Contantinople humans are functionalized as things like clocks (only the Sultan's human clock goes too fast because of a high fever — another sign of temporal disorder); on the moon reproduction is totally severed from the human body, "taken care of" by fruit trees. If *Münchhausen*'s social body is unstable, so are its human bodies. When Münchhausen rubs a black man, the color remains on his hands, as if to mock the doctrine of race and bodily markings so central to Nazism's stability. If Münchhausen comments early on that he has never seen a "completely grown up man" (which he would consider "boring"), we soon experience a time warp that instantaneously grows a mustache on a young boy (through Christian's magic ointment).

Most interesting in this respect is the film's recurring reference to bodies that lose their head — a metaphor that is purely pleasurable at first and becomes more and more literal and potentially violent. Münchhausen first wants to stop talking "reason" and "lose his head" in sexual pleasure in Catherine's boudoir (where his head is almost caught by a trap door in the floor; photo 64); in Constantinople he faces the threat of literally losing his head at the hands of the Sultan; he himself wants to "rip off the head" of Isabella's sadistic brother. The moon people drive the metaphor to its logical extreme, as they blithely separate head and body; Münchhausen flirtatiously congratulates the moon lady on locking up her body so she does not "do something stupid," even though she is headless. Finally, recounting the decades through which he has lived, Münchhausen refers to the French Revolution's reign of terror, in which heads were chopped off "in the name of Reason," bringing to full circle the metaphor's point of departure. This polysemic motif becomes one of the film's most compelling if we consider that in *Münchhausen* we have a social body that has indeed lost its head, that presents at best a facade of social authority, while in reality each "head" of state is weak and childish. Each space he enters is ruled by increasingly autocratic, irrational male figures (the film explicitly codes Catherine as a woman with balls, as a courtier remarks she should not be called "Katarina *die Grosse*," but "Katarina *der Grosse*," the latter being a masculine epithet). Only the moon seems to function with no state apparatus, its one man being literally vegetative; hence this is the only space Münchhausen exits without controversy. The resolution *Münch-hausen* strives for is, however, not, as in other films, the emergence of a

64 Münchhausen disappearing in a trap door in Catherine the Great's boudoir. The film plays literally and metaphorically with the motif of "losing your head."
65·66 Iconography links women with ornamental flowers in *Münchhausen*. Princess Isabella d'Este confined in a harem (*above*); the bodiless moon lady (*below*).
67 With one click of an electric light, Münchhausen thrusts us from what we think is the eighteenth to the twentieth century.

figure ready to redeem the social body, but an escape further into childhood. All of the film's grown-up children are outmaneuvered by the biggest child of them all, the supreme narcissistic individual Münchhausen. Whether we read the film as a cynical commentary by the Nazis on its own apparatus of illusions or as a longing for extrication from an existing community, in some way or another the film subverts Nazism's obsession with wholeness.

As our textual guide, Münchhausen reminds us of the impossibility not only of wholeness or pure community, but of desire itself. He cannot *fulfill* desire, but only pursue it in his stories and in the form of story, by telling and telling. Again as in *1001 Nights,* "sexual activity engenders and ultimately equals narrative activity; Scheherazade's nights with the king satisfy not only his sexual desire but his narrative desire as well."[9] The same holds true for Münchhausen's twentieth-century listeners (including the film audience), for whom narrative desire has to compensate for unfulfilled desire (which is explicitly sexual in the case of the girl who pursues him at the beginning of the film). Because desire is unfulfillable, Münchhausen's story can only end itself artificially, via the frame, and the only pleasures worth pursuing in his stories are those that remain elusive. Münchhausen's women are quickly spent, reduced from Things in Lacan's sense to everyday things, like the framed portrait of a former lover he noncommitally shows his father ("What can you do if love goes just like it comes — there are just too many pretty women!"), or former lover Luise la Tour, mocked by Münchhausen and the film alike. More desirable are the women who remain locked away: the princess "buried alive" by her brother or the moon lady whose lack of body only enhances Münchhausen's titillation ("Too bad my figure isn't here — it looks even younger!"). The iconic depictions of both of these women equate them with flowers; Isabella first appears ornamentally framed in the lattice of a decorative wall allowing petals to frame her face (photo 65); the moon lady's head sits on a flower stem, effectively replacing its bud (photo 66). As with nature, the iconography suggests, what is picked wilts and dies. This is also the lesson in the painting of the nude woman Cagliostro brings to life (when she turns to reveal her face and breasts, both men agree they "liked her better from behind"), as it is in Münchhausen's indifference to Luise la Tour's décolleté and in his gesture covering a nude statue. This understanding of the structure of desire sustains *Münchhausen*'s allegory

9. Naddaff, 45.

of film, which likewise offers a select glimpse, never the Thing itself, which is not only absent, but, as Lacan would put it, not.

Finally, this same insight motivates a little joke the film plays on us that I have left for the end, though it begins the film. As the minuet is danced at Münchhausen's rococo ball amid the glow of candles, the film gives us no clue that we are not "in" the eighteenth century, that we are really seeing, even on a diegetic level, a simulation of another time, a costume ball. Suddenly, however, Münchhausen passes on to the spectator the dose of reality with which he has dashed the hopes of the amorous girl: his lace-cuffed hand reaches to an electric light switch (photo 67). With one click the magic of illusion is broken; we're in the "present," but, like someone thrust from a dark room into bright sunlight, not quite ready for it. Imitating its lying protagonist, the film takes sadistic pleasure in disorienting us and proceeds to flaunt its anachronisms with exhibitionistic relish: wigged courtiers dance the tango to accordions, while the rococo-clad girl races off in a flashy sports car.

In several respects, Münchhausen's sobering gesture achieves what I have attempted to do in the study as a whole: first, to cast a cold light on Nazi cinema's world of pleasurable semblance, exploring its simulacra less as lies than as imaginary constructions that come from *somewhere,* and not only from the diabolical imagination of cynics. Second, I have explored the particular relation between an eighteenth century imagined in Nazi films and the present by and for whom it was imagined. *Münchhausen* is unusually accommodating by self-consciously foregrounding this relationship; it narrativizes only the eighteenth and twentieth centuries, while the intervening time is only *narrated* within the diegesis (Münchhausen sums it up). We saw how on the ideological level, manifested in its frame story, the film again reappropriates the eighteenth century's "universally human" virtue. Yet, ironically, *Münchhausen* alone releases the eighteenth century itself from the burden of morality. We have here more the eighteenth century of de Sade than of Schiller or Lessing; the dominant motif of calm (*Ruhe*) gives way to restlessness (*Unruhe*); grown-up men becomes bores. And while the other films use the past to imagine a trajectory toward a whole social body, this one allows that body to remain fragmented and euphorically self-centered, only pretending to cooperate with the sacrificial present.

Finally, *Münchhausen*'s opening scene sums up the tension responsible for both the contradiction and the energy of any study of classical cinema: between the cold-blooded technology that film *is* and the candles of illusion and desire that film *serves*. In keeping with its allegorical relation to cinema, *Münchhausen* might be thought of as a treatise on sources of light. The film ends as it begins, allowing two sources of light to compete. A servant holding a candelabra switches off an electric light to signal the end. Münchhausen's portrait again comes to life, leaning over three times to blow out the candles in the candelabra; their smoke rises to form the words "the end." Again this double ending articulates our ambivalent subject position vis-à-vis cinema; we "know" that it depends on the first light, the technological apparatus, but we don't care to know, much preferring Münchhausen's version of closure (just as he preferred Christian's moon death, a gentle fading into smoke, to the decay and rot of earthly death). This ending may also stand in for what I've suggested about Nazi cinema as a propaganda apparatus. Münchhausen, like our imagined subject of these movies, sits in his portrait, subdued and moralized, having taken his place in a temporal and sacrificial collective. But some surplus energy defies the gentrification and, not quite content to stay put within the boundaries of the frame, breaks out ever so slightly.

SELECT BIBLIOGRAPHY

Adorno, Theodor W. *Ästhetische Theorie*. Vol. 7 of *Gesammelte Schriften*. 11 vols. Frankfurt am Main: Suhrkamp, 1970.

Albrecht, Gerd. *Nationalsozialistische Filmpolitik: Eine soziologische Untersuchung über die Spielfilme des dritten Reiches*. Stuttgart: Ferdinand Enke, 1969.

———, ed. *Film im Dritten Reich: Eine Dokumentation*. Karlsruhe: Fricker & Co OHG + DOKU-Verlag, 1979.

Althusser, Louis. "Ideology and Ideological State Apparatuses." In *Lenin and Philosophy and Other Essays*. London: New Left Books, 1971. 127–86.

Anderson, Benedict. *Imagined Communities: Reflections on the Origin and Spread of Nationalism*. London: Verso, 1983.

Armstrong, Nancy. *Desire and Domestic Fiction*. New York: Oxford University Press, 1987.

Aronowitz, Stanley. "Film — The Art Form of Late Capitalism." In *The Crisis in Historical Materialism*. New York: Praeger, 1981. 201–24.

Bauer, Alfred. *Deutscher Spielfilmalmanach, 1929–1950*. 1950. Munich: Filmladen Christoph Winterberg, 1976.

Becker, Horst. *Die Familie*. Leipzig: M. Schäfer, 1935.

Becker, Wolfgang. *Film und Herrschaft*. Berlin: Volker Spiess, 1973.

Belach, Helga, ed. *Wir tanzen um die Welt: Deutsche Revuefilme, 1933–45*. Munich: Carl Hanser Verlag, 1979.

Benjamin, Walter. "Denkbilder." In vol. 4 of *Gesammelte Schriften*. Frankfurt: Suhrkamp, 1980. 305–438.

———. *Illuminations*. Trans. H. Zohn. New York: Harcourt, Brace, and World, 1968.

———. "Pariser Brief." 1936. In vol. 3 of *Gesammelte Schriften*. 4 vols. Frankfurt: Suhrkamp, 1980. 482–95.

———. "Theorien des deutschen Faschismus: Zur der Sammelschrift 'Krieg und Krieger' hrsg. von Ernst Jünger." 1930. In vol. 3 of *Gesammelte Schriften*. 4 vols. Frankfurt: Suhrkamp, 1980. 238–50.

Bergstrom, Janet. "Sexuality at a Loss: The Films of F. W. Murnau." *Poetics Today* 6.1 (1985): 185–203.

Bloch, Ernst. *Erbschaft dieser Zeit*. 1935. Frankfurt am Main: Bibliothek Suhrkamp, 1973.

Bock, Hans-Michael. "Georg Wilhelm Pabst: Documenting a Life and a Career." In *The*

Films of G. W. Pabst: An Extraterritorial Cinema, ed. Eric Rentschler. New Brunswick, N.J.: Rutgers University Press, 1990. 217–35.

Bormann, Alexander von. "Das nationalsozialistische Gemeinschaftslied." In *Die deutsche Literatur im dritten Reich,* ed. H. Denkler, K. Prümm. Stuttgart: Reclam, 1976. 256–80.

Bovenschen, Silvia. *Die imaginierte Weiblichkeit: Exemplarische Untersuchungen zu kulturgeschichtlichen und literarischen Präsentationsformen des Weiblichen.* Frankfurt: Suhrkamp, 1979.

Brandt, Hans-Jürgen. *NS-Filmtheorie und dokumentarische Praxis: Hippler, Noldan, Junghans.* Tübingen: Max Niemeyer Verlag, 1987.

Brecht, Bertolt. *Arbeitsjournal.* 2 vols. Frankfurt am Main: Suhrkamp, 1973.

———. "Briefe um Deutschland." In vol. 20 of *Gesammelte Werke.* 20 vols. Frankfurt am Main: Suhrkamp, 1967. 234–35.

———. "Der Dreigroschenprozess." 1931. In vol. 18 of *Gesammelte Werke.* Frankfurt am Main: Suhrkamp, 1967. 139–209.

———. "Die Horst-Wessel Legende." In vol. 20 of *Gesammelte Werke.* Frankfurt am Main: Suhrkamp, 1967. 209–19.

———. *Der Messingkauf.* In vol. 16 of *Gesammelte Werke.* Frankfurt am Main: Suhrkamp, 1967. 501–657.

Bredow, Wilfried von, and Rolf Zurek. *Film und Gesellschaft in Deutschland: Dokumente und Materialien.* Hamburg: Hoffmann & Campe, 1975.

Brockmann, Stephen. "The Cultural Meaning of the Gulf War." *Michigan Quarterly Review* 31.2 (Spring 1992): 149–78.

Bruck, Moeller van den. *Germany's Third Empire.* Trans. E. O. Lorimer. London: George Allen & Unwin, 1934.

Bürger, Christa, et al., eds. *Aufklärung und literarische Öffentlichkeit.* Frankfurt am Main: Suhrkamp, 1980.

Cixous, Hélène. "Fiction and Its Phantoms: A Reading of Freud's '*Das Unheimliche*' ('The Uncanny')." *New Literary History* 7 (Spring 1976): 525–48.

Comolli, Jean-Louis. "Historical Fiction: A Body Too Much." *Screen* 19 (Summer 1978): 41–53.

Coster, Didier. *Ten Steps to the Tale Told: Toward an Integrated Theory of Narrative Communication.* Minneapolis: University of Minnesota Press, 1989.

Courtade, Francis, and Pierre Cadars. *Geschichte des Films im dritten Reich.* Trans. Florian Hopf. Munich: Carl Hanser, 1975.

De Lauretis, Teresa. *Alice Doesn't: Feminism, Semiotics, Cinema.* Bloomington: Indiana University Press, 1984.

De Man, Paul. "Aesthetic Formalization: Kleist's *Über das Marionettentheater.*" In *The Rhetoric of Romanticism.* New York: Columbia University Press, 1984. 263–90.

———. "Kant and Schiller." Unpublished lecture, n.p.

DeMause, Lloyd. *Foundations of Psychohistory.* New York: Creative Roots, 1982.

———. *Reagan's America.* New York: Creative Roots, 1983.

Denkler, Horst, and Karl Prümm, eds. *Die deutsche Literatur im dritten Reich.* Stuttgart: Reclam, 1976.

Doane, Mary-Ann. *The Desire to Desire: The Woman's Film of the 1940s*. Bloomington: Indiana University Press, 1987.

Donald, James. "The Fantastic, the Sublime, and the Popular; Or, What's at Stake in Vampire Films?" In *Fantasy and the Cinema,* ed. James Donald. London: British Film Institute, 1989. 233–51.

Drewniak, Boguslaw. *Der deutsche Film, 1938–45: Ein Gesamtüberblick.* Düsseldorf: Droste, 1987.

Durgnat, Raymond. "Six Films of Joseph von Sternberg." In *Movies and Methods,* ed. Bill Nichols. 2 vols. Berkeley: University of California Press, 1976. 1:262–73.

Elias, Norbert. *Die höfische Gesellschaft: Untersuchungen zur Soziologie des Königstums und der höfischen Aristokratie mit einer Einleitung — Soziologie und Geschichtswissenschaft.* Berlin: Luchterhand, 1969.

Ellwanger, Karen, and Eva-Maria Warth. "*Die Frau meiner Träume.* Weiblichkeit und Maskerade: eine Untersuchung zu Form und Funktion von Kleidung als Zeichensystem im Film." *Frauen und Film* 38 (May 1985): 58–71.

Elsaesser, Thomas. "Primary Identification and the Historical Subject: Fassbinder and Germany." In *Narrative, Apparatus, Ideology,* ed. Philip Rosen. New York: Columbia University Press, 1986. 535–49.

———. "Tales of Sound and Fury: Observations on the Family Melodrama." In *Movies and Methods,* ed. Bill Nichols. 2 vols. Berkeley: University of California Press, 1985. 2:165–89.

Emmerich, Wolfgang. "'Massenfaschismus' und die Rolle des Ästhetischen: Faschismustheorie bei Ernst Bloch, Walter Benjamin, Bertolt Brecht." In vol. 1 of *Antifaschistische Literatur.* Kronberg/Ts: Scriptor, 1977. 223–90.

Feld, Hans. "Potsdam gegen Weimar oder Wie Otto Gebühr den Siebenjährigen Krieg gewann." In *Preussen im Film,* ed. Axel Marquardt and Heinz Rathsack. Reinbek bei Hamburg: Rowohlt, 1981. 68–73.

Ferro, Marc. *Cinema and History.* Trans. Naomi Greene. Detroit: Wayne State University Press, 1988.

Foucault, Michel. *Discipline and Punish: The Birth of the Prison.* Trans. Alan Sheridan. New York: Vintage, 1979.

———. *History of Sexuality.* 3 vols. Trans. Robert Hurley. New York: Random House, 1978, 1985, and 1986.

Friedländer, Saul. *Reflections of Nazism.* New York: Harper, 1982.

Friedman, Régine Mihal. "Die Ausnahme ist die Regel: Zu Romanze in Moll (1943) von Helmut Käutner." *Frauen und Film* 43 (December 1987): 48–58.

———. "Ecce Ingenium Teutonicum: Paracelsus." In *The Films of G. W. Pabst: An Extraterritorial Cinema,* ed. Eric Rentschler. New Brunswick, N.J.: Rutgers University Press, 1990.

———. *L'image et son Juif: Le Juif dans le cinéma nazi.* Paris: Payot, 1983.

———. "Male Gaze and Female Reaction: Veit Harlan's *Jew Süss.*" Trans. Angelika Rauch. In *Gender and German Cinema,* ed. Sandra Frieden et al. 2 vols. Providence, R.I.: Berg Publishers, 1993. 2:117–33.

Gilman, Sander. *The Jew's Body.* New York: Routledge, 1991.

Gleber, Anke. "Das Fräulein von Tellheim: Die ideologische Funktion der Frau in der nationalsozialistischen Lessing-Adaption." *German Quarterly* 59.4 (Fall 1986): 547–68.

——. "Masochism and Wartime Melodrama: *Komödianten*." In *The Films of G. W. Pabst: An Extraterritorial Cinema,* ed. Eric Rentschler. New Brunswick, N.J.: Rutgers University Press, 1990.

——. " 'Only a Man Must Be and Remain a Judge, Soldier, and Ruler of State' — Female as Void in Nazi Film." Trans. Antja Masten. In *Gender and German Cinema,* ed. Sandra Frieden et al. Providence, R.I.: Berg Publishers, 1993. 2:105–16.

Godzich, Wlad. "After the Storyteller. . . . " Foreword. In *Story and Situation: Narrative Seduction and the Power of Fiction,* by Ross Chambers. Minneapolis: University of Minnesota Press, 1984. xi–xxii.

Graumann, C. F., ed. *Psychologie im Nationalsozialismus.* Berlin: Springer Verlag, 1985.

Greimas, A. J. *Structuralist Semantics: An Attempt at a Method.* Trans. Daniele McDowell and Alan Velie. Lincoln: University of Nebraska Press, 1983.

Guerin, Daniel. *Fascism and Big Business.* New York: Monad Press, 1973.

Hansen, Miriam. "Pleasure, Ambivalence, Identification: Valentino and Female Spectatorship." *Cinema Journal* 25.4 (Summer 1986): 11–12.

Happel, Gerd. *Der historische Spielfilm im Nationalsozialismus.* Frankfurt am Main: R. G. Fischer, 1984.

Harlan, Veit. *Im Schatten meiner Filme.* Gütersloh: Siegbert Mohn Verlag, 1966.

Hausen, Karin. "Die Polarisierung der 'Gesellschaftscharaktere' — Eine Spiegelung der Dissoziation von Erwerbs- und Familienleben." In *Seminar: Familie und Gesellschaftsstruktur,* ed. Heidi Rosenbaum. Frankfurt am Main: Suhrkamp Verlag, 1978.

Heath, Steven. "Narrative Space." *Screen* 17.3 (Autumn, 1976): 68–112.

Hippler, Fritz. *Betrachtungen zum Filmschaffen.* Berlin: Max Hesse Verlag, 1942.

Hitler, Adolf. *Mein Kampf.* Trans. Ralph Manheim. 1925. Boston: Houghton Mifflin, 1943.

Hoffmann, Hilmar. *The Triumph of Propaganda: Film and National Socialism, 1933–1945.* Providence, R.I.: Berghahn Books, 1996.

Hollstein, Dorothea. *"Jud Süss" und die Deutschen: Antisemitische Vorurteile im nationalsozialistischen Spielfilm.* Franfurt am Main: Ullstein, 1971.

Horkheimer, Max. "Die Juden und Europa." *Zeitschrift für Sozialforschung* 1–2 (1939): 115–37.

——, and Theodor Adorno. *Dialectic of Enlightenment.* Trans. John Cumming. New York: Seabery, 1972.

Hull, David Stewart. *Film in the Third Reich.* Berkeley: University of California Press, 1969.

Huyssen, Andreas. *After the Great Divide.* Bloomington: Indiana University Press, 1986.

Jay, Martin. "The 'Aesthetic Ideology' as Ideology; or, What Does It Mean to Aestheticize Politics?" *New German Critique* 21 (Spring 1992): 41–62.

———. "The Jews and the Frankfurt School." *New German Critique* 19 (Winter 1980): 137–49.

Johnson, Sheila. "Ideological Ambiguity in Pabst's *Paracelsus*." *Monatshefte* 83.2 (Summer 1991): 104–26.

Jugendfilm im Nationalsozialismus: Dokumentation und Kommentar nach der Sonder-veröffentlichung Nr. 6 der Zeitschrift "Das junge Deutschland" hrsg. von Jugend-führer des Deutschen Reiches: A. U. Sander, Jugend und Film, Berlin 1944. Kom-mentar von Hartmut Reese. Münster: Lit, 1984.

Kaes, Anton. *From Hitler to Heimat: The Return of History as Film.* Cambridge, Mass.: Harvard University Press, 1989.

Kampen, Wilhelm van. "Das 'preussische Beispiel' als Propaganda und politisches Lebensbedürfnis: Anmerkungen zur Authentizität und Instrumentalisierung von Geschichte im Preussenfilm." In *Preussen im Film*, ed. Axel Marquardt and Heinz Rathsack. Reinbek bei Hamburg: Rowohlt, 1981. 164–77.

Kantorowicz, Ernst H. *The King's Two Bodies: A Study in Mediaeval Political Theol-ogy.* Princeton, N.J.: Princeton University Press, 1957.

Kaplan, Alice Yaeger. *Reproductions of Banality: Fascism, Literature, and French Intel-lectual Life.* Minneapolis: University of Minnesota Press, 1986.

Kehr, Eckhart. *Das Primat der Innenpolitik.* Berlin: de Gruyter, 1965.

———. "The Genesis of the Royal Prussian Reserve Officer." In *Economic Interest, Militarism, and Foreign Policy*, ed. Gordon Craig. Berkeley: University of Califor-nia Press, 1965. 97–108.

Klooss, Reinhard, and Thomas Reuter. *Körperbilder: Menschenornamente in Revue-theater und Revuefilm.* Frankfurt am Main: Syndikat Autoren- und Verlagsgesell-schaft, 1980.

Knilli, Friedrich, et al., ed. *"Jud Süss": Filmprotokoll, Programmheft und Einzel-analysen.* Preprints zur Medienwissenschaft. Berlin: Spiess, 1983.

Koch, Gertrud. "Der höhere Befehl der Frau ist ihr niederer Instinkt: Frauenhass und Männer-Mythos in Filmen über Preussen." In *Preussen im Film*, ed. Axel Mar-quardt and Heinz Rathsack. Reinbek bei Hamburg: Rowohlt, 1981. 219–33.

Koonz, Claudia. *Mothers in the Fatherland: Women, the Family, and Nazi Politics.* New York: St. Martin's, 1987.

Korte, Helmut, ed. *Film und Realität in der Weimarer Republik.* Munich: Carl Hanser Verlag, 1978.

Koselleck, Reinhart. "Terror and Dream: Methodological Remarks on the Experience of Time during the Third Reich." In *Futures Past: On the Semantics of Historical Time*, trans. Kenneth Tribe. Cambridge, Mass.: MIT Press, 1985. 213–30.

Kovel, Joel. *White Racism.* New York: Columbia University Press, 1984.

Kracauer, Siegfried. "Die Biographie als neubürgerliche Kunstform." *Frankfurter Zei-tung* 26.6 (1930).

———. *From Caligari to Hitler: A Psychological History of the German Film.* 1947. Princeton: Princeton University Press, 1971.

———. "The Mass Ornament." Trans. B. Lovell and J. Zipes. *New German Critique* 5 (Spring 1975): 67–76.

Kuhn, Annette, and Valentine Rothe. *Frauen im deutschen Faschismus.* 2 vols. Düsseldorf: Schwann, 1983.

Lacan, Jacques. *Écrits: A Selection.* Trans. A. Sheridon. New York: Norton, 1977.

———. *Four Fundamental Concepts of Psychoanalysis.* Ed. Jacques-Alain Miller. Trans. Alan Sheridan. New York: W. W. Norton, 1973.

———. *The Seminar,* Book 7. Ed. Jacques-Alain Miller. Trans. Dennis Porter. New York: W. W. Norton, 1986.

Laclau, Ernesto. "Fascism and Ideology." In *Politics and Ideology in Marxist Theory.* London: Verso, 1977. 81–142.

———, and Chantal Mouffe. *Hegemony and Socialist Strategy: Towards a Radical Democratic Politics.* London: Verso, 1985.

Lacoue-Labarthe, Philippe, and Jean-Luc Nancy. "The Nazi Myth." Trans. Brian Holmes. *Critical Inquiry* 2.16 (Winter 1990): 291–312.

Landy, Marcia. *Fascism in Film: The Italian Commercial Cinema, 1931–1943.* Princeton, N.J.: Princeton University Press, 1986.

Lefort, Claude. *Democracy and Political Theory.* Trans. David Macey. Minneapolis: University of Minnesota Press, 1988.

Leiser, Erwin. *Nazi Cinema.* Trans. G. Mander and D. Wilson. New York: Macmillan, 1974.

Leppert, Richard. *The Sight of Sound: Music, Representation, and the History of the Body.* Berkeley: University of California Press, 1993.

———, and Susan McClary, eds. *Music and Society: The Politics of Composition, Performance, and Reception.* Cambridge: Cambridge University Press, 1987.

Leppert-Fögen, Annette. *Die deklassierte Klasse: Studien zur Geschichte und Ideologie des Kleinbürgertums.* Frankfurt: Fischer, 1974.

Leuken, Verena. "Zur Erzählstruktur des nationalsozialistischen Films: Versuch einer strukturalen Analyse." *MuK 13* (Veröffentlichungen des Forschungsschwerpunkts *Massenmedien und Kommunikation* an der Universität — Gesamthochschule Siegen). Siegen 1981.

Link, Jürgen. "Collective Symbolism in Political Discourse and Its Share in Underlying Totalitarian Trends." Trans. Rita Westerholt and Linda Schulte-Sasse. In *The Public Realm: Essays on Discursive Types in Political Philosophy,* ed. Reiner Schürman. Albany: State University of New York Press, 1989. 225–38.

———. "Fanatics, Fundamentalists, Lunatics, and Drug Traffickers — The New Southern Enemy Image." Trans. Linda Schulte-Sasse. *Cultural Critique* 19 (Fall 1991): 33–53.

———. "Von 'Kabale und Liebe' zur 'Love Story' — Zur Evolutionsgesetzlichkeit eines bügerlichen Geschichtentyps." In *Literarischer Kitsch,* ed. Jochen Schulte-Sasse. Tübingen: Niemeyer, 1979. 121–55.

Loiperdinger, Martin. *Rituale der Mobilmachung: Der Parteitagsfilm 'Triumph des Willens' von Leni Riefenstahl.* Opladen: Leske & Budrich, 1987.

Lowe, Donald. *History of Bourgeois Perception.* Chicago: University of Chicago Press, 1982.

Lowry, Stephen. *Pathos und Politik: Ideologie in Spielfilmen des Nationalsozialismus.* Tübingen: Niemeyer, 1991.

Luhmann, Niklas. *The Differentiation of Society.* Trans. Stephen Holmes and Charles Larmore. New York: Columbia University Press, 1982.

———. *Love as Passion: The Codification of Intimacy.* Trans. Jeremy Gaines and Doris Jones. Cambridge: Harvard University Press, 1986.

Mann, Thomas. "Friedrich und die grosse Koalition." In vol. 11 of *Gesammelte Werke.* Berlin: Aufbau Verlag, 1956. 66–126.

Marcuse, Herbert. "The Affirmative Character of Culture." In *Negations,* trans. Jeremy Shapiro. Boston: Beacon Press, 1968. 88–133.

———. *One Dimensional Man.* Boston: Beacon, 1964.

———. "The Struggle against 'Liberalism' in the Totalitarian View of the State." 1934. In *Negations,* trans. Jeremy Shapiro. Boston: Beacon Press, 1968. 3–42.

Mehring, Franz. *Die Lessing Legende: Zur Geschichte und Kritik des preussischen Despotismus und der klassischen Literatur.* 1893. Stuttgart: Verlag das neue Wort, 1953.

Metz, Christian. *The Imaginary Signifier.* Trans. Celia Britton, Annwyl Williams, Ben Brewster, and Alfred Guzzetti. Bloomington: Indiana University Press, 1982.

Mitscherlich, Alexander. *Society without Fathers.* Trans. Eric Mosbacher. London: Tavistock Publications, 1969.

Möbius, Hanno. "Heimat im nationalsozialistischen Film." *Augen-Blick 5: Heimat,* Marburger Hefte zur Medienwissenschaft, 1988. 31–44.

Modleski, Tania. "Time and Desire in the Woman's Film." *Cinema Journal* 23.3 (Spring 1984): 19–30.

———. *The Women Who Knew Too Much: Hitchcock and Feminist Theory.* New York: Methuen, 1988.

Moritz, Karl Philip. "Das Edleste in der Natur." In *Moritz: Werke in Zwei Bände,* ed. Jürgen Jahn. Berlin: Aufbau, 1973.

Mosse, George L. *The Crisis of Ideology: Intellectual Origins of the Third Reich.* New York: Grosset & Dunlap, 1964.

———. *Nazi Culture: Intellectual, Cultural, and Social Life in the Third Reich.* Trans. Salvator Attanasio et al. New York: Grosset & Dunlap, 1966.

Mücke, Dorothea von. *Virtue and the Veil of Illusion: Generic Innovation and the Pedagogical Project in Eighteenth-Century Literature.* Stanford: Stanford University Press, 1991.

Mühr, Alfred. *Mephisto ohne Maske: Gustaf Gründgens Legende und Wahrheit.* Munich: Georg Müller Verlag GmbH, 1981.

Mulvey, Laura. *Visual and Other Pleasures.* Bloomington: University of Indiana Press, 1989.

———. "Visual Pleasure and Narrative Cinema." *Screen* 16.3 (Autumn 1975): 6–18.

Murray, Bruce. *Film and the German Left in the Weimar Republic: From Caligari to Kuhle Wampe.* Austin: University of Texas Press, 1990.

Naddaff, Sandra. *Arabesque: Narrative Structure and the Aesthetics of Repetition in 1001 Nights.* Evanston, Ill.: Northwestern University Press, 1991.

Neale, Steve. "Masculinity as Spectacle: Reflections on Men and Mainstream Cinema." *Screen* 24 (November–December 1983): 2–16.

———. "Melodrama and Tears." *Screen* 27.6 (November–December 1986): 6–22.

———. "Propaganda." *Screen* 18 (Autumn 1977): 9–40.

———. "Triumph of the Will: Notes on Documentary and Spectacle." *Screen* 20 (Spring 1979): 63–86.

Neue Gesellschaft für Bildende Kunst, ed. *Inszenierung der Macht: Ästhetische Faszination im Faschismus*. Berlin: Nishen, 1987.

Neumann, Franz. *Behemoth: The Structure and Practice of National Socialism*. Toronto: Oxford University Press, 1942.

The New Grove Dictionary of Music and Musicians. Ed. Stanley Sadie. 20 vols. London: Macmillan, 1980.

Nolte, Ernst, ed. *Theorien über den Faschismus*. 5th edition. Königsstein/Ts.: Verlagsgruppe Athenäum, Hain, Scriptor, Hanstein, 1979.

———. *Three Faces of Fascism*. Trans. Leila Vennewitz. London: Weidenfeld & Nicolson, 1963.

Nowell-Smith, Geoffrey. "Minelli and Melodrama." In *Movies and Methods*, ed. Bill Nichols. 2 vols. Berkeley: University of California Press, 1985. 2:190–94.

Parry, Geraint. "Enlightened Government and Its Critics in Eighteenth-Century Germany." *Historical Journal* 6.2 (1963): 178–92.

"Perspectives on the Fascist Public Sphere: A Discussion with Peter Brückner, Wilfried Gottschalch, Eberhard Knödler-Bunte, Olav Münzenberg, and Oskar Negt." *New German Critique* 11 (Spring 1977): 94–132.

Petley, Julian. *Capital and Culture: German Cinema, 1933–45*. London: British Film Institute, 1979.

Petro, Patrice. *Joyless Streets: Women and Melodramatic Representation in Weimar Germany*. Princeton, N.J.: Princeton University Press, 1989.

Plummer, Tom, Bruce Murray, and Linda Schulte-Sasse. *Film and Politics in the Weimar Republic*. New York: Holmes & Meier, 1982.

Polan, Dana. "A Brechtian Cinema? Towards a Politics of Self-Reflexive Film." In *Movies and Methods*, ed. Bill Nichols. 2 vols. Berkeley: University of California Press, 1985. 2:661–72.

———. *Power and Paranoia: History, Narrative, and the American Cinema, 1940–1950*. New York: Columbia University Press, 1986.

Postone, Moische. "Anti-Semitism and National Socialism: Notes on the German Reaction to 'Holocaust.'" *New German Critique* 11 (Winter 1980): 97–115.

Poulantzas, Nicos. *Fascism and Dictatorship: The Third International and Problems of Fascism*. London: NLB, 1974.

Preussen im Film: Eine Retrospektive der Stiftung Deutsche Kinemathek. Ed. Axel Marquardt and Heinz Rathsack. Reinbek bei Hamburg: Rowohlt Taschenbuch Verlag GmbH, 1981.

Prümm, Karl. *Die Literatur des soldatischen Nationalismus der zwanziger Jahre (1918–1933): Gruppenideologie und Epochenproblematik*. 2 vols. Kronberg/Ts.: Scriptor, 1974.

Rabenalt, Arthur Maria. *Film im Zwielicht: Über den unpolitischen Film des Dritten Reiches und die Begrenzung des totalitären Anspruches*. Hildesheim: Olms Presse, 1978.

Rabinbach, Anson. "Unclaimed Heritage: Ernst Bloch's *Heritage of Our Times* and the Theory of Fascism." *New German Critique* 11 (Spring 1977): 5–21.

————, and Jack Zipes. "Lessons of the Holocaust." *New German Critique* 19 (Winter 1980): 3–7.

Reich, Wilhelm. *The Mass Psychology of Fascism*. New York: Farrar, Straus and Giroux, 1970.

Reis, Thomas, ed. *Drehbuch zu dem Film "Friedrich Schiller: Der Triumph eines Genies" (1940)*. Frankfurt am Main: Fischer Verlag, 1983.

Rentschler, Eric. "Fatal Attractions: The Blue Light." *October* 48 (Spring 1989): 47–68.

————. "German Feature Films, 1933–1945." *Monatshefte* 82.3 (1990): 257–66.

————. "Mountains and Modernity: Relocating the *Bergfilm*." *New German Critique* 51 (Fall 1990): 137–61.

————. "Pabst umfunktionierter Paracelsus." *Germanic Review*. Special issue: German Film, 66.1 (Winter 1991): 16–24.

————. "There's No Place Like Home: Luis Trenker's *The Prodigal Son*." *New German Critique* 60 (Fall 1993): 33–56.

————. *The Ministry of Illusion: Nazi Feature Films and their Afterlife*. Cambridge: Harvard University Press, 1996.

————. "The Triumph of Male Will: *Münchhausen*." *Film Quarterly* 43.3 (Spring 1990): 14–23.

————. "The Use and Abuse of Memory: New German Film and the Discourse of Bitburg." *New German Critique* 36 (Fall 1985): 67–90.

————, ed. *The Films of G. W. Pabst: An Extraterritorial Cinema*. New Brunswick, N.J.: Rutgers University Press, 1990.

Riefenstahl, Leni. *Hinter den Kulissen des Reichsparteitagsfilms*. Munich: Zentralverlag der NSDAP, 1935.

Riehl, Wilhelm Heinrich. *Die Familie*. Vol. 3 of *Die Naturgeschichte des deutschen Volkes*. Stuttgart: J. C. Cotta, 1859.

Riess, Curt. *Gustaf Gründgens: Die klassische Biographie des grossen Künstlers*. Freiburg in Breisgau: Verlag Herder, 1988.

Rischbieter, Henning, ed. *Gründgens: Schauspieler, Regisseur, Theaterleiter*. Velber bei Hannover: Erhard Friedrich Verlag, 1963.

Romani, Cinzia. *Tainted Goddesses: Female Film Stars of the Third Reich*. Trans. Robert Connolly. New York: Sarpedon Publishers, 1992.

Rosenberg, Alfred. *Der Mythos des 20. Jahrhunderts*. Munich: Hoheneichen Verlag, 1930.

Rosenberg, Hans. *Grosse Depression und Bismarckzeit*. Berlin: de Gruyter, 1967.

Rotman, Brian. *Signifying Nothing: The Semiotics of Zero*. New York: St. Martin's Press, 1987.

Ruppelt, Georg. *Schiller im nationalsozialistischen Deutschland*. Stuttgart: Metzler, 1979.

Schiller, Friedrich. "On the Uses of the Chorus in Tragedy" (1803–1804). Preface to *The Bride of Messina*, in *The Works of Friedrich Schiller*, trans. Henry G. Bohn. London: Henry G. Bohn, 1854. 3:439–44.

————. *On the Aesthetic Education of Man in a Series of Letters*. Trans. Reginald Snell. New York: Frederick Ungar, 1965.

Schlüpmann, Heide. "Faschistische Trugbilder weiblicher Autonomie." *Frauen und Film* 44/45 (October 1988): 44–66.

——. "Politik als Schuld: Zur Funktion des historischen Kostüms in Weiblichkeitsbildern der Filme *Maria Ilona* (1939) und *Königin Luise* (1956)." *Frauen und Film* 38 (May 1985): 47–57.

Schmidt, Jochen. *Die Geschichte des Genie-Gedankens in der deutschen Literatur, Philosophie und Politik, 1750–1945.* 2 vols. Darmstadt: Wissenschaftliche Buchgesellschaft, 1985.

Schoenbaum, David. *Hitler's Social Revolution: Class and Status in Nazi Germany, 1933–39.* New York: Norton, 1980.

Schoenberner, Gerhard. "Das Preussenbild im deutschen Film: Geschichte und Ideologie." In *Preussen im Film,* ed. Axel Marquardt and Heinz Rathsack. Reinbek bei Hamburg: Rowohlt, 1981. 219–33.

Schulte-Sasse, Jochen. "Art and the Sacrificial Structure of Modernity." Foreword to *Framed Narratives,* by Jay Caplan. Minneapolis: University of Minnesota Press, 1985. 97–115.

——. "Electronic Media and Cultural Politics in the Reagan Era: The Attack on Libya and Hands Across America as Postmodern Events." *Cultural Critique* 8 (Winter 1987–88): 123–52.

——. *Literarische Struktur und historisch-sozialer Kontext: Zum Beispiel Lessings "Emilia Galotti."* Paderborn: Schöningh, 1975.

——. "Literarische Wertung: Zum unausweichlichen historischen Verfall einer literaturkritischen Praxis." *Lili* 18.71 (1988): 13–47.

——. "The Prestige of the Artist under Conditions of Modernity." *Cultural Critique* 12 (Spring 1989): 83–100.

——. "Toward a 'Culture' for the Masses: The Socio-Psychological Function of Popular Literatur in Germany and the U.S., 1880–1920." *New German Critique* 29 (Spring/Summer 1983): 85–105.

——, ed. *Briefwechsel über das Trauerspiel: Lessing, Nicolai, Mendelssohn.* Munich: Winkler, 1972.

——, and Linda Schulte-Sasse. "War, Otherness, and Illusionary Identifications with the State." *Cultural Critique* 19 (Fall 1991): 67–95.

Schwab, Gabriele. *Subjects without Selves: Transitional Texts in Modern Fiction.* Cambridge and London: Harvard University Press, 1994.

Silberman, Marc. "The Fascist Discourse in the Cinema: A Reading of Eduard von Borsody's *Wunschkonzert* (1940)." In *Intertextuality: German Literature and Visual Art from the Renaissance to the Twentieth Century,* ed. Ingeborg Hoesterey and Ulrich Weisstein. Columbia, S.C.: Camden House, 1993. 188–200.

——. "The Ideology of Re-Presenting the Classics: Filming *Der zerbrochene Krug* in the Third Reich." *German Quarterly* 57.4 (Fall 1984): 590–602.

Silverman, Kaja. *The Acoustic Mirror: The Female Voice in Psychoanalysis and Cinema.* Bloomington: University of Indiana Press, 1988.

——. "Fragments of a Fashionable Discourse." In *Studies in Entertainment: Critical Approaches to Mass Culture,* ed. Tania Modleski. Bloomington: Indiana University Press, 1986. 139–52.

———. *Male Subjectivity at the Margins*. New York: Routledge, 1992.

Skal, David. *Hollywood Gothic: The Tangled Web of Dracula from Novel to Stage to Screen*. New York: W. W. Norton, 1990.

Sontag, Susan. "Fascinating Fascism." In *Under the Sign of Saturn*. New York: Farrar, Straus and Giroux, 1972. 73–108.

Sorlin, Pierre. *The Film in History: Restaging the Past*. Oxford: Basil Blackwell, 1980.

Spiker, Jürgen. *Film und Kapital*. Berlin: Volker Spiess, 1975.

Stern, Fritz. *The Politics of Cultural Despair: A Study in the Rise of the Germanic Ideology*. Berkeley: University of California Press, 1961.

Stoker, Bram. *Dracula*. 1897. New York: Barnes & Noble, 1992.

Stollmann, Rainer. *Ästhetisierung der Politik: Literaturstudien zum subjektiven Faschismus*. Stuttgart: Metzler, 1978.

———. "Fascist Politics as a Total Work of Art: Tendencies of the Aesthetization of Political Life in National Socialism." *New German Critique* 14 (Spring 1978): 41–60.

Taylor, Richard. *Film Propaganda: Soviet Russia and Nazi Germany*. London: Croom Helm, 1979.

Theweleit, Klaus. *Male Fantasies*. 2 vols. Trans. Steven Conway (vol. 1); Erica Carter and Chris Turner (vol. 2). Minneapolis: University of Minnesota Press, 1987 and 1989.

Toelpitz, Jerzy. *Geschichte des Films*. 3 vols. Berlin: Henschelverlag, 1979.

Traub, Hans. *Die UFA: Ein Beitrag zur Entwicklungsgeschichte des deutschen Filmschaffens*. Berlin: Ufa-Buchverlag Gmbh, 1943.

Tribe, Keith. "History and the Production of Memories." *Screen* 18.4 (Winter 1977/1978): 9–22.

Twitchell, James B. *The Living Dead: A Study of the Vampire in Romantic Literature*. Durham, N.C.: Duke University Press, 1981.

Virilio, Paul. *War and Cinema: The Logistics of Perception*. Trans. Patrick Camiller. London: Verso, 1989.

Vogt, Sigrid. " 'Das blaue licht'. logik des entweder-oder." *Frauen und Film* 14 (December 1977): 28.

Vondung, Klaus. *Magie und Manipulation: Ideologischer Kult und politische Religion des Nationalsozialismus*. Göttingen: Vandenhoeck & Ruprecht, 1971.

———, ed. *Völkisch-nationale und nationalsozialistische Literaturtheorie*. Munich: Paul List Verlag, 1973.

Ward, Albert. *Book Production, Fiction, and the German Reading Public: 1740–1800*. Oxford: Clarendon Press, 1974.

Weber-Kellermann, Ingeborg. *Die deutsche Familie*. Frankfurt: Suhrkamp, 1974.

Weinberg, David. "Approaches to the Study of Film in the Third Reich: A Critical Appraisal." *Journal of Contemporary History* 19 (1984): 105–26.

Weinstein, Fred, and Gerald Platt. *The Wish to Be Free*. Berkeley: University of California Press, 1969.

Welch, David. *Propaganda and the German Cinema, 1933–45*. Oxford: Clarendon Press, 1983.

330

Werner, Renate. "Der Zeitschichtsroman in der Weimarer Republik." *Heinrich Mann Jahrbuch* 1 (1983): 121–44.

———. "Transparente Kommentare: Überlegungen zu historischen Romanen deutscher Exilautoren." *Poetica* 3–4 (1977): 324–51.

Wetzel, Kraft, and Peter Hagemann. *Liebe, Tod und Technik: Kino des Phantastischen, 1933–45.* Berlin: Verlag Volker Spiess, 1977.

———. *Zensur: Verbotene deutsche Filme, 1933–45.* Berlin: Verlag Volker Spiess, 1978.

White, Hayden. "The Value of Narrativity in the Representation of Reality." In *On Narrative,* ed. W. J. T. Mitchell. Chicago: University of Chicago Press, 1980.

Wiggershaus, Renate. *Frauen unterm Nationalsozialismus.* Wuppertal: Peter Hammer, 1984.

Williams, Linda. "When the Woman Looks." In *Re-vision: Essays in Feminist Film Criticism,* ed. Mary-Ann Doane, Paricia Mellencamp, and Linda Williams. Los Angeles: American Film Institute, 1984. 83–99.

Winkler, Heinrich August. "Die 'neue Linke' und der Faschismus: Zur Kritik neomarxistischer Theorien über den Nationalsozialismus." *Revolution, Staat, Faschismus.* Göttingen: Vandenhoeck & Ruprecht, 1978. 65–117.

Witte, Karsten. "Die Filmkomödie im dritten Reich." In *Literatur des dritten Reiches,* ed. H. Denckler and K. Prümm. Stuttgart: Reclam, 1976. 347–63.

———. "How Nazi Cinema Mobilizes the Classics: Schweikart's *Das Fräulein von Barnhelm.*" In *German Film and Literature: Adaptations and Transformations,* ed. Eric Rentschler. New York: Frederick Ungar, 1984. 103–16.

———. "Introduction to Kracauer's 'The Mass Ornament.'" *New German Critique* 5 (Spring 1975): 59–66.

———. "Visual Pleasure Inhibited: Aspects of the German Revue Film." *New German Critique* 24–25 (Fall/Winter 1981–82): 238–63.

Wulf, Joseph. *Theater und Film im dritten Reich.* Reinbek bei Hamburg: Rowohlt, 1966.

Wülfing, Wulf. "Die heilige Luise von Preussen: Zur Mythisierung einer Figur der Geschichte in der deutschen Literatur des 19. Jahrhunderts." In *Bewegung und Stillstand in Metaphern und Mythen,* ed. Wulf Wülfing and Jürgen Link. Stuttgart: Klett-Cotta, 1984. 233–75.

Zielinsky, Siegfried, and Thomas Maurer. "Bausteine des Films 'Jud Süss.'" In *Jud Süss: Filmprotokoll, Programmheft und Einzelanalysen,* ed. Friedrich Knilli et al. Berlin: Spiess, 1983. 19–56.

Žižek, Slavoj. *Enjoy Your Symptom! Jacques Lacan in Hollywood and Out.* New York: Routledge, 1992.

———. *Everything You Ever Wanted to Know about Lacan, but Were Afraid to Ask Hitchcock.* London: Verso, 1992.

———. *For They Know Not What They Do: Enjoyment as a Political Factor.* London: Verso, 1991.

———. *Looking Awry: An Introduction to Jacques Lacan through Popular Culture.* Cambridge, Mass.: MIT Press, 1991.

———. *The Sublime Object of Ideology.* London: Verso, 1989.

FILMOGRAPHY

Diesel (1942)
Director: Gerhard Lamprecht
Script: Frank Thiess, Gerhard Lamprecht, Richard Riedel, after Eugen Diesel's biography
Actors: Willy Birgel, Paul Wegener, Hilde Weissner, Arthur Schröder, Josef Sieber, Erich
    Ponto, Hilde von Stolz, Walter Janssen
Production: Ufa
Camera: George Krause
Music: Hans-Otto Borgmann
Approved for release: October 16, 1942
Predicates: politically and artistically valuable, valuable for the People
Premiere: November 13, 1942
Availability: on video through German Language Video Center (no subtitles)

For Human Rights (Um das Menschenrecht, 1934)
Director: Hans Zöberlein and Ludwg Schmid-Wildy
Script: Hans Zöberlein
Actors: Hans Sclenck, Kurt Holm, Ernst Matens, Beppo Brem, Ludwig ten Kloot, Erich
    Pfleger, Paul Schaidler
Production: Arya-Film GmbH
Camera: Ludwig Zan, Bartl Seyr
Music: —
Approved for release: December 22, 1934
Predicates: artistically valuable
Premiere: December 28, 1934
Availability: available for screening at Library of Congress, Washington, D.C.

Fridericus (1935)
Director: Johannes Meyer
Script: Erich Kröhnke, Walter von Molo, after novel of same title by von Molo
Actors: Otto Gebühr, Hilde Körber, Lil Dagover, Agnes Straub, Käthe Haack, Bernhard
    Minetti, Paul Klinger, Carola Höhn, Paul Dahlke, Lucie Höflich, Wilhelm König
Production: Diana Tonfilm im GmbH (In the Tobis Corporation)

Camera: Bruno Mondi
Music: Marc Roland
Approved for release: December 11, 1936
Predicates: politically valuable
Premiere: February 8, 1937
Availability: on video through German Language Video Center and International Historic Films, Inc. (no subtitles)

Friedemann Bach (1941)
Director: Traugott Müller
Script: Helmut Brandis, Eckart von Naso, after a film novella by Ludwig Metzger
Actors: Gustav Gründgens, Eugen Klöpfer, Wolfgang Liebeneiner, Leny Marenbach, Camilla Horn, Johannes Riemann, Lina Lossen, Lotte Koch, Gustav Knuth, Wolf Trutz
Production: Terra
Camera: Walter Pindter
Music: Mark Lothar, using works by Johann Sebastian Bach and Friedemann Bach
Approved for release: June 20, 1941
Predicates: artistically valuable, culturally valuable
Premiere: June 25, 1941
Availability: on video through German Language Video Center and International Historic Films (no subtitles); 16 mm rental through West Glen Films and Trans-World Films (both with subtitles)

Friedrich Schiller — Triumph of a Genius (Friedrich Schiller, Der Triumph eines Genies, 1940)
Director: Herbert Maisch
Script: Walter Wassermann, C. H. Diller, after an idea by Dr. Paul Joseph Cremers
Actors: Horst Caspar, Heinrich George, Lil Dagover, Eugen Klöpfer, Paul Henckels, Friedrich Kayssler, Walter Franck, Herbert Hübner, Dagny Servaes, Hannelore Schroth, Paul Dahlke, Hans Nielsen
Production: Tobis
Camera: Fritz Arno Wagner
Music: Herbert Windt
Approved for release: November 11, 1940
Predicates: politically valuable, artistically valuable, valuable for youth
Premiere: November 13, 1940
Availability: on video through German Language Video Center; 16 mm rental through Trans-World Films (no subtitles)

Gold (1934)
Director: Karl Hartl
Script: Rolf E. Vanloo
Actors: Hans Albers, Brigitte Helm, Lien Deyers, Michael Bohnen, Friedrich Kayssler, Eberhard Leithoff, Ernst Karchow, Willi Schnur, Rudolf Platte, Walter Steinbeck

Production: Ufa
Camera: Günther Rittau, Otto Baecker, Werner Bohne
Music: Hans-Otto Borgmann
Approved for release: March 26, 1934
Predicates: artistic
Premiere: March 29, 1934
Availability: on video through German Language Video Center and International Historic Films (no subtitles)

The Great King (Der grosse König, 1942)
Director: Veit Harlan
Script: Veit Harlan
Actors: Otto Gebühr, Kristina Söderbaum, Gustav Fröhlich, Hans Nielsen, Paul Wegener, Paul Henckels, Elisabeth Flickenschildt, Kurt Meisel, Hilde Körber, Herbert Hübner, Franz Nicklisch, Claus Clausen, Claus Detlef Sierck
Production: Tobis
Camera: Bruno Mondi
Music: Hans-Otto Borgmann
Approved for release: February 28, 1942
Predicates: "Film of the Nation"; especially valuable and artistic; culturally, nationally valuable; educational; valuable for youth
Premiere: March 3, 1942
Availability: on video through German Language Video Center and International Historic Films (no subtitles)

The Great Love (Die grosse Liebe, 1942)
Director: Rolf Hansen
Script: Peter Groll, Rolf Hansen, from an idea by Alexander Lernet-Holenia
Actors: Zarah Leander, Viktor Staal, Paul Hörbiger, Grete Weiser, Hans Schwarz Jr., Wolfgang Preiss, Viktor Janson, Leopold von Ledebur
Production: Ufa
Camera: Franz Weihmayr
Music: Micheal Jary
Approved for release: June 6, 1942
Predicates: politically and artistically valuable, nationally valuable
Premiere: June 12, 1942
Availability: on video through German Language Video Center and International Historic Films (no subtitles)

Hans Westmar (1933)
Director: Franz Wenzler
Script: Hanns Heinz Ewers, after his book *Horst Wessel*
Actors: Emil Lohkamp, Carla Bartheel, Grete Reinwald, Arthur Schröder, Paul Wegener, Carl Auen, Heinrich Heilinger
Production: Volksdeutsche Film GmbH

Camera: Franz Weihmayr
Music: Giuseppe Becce, Ernst Hanfstaengl
Approved for release: November 23, 1933
Predicates: —
Premiere: December 13, 1933
Availability: available for screening at Library of Congress, Washington, D.C.

Hitler Youth Quex (Hitlerjunge Quex, 1933)
Director: Hans Steinhoff
Script: K. A. Schenzinger, B. E. Lüthge, after the novel of the same title by K. A. Schenzinger
Actors: Heinrich George, Berta Drews, Claus Clausen, Hermann Speelmans, Rotraut Richter, Karl Meixner, Hans Richter, Rudolf Platte
Production: Ufa
Camera: Konstantin Irmen-Tschet
Music: Hans-Otto Borgmann
Approved for release: September 7, 1933
Predicates: artistically especially valuable
Premiere: September 19, 1933
Availability: on video through German Language Video Center and International Historic Films (no subtitles); 16 mm rental through Museum of Modern Art (no subtitles; written English commentary by Gregory Bateson)

Holiday on Word of Honor (Urlaub auf Ehrenwort, 1937)
Director: Karl Ritter
Script: Charles Klein, Felix Lützkendorf, after ideas by Kilian Koll, Walter Bloem, and Charles Klein
Actors: Ingeborg Theek, Rolf Moebius, Fritz Kampers, Bertha Drews, René Deltgen, Heinz Welzel, Carl Raddatz, Jakob Sinn
Production: Ufa
Camera: Günther Anders
Music: Ernst Erich Buder
Approved for release: December 31, 1937
Predicates: especially valuable politically and artistically
Premiere: January 11, 1938
Availability: on video through International Historic Films (no subtitles)

Jew Süss (Jud Süss, 1940)
Director: Veit Harlan
Script: Ludwig Metzger, Eberhard Wolfgang Möller, Veit Harlan
Actors: Ferdinand Marian, Kristina Söderbaum, Heinrich George, Werner Krauss, Eugen Klöpfer, Hilde von Stolz, Malte Jäger, Albert Florath, Theodor Loos, Walter Werner, Charlotte Schulz, Anny Seitz
Production: Terra
Camera: Bruno Mondi

Music: Wolfgang Zeller
Approved for release: September 6, 1940
Predicates: especially valuable politically and artistically, valuable for youth
Premiere: September 24, 1940
Availability: on video through International Historic Films (subtitles)

Kolberg (1945)
Director: Veit Harlan
Script: Veit Harlan, Alfred Braun
Actors: Heinrich George, Kristina Söderbaum, Paul Wegener, Horst Caspar, Gustav Diessl, Otto Wernicke, Irene von Meyendorff, Kurt Meisel, Claus Clausen, Jaspar von Oertzen
Production: Ufa
Camera: Bruno Mondi
Music: Norbert Schultze
Approved for release: January 26, 1945
Predicates: "Film of the Nation," especially valuable politically and artistically, culturally valuable, nationally valuable, commendable, educational, valuable for youth
Premiere: January 30, 1945
Availability: available on video through International Historic Films (no subtitles)

Komödianten (1941)
Director: G. W. Pabst
Script: Axel Eggebrecht, Walter von Hollander, G. W. Pabst, after the novel *Philine* by Olly Boeheim
Actors: Käthe Dorsch, Hilde Krahl, Henny Porten, Gustav Diessl, Richard Häussler, Ludwig Schmitz, Friedrich Domin, Sonja-Gerda Scholz
Production: Bavaria, München
Camera: Bruno Stephan
Music: Lothar Brühne
Approved for release: August 13, 1941
Predicates: especially valuable politically and artistically, culturally valuable, educational
Premiere: September 5, 1941
Availability: 16 mm rental through Trans-World Films (subtitles)

Lady von Barnhelm (Das Fräulein von Barnhelm, 1940)
Director: Hans Schweikart
Script: Ernst Hasselbach, Peter Francke, after the comedy *Minna von Barnhelm* by G. E. Lessing
Actors: Käthe Gold, Ewald Balser, Fita Benkhoff, Theo Lingen, Paul Dahlke, Fritz Kampers, Erich Ponto
Production: Bavaria, München
Camera: Carl Hoffmann, Heinz Schnackertz
Music: Alois Melichar

Approved for release: October 9, 1940
Predicates: artistically valuable
Premiere: October 18, 1940
Availability: 16 mm rental through Trans-World Films (subtitles)

Münchhausen (1943)
Director: Josef von Baky
Script: Berthold Bürger (alias Erich Kästner)
Actors: Hans Albers, Brigitte Horney, Ilse Werner, Käthe Haack, Marianne Simson, Leo Slezak, Hermann Speelmans, Wilhelm Bendow, Walter Lieck, Ferdinand Marian, Gustav Waldau, Eduard von Winterstein, Micheal Bohnen
Production: Ufa
Camera: Werner Krien, Konstantin Irmen-Tschet
Music: Georg Haentzschel
Approved for release: March 3, 1943
Predicates: especially valuable artistically, valuable for the People
Premiere: March 5, 1943
Availability: 16mm rental through West Glen Films, on video through German Language Video Center and International Historic Films (subtitles)

The Old and the Young King (Der alte und der junge König, 1935)
Director: Hans Steinhoff
Script: Thea von Harbou, Rolf Lauckner
Actors: Emil Jannings, Werner Hinz, Leopoldine Konstantin, Carola Höhn, Marieluise Claudius, Claus Clausen, Friedrich Kayssler, Georg Alexander, Walter Janssen, Theodor Loos
Production: Deka-Film GmbH
Camera: Karl Puth
Music: Wolfgang Zeller
Approved for release: January 29, 1935
Predicates: especially valuable politically and artistically
Premiere: January 29, 1935
Availability: 16 mm rental, West Glen Films and Trans-World Films (the latter with subtitles)

Paracelsus (1943)
Director: G. W. Pabst
Script: Kurt Heuser
Actors: Werner Krauss, Mathias Wieman, Annelies Reinhold, Martin Urtel, Fritz Rasp, Josef Sieber, Herbert Hübner
Production: Bavaria
Camera: Bruno Stephan
Music: Herbert Windt
Approved for release: March 4, 1943
Predicates: politically and artistically valuable

Premiere: March 12, 1943
Availability: on video through German Language Video Center and International Historic Films (no subtitles); 16 mm rental through Trans-World Films (subtitles)

Pour le Mérite (1938)
Director: Karl Ritter
Script: Fred Hildenbrand, Karl Ritter
Actors: Paul Hartmann, Jutta Freybe, Albert Hehn, Herbert A. E. Bühme, Carsta Lück, Fritz Kampers, Paul Otto, Joseph Dahmen, Willi Rose
Production: Ufa
Camera: Günther Anders, Heinz von Jaworsky (aerial shots)
Music: Herbert Windt
Approved for release: December 7, 1938
Predicates: especially valuable politically and artistically, valuable for youth
Premiere: December 22, 1938
Availability: available for screening at Library of Congress, Washington, D.C.

Request Concert (Wunschkonzert, 1940)
Director: Eduard von Borsody
Script: Felix Lützendorf, Eduard von Borsody
Actors: Ilse Werner, Carl Raddatz, Joachim Brennecke, Ida Wüst, Hedwig Bleibtreu, Heinz Goedecke, Malte Jäger, Heinz Schaufuss
Production: Cine-Allianz-Tonfilmproduktion GmbH
Camera: Franz Weihmayr, Günther Anders, Carl Drews
Music: Werner Bochmann
Approved for release: December 21, 1940
Predicates: politically valuable, artistically valuable, nationally valuable, valuable for youth
Premiere: December 30, 1940
Availability: on video through German Language Video Center and International Historic Films (no subtitles)

Robert and Bertram (Robert und Bertram, 1939)
Director: Hans Heinz Zerlett
Script: Hans Heinz Zerlett, after a farce of the same title by Gustav Raeder
Actors: Rudi Godden, Kurt Seifert, Carla Rüst, Fritz Kampers, Heinz Schorlemmer, Herbert Hübner, Tatjana Sais, Ursula Deinert, Robert Dorsay, Erwin Biegel, Hans Stiebner
Production: Tobis
Camera: Friedl Behn-Grund
Music: Leo Ieux
Approved for release: June 20, 1939
Predicates: —
Premiere: July 7, 1939
Availability: on video through International Historic Films (no subtitles)

The Ruler (Der Herrscher, 1937)
Director: Veit Harlan
Script: Thea von Harbou, Curt J. Braun, freely adapted from Gerhard Hauptmann's
    Vor Sonnenuntergang
Actors: Emil Jannings, Marianne Hoppe, Harald Paulsen, Hilde Körber, Paul Wagner,
    Maria Koppenhöfer, Hannes Stelzer, Käthe Haack, Herbert Hübner
Production: Tobis-Magna-Filmproduktion GmbH
Camera: Günther Anders, Werner Brandes
Music: Wolfgang Zeller
Approved for release: March 15, 1937
Predicates: especially valuable politically and artistically; National Film Prize 1937
Premiere: March 17, 1937
Availability: available for screening at Library of Congress, Washington, D.C.

S.A. Man Brand (S.A. Mann Brand, 1933)
Director: Franz Seitz
Script: Joseph Dalman, Joe Stöckel
Actors: Heinz Klingenberg, Otto Wernicke, Elise Aulinger, Rolf Wenkhaus, Joe Stöckel,
    Max Weydner, Manfred Pilot
Production: Bavaria-Film A.G., Munich
Camera: Franz Koch
Music: Toni Thoms
Approved for release: June 9, 1933
Predicates: artistically especially valuable, educational
Premiere: June 14, 1933
Availability: on video through International Historic Films (no subtitles)

INDEX

Linda Schulte-Sasse is Associate Professor in the
Department of German and Russian, Macalester
College. She is the co-editor of *Film and Politics in the
Weimar Republic.*

Library of Congress Cataloging-in-Publication Data
Schulte-Sasse, Linda.
Entertaining the Third Reich : illusions of wholeness in
Nazi cinema / Linda Schulte-Sasse.
p.   cm. — (Post-contemporary interventions)
Filmography: p.
Includes bibliographical references and index.
ISBN 0-8223-1830-X (cloth : alk. paper). —
ISBN 0-8223-1824-5 (paper : alk. paper)
1. National socialism and motion pictures.   2. Motion
pictures — Political aspects — Germany.   I. Title.
PN1995.9.N36S38   1996
791.43'6358 — dc20   96-17882 CIP